Rick Ferrell, Knuckleball Catcher

A Hall of Famer's Life Behind the Plate and in the Front Office

KERRIE FERRELL

with WILLIAM M. ANDERSON

Foreword by DONALD HONIG

McFarland & Company, Inc., Publishers
Jefferson, North Carolina, and London

LIBRARY OF CONGRESS CATALOGUING-IN-PUBLICATION DATA

Ferrell, Kerrie.
    Rick Ferrell, knuckleball catcher : a hall of famer's life behind
the plate and in the front office / Kerrie Ferrell with William M.
Anderson ; foreword by Donald Honig.
      p.   cm.
    Includes bibliographical references and index.

    ISBN 978-0-7864-4796-1
    softcover : 50# alkaline paper ∞

    1. Ferrell, Rick, 1905–1995.   2. Baseball players— United
States— Biography.   3. Baseball managers— United States—
Biography.   4. Detroit Tigers (Baseball team)— History.
I. Anderson, William M. (William Martin), 1938–   II. Title.
GV865.F425F47   2010
796.357092 — dc22   2010001712
  [B]

British Library cataloguing data are available

Front cover: Youthful St. Louis Browns catcher Rick Ferrell smiles
for the camera in a photograph taken in the early 1930s as his
baseball skills were becoming widely recognized (Kerrie Ferrell
collection); background ©2010 Shutterstock

Manufactured in the United States of America

McFarland & Company, Inc., Publishers
 Box 611, Jefferson, North Carolina 28640
  www.mcfarlandpub.com

Acknowledgments

First, I would like to thank Ferrell family members Bonnie Ferrell Waynick, Gwen Ferrell Gore, Wes Ferrell, Jr., and George Ferrell, Jr., for their assistance with photographs, details, and chronology of Ferrell family history.

Many heartfelt thanks to author Bill Anderson for his text and photographic contributions; baseball historian and author Donald Honig for generously writing the book's introduction; the tireless staff at the National Baseball Hall of Fame and Museum, especially Bill Haase and Tim Wiles for their help with baseball research, and Pat Kelly for assistance obtaining historical photographs; Patricia Kenney for sharing her Rick Ferrell photos and memories from the Detroit Tigers; the Fetzer Institute library staff for help locating Detroit Tigers' executive files and permission to use same; the staff at Guilford College for digging up old transcripts and athletic histories; Sharon Arend of Ilitch Enterprises for her generosity in providing historical photographs from the Detroit Tigers' archives; the folks who supplied access to the Harwell Collection at the Detroit Public Library, and the incredibly patient and helpful library staffs at the University of Michigan Graduate Library and the Michigan State University Library; and the reference librarians at the Ann Arbor Public Library for obtaining microfilm of several historical newspapers through their inter-library loan services.

Finally, so much appreciation is extended to the baseball players and associates in my father's life who provided personal interviews for this book: Elden Auker, Floyd Baker, Wilt Browning, Bobby Doerr, Bill Freehan, Joe Ginsburg, Ted Gray, Don Gutteridge, Ernie Harwell, Ralph Houk, Sid Hudson, George Kell, Hillis Layne, Buddy Lewis, Lew Matlin, John McHale, Virgil Trucks, Mickey Vernon, Bill Werber, and Eddie Yost. —K.F.

To the memory of my father,
who played his hand with
wisdom, strength, and grace
— *K.F.*

Table of Contents

Preface

Many modern baseball fans are unfamiliar with my father, Hall of Fame catcher Rick Ferrell, and the baseball career that led to his 1984 induction into the National Baseball Hall of Fame. His life spanned most of the twentieth century, from 1905 to 1995, and his professional baseball career lasted 66 of his 89 years. Rick caught in the American league for 18 years during the Great Depression and World War II. Afterwards he coached for, and worked his way up to, general manager and vice president of the Detroit Tigers. Years after his 1995 death, I decided to write the story of my father's baseball life, focusing on his athletic accomplishments, executive contributions, and the extraordinary character that propelled him to success in professional baseball. To achieve this goal, I enlisted the assistance of baseball historian Bill Anderson.

When I began researching my father's career in 2003, I had no idea the manuscript would take more than six years to complete. I researched almost all of the 1,884 games in which he played. Sources included the on-line ProQuest database of historical newspapers, baseball reference books, family scrapbooks, print articles, and the recollection of family members and baseball contemporaries.

This biography examines Rick's baseball career, both as a major league catcher and baseball executive, with attention also given to Wes and George, his baseball-playing brothers.

The narrative begins with Richard's early family life, when he played baseball with his six brothers on their parents' North Carolina dairy farm, and his struggle to break into professional baseball. Subsequent exploits are related as he built a career as an American League catcher from 1929 to 1947, playing for the St. Louis Browns, Boston Red Sox, and Washington Senators.

In 1929, Rick broke into the big leagues with the St. Louis Browns after gaining free agency from the Detroit Tigers by Baseball Commissioner Landis. In 1933, manager Connie Mack chose Ferrell to catch the entire first All-Star Game for the American League team, which included Babe Ruth, Lou Gehrig, Wes Ferrell, Bill Dickey, and Charlie Gehringer. Ferrell was named to eight All-Star teams during his career. During the mid–1930s, Rick and his pitching brother, Wes Ferrell, a six-time 20-game winner, comprised the Ferrell broth-ers battery for the Boston Red Sox and Washington Senators.

Defensively, Rick Ferrell possessed a laser-accurate throwing arm and the rare ability to handle the knuckleball pitch. During the 1944 and '45 seasons at ages 38 and 39, he accomplished the historic task of regularly catching four Washington Senators knuckleball starters: "Dutch" Leonard, Mickey Haefner, John Niggeling, and Roger Wolff. At that time, few catchers would even call for the unpredictable "butterfly pitch" because they couldn't catch it, and the errors made in attempts made their stats look weak. For 43 years, from 1945 to 1988, he held the American League record for most games caught (1,806) until Carlton Fisk of the Chicago White Sox broke it in August 1988.

After retiring as a Senators coach, in 1950, Rick ironically returned to coach the Detroit Tigers, rising through their organizational ranks for the next 42 years as general manager, vice president, and executive consultant. The Tigers won the American League pennant and World Series twice (1968, '84) and the A.L. East championship three times during Ferrell's tenure. In 1961, Ferrell succeeded Hank Greenberg as one of three American League members on the nine-member Major League Baseball Official Playing Rules Committee, on which he served for twenty years. Game changes like baseball expansion, the designated-hitter rule, and the reserve clause were influenced by Rick's per-spective and vote.

Ferrell's greatest pinnacle came in 1984 when at age 78 he was elected to the National Baseball Hall of Fame in Cooperstown, New York, by its thirteen-member Veterans Committee. Joining fellow inductees Don Drysdale, Pee Wee Reese, Luis Aparicio, and Harmon Killebrew in August 1984, Rick became the eleventh catcher ever inducted into the Baseball Hall of Fame.

The catcher was never considered a home-run hitter, which spun some controversy around the legacy of the supremely non-controversial Rick for the first time. A few statisticians balked at "28 career home runs." Offensively, a contact hitter rather than a power hitter, Ferrell's dangerous clutch hitting often won games during a career in which he finished with a .281 batting average. His .378 on-base percentage is fourth out of sixteen current Hall of Fame catch-ers (as of 2009). The fact that he played on losing, second-division teams had more to do with poor player rosters, the tyranny of management during the 1930s and '40s, and the absence of a players union than with Rick's superb pro-fessional skills. One wonders what successes Rick would have accomplished had he played for the New York Yankees or another strong, winning team.

Certainly Ferrell's Hall of Fame election was based more on outstanding defense and his unique ability in catching four regular knuckleball starters for the 1944–45 Washington Senators at ages 38–39, a team that almost took the pennant in 1945. In terms of character, statistics, longevity, and accomplish-ment, Ferrell represents a Hall of Famer of the classiest kind.

Serving under nine baseball commissioners over eight decades, Rick witnessed dramatic changes in the major leagues. Train travel gave way to airplane flights, minorities integrated formerly all-white teams, and the knuckleball was supplanted by the split-finger pitch. In addition, leagues expanded along with player salaries, the Players Association displaced the supreme authority of the powerful owners, and free agency became the norm.

I was born after my father's playing career ended and never was able to see him play. Yet researching his life story has permitted me to visualize in my imagination some of his games from a past century, and the trials and jubilation accompanying them. This book is for anyone curious about the path a slender North Carolina farm boy took to catch his way to the top of the major league baseball game and wind up as one of only sixteen catchers in the National Baseball Hall of Fame at Cooperstown, New York.

Kerrie Ferrell • *February 2010*

Foreword

by Donald Honig

I had the pleasure once of meeting Rick Ferrell. This was in the summer of 1984 when Ferrell was being honored at Fenway Park after his recent election to the Hall of Fame at Cooperstown. I was finishing my meal when I looked across the Fenway dining room and saw the old catcher sitting at a table. People were stopping by to shake his hand and offer a few words of congratulations, to which Ferrell responded with as much appreciation as his diffident personality would allow, smiling shyly and nodding his head.

You wouldn't have taken him for one of the finest catchers in baseball history. In his prime he stood 5'10" and weighed around 160 pounds, not a typical catcher's physique, yet when he retired in 1947, it was with the American League record for games caught (1,806) that remained in the books until broken by Carlton Fisk more than forty years later.

There was no question that the placid gentleman across the room had been plenty tough, as there was no question that he had been born with plenty of resolve. When just a youngster the North Carolina farm boy saved his pennies and bought himself a secondhand catcher's mitt. Young Rick had a goal and he never lost sight of it. That he achieved it with honors is now part of baseball history, and that in spirit, the farm boy never strayed far from the farm is best illustrated by a telltale remark he once made. While sitting in the dugout watching a game one day, Rick turned to a teammate and said, "Can you imagine, getting paid to do this?"

Just how good a player was Rick Ferrell? Well, like many quiet men, Ferrell let the record book speak for him. At the time of the first All-Star game, played in Chicago in 1933, the American League had in its ranks two of baseball's most eminent catchers, New York Yankee Bill Dickey and Philadelphia Athletic Mickey Cochrane, each then in the midst of their splendid careers. But if you check the box score of that historic game you will find that the man who caught all nine innings for the victorious American League team was Rick Ferrell of the Boston Red Sox. The team's manager, the estimable Connie Mack, thought that highly of Ferrell.

5

Years later, while sitting in his Greensboro, North Carolina, home with Wes Ferrell, Rick's younger brother and sometime battery mate (with the Red Sox and Washington Senators), I asked the six-time twenty-game winner about that game. Had Mack ever explained his decision?

"He didn't have to," Wes said with brotherly pride. "It spoke for itself."

A lot of things spoke for themselves where Rick Ferrell was concerned. He was one of baseball's "quiet men." He let you find out for yourself just how good he was.

"Tougher than he looked," Detroit's own "quiet man" Charlie Gehringer said. "When you ran into him at home plate, it was like he was anchored. You would have sworn he was twice his size."

No doubt the anchor was shaped by that boyhood goal. Rick Ferrell always knew who he was, and that type doesn't yield easily, if at all.

Given the vagaries of baseball memory, it is not as a record-setting catcher or Hall of Famer for which Rick Ferrell is chiefly remembered; it is for what he did in 1945 while catching for the Washington Senators. It is a given among the catching fraternity that nightmares come in the shape of knuckleball pitchers. The classic line belongs to the witty former catcher Bob Uecker, who said the best way to handle a knuckleball is to wait until it stops rolling and then run and pick it up. Well, in 1945, Rick handled no less than four of the challenging breed — Roger Wolff, Johnny Niggeling, Mickey Haefner, and Dutch Leonard. In nursing this quartet to 60 victories that season, Ferrell turned in what his manager Ossie Bluege called the finest sustained catching performance he had ever seen.

I couldn't let the opportunity pass that day at Fenway Park. When I felt the moment was ripe, I got up and crossed the room, heading for the brand new Hall of Famer, who in his dignified serenity might have been a retired banker or school principal. He invited me to join him. We spoke of his brother Wes, then some years deceased.

"We started playing ball together," Rick said. "Right out of the cradle."

I mentioned the catcher's mitt he had bought as a boy.

"For a dollar and a half," he said. "I saved up for it. A few pennies at a time."

"It seems you had your goal in mind even back then."

"I guess I did."

I asked if he still had the mitt. He laughed.

"No," he said. "I wish I did, but it's long gone."

The mitt may have been long gone, but the goal remained, never lost to heart or time. The proof of that is on the wall at Cooperstown.

Veteran baseball historian Donald Honig has been a baseball devotee since his youth in New York City and has written 39 authoritative baseball history books. His latest publication is The Fifth Season: Tales of My Life in Baseball *(2009).*

PART I
Behind the Plate

1

❖ ❖ ❖

1905–1928

Early Life in North Carolina and the Minors

At the end of summer in 1928, 22-year-old North Carolina catcher Richard Ferrell was a man on a curious mission. After a superlative third season playing minor league baseball in the Detroit Tigers' system, he still had not been called up to the major leagues. Playing in 126 games for the Columbus (Ohio) Senators, a seventh-place AA team, Ferrell had struck out only four times in 339 at-bats. His 113 hits had included 21 doubles, 5 triples, plus 65 RBIs — stats that had earned him a spot on the American Association All-Star team. But still no call to the majors, while his brother, Wesley, two years younger, was already pitching for the Cleveland Indians.

During the season Richard had traveled by bus to Detroit, his supposed parent club, to see what plans Tigers owner Frank Navin had for him, but was dismissed back to Columbus and advised to be patient. But when another catcher, Hugh McMullen, was called up in September by the Cincinnati Reds, Rick began to question which club actually owned him, Detroit or Cincinnati? Mystified, Ferrell had then visited the Cincinnati brass, inquiring if that club had plans for his promotion, but again was told to return to the minors and keep playing. What Richard did not know was that the Cincinnati Reds had secretly purchased the Columbus club in February 1927, including the contracts of its thirty-four players.

Having studied his season contract with close attention, the catcher suspected he was being illegally held back in the minor leagues. Something smelled fishy, with too many unanswered questions. His urgent mission now was to figure out which major league baseball team actually owned him before he returned home for the off-season. His father thought he should be cultivating the Ferrell family farm instead of wasting precious time playing professional baseball. But his confident son knew he could succeed as a ballplayer if given half a chance, and he surely didn't want to play for Columbus again, ever! He saw no choice but to take his plight all the way to baseball's ultimate power: the baseball commissioner, Judge Kenesaw Mountain Landis.

On September 24 in Louisville, Kentucky, after the last game of the 1928 season, Ferrell boarded the northern train to Chicago, aiming to have a conference with Landis. The catcher was certain the Detroit Tigers and the owner of the Columbus team had made a deal to hide him in the minor leagues rather than promote him to the majors, a common, though illegal, practice at the time.

In the large, bustling metropolis of Chicago, the small-town farm boy found his way to the Office of the Commissioner of Baseball, but with no appointment, sat on a hard bench, waiting the entire day, without getting in to see Judge Landis. At last, the commissioner's secretary, Francis O'Connor, told the prospect to return to North Carolina and address his complaint in writing to Landis, which Ferrell did.

In the meantime Tigers owner Frank Navin got wind that his silent partner, Columbus-owner Joe Carr, creator of the N.F.L., was marketing Ferrell. In a phone conversation Carr admitted having received a $50,000 offer for the young prospect; however, Navin stated that the catcher was his property. Supposedly Carr countered by telling the Tigers' owner that there was nothing in writing to substantiate the claim, although Richard had signed a Detroit contract. Navin, himself, called Commissioner Landis to protest. On November 8, 1928, Landis conducted a hearing. After careful consideration of the facts, the commissioner declared Richard Ferrell free to bargain with any club, except the Detroit Tigers, making him one of baseball's first free agents.

An old family scrapbook news article stated, "What is known in the baseball business as the 'old cover-up' has been worked ever since the passing of regulations intended to protect the young players in the minors.... A major league club has a promising player who needs more experience or time. The club is expected to dispose of the player. It covers him by 'selling' him to a friendly minor league club that, within a year or two, 'sells' him back to the major league club."

Back home and free now to bargain his services with any team, word traveled like wildfire. Several American League teams expressed interest: the Boston Red Sox, New York Yankees, St. Louis Browns, Chicago White Sox, and Washington Nationals. Boston offered Ferrell an $18,000 contract. The National League Pittsburgh Pirates and New York Giants also pursued him.

A March 26, 1938, *World Telegram* article described the confusing events in retrospect. Detroit's Frank Navin phoned friend Philip De Catesby Ball, owner of the St. Louis Browns, encouraging him to sign Ferrell. Phil Ball offered a three-year contract plus a $25,000 bonus to the young player, who immediately agreed to terms. Browns' business manager Bill Friel traveled to Greensboro and gave Ferrell his $25,000 bonus check, all the money in the world back then. A 1928 *Greensboro Daily News* article confirmed, "When the Columbus club learned Ferrell was to be freed, they quickly offered him $2,000 to sign with them, but he declined. He was sorry, but he had already signed with the

St. Louis Browns for $25,000 and wasn't interested in pin money." Ferrell later recalled the signing: "I thought I was doing the smart thing to sign with the Browns. They had just finished third in 1928, and they had a couple of old-timers, Steve O'Neill and Wally Schang, catching. I figured I could step right in and take over the catching job." Rick Ferrell was on his way as a major leaguer, but soon discovered that reality would not quite match his expectations.

The earliest Ferrells had settled in the Piedmont Crescent area of central North Carolina after arriving in North America from the British Isles and Ireland in the mid–1700s. In 1873, Rick Ferrell's father, Rufus Benjamin Ferrell, was born in Oak Grove, North Carolina (Wake County), where he grew up and married Clora Alice Carpenter, a local girl six years his junior, in 1898.

In the early 1900s, they moved to Greensboro in nearby Guilford County where Rufus worked twenty-five years with Southern Railway, first as a fireman and later as a railroad engineer. Guilford County had been the site of several historical events. During the Revolutionary War in 1781, General Nathanial Greene and his Colonial troops had defeated Cornwallis and the British in the Battle of Guilford Courthouse. In 1808, Greene had founded the city of Greensboro. North Carolina had joined the Confederacy during the Civil War (1861–65).

Alice ("Mother Ferrell"), educated, soft-spoken, yet strong-willed, supported Rufus at every step and she taught the illiterate "Daddy Ferrell" to read. From 1899 through 1913, Alice gave birth to seven healthy sons. The eldest was Basil ("Slats") in 1899, and the next was William Kermit ("Pete") in 1902. Then came the baseball-playing boys, George Stuart, third (1904), Richard Benjamin (1905) fourth, and Wesley Cheek, the fifth son (1908). The final two children were Issac Marvin, sixth (1910), and Thomas Ewell ("Chubby"), the seventh son (1913). Richard Benjamin Ferrell was born Columbus Day, October 12, 1905, at his grandmother's home in nearby Durham and lived a happy, Spartan life, growing up playing baseball in the Greensboro streets.

A 5'8", 150 pound mass of muscle-power and gristle, Rufus Ferrell was as tough as the steel trains he drove and greatly influenced his sons. In April 1911, when Richard was five, his dad was involved in a fiery train crash at work that left him pinned under hot steel. When rescuers arrived, Ferrell calmly directed them where to dig for him, despite having broken arms and scalding hot metal stretched across his lower limbs. During an agonizing two-and-a-half hours, not one word of complaint came from him. When finally rescued, Rufus said, "Well, things look a good deal better now than they did for a while this evening, and I guess I'll make it now all right."[1] Tough "Daddy" Ferrell recovered, bearing permanent facial scars and a limp from the accident.

Rick's maternal grandmother, Geneva Phipps, first introduced the boys to ball games. Rolling her old cotton stockings tightly together into homemade "sock balls," Geneva tossed them to her young grandsons to catch and throw back to her. Growing up, they enjoyed playing recreational baseball games in the city lots. In 1917, just before Rick's twelfth birthday, "Lonnie," as locals called Rufus, moved his growing family out to a 150-acre farm off of the U.S. 421 highway, land that he had been gradually acquiring since 1910.

On the farm stood the large white, two-story house that initially lacked electricity, indoor plumbing, or running water, all of which were installed later. Facing south, a wrap-around porch encircled the front and west side with rocking chairs where everyone gathered in the evenings to talk and play checkers. On the first floor was a formal living room, the parents' bedroom and an adjoining sitting room, plus a dining room and kitchen. Upstairs were four bedrooms for the seven sons. In back was the out-house; in front, a fresh-water well where passing horses and their thirsty riders stopped for water.[2]

Typical of early nineteenth century American farms, there was a white cow barn housing about sixty milking cows, by the smaller milk house where butter, cream, and cottage cheese were processed. In addition to a mule barn and hog pen, there was a chicken coop housing seventy-five chickens. The Ferrells grew fruits, vegetables, white cotton, and brown tobacco. Lonnie collected honey from his beehives.

The Rufus B. Ferrell and Sons Dairy Farm grew into the family business. Basil and Kermit delivered milk, butter, and cottage cheese in town and sold vegetables, molasses, honey, and eggs. Farm chores like plowing, planting, harvesting, chopping wood, baling hay, milking cows twice daily kept all the boys busy and strong. When not at school, Richard and his brothers fished for lake trout, hunted for squirrel in the sixteen acres of pine woods, and enjoyed playing baseball. Always together for company, there was never a dull minute. Intensely loyal to each other and deeply proud of their "Ferrell" name, the seven brothers lived by the motto: "All for one, and one for all!"

Richard's parents instilled high, Christian morals in him, that "right was right, and wrong was wrong"— that he must always do the right thing in life. Education was a top priority; all the sons completed high school in the Guilford County Schoolhouse. Richard's teacher there, Miss Leah Stanley, once commented about him in an interview: "He's such an earnest, well-bred, and well-behaved student, always curious and asking questions, especially about North Carolina history." An undated *Greensboro Daily News* article in a Ferrell scrapbook described Miss Stanley's asking the class what they wanted to be: "I plan to be a doctor," one student said eagerly. "And I, a lawyer," another kid called out. A third boy replied, "A minister!" Richard then announced, "I'm determined to become a baseball player, Miss Stanley!" much to the raucous laughter of his classmates at the small boy with such big dreams!

Even then, Richard had made up his mind. Unlike his father, he disliked farming and despite his 5'10", 145 pound stature, his singular consuming drive was to become a professional baseball catcher, a vision he had vowed to create. When not farming, playing ball, training, eating proper food, and maintaining regular hours constituted the boy's daily routine. He'd set rabbit traps

The 1918 Guilford High Baseball Team: Rick Ferrell is the little boy with arms crossed standing in the center of the team, copying his eldest brother, Basil (Slats), who is standing second from left with his arms crossed. Pete Ferrell sits in the middle of the first row.

at quarter-mile intervals over a four-mile stretch and get up before daylight to wind-sprint his course at dawn, stopping only to snatch the dead rabbits. Wearing boxing gloves, he pounded a punching bag hung from the barn beams and also lifted a fifty-pound rock to develop muscles.

Richard's initial exposure to Organized Baseball occurred when "Slats" took him and his brothers across town to the local Cone Mills Park to watch the Piedmont League play their baseball games. In his book, *The Ferrell Brothers of Baseball*, Dick Thompson relates a Ferrell family story of the day "Slats" found a season pass and used it to gain entrance to the baseball game. He then tossed a cigar box containing the ticket over the fence to his waiting brothers for another one to use to gain admission to the ball park. All the Ferrells eventually entered the game that day, free of charge.

Sometimes when Daddy Ferrell drove the horse-drawn buggy to town for supplies, the brothers would quit working in the fields and race out to play baseball on their make-shift baseball diamond. All but Richard considered themselves to be pitchers. The young catcher had saved his pennies to eagerly buy a catcher's mitt for $1.50, but its flimsy quality had proven a disappointment. Nonetheless, crouching down, he caught their experimental fastballs, curves, changeups and sliders, learning to catch anything they threw at him.

On weekends the brothers held hitting contests in the field as a form of batting practice. If one boy hit his ball a long way, a stick was put in the ground to mark where the ball landed. When someone hit the ball farther, the stick was moved to where that ball landed, to measure which ball went the farthest. "Stick a stick up on THAT one!" they would yell, after powering a particularly strong blast. The sportsmanship, competitive drive, and a cooperative team spirit that Rick developed during these family contests cannot be underestimated. The skills required of a professional athlete — ability, strength, playing by the rules, hustle, hard work — young Rick learned with his brothers as a youngster playing baseball on his family's North Carolina farm.

By 1918, the 13-year-old farm boy still determined to mold himself into a catcher. Despite being the smallest member of the Guilford High School baseball squad, he worked out at every chance. Playing with his brothers, he caught pick-up games with the many textile mill teams around town and played on the local Guilford County League team at Cone Mills Park. Of the Ferrells on the team, Rick caught, "Slats" played first base, Pete was a middle infielder, and George and Wes, in addition to pitching, could play anywhere.

The Ferrell clan helped the local Glenwood team win the final 1921 County League championship game against Buffalo, 2–1. The pitcher Wes, 15, struck out eleven batters as "Dick" (Richard), 17, caught, and outfielder George, 19, got the game's big hits for the victory. In an article years later for *The Sporting News*, Harry Bundridge described the event. As George raced in to congratulate Wes when the game was over, he shouted excitedly: "You're a cinch for the big league some day!" Wes replied, "Aw, it was Dick's catching. He made me look good, that's all. He's sure to be in the big leagues in a year or two. He's a great catcher." Issac Marvin Ferrell, 12 years old, watched the game from the Glenwood bench and joined his brothers. "George's hitting won the game! You'll all three be big league players one of these days, and so will I!" "Me, too!" piped Ewell Ferrell, the nine-year-old bat boy."[3]

Of all the brothers, the best ball player, Pete, the second son, remained on the farm along with "Slats" to help out Daddy Ferrell rather than pursue an athletic career. Married in 1922, Pete had five children and worked for Duke Power and Electric Company in Greensboro.

In 1920 at age fifteen, while playing on his high school team, young Richard began working out with the Guilford College Quakers, the best college baseball team in North Carolina, benefitting from their excellent coaches. He figured college would not only provide an academic foundation, but also a ticket into professional baseball.

Following his Guilford High School graduation in the spring of 1923 at age seventeen, Richard enrolled in the lovely Quaker campus of Guilford College for fall term, taking eleven credits in English, history, math, and also German.[4] The German course proved an ultimately unwise choice.

His older brother George, already a Guilford College student, walked with Richard the two miles to college daily. For winter term in 1924, Richard, 18, took history, English, biology, and Sunday school, with perfect attendance.[5] Like George and his friend, pitcher Rufus "Shirt" Smith, Richard played forward on the Guilford College varsity basketball team from 1924 to 1926, earning varsity letters in the sport. In 1926, he averaged about eight points per game.

In the spring of 1924, Ferrell joined George, a pitcher, on Coach Bob Doak's Guilford College varsity baseball team as starting catcher. Among his teammates were North Carolina native sons Frank Smithdeal, southpaw "Shirt" Smith, and brothers "Shorty" and Charlie Frazier. Later major league Tar Heels Tom Zachery and Ernie Shore also graduated from the Guilford College baseball program.

Since he had never played for an organized team before in his life, getting his first maroon and gray Guilford Quakers baseball uniform in college filled Richard with pride. The catcher wore the college's striped shirt and baggy flannel pants, gray baseball cap with a maroon "G," leggings, and undershirt, cleaning and caring for that first uniform as if it were a symbol of status and hope for his future.

Under Coach Doak's tutelage Rick's defensive catching skills quickly improved as he practiced the fine points of how to judge batters, work with different pitchers, call games, block home plate, and make the long, straight throw to second. Through April 1924, "Dick" (as Rick was then called) and the Guilford Quakers played home games at Cone Park and traveled by team bus to Lynchburg, Virginia, and Hampden Sidney, North Carolina, and other college towns for away games, batting eighth in the lineup initially, then finishing the season batting fourth.

In order to pay for their college tuition from 1923 to 1925, George and Richard took up amateur boxing in Greensboro. One bout earned a whopping $35 per fight on weekends at Neese's Hall, a second-floor boxing ring above Hobbs Grocery store at South Davie and Washington streets. Richard fought as a lightweight, later moving up to the 150-pound class. George was a welterweight. Sometimes 2,000 to 3,000 people would show up to watch the matches. Through boxing, Rick further developed his timing and athleticism, as well as gaining experience performing in front of large crowds.

Fighting under the name of "Kid Corbett" after the heavyweight boxer "Gentleman Jim" Corbett, Ferrell won ten straight bouts in the lightweight category. Once in a welterweight match, a tough old sergeant from Fort Bragg knocked him down for the count at the Grand Theater. "How sweetly the birdies did sing to me as I lay there on the canvas," Rick later said in an undated scrapbook article. "They had to carry me to my corner, but I left the ring under my own steam." When a boxing promoter suggested he and George battle each other in the ring, they refused, never wanting to fight against each other, in or out of the ring.

To *Greensboro Daily News* reporter Wilt Browning, Rick described a prospective fight that never happened. "The fight game was a big racket, and you had to take your chances. I was supposed to spar a few rounds with a fighter named Young Stribling in the Grand Theater. But Stribling had not made a name for himself yet, and he failed to show up for the exhibition. That really upset me because I wanted to try him out. Later I found out I was probably lucky he didn't show up." Stribling later became 1928's top heavyweight fighter.[6]

After the single loss, Richard won eight or nine more bouts for a total of eighteen or so, to become North Carolina's Welterweight Boxing Champion, gaining a scary reputation for himself as an amateur boxer. But from Guilford College, Coach Doak warned that if the catcher continued boxing, he'd be considered a professional and thus be ineligible to play college baseball. In addition, a severe boxing injury could ruin his chances for a successful baseball career. In the same Browning article, Ferrell conceded, "So, as the country at large did not seem to offer any clamorous objections, I left the ring flat. By flat, however, I do not mean that I was carried out. I'd probably be punchy by now any way, and never could have had a major league career!" Interestingly, Wes never did enter the boxing ring, professing a desire to become a doctor.

In the summer of 1924, Rick, 18, was offered $135 per month to catch professionally for the Newberry, South Carolina, team in the Palmetto League, where "Shirt" Smith was pitching. There Ferrell assumed the name "Jim Richards" to preserve his amateur status for college baseball.

Returning to Guilford College in the fall to continue his sophomore studies, Richard registered for classes in English, education, history, and German, but ultimately flunked the German class, as the pronunciation did not blend well with his Southern accent. Having earned 78 credits in pursuit of his college degree, he pressed on with five courses for winter term in 1925: history, English, Teaching Religion, education, and The Life of Christ, with perfect attendance. Like his mother, Ferrell valued education and learning as a way toward self-improvement,

Academics were, however, a back-up to a baseball career. In the spring of 1925, St. Louis Cardinals scout Charley Barrett offered Richard a $1,000 bonus to sign a contract with the Cardinals organization. On May 13, 1925, Ferrell eagerly withdrew from Guilford College "to accept a position as a baseball player." Working with the St. Louis Nationals and the Syracuse Internationals, he only played in exhibition games.

While at Newberry, South Carolina, that summer, Richard overheard his manager say one day that he needed an outfielder. Knowing that his brother George needed a job, Rick asked his manager if George could come down for a tryout. After getting the approval, Rick contacted George, who immediately

The Ferrell family assembled for this family portrait taken on the Ferrell farm in spring 1928. Seated from left to right: Ewell, Alice (Mother Ferrell), Rufus (Daddy Ferrell), and Marvin. Standing in back: Rick, George, Kermit, Basil, and Wesley. (Bonnie Ferrell Waynick)

joined him in Newberry. Since George had always been a pitcher, before the tryout, Richard spent the entire day batting fly balls to the outfield for George to catch or run down. Lo and behold, George made the Newberry team as an outfielder that summer and finished his long minor-league career at the same position. "One for all, and all for one!"

In the fall of 1925, after the season ended, a hopeful Rick traveled by train to St. Louis to finally sign the agreement with the Cardinals brass: Manager Rogers Hornsby, GM Branch Rickey, and President Sam Breadon. But when Rick met with Branch Rickey to collect the $1,000 signing bonus he'd been promised by Barrett, Rickey handed Ferrell a check for $600, saying, "That's the best I can do, Kid. $600, take it or leave it." Ferrell balked when he saw the reduced amount, protesting that he had been promised $1,000. When Rickey held firm, the young Southerner took the $600 check and slowly tore it up into several pieces before putting them back down on the general manager's desk. An angry Ferrell silently exited Rickey's office, boarding the eastbound train from St. Louis back to Guilford County — unsigned, no baseball contract, broke with no cash, but with his stubborn pride intact. No one was going to take advantage of him financially.

With increased resolve, Ferrell returned again for the 1926 winter term at Guilford College, taking English, English history, education, and French this time, rather than German, for his foreign language requirement. Undaunted, he resolved to play on the Guilford baseball team in the spring and wait for another chance at a baseball contract. Finishing the college baseball season that May, Rick earned a .360 batting average hitting cleanup, with 27 hits in 75 tries.

That spring of 1926 finally proved to be Rick Ferrell's big break. Ivory hunters from all over — the New York Yankees, Detroit Tigers, Philadelphia A's, Washington Nationals— were coming to scout the Guilford College Quakers and the battery of pitcher "Shirt" Smith and catcher Rick Ferrell. The Detroit Tigers' scout for the southern territory, Billy Doyle, had watched Ferrell catch several games and offered him $1,500 to sign with his club. The young catcher didn't take long making up his mind, soon accepting the offer to join the Detroit Tigers' organization. Again with high hopes, he withdrew from Guilford College "to accept a position as a baseball player," having completed 129 credits toward his bachelor's degree. This time Ferrell wouldn't return.

The Tigers immediately instructed their new recruit to report to spring training camp in San Antonio, Texas. Although unrecorded, one can only imagine the awe Ferrell must have felt to be at spring training with the immortal Ty Cobb running the ball club. Richard was farmed out to the Kinston Eagles in the Class B Virginia League for the 1926 season. Made up of six teams, the league played a 152-game schedule with clubs called the "Bugs," "Truckers" and not surprisingly in Norfolk, the "Tars." Ferrell made his minor league debut as catcher on May 24. Although inexplicably absent from the line-up during July, probably due to an injury, Detroit gave him a brief look at a higher level when he was called up to Columbus late in the season to replace fellow catcher and Guilford County resident Ray Hayworth, who'd moved up to the Detroit Tigers roster.

In 1926, Ferrell, 20, got into five games with the AA Columbus Senators in closing out his first season in minor-league ball. He had played in 64 games, earned a .266 batting average in 192 trips to the plate, and connected for 52 hits, among them two home runs. The Kinston Eagles finished in fifth place with a 69–83 record.

Meanwhile in school at Oak Ridge Institute near Greensboro, Wesley joined both the basketball and baseball teams. Under well-known baseball coach Earl Holt, Wes won a game against Duke University in which future big-leaguer and teammate Billy Werber played third base. The pitcher also played right field.

The 1926 season had proven to be disappointing as the parent club, the Detroit Tigers, finished sixth and player-manager Ty Cobb felt ready to retire.

In six seasons Cobb had been unable to produce a pennant-winning ball club. The Detroit Tigers had made their best showing in 1924 when they finished runner-up while setting an all-time attendance record in breaking the million-mark for the first time in franchise history.

For the 1927 season, Rick returned to Columbus, Ohio, where he played the entire year. However, unknown to Ferrell, that February the Columbus club had been purchased quietly from the Detroit Tigers by the Cincinnati Reds organization. Also pursuing a baseball career, Wes was pitching semi-pro ball in East Douglas, Massachusetts, with Guilford College pitcher "Shirt" Smith for $300 a month, plus food and lodging.

The American Association, an eight team AA league, possessed the highest minor league ranking at this time. Under manager Ivy Wingo, Columbus had had a terrible previous year in 1927. After losing 108 games, the team had finished dead last, 41 games behind the pennant-winning Toledo Mud Hens. The local *Columbus Clipper* newspaper reported that the local club had "ended the 1927 season as they started it — with a defeat."[7]

Although quickly promoted in 1927, "Dick" Ferrell acquired marginal stats. In 104 games, he managed a .249 batting average with 86 hits in 345 at-bats. While still learning his trade behind the plate, Ferrell committed 15 errors. Bobby Veach, another Tiger farm hand, played for Toledo and made the Association All-Star team, knocking in a league-leading 145 runs. Soon-to-be-known shortstop Leo Durocher played for rival St. Paul. Meanwhile brother Wes, 19, had been called up to "The Show" from East Douglas, joining the major league Cleveland Indians team in the fall to pitch — side-stepping the minors altogether. Over in Tennessee, George had hit .292 for Memphis in the Southern Association. After their respective seasons had ended, the Ferrell brothers all reconvened back home on the farm in the fall to help Daddy Ferrell harvest, swap stories with the family, and practice their baseball skills.

Rick spent late February and March of 1928 in spring training with the Detroit Tigers. In April, he was sent back to the minors in Columbus by his supposed parent club, the Tigers. For the 1928 season Columbus' ownership brought in Nemo Leibold to manage, a veteran outfielder who had played thirteen years (1913–1925) in the majors with Cleveland, Chicago, Boston and Washington. Unfortunately the change in field leadership didn't change anything with the Columbus Senators who, saddled with weak pitching, were deep in the cellar by the third week of May. In an early season series against the Kansas City Blues, Ferrell met young infielder Joe Cronin, third baseman for the Blues, who, like Ferrell, would have a distinguished career in the majors, ultimately becoming both Rick's teammate and manager.

In 1928, Richard Ferrell got hot early, hitting nearly .300 in his first 71 at-bats. He cracked his first home run on May 5 and had multiple-hit games on May 22, 24, and 29. Defensively during this stretch, he threw out six basestealers in two games, but 10 consecutive losses left the Senators in the cellar —

Though Rick Ferrell was initially signed by the Detroit Tigers, he never played with the club at the major league level, staying in their minor leagues for three years, 1926 through 1928. Following his 1928 season at Columbus, a determined young ballplayer suspicious that the Tigers were manipulating his contract to "bury" him in the minors, challenged the system. Commissioner Kenesaw Mountain Landis declared him a free agent. This photograph was likely taken in spring training. (William M. Anderson)

soon-to-be familiar surroundings. Kansas City led the pack with a 16–6 record. St. Paul held second place just a half-game back, followed by Milwaukee, Indianapolis, Minneapolis, Louisville, Toledo and the battered Columbus Senators.

Ferrell sustained a hand injury after the first week of May and was out until May 20 while his team continued to lose. Returning home after losing 17 of 18 games, only 859 fans showed up at Neil Field for the homecoming.[8] Ferrell returned to the lineup later in the month and immediately resumed his fine hitting, but by the end of May, Columbus' record stood at 13–35.

On June 25, Columbus split a doubleheader with Indianapolis and in a blistering day at the plate, Ferrell got six hits in nine appearances, increasing his batting average to .402, with 51 hits in 127 at-bats. When Columbus pitcher Joe Stripp was strangely called up to join the Cincinnati Reds in late June, some minds questioned why Joe hadn't joined the Detroit Tigers, their supposed parent club. After Ferrell's hitting cooled off some, he was frequently used as a pinch-hitter. By August 9, the team was still entrenched in the basement with a 48–71 record. While sharing the catching duties with another receiver, Rick got back on track and began to hit, generating a .431 average for September.

With younger brother Wes already pitching for the major-league Cleveland Indians, Rick kept wondering when he would be called up to sample "The Show," either with the Tigers or with Columbus' new parent club, the Cincinnati Red Legs. An undated Ferrell family scrapbook news article from the time described Rick's curious situation: "Ferrell is, without a doubt, possessor of one of the greatest throwing arms in the history of the American Association. He catches runners at second base without apparent effort and seems to have more enthusiasm for his work than at any other time since joining the Senators.... Class is written all over him, and when all is said and done, it might safely be said that he is a better major league prospect than even Joe Stripp. It's laughable the way he picks runners off as they attempt to steal bases."

In late September of 1928, the Senators finally were able to reel off seven straight wins to slip by the Louisville Clippers and avoid the basement by finishing seventh. Ferrell had enjoyed a breakout season, hitting .333 and earning a spot on the American Association's All-Star team. He was joined on that team by several other future big leaguers: first baseman Joe Kuhel, third baseman Fred Haney, and Kansas City outfielder Ernie Orsatti. After the Louisville game, a mystified yet resolute Southern catcher had contacted Commissioner Landis, who then made Ferrell one of the first free agents in baseball history. The catcher couldn't wait to play baseball as a major leaguer.

When "Dick" Ferrell enthusiastically joined the St. Louis Browns as a rookie in spring training 1929, his club was coming off a miserable preceding year, winning just 59 games and narrowly escaping last place. The Browns franchise is best remembered as the team that won only one pennant (1944), drew poorly, and suffered through eight seasons of losing at least 100 games in a 52-year history in St. Louis.

However, during the 1920s, the club had finished in the first division eight times, topped by its greatest winning season in 1922, when the Browns won 93 games and lost out to the New York Yankees by a single game. The fall from the heat of the pennant race in 1922 to their dismal finish in 1927, 50½ games behind the again-champion Yankees, had been immense. Had Richard Ferrell possessed a crystal ball that foretold the Browns' future, he might have selected a different club.

After the disappointing 1928 season, tempestuous, exasperated Browns' owner Phil Ball began rebuilding his team. The Browns acquired excellent hitting outfielder Heine Manush and first baseman Lu Blue, a .295 hitter, from the Tigers. Ball sent Bing Miller (.300) to the Philadelphia Athletics in return for pitcher Sam Gray, who immediately won 20 games for the Brownies. All-Star George Sisler was sold to Washington for $25,000. Signing rookie Dick Ferrell on November 11, 1928, as his receiver-of-the-future gave Ball the freedom to release catcher Steve O'Neill, 36, the next day.

When Richard received his $25,000 signing bonus, he promptly handed over the bulk to Daddy Ferrell, helping him save the Ferrell family farm from financial difficulties. Suddenly, Daddy Ferrell saw baseball as a bright career for his son. At about this time, the catcher's nickname "Dick" became "Rick" as his first major league season beckoned.

2

❖ ❖ ❖

1929–1932

Rookie Years with the St. Louis Browns

In mid–February 1929, a hopeful 23-year-old Ferrell began his major league rookie season at the Browns' spring training camp in West Palm Beach, Florida, as second-string catcher behind Wally Schang, 38. Brother Wes headed to Cleveland to pitch for the Indians, George had left the farm for Memphis in the Southern Association to play outfield, while Marvin was at Oak Ridge.

Rick Ferrell had never played in a major league ballpark before. Sportsman's Park, the home stadium of the St. Louis Browns and the National League's St. Louis Cardinals, had hosted its first game on April 23, 1902, when the Browns joined the American League, then in its second year of existence. The Cardinals played their first game there on July 1, 1920.[1]

Following the 1925 season, owner Phil Ball expected attendance to dramatically increase, so had the stands double-decked in horseshoe fashion, stretching from the left-field corner to the right-field corner. Wooden bleachers were replaced with concrete structures and a roof was installed over the single-deck right-field stands, a massive overhaul that increased seating capacity to 34,000.

The dimensions of the "new" Sportsman's Park were fairly typical of most major league stadiums: 351 feet down the left-field line, 422 to the fence in dead center-field, and an enticingly short right-field just 310 feet along the line.[2] In July 1929 during Ferrell's first season, the Browns erected a thirty-three-foot-high screen in front of the right-field pavilion that extended from the foul pole into right-center field. That strategic decision was made the day after the Tigers left town following a four-game series in which they hit eight home runs. The right-field pavilion with its high screen became the most distinguishing feature of this ballpark.

Ferrell would catch a Browns pitching staff that included Bill "Dolly" Gray, "General" Alvin Crowder, George Blaeholder, and Tennessee southpaw Walter "Lefty" Stewart. His teammates in the infield consisted of veteran first baseman Lu Blue, second base Oscar Melillo, better known as "Ski" or "Spinach," shortstop Red Kress, and third baseman Frank O'Roarke. Roaming the outfield were Heine Manush, plus Fred Schulte, Frank "Beauty" McGowan, and Morris "Red" Badgro.

Having always played baseball with a sense of team camaraderie, Rick was not prepared for the chilly reception to "The Show" he first received. In these times competition for positions on a ball team was so intense that a newcomer received little assistance from his peers, and Rick was no exception. His enormous $25,000 signing bonus perhaps prejudiced some Browns players, who possibly resented the rookie catcher and wanted to see what this kid could really do. Without any coaching assistance, Ferrell improved his skills on his own through keen observation, self-correction, and diligent practice. As he progressed through the majors, however, Rick eschewed this cold treatment toward young rookies and was always the first one to greet a new guy, make him feel welcomed to the squad, and help him improve in any way possible.

Ferrell's major league debut came on April 19, 1929, at Sportsman's Park in a game Chicago won, 5–4. In the bottom of the eighth with a 4–4 tie, the Browns' skipper sent lefty Tom Jenkins up to bat for second baseman Oscar Melillo. When White Sox manager Lena Blackburne countered with a left-handed relief pitcher, Dan Dugan, the managerial chess game continued. Manager Dan Howley then called on rookie Rick Ferrell, a right-handed hitter, to pinch-hit for Jenkins. Dugan retired the young catcher, and Chicago won in the ninth. Ferrell's first major league base hit occurred two days later on Sunday, April 21, in a 16–9 loss to Detroit.[3]

The 1929 Browns blasted off, leading the pack in the early season. On May 1, they recorded their fourth straight victory by edging the Cleveland Indians, 4–3. Rick's younger brother Wes pitched and was beaten by the Browns' seasoned starter General Crowder, a 20-game winner in 1928. But Wes Ferrell would have his breakout season in 1929, winning 21 games. Rick did not challenge his brother at the plate; Howley used his veteran catcher Schang.

From May 10 to 12, the Brownies took two of three from Boston. The May 12 St. Louis Post-Dispatch commented on Ferrell's quick throw to second: "There may be better arms in baseball than Rick Ferrell's, but they haven't been on view here thus far. Red Sox center fielder [Jack] Rothrock is a fast man, but attempting to steal on Ferrell, he was out by several feet."

From June 1 to 18, the Browns traveled by train from Union Station through the entire circuit, playing against all the American League teams except Chicago. On June 5 at Philadelphia's Shibe Park, Ferrell's catching skills caught the eye of the A's manager Connie Mack, a former catcher, who told the youngster how much he admired his skills behind the plate. A year later, a newspaper article by Hersh quoted the Athletics' manager as saying: "Rick Ferrell is not a good catcher — he's far better than good. 'Good' does not explain him."

The next stop after the City of Brotherly Love on that first road trip of 1929 was Yankee Stadium on June 8. Rick described his first time in New York

City in an August 12, 1984, *Detroit News Magazine* interview with Detroit sportswriter Joe Falls, who paraphrased: "[Rick] was making his first trip into New York City and didn't want anyone to know he was a rookie. When the train pulled into Grand Central Station, the young catcher decided he would pick out one of the veteran players and follow him to the hotel. He chose Lu Blue, the longtime first baseman, and would do whatever he did. Old Lu would know where to go. Blue got off the train; Ferrell got off the train. Blue picked up his bag; Ferrell picked up his bag. Blue started walking away, and Ferrell started following him. Blue went down a flight of stairs; Ferrell went down a flight of stairs. Blue walked under the station and started up another flight of stairs. He noticed Ferrell following him. 'What are you doing?' Blue turned around and asked. 'I'm following you,' said Ferrell. 'That's fine with me ... but I'm going to my home in New Rochelle,' replied Blue," whereupon Rick backtracked to get himself to the team's hotel.

Through June the Browns primarily held down third place behind New York and Philadelphia. Batting below .200, Rick had progressed slowly at first, having gotten into only seven games in five weeks. However in a June 15 game against the Red Sox at Fenway, Ferrell proved himself with the game on the line. Summoned to pinch-hit in the top of the eighth inning, he blasted a two-run double that led to a 12–8 win for the Browns' Dolly Gray. Game-winning clutch hitting would define Rick's offensive production countless times over the course of his long major league career.

Ferrell caught Walter Stewart twice and won twice during a four-game series vs. Cleveland from June 24 to 26. In the second game of a Sunday doubleheader on June 25, Stewart pitched an 8–0 shutout, giving up only two hits with Rick behind the plate. Finding his stride, catcher Ferrell drove home two runs on two hits and had two walks. Three days later at Comiskey Park on June 29, the Browns swept a doubleheader from Chicago in which again the battery of Stewart and Ferrell won the second game, 12–4. In this outing Rick scored three times, getting two RBIs on two hits. Suddenly, at the end of the month, first-string catcher Clyde Manion left the Browns due to his wife's unexpected death and would be absent until August. During this time, back-up catcher Rick played more frequently.

From July 2 to 21, St. Louis played a three-week home stand at Sportsman's Park, garnering a 10–13 record. In a double-loss to Washington on July 20, a pitch that bounced hard off Ferrell's knee put him out of the lineup for several days. However, despite his bench time, Rick's batting average had reached .200 and during August he got on base 17 times in 30 at-bats. He caught two of four games in back-to-back doubleheaders vs. the A's on August 5 and 6 and belted out four hits. In a third game, his pinch-hit single helped St. Louis to a two-two split of the series.

Rick and Wesley saw each other throughout the season whenever the Browns and Indians played. Usually however, when Wes pitched, Rick had the day off. On September 28, Wes pitched a brilliant two-hitter to shut out St. Louis, 4–0, in Cleveland for his twentieth win, but his older brother did not play. On October 3, pitcher Alvin Crowder out-dueled Wes Ferrell in a ten-inning affair as the Browns managed a 3–2 victory. In this contest, Rick faced Wes for the first time as a hitter in a professional game, grounding out.

The day before the season ended on October 6, manager Dan Howley announced his plans to leave the Browns, stating dissatisfaction with the conditions and his disinterest in even discussing future changes with owner Phil Ball. Howley said: "I'm merely going to see him and say good-bye."[4] Howley's gang enjoyed a strong final day, beating the visiting Indians twice, 4–2 and 4–1, to finish the 1929 season in fourth place. With less than 340,000 in attendance, the Browns never became a strong draw for fans. St. Louis baseball fans favored the National League Cardinals, co-tenants of Sportsman's Park.

Over in Cleveland 21-year-old Wesley Ferrell became the ace of the Indians' 1929 pitching staff in his first full season, winning 21 games (3.50 ERA). His strong consistent pitching helped the Indians finish in third place, just in front of the Browns.

Starting slow as St. Louis' first-year bonus-baby in 1929, Rick Ferrell played in 64 games as the back-up catcher, garnering meager stats. In 144 at-bats he totaled 33 hits, walked 32 times, and drove in 20 runs to account for a .229 batting average, the lowest of his 18-year playing career. A line-drive hitter, he would later stroke a considerable number of doubles; he had six in his first season in the big time. An undated 1931 article in Rick's Hall of Fame file referred to his 1929 season: "But 1929 was a disappointment to the young catcher. He was dissatisfied with the little work that manager Dan Howley allotted to him, and he voiced displeasure, which didn't hasten his daily appearance in the line-up. Rick was too ambitious to be content with an occasional major assignment or working exhibition games. His $25,000 bonus, followed by irksome bench duty, plus the swift gait of brother Wes, also a 1929 rookie, combined to make Rick look bad. The superficial public was misled."

That fall Rick returned to his Guilford family home where his parents and brothers celebrated his 24th birthday on October 12. Rick, Wes, and George brought out their Hawaiian guitars and banjos to sing and play music with their cousin Hally Jones, as all possessed considerable musical talent.

Almost two weeks later while walking in Greensboro, Rick came upon a noisy group of men screaming and pounding on the locked doors of the local bank. At mid-afternoon the bank was closed! The date was October 24, 1929, to be known as "Black Tuesday." The American stock market had crashed, families suddenly lost all of their deposited money in bank failures, and a ruinous economic Depression unlike any other had invaded the country.

Over the winter owner Phil Ball had replaced Dan Howley with Browns coach Bill Killefer, a former thirteen-year major league catcher and battery-mate of Grover Cleveland Alexander. Rick joined the Browns in West Palm

Beach, Florida, for 1930 spring training. George Ferrell had transferred from the Memphis club to play for the Winston-Salem (N.C.) team in the Piedmont League, while Wes was pitching for the Cleveland Indians.

Based on their performance in 1929, St. Louis had a competitive team, at least against seven of the eight teams. Playing at a higher caliber, Philadelphia won 104 games and dropped only 46, to finish 18 games ahead of its nearest rival. But the Browns appeared to have a solid nucleus with outfielders Heinie Manush (.355) and Fred Schulte (.307) and infielders Ralph Kress (.305), Oscar Melillo (.296, and the league leader in assists), and Lu Blue (.293, with the league's most putouts). Their respectable pitching staff was headed by Dolly Gray, who had finished with 18 wins after pitching a league-leading 305 innings. The number two and three hurlers, Alvin Crowder (17–15) and George Blaeholder (14–15), were also workhorses. Lack of offensive power underscored the team's worst weakness; the players hit only 46 home runs collectively, a number equaled individually by Babe Ruth in 1929.

With Wally Schang traded back to the A's during the off-season, Rick Ferrell became first-string catcher, sharing duties with Clyde Manion, a part-timer who had caught a career-high 76 games for the 1928 Browns. The opportunity was open for Rick Ferrell to emerge as the regular catcher under manager Killefer. After practicing all winter, Ferrell adopted a game plan aimed at improving his batting average, later stating in an interview: "I tried to be an all-around player. I knew I wasn't going to be a home run hitter. I more or less concentrated on average and line drives."[5]

On Tuesday, April 15, 1930, the Browns opened the season in Detroit, but the Tigers spoiled the day with a 6–3 victory. Manion drew the starting assignment early in the season as cold weather forced the cancellation of several games, but my month's end, Ferrell was beginning to see action and was hitting the ball at a .353 clip. St. Louis strung together five wins, vaulting into second place. Impressed with his young catcher's work behind the plate, first-year manager Bill Killefer remarked: "Ferrell is the first young catcher I ever saw come up knowing everything." Near the end of the month, St. Louis looked like a world-beater, downing the White Sox, 12–0.

On May 21 at Cleveland's League Park, right-hander George Blaeholder nosed out Wes Ferrell, 6–5, as the Browns took three-out-of-four from the Indians. Two days later Wes returned to relieve in the eighth inning, but the Indians were edged, 5–4, by the Lefty Stewart-Rick Ferrell battery. Despite taking the series, the Browns, at 14–19, were not winning consistently, with mediocre play that shoved them back into sixth place, already 9½ games out.

May 28 topped off a three-game losing streak by the Detroit Tigers as the Browns fell in a 16–11, free-for-all loss. Ferrell scored one run in a one-for-five day at the plate, but drew the ire of his manager for not executing a play. In its May 28 issue, *The World* published a short story carrying the headline, "Ferrell Fined $50 for Bonehead Play." According to the account, Tiger runners were

Rick stands in the middle of Sportsman's Park in St. Louis in 1930 during the first of two stints with the St. Louis Browns, arm outstretched, ready to catch whatever comes his way. (Patricia Kenney)

on first and second when pitcher Vic Sorrell laid down a bunt that first rolled outside the baseline, then back into fair territory. Ferrell fielded the fair ball, but then momentarily held on to it, resulting in a bases-loaded situation. Although manager Killifer called Rick's hesitation a "dumb play," the $50 fine seemed severe and knee-jerk, perhaps reflecting the skipper's personal hostility while watching his team give up 16 runs.

In a three-week home stand from May 25 to June 17, St. Louis continued its lackluster play, winning 10 and losing 12, yet the competition allowed the Browns to move into the first division. Ferrell's early hitting binge cooled, and he had leveled off at .255 after 18 games.

During this home stand, owner Ball engineered a memorable trade with Washington, giving up his best hitter, Heinie Manush, and his best pitcher, Alvin Crowder, in return for slugging outfielder Goose Goslin.[6] Manush's spring holdout and the general lack of punch in the Brownie lineup certainly influenced a bad decision. Although Goslin was a great hitter, destined for Cooperstown, Ball had traded his own would-be member of the Hall in Manush, and Crowder would win 15 games for his new club during the rest of the season before going on a four-year winning spree, and earning the league's best record for wins in the 1932–33 period, with 26 in '32 and 24 in '33. Some of Ball's ire with Crowder centered around the angry pitcher's hurling a ball into the stands that almost hit Ball's guests who were seated in his private box.

In almost storybook fashion, the Nats then faced the Browns on June 14, 1930, at Sportsman's Park. Sam Gray pitched well, allowing only four Washington safeties; St. Louis won the contest, 5–4, with Rick Ferrell carrying the offensive load. He figured in all the scoring and only a triple denied him from hitting for the cycle. Rick's perfect day at the plate included his first career home run off southpaw and fellow North Carolinian Garland Braxton in the seventh inning; his three hits drove in four runs. A good-sized crowd of 7,000 saw Ferrell enjoy a career offensive day and their new long ball hitter, Goose Goslin, go one for four, while the just-departed Heinie Manush managed one hit in five trips to the plate.[7] Ferrell's home run made a sports headline in the *Washington Post*, his first such notoriety in the big time. Before the Nationals left town they were felled again when the Browns rallied for six runs in the eighth to claim a 12–9 victory. Newly-acquired Goslin paid big dividends with a three-hit game, including a home run and a double. Ferrell's hot hitting continued with a three-for-four day plus a walk, adding three RBIs.

On July 9, 1930, the Browns fought the Indians and Wes Ferrell, but the tenacious Cleveland right-hander hung on to win a 9–5 decision, despite giving up ten hits and four walks. In a rare occurrence, Rick faced his brother, getting one hit in two official at-bats. By the end of July, the Browns' slide continued as they stood 40–60 in seventh place, 26½ games behind the league-leading New York Yankees. On July 26, Goslin again provided the difference in St. Louis' 6–3 win over Boston with a three-hit game that tallied four runs while he clubbed his eighteenth round-tripper. Rick caught the game before a crowd that Wray, in that day's *St. Louis Post-Dispatch* column, called "hardly enough present to give a husky cheer or a good jeer." Ferrell was now hitting .274.

In the first week of August, Wes Ferrell came back to town to win his eighteenth victory by a 5–2 score. Again, Rick sat that one out, as well as several more games until August 12, for some unknown reason, probably an injury. Though the Browns slumped, Goose Goslin reminded owner Ball why he had coveted his services. In a 7–2 victory over the Red Sox with Rick catching on August 13, he drove home four runs. A week later he hit successive home runs in three plate appearances to help propel the offense to a 7–0 victory over Philadelphia. In the same series with the A's, St. Louis was victimized by the A's "Lefty" Grove when he notched his twentieth season win by a 4–2 margin. The Browns touched him for ten hits, with two coming off the bat of Rick Ferrell.

The "Dog Days of Summer" epitomize a time in the season when players are tiring and heat can be oppressive. In a Mississippi River town like St. Louis, the combination of heat and humidity adds a whole layer of fatigue to the game of baseball. Ferrell would recall to friends those steamy temperatures that sapped energy as St. Louis was the hottest place in the league to play. He could lose as much as ten pounds in a doubleheader, and September was always his worst month, as he was tiring by then.

In late August, St. Louis faced-off twice with Detroit, first at Navin Field in the Motor City, then in a five game series at home from August 25 to 30 to close out the month. On August 25, the Tigers introduced highly-prized rookie pitcher Tommy Bridges in his first starting assignment. Though he hung around for eight and two-thirds innings, Bridges experienced a shaky outing, allowing seven hits and twelve walks. In the bottom of the ninth inning with two outs and Detroit leading, 5–4, catcher Rick Ferrell blasted a bases-loaded clutch triple, winning the game for St. Louis, 7–5. Ferrell continued to get timely hits as the Browns took four out of the five games from Detroit. In the series finale, he went 2–4 in a thirteen-inning, 6–5 win.

On Monday, September 1, the Tribe won a doubleheader as Cleveland out-slugged St. Louis, 13–8, in the opening game. Rick Ferrell contributed a single and a sacrifice bunt to knock in a run, as the two teams combined for thirty-three hits. Wes Ferrell mastered the Browns in the second game for his twenty-fourth victory as Rick watched his teammates bow, 9–5.

The Browns experienced a disappointing season in 1930, finishing a distant 38 games behind the repeating American League champion Philadelphia Athletics. Losing 90 games, they only competed with the tail-end teams. Attendance reflected their level of inept play with only 280,000 fans passing through the turnstiles, a drop-off of 140,000 paid customers from the previous campaign. Goslin produced as expected, batting .326 with 30 home runs and an even 100 RBIs. Kress came back with another fine season, finishing with a .313 average and a team high 112 runs driven in. Lefty Stewart won twenty games.

In his second major league season, Rick Ferrell showed marked improvement, increasing his batting average almost forty points, from .229 to .268, and improving his slugging average to .360. He caught a majority of the games, 101, and nearly tripled his hit total with 84. As a defensive receiver he was beginning to make his mark, skillfully handling his position for a fielding average of .983. After the season, the two major league brothers headed back to North Carolina to help their father on the family farm, meet with the other Ferrells, and prepare for the next campaign.

Surely the Ferrell family must have felt great pride with three sons playing professional baseball, George at the AAA level, and Rick and Wes in the majors with their careers advancing rapidly. In just his second full season, Wes had compiled an outstanding record in 1930, winning a second-best 25 victories, three short of Lefty Grove. He ranked second in the league in earned-run-average (3.31) and innings pitched (297), third in complete games (25), and fourth in winning percentage (.658) and strikeouts (143).

Rick Ferrell could reveal a remarkable openness, especially for a person generally thought to be quiet, modest and protective of his personal life. In a letter from December 16, 1930, to a St. Louis sportswriter and published soon after in the *St. Louis Post-Dispatch*, he wrote:

Dear Willie,

I was pleased to receive your letter and to learn that everything is going along nicely with you and the St. Louis Browns. I am a little late in answering, but nevertheless, I will give you an idea how my brother and I have been spending the winter months.

All of my brothers are spending the winter at home at Guilford and we sure have a wonderful time together. Unlike most ball players, we have a firm belief in keeping in good condition the year around. We do not figure our year's work has been entirely completed at the end of the playing season, but that we must keep in good shape preparing for next spring and another season.

Our daily routine of exercises consists of golfing, hunting, and light workouts at the gymnasium. By working in this manner each and every day, we succeed in keeping in the best of health and splendid physical condition.

Our "foursome" in golf is made up of my brother Wes of Cleveland; the pitcher Garland Braxton, Chicago southpaw; Tiny Stewart, Cardinal scout at Greensboro; and myself. I have just recently taken up golf and I find it very fascinating. Most every day, you could find me on the links trying to improve in every way. I won my first prize in a tournament at a local golf course just recently. One hundred players entered the contest. We were all "ham and eggers," but anyway, I got a kick out of winning.

Hunting has been good here this year. We have mountains on one side of us and the seashore on the other. In either direction, there is plenty of game. Duck shooting on the coast has been especially good. Tom Zachery, Boston Braves pitcher and former Brownie, is our hunting partner.

I am expecting to pay St. Louis a visit in the near future, but I have not decided just when I will make this trip. I suppose you are having a great deal of cold weather, and that doesn't exactly suit me. I much prefer the weather of the sunny South. It isn't very sunny right now, as we are sharing the cold weather with you. In closing, I wish you all the very best of luck and a delightful winter.

Rick Ferrell

In February 1931, the three Ferrell brothers left their Guilford County farm to play professional baseball — Rick again traveled to West Palm Beach to join the St. Louis Browns, Wes reported to Sarasota, Florida, to the Cleveland Indians spring camp, and George Ferrell, Buffalo Bisons outfielder, also left for spring training in Florida. The Ferrell family presence continued to grow when 20-year-old brother Marvin, then an aspiring pitcher, joined Rick in West Palm to try out with the Browns. Having played three years of semi-pro baseball in North Carolina and Pennsylvania, he was hoping to sign a professional contract. After working out with St. Louis hurlers Sam Gray, George Blaeholder, and Dick Coffman, young Marvin impressed the Browns' upper echelon enough to be granted a minor league contract and an assignment to pitch for the Wichita Falls club in the Texas League.

During the off-season, the Browns had done little to strengthen a sub-par team lacking front-line pitching and, other than Goslin and Kress, firepower. The Browns' season opened on April 14, 1931, at home against the Detroit Tigers, whom they defeated in the first two games by scores of 7–3 and 6–4. However, these victories were followed by a dismal nine-game losing streak.

In six of his first thirteen games, Ferrell, wearing number 8 on his uniform, went hitless, including an historic game for the record books played out on April 29, 1931, in Cleveland — a day Rick and the Browns were at League Park to compete against the first-place Indians and Wes Ferrell. The game began with the Browns' lead-off man hitting a ground ball to shortstop, but Bill Hunnefield booted it and Jim Levey was on base. After the Browns' best hitter, Goose Goslin, lined into a double play, "0 runs, 0 hits and 1 error" displayed on the scoreboard for six innings.

When a no-hitter stretches past the sixth frame, spectators start counting the outs remaining. While Wes Ferrell was handcuffing the Browns' lineup, his hitting approached the magnificence of his pitching. In the fourth inning, he drove a pitch over the wall in left field for a two-run homer. In the eighth, Wesley connected again, banging a long drive off the right field wall, barely missing a second homer, and instead settling for a long double that scored two more runs.

The dramatic eighth inning started with Goslin cracking a wicked line drive headed through the box and Wes, almost in self-defense, made his own saving play by knocking it down and retiring the Goose with a toss to first. Next, Ferrell struck out the ever-dangerous Red Kress, setting the stage for an encounter with another tough out — his brother Rick.

This sibling confrontation in what turned out to be an historic game is even more interesting when one remembers that generally Rick's managers kept him out of the St. Louis lineup when Wes was slated to hurl for the Indians. In the third inning, Rick had grounded out to second baseman Johnny Hodapp. In the sixth, he again grounded out, this time to shortstop Hunnefield. Not about to give ground, Rick stepped up in the eighth frame of the hitless game and smashed one into the hole, digging hard toward first base. Hunnefield snared the ball and made the long throw, which pulled the first baseman off the bag. The umpire cried "Safe!" and Wes Ferrell's no-hitter appeared to be broken up by his brother Rick. But moments later, the official scorer changed the decision: Rick Ferrell was declared safe on a throwing error, not a base hit! The final inning was less heart-stopping, a walk to Goslin sandwiched between a ground out and a whiff that brought outfielder Fred Schulte to bat. He slapped one to second sacker Hodapp for an easy 4–3 putout, and Wes Ferrell won his no-hit masterpiece, 9–0, while striking out eight Brownies.

In a newspaper interview in Chicago a few days later, Rick recounted the close play at first. "I didn't want a base hit, but I had to get up there. Anyway, I was up there, doing my best to knock my kid brother off his perch in the Hall of Fame. Wes didn't say a word, but I knew he was going to bear down plenty, and he's never been any easier for me to hit than any other pitcher either! With the count two and two, I got a hold of a shoulder high fastball and lit out for first base. I just flew down there. It was a pretty well hit ball, but Hunnefield came up with it and gunned it over to first. His peg was a little wide and pulled [Lew] Fonseca off the bag and I was safe. Wes walked over and said, 'You wouldn't take that one, would ya, Rick?' He was smiling, but I bet he felt kind of choky about it, at that. Then, they decided it was a bum throw instead. I love my bingles just as much as the next ball player, but there's one time 'just another at bat' didn't make me mad.'"[8]

While in Chicago on this grueling road trip in which they had lost seven games in a row, St. Louis ran into a hot White Sox club and on May 2, the Browns couldn't take advantage of six errors committed by their hosts in a 2–1 defeat. Ferrell went one-for-three as his mates collected only four safeties.

On the following day, the Browns finally snapped their long losing streak, getting their first road win of 1931 at the expense of Chicago by a 9–5 score. St. Louis broke the game open in the sixth, scoring seven runs. Rick Ferrell led the 15-hit attack with four safeties including two doubles. With this hot performance at the plate, Ferrell's hitting gained greater consistency: in five games leading up to May 12, he had piled up 12 hits in 17 at-bats to achieve a sizzling .706 average, upping his season average to .371.

Gasping for breath, the sinking Browns rose up the next day, June 21, and in a two-game set, topped the mighty Yankees twice, 9–7 and 8–2. Their victories were particularly sweet given their combined 22 hits and 17 runs when primarily facing the slants of two fine hurlers, George Pipgras and youngster Vernon "Lefty" Gomez. Manager Killifer rested Ferrell in the opener, but Rick was behind the plate for the second game and delivered a home run in his first time at bat, staking the Browns to a 2–0 lead. On Monday, June 22, St. Louis made it three in a row over New York by clipping their high-flying wings, 14–10, in another offensive outburst featuring a four-hit game from Rick Ferrell.

Throughout his distinguished career, Rick was often eclipsed by his flamboyant and highly-talented brother Wes, and the two were very different personalities and players. A pitcher is like a quarterback, always at the center of the action with lots of opportunities to draw raves. A catcher assumes a supporting role, regardless of ability and leadership, and seldom is credited with making the difference in a game. Given superior ability, the pitcher is the key to victory in every game he pitches, and Wesley Ferrell was certainly a dominant hurler. Being handsome and gregarious, he seemingly had everything going for him and he provided good copy. To top it all off, he was one of baseball's greatest power-hitting pitchers, while Rick was primarily a singles and doubles hitter. Their respective behaviors defined their differences even more sharply. Rick was nearly always a model citizen, while Wes could be emotionally combative and confrontational, making headlines both because of his exceptional

Rick swings a bat wearing a St. Louis Browns cap in a photograph probably taken in 1929. Note the baggy flannel pants worn at the time.

performance and the controversy that accompanied his sometimes volatile behavior.

The August 1931 issue of *Baseball Magazine* ran an article about Rick that said, "Rick of the Browns is quite overshadowed by the spectacular triumphs of Wes. But who in authority would care to predict that Rick's future won't be equally as bright? ... [Rick] is ambitious to excel, and after an hour's chat with him, one is convinced that he will. His confidence in himself is supreme — but it is quiet. There is nothing obnoxious about it. Then too, he has unusual baseball sense, a keen alertness, and good judgment. He handles pitchers well. Mentally or physically, he has no defective kinks in his armor."

Although Wes was exonerated of any blame, he became a principal character in a controversy involving Indians manager Roger Peckinpaugh, umpires William McGowan and Thomas Connolly, and league president William Harridge. In the final game of a series in Detroit on May 31, Peckinpaugh summoned Ferrell from the bullpen in the seventh inning to replace Indians pitcher Willis Hudlin. After warming up on the mound, McGowan signaled, "Play ball." Peckinpaugh, Ferrell, and catcher Luke Sewell challenged the umpire-in-chief, claiming that the pitcher could throw as many pitches as he wanted. McGowan disagreed, yet allowed Ferrell to throw a tenth pitch. "I motioned the batter to step into the box, and took my stance behind the plate. Ferrell then waved the batter aside and started to throw another ball. I held up my hand and told him that I was going to call balls on him if he threw any more balls. I called "Play Ball!" and Sewell stepped out ten or fifteen feet, and took another toss from Ferrell." When the game continued and the Indian bench began to razz McGowan, he reacted quickly and tossed Peckinbaugh out of the game.

Letters from the Baseball Hall of Fame files indicate that the umpire wrote to Harridge insisting he had handled the situation correctly. Within the week, Harridge wrote McGowan, stating there was not a rule regulating how many warm-up pitches a reliever could throw. Instead the matter was left up to the home plate umpire's judgment. "In the case referred to," wrote Harridge, "I do not believe it would have done any harm for you to have gone a little farther with Ferrell. He is a valuable asset, and pitching a few more balls would have made no particular difference. It is incidents of this kind that cause all of the trouble for the umpire."

Playing at home over the Independence Day holiday, the Browns split a twin bill on July 5 as Rick Ferrell caught both contests, contributing an RBI in each game while going two-for-five for the day. With constant effort, he'd raised his batting average to a strong .333, getting two more hits in a 7–1 victory over Detroit at Navin Field on July 13. The team went on to Boston and took three out of four. Rick came through with a two-for-three game in the series opener. The Browns prevailed, thanks to a three-run rally in the sixth inning when Ferrell delivered a clutch hit to drive in a run with two outs.

On July 14, Ferrell suffered his first serious injury in the opening game of a doubleheader with the Red Sox. On a bang-bang play at the plate, he put the tag on a hard-sliding Urbane Pickering, who had raced home to score from third base. The runner and catcher collided, with Ferrell hanging onto the ball and getting the out. But the hard impact resulted in what Ferrell thought was only a bruise; he told manager Killefer his hand was a bit sore the next day. However a medical examination discovered a broken bone in his right hand, whereupon Rick was promptly dispatched on the twenty-six hour train ride back to St. Louis to see the team doctor. During his projected three-week absence, the Browns would use backup catchers Russ Young and Benny Bengough to fill in.

According to the July 16 *Post-Dispatch*, Ferrell's loss to the Browns' progress was a major blow. Referring to Ferrell as a star, the writer, Regan, wrote: "The loss of Ferrell will probably affect the team more than the loss of any two or three of the other athletes. Besides Rick's steadying influence and his right smart hitting with men on bases, the lad was a great coach not only to the pitchers, but to every individual on the team."

On September 8, St. Louis moved up a notch in the standings to the fifth rung, following a 3–2 triumph over Detroit in which number 8, Rick Ferrell, blasted a solo home run. All in all, August was a disastrous month for St. Louis, winning 10 games, losing 24, and ultimately playing under .300 baseball. Winning three out of four from the hapless Chicago White Sox allowed the Browns to sneak into a fifth-place finish in 1931.

Although the Browns piled up 91 losses in 1931, its fifth-place finish would prove to be its best standing in the twelve years stretching from 1930 through 1941. St. Louis led the league in fewest walks allowed and double plays made. Individually, the players did not achieve any distinction. Ferrell, at 25, had the best season in his young career by batting .306, with 118 hits, hitting a high percentage of doubles (30), and driving in 57 runs. Though never a long ball hitter, his three home runs were three times as many as he hit in his first full season. Most importantly, he had become the Browns' regular receiver, catching 118 games.

The initial three-year contract Rick signed in November 1928 had expired. On January 29, 1932, he told the *Greensboro Daily News* that without a $2000 salary raise, he expected to "have trouble getting together with the Browns for 1932." The paper reported that on February 12 Ferrell had returned his contract to Ball, unsigned, calling the terms "very unsatisfactory." Despite America's dreadful economic depression and the Browns' dismal 1931 season, Ferrell remained firm, ultimately refusing to accept three contracts that had been offered. Shirley Povich lent support in the February 1 *Washington Post*, writing that "Rick Ferrell of the Browns is rapidly approaching the stardom as a catcher that Wesley Ferrell is enjoying as a pitcher with the Indians." Also holding out for more money were star shortstop Red Kress, big hitter Goose Goslin, starting pitcher Lefty Stewart, and second tier players Benny Bengough and Harry Collins.

The *Washington Post* reported on March 11 that Ball had signed Goslin, and given his stature, this news undoubtedly influenced others to come around; however, both Ferrell and Kress held tough. By March 15, an exasperated Phil Ball issued an ultimatum, stating "the hold-outs would either sign at what we've offered, or they can pick fruit all summer."[9] About a week later, Ferrell folded his hand and signed a one-year contract with his old buddy, Browns business manager Bill Friel.

Although he reported late on March 20, Rick got going in a hurry. His five RBIs in one game with Buffalo reflected his strong hitting in exhibition games, and he was quickly establishing himself as a premier major-league catcher. Certainly new Browns coach Allan Sothorn was impressed after watching Ferrell in spring training.

Off the field, Rick Ferrell could have been mistaken for a banker or college professor. Here he sits for a posed studio portrait, probably taken around 1930, dressed in his fine striped suit and polka dot tie.

"I don't think there's a better catcher in baseball. I had heard and read a lot about him, but he was really better than I believed he could be," Sothorn was quoted in the April 1, 1932, *St. Louis Post-Dispatch*.

The 1932 Browns team remained largely unchanged from 1931, excepting Ball parted with Red Kress, one of the key cogs in the Browns lineup, sending him to the White Sox in exchange for pitcher Bump Hadley and a young outfielder, Bruce Campbell. Kress had annoyed the owner with his prolonged hold-out. Ball did not like players who bucked his authority, and he was eager to bolster his inept starting rotation. Hadley had won 11 games for Washington in 1931 and brought a mark of 1–1 when he joined his newest team. Hardly much of a contributor, the Browns' new right-hander won 12 and lost 19 over the remainder of the season. Offensively, the Browns could hit fairly well, but their pitching remained a major weakness.

St. Louis opened the 1932 season on April 12 at Comiskey Park and, despite 13 hits apiece, lost to Chicago, 9–2. Goslin (three hits) and Ferrell (two hits) made the most noise for the Browns, each accounting for the team's total scoring. *Chicago Daily Tribune* reporter Edward Burns' game account referred to the Browns catcher as "the dangerous Rick Ferrell." Goslin also made news when the home plate umpire would not allow the Goose to use a white bat with dark stripes, calling it a "camouflage bat."

As would often happen in this season, the Browns would sweep or win a series hands-down, and then experience exactly the opposite with the next opponent. The next visitors to arrive in town were the Indians, who left with three victories in a row, the finale won by nemesis Wes Ferrell. Although his team lost 10–5 on April 25 against the Tribe, Rick Ferrell, again wearing number 8, represented much of the Browns' offense by getting three of his team's six hits, including a solo home run. After a slow start, the Browns heated up by winning with greater regularity, yet were still capable of completely blowing a series. They concluded April in fifth place, winning two out of three from the Tigers, with each game decided by a single run.

Rick was spare, but muscular, with very strong hands. He didn't swing from the end of the bat and didn't try to hit home runs. As a contact hitter, he tried to put the bat on the ball, generally getting more hits to center field and right-center than down the third base line.

From May 2 to 29, the Brownies launched a 20-game road trip. The Tribe had racked up nine straight victories until they succumbed to a 16-hit St. Louis attack on May 3, in which Rick Ferrell slammed three hits. As so often happened with this hot and cold team, they next handled the Red Sox by winning three of a four-game series. In a free-swinging affair against Washington on May 18, the Nats and Browns combined for thirty-three hits in an 11–7 St. Louis victory. Goslin reminded his former owner what he had given up by driving in four runs. Ferrell, continuing to hit in the fifth spot, scored three runs on the afternoon, stinging the ball with two hits, one a triple that scored two runs.

Suddenly from June 2 to 18, St. Louis began to play their best baseball of the season as pitching and hitting suddenly took off: the home team won the next 10 out of 12 games. In the 9–8 win on June 15, Rick Ferrell powered his club to victory with three hits that included a double and a triple that cleared all the bases. For the day, the catcher scored twice and drove in four runs, including the winning tally. For the season his batting average stood at .312. But during the second game of a doubleheader at home on June 19, A's pitcher George Earnshaw threw a pitch that broke hitter Ferrell's hand, an injury that benched him for three weeks.

The Browns had flourished, winning 11 of 17 games in the home stand, and writer Gould had difficulty restraining his excitement in his June 24 *Post-Dispatch* column: "You can almost hear Bill Killefer, manager of the fighting Browns, paraphrasing history to announce today, 'We have met the East and they are ours.'" St. Louis continued their roll, winning five of the next eight to end June. The headline of the June 28 *Post-Dispatch* blared, "Browns Setting .636 Pace for 22 Games, All Primed for Big Drive."

With a rehabilitated hand, Rick returned to action on July 10 at Yankee Stadium to help his team whip the Yankees twice on a Sunday afternoon, 10–9 and 8–7. Goslin went on a rampage in the opener going five-for-five and knocking in four runs. Ferrell's clutch hit drove in the deciding run to win the nightcap.

But, true to form, from July 11 to 20, the home team again struggled through a sustained losing streak, dropping 11 straight games that put them 22 games out, yet still in sixth place. In a tight 3–2 Browns win vs. the Nationals on July 26, Ferrell went two-for-three, getting two runs with an RBI and a run scored.

The Browns' August performance wasn't pretty. They captured only nine wins against 17 defeats, including six straight losses to close out the month. But, individually, Rick Ferrell was on a personal roll in 1932, blasting offensive highlights during the month with his strong bat. The first thrill came on August 5 when his two-run double in the bottom of the tenth inning erased a one-run Athletics margin and pinned a 9–8 loss on All-Star hurler Lefty Grove, pitching in relief. On August 9 in a losing effort at Sportsman's Park, Rick homered off the Yankees' Lefty Gomez, who won his nineteenth game of the season, 5–3. Then on August 18 at Fenway Park, Ferrell blasted four hits and a sacrifice in six at-bats in a disappointing 7–6 loss to Boston. In the next game he caught, Ferrell went hitless, breaking his 20-game hitting streak. With a season-high .339 batting average, Rick, the powerhouse, was hitting sixth-best in the league.

As August wound down, both Ferrells were receiving extra press coverage. Fans were awaiting the selections for the Babe Ruth All-American team, with Rick considered a top nominee. In recognizing the tough competition among several outstanding catchers, Damon Kerby of the *Post-Dispatch* stated, "For instance, Rick Ferrell of the Browns is having a great year. One of most accurate throwers and a steady receiver, Ferrell is recognized as an outstanding hitter. Ferrell's throwing and hitting have bettered Mickey's

Babe Ruth steals home on St. Louis Browns catcher Rick Ferrell in a game at Yankee Stadium on August 4, 1932, when Ruth was nearing forty. Pitcher Lefty Stewart was wild in his delivery. Frankie Crosetti is the batter.

[Cochrane] performances this season. The Browns' catcher has been named more frequently that any other player on either St. Louis team, and with plenty of reason. Ferrell ranks among the top-notchers in catching this season, both behind the plate and at bat."[10]

Although Wes had already won his twentieth game, marking the fourth consecutive season with 20 or more victories, he had drawn a ten-day suspension by his manager for insubordination. Peckinpaugh jerked his star pitcher in the first inning of a game with Boston on August 30 after Ferrell had allowed three hits and a walk. The temperamental hurler vigorously objected, kicking up dirt, and only after being ordered to leave did he make his exit. After beating the Browns eight straight times over the past two seasons, St. Louis would escape seeing Wes in their final seven games against the Indians.

September represented the low point in the Browns' 1932 season, as they managed only seven victories in the remaining 29 games. In a humiliating 10–4 loss against the Senators on September 10, Rick had a rare off-day behind the plate. He dropped a throw home allowing a run to score and was charged with a passed ball — all in one inning. He compensated for that lapse by later slamming a double that plated two runs.

Mercifully, the season ended on September 25 with St. Louis replicating its prior year's finish of 63 wins and 91 losses, but one rung lower in sixth place, 44 games behind the pennant-winning New York Yankees. Seven position players hit .280 or better for the season, with Rick Ferrell achieving the best mark on the team with a career-high .315 average. Over 126 games, Ferrell's production included 67 runs scored and 65 runs driven in. Among his 138 hits were 30 doubles, five triples, and two home runs. In 438 at-bats, he struck out 18 times and drew 66 walks.

Behind the plate, Rick caught 120 games for a .986 fielding average with 486 putouts.

Rick's stats had gradually improved over his first four years in "The Show," and he had just completed his best personal season in 1932. What he did not know was that the tenure with his first big league club was about to come to a merciful and abrupt end. Over in Cleveland, Wes had just finished with an outstanding 23–3 record (3.60 ERA) in his fourth full season with the Indians.

3

❖ ❖ ❖

1933–1934

The Red Sox, First
All-Star Game, and Wes

Franklin D. Roosevelt was about to be sworn in as the 32nd president of the U.S. Due to the Depression, Commissioner Landis cut his own salary by 40 percent in January 1933, signaling that all baseball salaries should be similarly slashed during the tough economic times.[1] After Rick's 17 percent pay cut ($2,000) in 1932, ownership intended to impose another reduction in pay, despite a strong season in which he had led his team in hitting. The press intimated that the Browns' star catcher was being offered a contract in the range of $7,500 to $8,000. Ferrell, an able negotiator, was naturally upset.

Several major leaguers became holdouts to protest their salary cuts, including Babe Ruth and Lou Gehrig. That January, Rick and Wes Ferrell again teamed up by both holding out and refusing to sign the contracts offered them. Boss Phil Ball, always the bully, assumed his usual "take-it-or leave it" stance. According to a story in *The Sporting News*, "The St. Louis owner, advised of Ferrell's intention [to hold out], insisted Rick had received the best — and only — offer he was going to get and that he had best be prepared to go to work at his trade."[2]

When Ferrell succeeded in getting free agency from Commissioner Landis in 1928, he had shrewdly offered his services to the highest bidder and secured what many people in baseball considered a fine deal from the Browns. Along with the $25,000 bonus, St. Louis paid Ferrell $12,500 for the first year of his three-year contract. But once he had the catcher locked up, owner Ball began to whittle away at the premium deal given Ferrell. Probably thinking his case would be reported sympathetically, Ball summarized to the papers the amount he had invested in his young catcher. Right on cue, *The Sporting News* editorialized by writing: "That may have been some kind of record for a first-year player." The "Baseball Bible" reporter asked Ball, "'Is there any chance for a compromise with Ferrell?'—'Yes,' answered Phil, 'that compromise comes when he signs at our figures.' And he insisted that the club's figures, in the catcher's hands for some time, are the last Rick will receive."[3]

By waiting for a larger contract, Ferrell missed much of spring camp in March and only succeeded in alienating the owner, whose uncompromising position had soured the talented receiver. Ferrell's catching talent was recognized throughout the league and no less than the Yankees' speedy basestealer Ben Chapman said in a March 16 *New York Times* interview, "The fellow I find the hardest to steal against is Rick Ferrell of the Browns. He gets that ball down there where the second-baseman wants it."

Amid this contentious period, the whole Ferrell family was unexpectedly hit with deep, tragic emotional pain. While Rick and Wes were holding out at home in Greensboro, several Ferrell brothers got together the evening of March 6, 1933, for a card game at Marvin's home. One of them was the youngest, 20-year-old Ewell, "Chubby," also an aspiring baseball player. After some time passed filled with conversation, Ewell abruptly got up from the game at the table and, for reasons unknown, left the room. Later, nobody recalled what exactly had been said. Immediately afterward, a gun shot blast sounded behind the door of the next room, and when Marvin raced to investigate, he found his young brother prostrate on the floor, bleeding from a bullet wound in his head, with a .22 caliber pistol laying nearby. Unconscious, Ewell was rushed to the local hospital, but died from the head wound the next day. Despite the absence of an inquest, the bereft family believed that the self-inflicted wound was an act of inexplicable suicide.

As could be expected, this tragic loss stunned the entire family, impacting each member in profound ways. The remaining six Ferrell brothers mourned deeply, quietly. George, an outfielder, and Marvin, a pitcher, reported to the minors. The two major leaguers, Rick and Wes, soon abandoned the battle for more favorable salary adjustments. In the end Rick capitulated and signed with St. Louis, although he went to camp actually hoping to be traded to another team more appreciative of his talents. Holdout Wes also accepted the Indians' offer.

An April 13, 1933, *Greensboro News and Record* newspaper article read: "One day, without saying a word to anyone, the brother battery packed their suitcases and left Guilford. The next thing the home town folks knew, both of them had signed. Rick, in particular, took the loss of his brother hard, and it is reported he was unable to sleep for several nights after he arrived at the Browns' training camp because of his sorrow. 'I can't sleep a wink since that kid died,' he lamented." The ever-generous Rick had purchased a new car for his little brother on his sixteenth birthday.

Only Ball's obstinence and shaky financial situation accounted for the way he battled Ferrell over salary, for this catcher was highly regarded after his four seasons at the major league level. On April 13, 1933, less that a month after agreeing to another pay cut, *The Sporting News*, published in St. Louis, carried a feature column on Ferrell recognizing how quickly he had progressed to a level of excellence, singling out his skills as a receiver with exceptional throwing ability. "Ferrell's catching form is near perfection. It is reminiscent of Muddy Ruel when Muddy was at the height of his career. There isn't a better thrower in either big league, and at bat, he is a line-drive batter of the most dangerous type. He never says much these days, but sort of cherishes the idea he might be making a higher salary if he hadn't got all that money his first year in the majors. In contrast to his battling spirit on the field, Ferrell, off the diamond, is as mild-mannered a chap as one would wish to meet. But if you heed the testimony of American League umpires, he's a pretty hard guy to please back of the plate. One arbiter said last year, 'Ferrell gives me more of a battle than any six catchers in the league.'"

By late April, a lackluster Rick possessed the second-highest batting average on the team: a paltry .239, with Reynolds hitting .288. Perhaps still distressed by Chubby's suicide, for the most part Rick was as cold as his ball club, not able to regain the hitting level he had established during the past two seasons. Amid this slump, Ferrell had an occasional bright moment when his bat contributed to a beleaguered St. Louis attack. On May 6, when the Browns offense drove Philadelphia's ace hurler Lefty Grove to the showers in an 8–6 loss, Ferrell collected two hits, including a home run. As the weather warmed, Rick's average increased to .250 by May 8.

But with no warning on May 10, 1933, the news announced that Rick Ferrell, along with pitcher Lloyd Brown, had suddenly been traded to the Boston Red Sox in exchange for veteran catcher Merv Shea and cash. The press suggested that St. Louis likely received an amount of around $50,000. The baseball scribes readily concluded that Boston got the better end of the deal by taking advantage of a cash-strapped St. Louis Browns franchise and an owner who was still sore at his catcher's recalcitrant contract behavior. Surely Rick's slow start (he went hitless on May 9, his last game in a Browns uniform), as well as the owner's financial needs, contributed to Phil Ball's willingness to part with one of his best players.

Calling the deal a surprise, the May 10 *St. Louis Post-Dispatch* sought to explain why the Browns' owner would part with Ferrell. "Rick Ferrell, one of the greatest catchers in the game, who received many votes for the post of catcher on Babe Ruth's All-America Team last year, has been sold 'up North' by the Browns. This will surprise fans who felt this player was one of the most important cogs in the machine, both on attack and defense.... It is entirely probable that sending Ferrell away from St. Louis had in it some part of discipline. Rick reported very late to training camp and, while he agreed to terms in West Palm Beach, plainly showed his dissatisfaction at provisions of his playing agreement. He often expressed a wish to be traded, having the idea that the numerous cuts of salary he had received were because of the great sum — $25,000 — paid him when he was a free agent in 1928."

For Ferrell there had been no hint that the trade, engineered during a special meeting of the American League owners in Cleveland, was imminent. Manager Killifer, himself, had learned of the trade by reading about it in the newspapers, which began a personal feud with his owner. The May 17 *Boston Globe* reported that Killefer wanted Red Sox GM Eddie Collins to know: "As for Ferrell, you can tell the world for me that I regard him as one of the best I have seen — and surely with Bill Dickey of the Yankees— outstanding in our league. He will catch great ball for you, Eddie. He will hit for you, and he will get all there is to get out of your pitchers. There is no laugh for me in losing ballplayers like that." Poor manager Killifer ultimately resigned abruptly in mid–July. After replacing him with Rogers Hornsby, owner Phil Ball, himself, became critically ill and was hospitalized from stress and exhaustion. He passed away on October 22, 1933, his sixty-fourth birthday.

When the unexpected trade was announced, Rick was pleased, though cautious, in revealing his true feelings. "Of course, I'm sorry in a way to leave St. Louis for I have made many friends here, but under the circumstances, I figure I got a break."[4] Despite a slow start, he had hit a .290 average during his four years with the Browns.

Far from Midwestern St. Louis, Boston was located in New England on the Charles River in Massachusetts. Born in Detroit, novice Red Sox owner Tom Yawkey was the nephew of one-time Tigers owner William Yawkey. He grew up an American Leaguer and stayed a baseball fan all his life. Having made a boatload of money in the lumber business, Tom Yawkey purchased the hapless Red Sox for a reported $1,500,000 from debt-ridden owner Bob Quinn, consummating the deal in 1933 at the very young age of thirty. Apparently wiser heads in the baseball world laughed at the foolishness of this seemingly gullible youngster and would-be owner. The reaction of more experienced baseball gurus was not without cause considering how pitifully the Boston Red Sox had played the past decade. The team had finished in last place nine times, seventh once, and reached their pinnacle of success in 1924 when they claimed sixth place while losing 87 games. In that period of poor major league play from 1922 through 1932, the year before Yawkey purchased the club, the Red Sox averaged 98 losses per season.

This trade elevated Rick Ferrell's public profile, casting him into the spotlight of his ascending career by relocating him from the western-most American League city to a northeastern metropolitan area with a much stronger media market. The warm welcome in Boston obscured his earlier, chilly start with St. Louis. The *Boston Globe* proclaimed "Rick Ferrell — Great Catcher" in its May 10 headline story announcing the trade with St. Louis. "Ferrell is a great catcher. A hard-hitting one. A fellow right in his prime possessing a true throwing arm. He should help the Red Sox right where they need plenty of help." New Boston general manager Eddie Collins was comparing him to the great Mickey Cochrane in his prime.

On May 24, two weeks later, Gene Mack of the *Globe* featured Ferrell again, this time with the headline, "Old-Timers Say Ferrell's Throwing Nearest Thing to Criger's They've Seen." The story presented a drawing characterizing Rick Ferrell down in his crouch surrounded by smaller depictions of six other past Red Sox catchers. Lou Criger, venerable catcher with Boston from 1901 (the inaugural year of the American League) to 1908, had set the standard of excellence for superior throwing catchers in Beantown. "Certainly it has been a long time since the Red Sox have had such a stylish throwing catcher as Ferrell," wrote Mack. "His pegs travel like lightening, dead to the mark and with little effort." Despite his velocity, Rick didn't throw a heavy ball, making it easy for the fielders covering the bags. Built like the wiry Criger, Ferrell began his career in Boston with a new-found stature. "Good catchers are scarce in the majors, and Fenway Park rooters are tickled that they have one of the best in Rick Ferrell."

Fenway Park was no stranger to Rick as he had played there many times before, but now it was his home ballpark. A distinctive facility and cozy place, its seating capacity held only 35,000 fans. The old ballparks possessed unique personalities and character that perhaps offered a home field advantage. Fenway had often been labeled a graveyard for left-handed pitchers, and right-handed batters could easily be seduced by the short left-field fence into becoming dead pull hitters, even if that was not a natural swing.

This venerable ballpark opened on April 20, 1912, pitting the home team against the New York Highlanders in an exciting contest won by Boston, 7–6. Its dimensions remained intact by the time Rick arrived in 1933: 321 feet down the left-field foul line; the outfield fence veered out sharply toward center, reaching a depth of 388 feet in the power alley; the outfield wall continued to retreat away until it reached dead center, 550 feet from home plate; the outfield wall then turned toward home, stretching out to right-center field at the 402 foot mark, and finally reaching the right-field foul pole a puny distance of 314 feet from the hitter.

The "friendly confines" of Fenway Park twisted with more than the normal nooks and crannies, most dictated by the proximity of an urban environment. The "Green Monster," a twenty-five-foot-high left-field wall, was its most well-known feature and thwarted many line drives from becoming home runs. Thus in 1934, the owner decided to make the high wall even higher, raising it to thirty-seven feet, converting would-be home runs into doubles for Ferrell.

Rick Ferrell may have been pleased to be rid of the autocratic, unappreciative Phil Ball, but he was about to join another team in deep distress in seventh place, with a 6–14 record, seven games out. May 11 marked Rick's debut with the Boston Red Sox, as well as his introduction to catching the slants of the Boston pitching staff. He began by catching starter Ivy Andrews, 26, in his first full season with Boston, who after six innings gave way to Johnny Welch, a spot starter with 40 relief appearances in 1933. Cleveland's Mel Harder threw a six-hit complete game as the host Indians triumphed over Boston by a 4–1 score.

Both the *New York Times* and the *Boston Globe* reported Rick's impressive day swinging the bat. In the hometown account, the writer stated, "Rick Ferrell, the catcher obtained by the Red Sox in a deal with St. Louis, donned a Boston uniform today for the first time and poled out a double and single in four trips to the plate, scoring the only tally credited to the Red Sox." With his new team, Ferrell wore the number "9" on the back of his new Red Sox uniform. Daniel M. Daniel wrote in his May 11, *Boston Globe* column, "Daniel's Dope," "Rick Ferrell is the third best catcher in the league behind Bill Dickey and Mickey Cochrane." In his May 18 column, the writer reiterated, "[Ferrell] is a great receiver with a fine arm and is a good hitter."

In addition to the trade that brought Ferrell to Boston, Yawkey opened his wallet and purchased right-handed starter George Pipgras and rookie third baseman Bill Werber from the New York Yankees in an unprecedented move. The sale of players had normally been in the other direction.

Although Ferrell was pleased to be playing for Boston, he must have thought he was back in St. Louis after becoming acquainted with his new mound crew. Among the eight hurlers, only the two new guys, Lloyd Brown and George Pipgras, had won consistently in 1932. As the season progressed, no ace on the Red Sox staff excelled. Pipgras, with a 9–8 record, and Hank Johnson, 8–6, were the only pitchers with winning records, and Gordon Rhodes, who threw the most innings, would be the top winner with a 12–15 record and the only ERA under 4.00. At a time when nicknames were legendary, Ferrell would catch a staff of "Dusty" Rhodes, "Lefty" Weiland, "Gimpy" Brown, "Poison Ivy" Andrews, and "Junior" Kline.

The new player acquisitions did not result in an early turnaround. Boston continued to lose, dropping five of its first seven games with newcomers Ferrell, Pipgras, Werber and company. The May 16 *Globe* printed their observations, "Rick Ferrell has already shown what great value he is likely to be for the McManus outfit. Had his straight-away hitting been with the club right along, the Sox easily could have won several more of these closest of ball games."

In the middle game of a series with Detroit, Ferrell had two singles and drove in one of the tallies. In the finale, Lloyd Brown turned in a clean six-hitter for a 2–0 shutout, while Rick picked off three Tiger runners trying to steal. "What an arm that Rickey Ferrell has!" observed the *Boston Globe* the next day.

On May 26, Boston hosted Cleveland and won two-of-three, their only defeat coming at the hands of Wes Ferrell in the middle contest. In the opener Rick connected for three singles which scored two runs in a 6–5 victory. Still on May 30, Boston was far down in eighth place with a record of 13–25, 12 games out.

At Griffith Stadium, Bill Werber debuted at shortstop on June 1 where Boston defeated the Nats, 7–5. In a twin bill played on June 8 with Washington, the two teams split, with Boston getting the win in the first game on the strength of a two-run rally in the ninth inning. Ferrell started the inning with a double, and then came around to score the tying run. The second game was all Washington's in a 12–3 laugher. Ferrell caught both games, but couldn't buy a hit in the nightcap.

Infielder Bill Werber deeply appreciated Rick's help as a newcomer to the team. In a telephone interview in 2003, Werber recalled: "In the early stages of 1933, Rick did me a favor that started us off on a good note. I was playing short-stop for Boston and one day in Boston, I made four errors, throwing the ball over the first base man's head, clear up into the stands. The people all booed me. After the game I sat in front of my locker and I just cried, like my heart would break. But your dad waited until after the clubhouse had cleared out, and he said, 'Come on, Bill. We're going to have some dinner.' He was so nice. He took me to dinner, and stayed with me, and walked me back to the hotel, and was a great comfort to me. A nice, sympathetic guy and a kindly man. He wasn't foul-mouthed. He never got upset about too much."

On June 14 in the final game of a Yankee series at Fenway, Boston won a decisive 13–5 victory from New York pitching ace "Lefty" Gomez, with Rick's substantial assistance. In a spectacular day at the plate, Ferrell went three-for-four, hitting a home run and driving in four runs. Then after a two-for-two day when he drove in two runs, Rick suffered a foul tip that slammed off the middle finger to injure his throwing hand, putting him out for the next six games.

Melville Webb, writing for the *Globe*, assessed the new players. "So far at least, the five most recent additions to the Red Sox personnel have not made a very important difference to the club. The big value may be said to be in Rick Ferrell. He has helped out in grand old fashion back of home plate, and he has just begun to hit the ball."[5]

In late June, a series in St. Louis took the catcher on his first trip back to Sportsman's Park as a member of the opposing team. On June 25 Boston lost a Sunday doubleheader, 10–6 and 6–4. Ferrell caught both games, demonstrating excellent offense against the Browns. He collected four hits in seven tries, drove in three runs, and hammered a double and a homer in the second game, to show the Browns the mistake they made in giving him up. Boston won the last two games, with Ferrell's sizzling bat stroking three more hits in a 5–4 victory on June 27 before leaving town on the train for the "Windy City."

The grand finale of a six-game winning streak that began June 26 culminated on the Fourth of July in a Sunday doubleheader in Philadelphia when the Red Sox battered A's pitching for 25 hits and 23 runs to take both games, 14–4 and 9–1. Rick Ferrell showed little mercy, hitting two doubles in the morning game and four safeties in four at-bats in the afternoon contest. He drove in two runs and scored another in that game.

Playing in Boston did wonders for Rick Ferrell's rising star and recognition of his unique talents as his outstanding play attracted attention. Joe Cashman, in an undated *Boston American* scrapbook article written before the first All-Star Game, claimed that Ferrell was the prototype of a smallish, lean, and agile receiver in a feature article entitled, "Rick Ferrell Disproves Old Catching Myth." "You don't have to be a giant of a man or bulky to be a great catcher" was Cashman's thesis. "He's the lightest player on the squad. No smaller hands, shorter fingers, frailer arms than Rick's could be found in the majors. Yet, he's generally rated as the best all-around catcher in the game today. Those small hands receive all types of pitching flawlessly, those short fingers snap a throw that is feared by the fleetest of baserunners, those thin arms consistently hit over .300." The photo caption read, in part, "Ferrell's digits are so small they can barely encircle a regulation baseball, as the inset shows. But he gets a firm grip on it nevertheless, to discourage would-be base-stealers."

The July 6 *Boston Globe* presented a large photograph of the team's star catcher, showing him wielding three bats as he came out of the dugout, with the headline, "Rick Ferrell Puts Fight in Red Sox: Backstop Has Improved His Batting 103 Points with Boston Club." Summarizing Rick's amazing play during his short tenure with the team, in forty games, along with not making a single error, he had driven in twenty-three runs and hit a sizzling .339. Recognizing his exceptional value to the team, the writer concluded, "The Sox did not begin to climb the moment Ferrell arrived, but it did not take long. The pitchers were going every which way, and Ferrell slowly began to straighten them out. He played great ball himself, holding to his remarkable fielding, and is gradually beginning to hit. Now Rick is well up at the top of the American League pile of backstops. He has proved to be the most valuable of the Sox recently acquired assets, and he has been the fulcrum to stand the pressure of the uplifting lever. It was a great day when the Sox got Ferrell. It is not often that just one man has meant so much to a ball club. And how Rick has been going over the past happy Red Sox stretch."

That surge, and his performance over the past several seasons, earned Rick Ferrell's selection in 1933 to the first major league All-Star game in history. The idea was promoted by Arch Ward, sports editor of the *Chicago Tribune*, who envisioned a "dream game" showcasing baseball's elite players from each league competing as part of Chicago's grand Century of Progress Exposition. Remarkably, Ward was able to gain the approval of Commissioner Landis, given that the baseball schedule had been set for many months. July 6 was the date the Game of Stars was to be played, and the owners voted unanimously in support. With fans selecting the players, strong-armed, hard-hitting White Sox outfielder Al Simmons garnered 320,291 votes, the most among the thirty-six players selected. Another Yankees outfielder, Babe Ruth, was sixth in the polling, with his advancing age undercutting his immense popularity and the first season in eight when his home run total dipped below 40. Connie Mack managed the American League start; John McGraw served as field boss for the National Leaguers. The serious Mack, seated in the dugout dressed in suit and tie rather than a uniform, aimed to win and made just one substitution the entire game among his position players.

The First American League All-Star Team in 1933 at Chicago's Comiskey Park: *Kneeling*, (left to right): Trainer Doc Schacht, Eddie Collins, Tony Lazzeri, Alvin Crowder, Jimmy Foxx, Coach Art Fletcher, Earl Averill, Ed Rommel, Ben Chapman, Rick Ferrell, Sam West, Charlie Gehringer, (Clyde McBride and batboy, cut off). *Standing*: Batting practice catcher Bill Conroy (partial image), Lou Gehrig, Babe Ruth, Orville Hildebrandt, Manager Connie Mack, Joe Cronin, Lefty Grove, batboy Harry Colledge, Bill Dickey, Al Simmons, Lefty Gomez, Wes Ferrell, Jimmy Dykes, clubhouse man Eph Colledge. (National Baseball Hall of Fame Library, Cooperstown, N.Y.)

Many years later in an interview with Ernie Harwell for the *Detroit Free Press*, Rick Ferrell recalled that Mack held a skull session before the game. "He called us together at the Del Prado Hotel and talked to us. He said, 'You are all great ballplayers, but don't be upset if some of you don't get to play today. We came here to beat McGraw and those Nationals.'" Apparently Mack liked to sit next to his catcher on the bench and talk about how to pitch to various hitters and discuss the strategy of the game. Thus Ferrell enjoyed a privileged seat and conversation while the American League batted. "He kept asking me about pitchers and waving his scorecard to position his defense."[6]

Reflecting back on this historic game from the perspective of the 1949 All-Star game, Ferrell stated with confidence and obvious pride: "That first All-Star team in the American League was the best ever chosen and could beat this one every day of the week.... No comparison with this year's team, man for man or any way you want to figure it. Baseball is getting better, but it will be several years before the majors return to the pre-war peak.... We had Gehrig at first, Gehringer at second, Cronin on short, Dykes at third, Simmons in left, Averill in center and Ruth in right. That's a real ball club."[7] Wes Ferrell had also been voted to the American League team, but did not see action.

With 47,595 lucky fans in their seats at Comiskey Park, the historical game began at 1:15 P.M. St. Louis Cardinals ace hurler Wild Bill Hallahan started for the National League and Yankee star pitcher Lefty Gomez took the mound for the American League. With Mickey Cochrane injured, Bill Dickey and Rick Ferrell had been chosen as American League catchers. Ferrell expected Dickey, who was Gomez's battery mate with New York, to get the starting nod. However, Dickey had sustained an injury in the pre-game practices, and Mack inserted Ferrell into the starting lineup. The Boston receiver would catch the entire historic game.

The two teams went quietly in the opening frame with only Charlie Gehringer reaching first base for the junior circuit. The American League broke through to score a run in the bottom half of the second inning. The notoriously weak-hitting Gomez slapped a sharp single to center, and Jimmy Dykes crossed home plate.

After the National League hitters were retired again to start the third, Gehringer led off with his second free pass. And the moment came that everyone was hoping for: the Babe connected on a one-one pitch, driving the ball into the right-field stands for a two-run homer. The fans were exhilarated! The National League finally got on the board with two runs in the sixth inning, making it a 3–2 game; the Americans countered with a run in the same frame to finally win, 4–2.

Rick came to the plate four times without a hit. He faced Hallahan in his first at-bat in the second inning and flied to right-fielder Chuck Klein. At bat again in the fourth with Lon Warneke on the hill, he lifted another fly to Klein. With Joe Cronin on first and no one out in the sixth, Ferrell moved him along with a sacrifice bunt to first baseman Bill Terry, who tossed to Frankie Frisch covering the bag. His final chance came in the seventh, when he grounded out second to first to end the inning. Ferrell caught three great pitchers in this historic game (with 1933 records): Lefty Gomez (16–10), Alvin Crowder (24–15), and Lefty Grove (24–8).

The first All-Star Game was experimental, a one-time special, and no one seemed to think it would become an annual celebration of baseball's finest performers. Even American League President Will Harridge considered it a one-time game, feeling that if it were to be made an annual event, it might sink to the level of an ordinary ballgame. Yet this history-making game must have meant a lot to the chosen few who played in Chicago on July 6. Rick recalled that after the first game, Frank Frisch sent a photo of his hitting a home run in the game. Since Ferrell was also catching in the picture, Frisch asked him to inscribe it. Ferrell wrote: "To a great hitter from the fellow who called the wrong pitch."

Boston began a 22-game homestand on July 8. A series finale against the Cleveland Indians on Sunday, July 19, found the Ferrell brothers competing against each other in another hitting contest. Wesley started for Cleveland,

During the first All-Star Game in Chicago in 1933, the National League's Frankie Frisch slams a home run while American League catcher Rick Ferrell watches. Later, Rick autographed this photograph for Frisch, signing it: "From the fellow who called the wrong pitch."

opposing Boston's Hank Johnson. In the bottom of the fourth inning, Rick came to bat and slammed one of Wes' pitches for a home run into the left-field seats. Circling the bases at third, he taunted Wes, who was kicking up dust on the mound, "Hey Wes—stick a stick up on that one!" Wesley glared and kicked the dirt, but would have the last laugh. In the next inning the pitcher came to bat and defiantly blasted his own homer over the left-field wall. Stepping on home plate, a triumphant Wes retorted, "Hey Rick, looks like you're going to have to go move the stick!"

For almost three hours, 3,000 fans watched the 13-inning game before Cleveland nosed out Boston, 8–7. Rick drove in three runs on a single and a home run. Wes did not make it through the seventh inning, but like his brother, also scored three runs on a single and a home run. This was one of the few times in baseball history that brothers on opposing teams homered in the same game. The July 20 *Boston Globe* commented, "That two brothers on opposing teams should each make a home run was a novelty that aroused comment among fans. It was amusing to see Wes Ferrell kick the ball the umpire threw out while Rick was circling the bases." Unbeknown to them, this would be the last game the Ferrells would ever play against each other.

On July 20, the Red Sox got red hot and in an eleven-day stretch, won nine and lost only one, for a 13–9 record by July 30 that included a five-game sweep of Chicago. In the second White Sox contest, Rick Ferrell pounded three hits in four trips to the plate, plus scored twice and drove in another tally. Chicago starter Milt Gaston gave up 18 hits to Boston batters, who savaged the White Sox, 12–2. Following a 2–0 loss to the Yankees, Boston reeled off four victories in a row.

Unfortunately, the team's improved play in July did not allow the Red Sox to gain any significant ground in the 1933 standings. Yet, Rick was never a blame-fixer or critical with his pitchers. He was smarter than most of the pitchers and led by example, but not through criticism, and wasn't argumentative or controversial. Despite their swan dive in the last two months of the season, Boston had lost 25 fewer games than in 1932.

Rick recovered from his slow start in St. Louis to produce a solid offensive season in 1933, batting .297 in 424 at-bats and hitting a career-best 77 RBIs. A patient hitter, Ferrell walked 70 times along with his 130 hits for a .345 on-base percentage and struck out only twenty times. Although Rick played in 140 games for both St. Louis and Boston, he caught a total of 136 games for a career-high .990 fielding average. He executed 591 putouts, the most of his eighteen-year career, while making only seven errors.

Post-season, as always, Ferrell returned to his Carolina farm to work and regroup with his family, minus Chubby. Both George and Marvin had played at Scranton, Pennsylvania, in the New York–Pennsylvania league, where George hit .301 and Marvin became an outfielder.

On December 5, 1933, Congress repealed the Prohibition Act so that now drinking alcoholic beverages in public in the United States was legal, without crime and punishment. Many people, including some Red Sox players, could imbibe spirits in public, although Rick always adhered to a two-drink limit.

Needing to improve their lowly seventh-place status, Mr. Yawkey and company had been busy making changes to the team during the 1933 off-season. Releasing manager Marty McManus in early October, Boston hired Detroit's ex-manager Bucky Harris as the new skipper, who had been fired at the tail-end of 1933 after nearly five years with the Tigers. At 37, Harris was still a young man, but would have a short one-year stay at the helm of the Red Sox before being supplanted by his former teammate, Joe Cronin, in 1935. Harris would, however, return for a longer term as manager of the Senators and, before his career ended, would have three managerial stints with Washington and two with Detroit.

Yawkey made a big catch in mid–December when the Red Sox shipped two very average players, pitcher Bob Kline and infielder Rabbit Warstler, along with $125,000 to Philadelphia for pitchers Lefty Grove and Rube Walberg, plus Max Bishop, the A's regular second baseman. Grove, 33 when the season began, had racked up 195 victories en route to Cooperstown, and Walberg, 36, had recorded 134 wins. This was another lopsided trade in which a millionaire owner took advantage of a Depression economy to strengthen his ball club.

All of this activity meant that Rick Ferrell would face a much different starting rotation in 1934. Holdovers Johnny Welch, Gordon Rhodes and Hank Johnson remained. Grove and Walberg would provide a veteran presence, and Fritz Ostermueller, 26, was about to make his big league rookie debut. To start the New Year, in January 1934, Boston signed free-agent pitcher Herb Pennock.

As the Red Sox traveled north by train from spring training to Boston, the team stopped off in Greensboro, and Wes, again an Indians holdout, practiced with the club. The fastballs he fired from his supposedly dead arm impressed Bucky Harris enough that he recommended to Eddie Collins that they try to sign Wes. At the time Collins strongly opposed the idea.

On Opening Day, April 17, Boston got out of the gate playing like an invigorated ball club. New skipper Harris started Dusty Rhodes, the team's top winner in 1933, against the defending champion, the visiting Washington Senators. The 5–5 tie score remained knotted until the eleventh inning when the Nationals scored an unearned run to win, 6–5. Rick Ferrell, wearing uniform number "7" this year, opened his season with two hits and a run-batted-in.

During a high point in early May, the Red Sox drubbed Detroit, 14–4, to go two games over .500, while winning its ninth game of the season. In a phenomenal fourth inning, Boston scored twelve runs, highlighted by four consecutive triples. Rick Ferrell scored two of the Red Sox runs and hit one of the barrage of triples.

At 160 pounds, Rick was always very slight and couldn't keep weight on during the summer. One day in Boston, he visited a physician who recommended that when the ballgame was over, he should go to a cool place and order a bottle of beer and drink it slowly to help keep his weight up. After the games were over, Rick would sometimes go out with Bill Werber. Each town had a beer that was his favorite. In St. Louis, it was Michelob. Different places, different beer. Toots Shor in New York was a Jewish promoter who used ballplayers to advertise his restaurant.

On May 25 while Cleveland was annihilating the Red Sox, 18–3, at League Park, GM Collins, with the boss's check book, was completing a trade with the Tribe to finally acquire pitcher Wesley Ferrell and outfielder "Twitchy" Dick Porter for hurler Bob Weiland, outfielder Bobby Seeds, and an undisclosed sum of cash. New manager Harris's urging had convinced Yawkey and Collins to take a chance on Wes. During 1933, Wes Ferrell had suffered through his second season with a chronic sore arm, caused largely by overuse, winning only 11 games and losing 12. Considered a career-threatening injury, Wes had asked to play outfield in the closing games of 1933, but the experiment did not work well due to his weak defensive play.

Like all hurlers trying to make a comeback, Wes Ferrell tried to persuade the Red Sox during spring of 1934 that he was a new man with a rested arm and renewed velocity. Yet the pitcher brought a well-documented temperament to his new team, along with questionable remaining skills. The more cerebral Rick Ferrell was being relied on to steady his emotional brother.

Wes' chief advocate had actually been his older brother Rick. Fifteen years later in an interview with Shirley Povich for the *Washington Post*, Rick related his role in the trade. Yawkey had sought Rick's advice on whether to acquire Wes. "I told him to grab Wes quick, even if it cost him a lot of money," recalled Rick. "Wes was holding out for an $18,000 salary from the Indians and refused to report."[8] Rick helped convince Yawkey that his brother's arm had come back, and soon after, Wes joined his new team and his brother Rick to form one of the first brother batteries in baseball history, and one of the longest lasting, at five years together.

The SABR.org website states that one of the few brother batteries in the American League before the Ferrells played together for Boston in 1934 was Milt and Alex Gaston (Boston, 1929). Later during the mid–1950s, Bobby and Billy Schantz played for three A.L. teams. The National League had produced John and Buck Ewing (New York, 1891) and Mike and Jack O'Neill (St. Louis, 1902, '03). The famous Cooper brothers, Mort and Walt, would play for St. Louis (N.L.) from 1940 to 1945, as well as Larry and Norm Sherry for Los Angeles (1959–62).

Rick's judgment in recommending Wes would be tested in a May 30 game at Shibe Park. "That day in Philadelphia, I thought it was going to be just a matter of minutes before Mr. Yawkey fired us both," recalled Rick. "Wes started throwing his six warm-up pitches, and the ball didn't have enough on it to break out of a cellophane wrapper. God knows what had happened to that fast ball he showed me in Greensboro during the winter, but I swear I could throw the ball back to him left-handed with more stuff than he was throwing me." Greatly concerned when the first batter Wes had to face stepped into the batter's box, Rick said: "Eric McNair was up, and here comes Wes' first pitch, and it looked as fat as a balloon, and I say to myself, 'Here's where we both get canned,' and then we got lucky. McNair popped it straight up over the plate, and I took it for the third out, and we were out of the inning. Wes shut 'em out in the ninth."[9]

With rare exception, effective starting pitchers rely on their fastball, which sets up everything else in their arsenal. Despite the sales job by Wes, his arm never re-acquired the high, hard one. Rick, of course, provided the best testimony stating, "He could throw more junk up to the plate than any man I ever caught. He threw slow curves, and slower ones, and dipsy-doodles and knucklers and gave them nothing good to hit."[10] Being Wesley's catcher at this stage of his career may have served as an apprenticeship for Rick when a few years later he caught a Washington rotation that relied on the knuckleball pitch.

Bringing the two brothers together on the same ball club also gave rise to an open recognition of their differences. Shirley Povich of the *Washington Post* provided a very contrasting characterization of the two siblings. "They could

Rick (left) was joined on the Boston Red Sox by his pitching brother Wes (right) in 1934, where they formed one of baseball's few brother batteries. They played together in Boston for three seasons until early 1937, and after being traded together to the Washington Nationals, for 1937 and part of the 1938 season before Wes's release. Rick remained with Washington until early 1941. (Gwenlo Ferrell Gore)

have been anything but brothers. Rick was short; Wes was tall. Rick was bald; Wes was wavy-haired and the matinee-idol type. Rick was quiet and soft spoken. Wes was loud and temperamental. Rick took the club's defeats philosophical[ly], Wes went into tantrums." Though an accurate portrayal, Rick also possessed a fiery will and given enough provocation, he, too, could become steamed and confrontational. One can only imagine how Rick must have felt about some of the ways his immensely talented younger brother acted out his personal frustrations. To Povich, he only said, "He never got mad at anybody but himself," which was the reality behind Wes' temper.[11]

From June 5 to 27, the team played three weeks at home in Fenway. In Boston, Rick and Wes lived together at the Sheraton Hotel, off Commonwealth Avenue, with its very serene view overlooking the Charles River. Rick drove a fancy, gray Packard then, which he would park directly in front of the hotel.

The crowd's electric anticipation filled the afternoon of June 10: Wes Ferrell would take the hill in his Red Sox home debut. With Rick catching, he pitched gamely, allowing eight hits while striking out four. After pounding a double, Wes scored Boston's third run to tie the score at 3–3. In the ninth inning with the lead runner on third, Wesley slugged a long sacrifice fly, allowing Reynolds to cross home plate with the winning run, 4–3. Wes Ferrell was 1–and–0 with his new club.

Shirley Povich, sports editor for the *Washington Post*, heralded Wes Ferrell's gutsy performance in his June 11 column. "Ferrell shut 'em out after that third inning, while Bill Cissell's [Boston's second baseman] homer after two were out in the fifth, tied the score. [Cecil] Travis did get to third with two out in the sixth, but with the big mitt of Brother Rick beckoning encouragement to the Boston pitcher, the Nats were hamstrung and hogtied by Ferrell's blazing curve." That victory pulled the Red Sox to an even .500 in the won/loss column at 24–24.

The Red Sox fell into a mode of winning and losing with consistency and bouncing from third to fifth position on consecutive days. The Sox were home for the big Fourth of July celebration in Boston to play the Yankees. Wes Ferrell started the opener of the Wednesday afternoon doubleheader, but left in the fifth with the score tied. Reliever Ostermueller pitched scoreless ball the rest of the way to win, 8–5. Rick caught the entire first game, going two-for-five, scoring twice, and driving home two more runs. His two-run double in the fifth inning of the opening game helped Boston prevail, although fortunes reversed in the second game when New York knocked off Boston, 10–4.

For a pitcher with a weary arm, Bucky Harris wasn't giving Wes any breaks in his work load. After pitching into the fifth inning on Independence Day, the manager gave him the ball again on July 6; Boston hadn't had a complete game pitched by its starters in nine days. Despite surrendering six runs on 11 Philadelphia hits, Ferrell pitched courageously the full nine innings for an 18–6 Red Sox victory after his team exploded for nine runs in the sixth. Bill Werber collected four hits and scored five of his team's 18 runs. The Ferrell brothers generated a field day of their own, going six-for-ten, scoring three runs, and driving in four more.

The second All-Star classic was played at the Polo Grounds on July 10, 1934. Rick was Boston's sole representative on the A. L. squad as reserve catcher behind both Bill Dickey and Mickey Cochrane; he did not play. The junior circuit won, 9–7, with the memory of pitcher Carl Hubbell fanning five All-Stars in a row — Babe Ruth, Lou Gehrig, Jimmy Foxx, Al Simmons and Joe Cronin — becoming legendary.

Beginning on July 19, Boston played eight games in seven successive road days against Cleveland and Detroit that produced merely two victories. Wes Ferrell intervened once by salvaging the only win in the five-game series with Cleveland. During the July 23–26 games with the first-place Tigers, Rick slugged out nine hits in 16 at-bats for a Boston series split. A victory over the Senators on July 30 when Ferrell pitched an 8–0 shutout pushed the Red Sox to their best mark of the campaign, seven games over .500 for a 52–45 season. Despite a 16–15 July team record, individually, Rick's hot hitting had reached a .410 batting average, and on July 26, he sported a season-high .348, sixth in the American League.

Having Wes nearby perhaps provided competitive inspiration and support for the catcher. Wes started August 8 against the A's in Philadelphia, batting ninth behind Rick. In the second with two runners on, Rick tripled to drive in two runs and Wes then scored his brother. Next inning, Rick doubled and Wes again drove him home. But with a 10–1 Boston lead in the bottom of the third, first Jimmy Foxx blasted a grand slam off Wes, then Ed Coleman slugged a two-run homer to send the enraged pitcher to the locker room, where he socked himself in the jaw so hard he fainted. The Red Sox ultimately prevailed, 11–9.

A doubleheader on Sunday afternoon, August 12, provided the perfect historic stage for Babe Ruth's farewell to Fenway Park. With abundant appreciation for the beloved Bambino, 46,766 fans passed through the turnstiles that day, the largest home attendance in history. Supposedly another 15,000 more were denied admission because the house was full. After his hitting heroics the previous afternoon, it was Wes Ferrell's privilege to pitch the opener on this memorable day.

As with all baseball players, time catches up with the aging veteran. In his game account, a writer for the August 12 *Chicago Daily Tribune* recalled the time back in 1914 when a youthful Ruth strode out to the mound for his first appearance in a Red Sox uniform. Against that backdrop he described: "Today the once-lithe young man bore the portly bulge of middle-age about his belt, and chubby jowls softened the generous lines of his mouth. Only the pipe-stemmed legs, which long have seemed too fragile to bear his bulk, remained the same. It was his youth then that made his debut inconspicuous, and it was his old age today that robbed his farewell of some of his glory. For where once in such a setting, the Babe most assuredly would have collided with one of his famous homers as a fitting climax to the occasion, he was unequal to the tasks today."

With twelve hits each, Boston bunched its offensive in the eighth inning to score three big runs, enough to insure a 6–4 victory. Wes Ferrell pitched a complete game, as the Babe doubled, singled, and scored once. In the second game New York cruised to a 7–1 victory; Ruth only got one official at-bat while drawing a couple of walks. Rick Ferrell caught both ends of the doubleheader, but like the other twenty-four players who appeared, they were all members of the supporting cast. When the Babe walked off the field after the last out, the mass assembly rose to its feet and gave him a "final thunderous cheer."

In the August 14 victory, Lefty Grove beat the Browns, 7–3, in a complete game. Rick tripled and scored a run, then doubled later on and scored.

One of Wes' highlight victories came on August 22 in a 3–2 win over

Chicago at Fenway. Pitching the complete game, the pitcher homered in the eighth to tie the game, 2–2, and homered again with two outs in the bottom of the tenth to win it amid much fan clamoring! Rick slugged two of Boston's ten hits.

Wes lost a closely-fought 3–2 game against Cleveland in the front end of a Sunday, August 26, twin bill. This day Rick Ferrell out-shone his brother, catching both games and collecting four hits that scored three runs and drove in another. Boston came back to win the second contest, 5–2, giving them seven tallies in the two games, with Rick scoring nearly half of the total. Although both brothers were very competitive, they shared a relationship of mutual respect and pulled for each other to succeed.

On August 31, Boston held fourth, with a 65–62 record. On September 3, according to Thompson's book, the batting averages of the three best A.L. catchers were comparable, with Dickey batting .324, Cochrane .323, and Ferrell .319. Rick had led most of the season.

Boston won only one game (September 6) of four in their final brush with Cleveland, and that day, their usually self-controlled catcher projected his frustration in a stunningly uncharacteristic manner. In the fourth inning with a streaking runner coming in from third, Rick Ferrell dropped the throw home and Cleveland's second baseman, Odell "Bad News" Hale, scored. In a letter later sent to American League President William Harridge, home plate umpire E. T. Ormsby wrote: "I called Hale safe and Farrell [sic] immediately gave me a push and knocked me off balance and called me a Dirty S — of a B — —. I then told him he was thru for the day. He kept arguing until Manager Harris came up who said, 'It's the same old story of trying to cover up your mistakes by putting Farrell out.' Farrell [sic] then took off his mask and threw it at least sixty feet toward the Boston bench, next took off his glove and threw it toward the Cleveland bench, then threw his protector towards the Boston bench and ended by taking off and throwing his shin guards on the home plate." He then left the field.

Ormsby concluded by offering his opinion about the catcher's behavior. "Farrell's [sic] actions were something I don't think the American League wants to tolerate." Punishment was quickly administered. Harridge wired manager Bucky Harris that same evening that Rick Ferrell was suspended for three days, fined fifty dollars, to be paid within five days, and would be reinstated and eligible to play on Sunday, September 9. The player paid his fine two days later.

With Rick "serving time," the Red Sox took on the Indians again in a September 8 doubleheader. In a rarity Wes would pitch without his brother behind the plate and give up 14 hits and four walks for a 5–1 Cleveland victory. Having Rick as his catcher in large part enabled Wes' pitching success at this stage of his career. The Red Sox lost the second game, 3–2.

Nearing the end of their road journey, the team took on the St. Louis Browns at Sportsman's Park, a ballpark Rick knew well. In a bizarre game played on September 18, Boston won a 10-inning affair by a score of 2–1 with only one hit, while St. Louis collected 10 safeties. But the fans had hardly settled in their seats before the Ferrell brothers became embroiled in a fight with the home plate umpire. When Wes struck out in the second inning, he vigorously disputed the call. When his brother exploded, both Ferrells were ejected. Umpire Kolls immediately sent a telegram to President Harridge, giving a shorthand version of the confrontation.

Kolls claimed that Wes had objected strenuously to the called third strike and began shouting foul names at the umpire. Wesley next hurled his bat in the direction of the Boston dugout. After being told that was enough, he retreated to the dugout and continued his coarse harangue. Kolls tossed the pitcher from the game. Brother Rick then joined the fray, allegedly spouting degrading language, with both Ferrells yelling loudly for all to hear their verbal tirade. Rick netted an exit pass too, but before leaving the field, the two angry players confronted the umpire at home plate. According to Kolls, he was physically threatened, saying they were ready to fight him under the stands after the game. And all the time the ball players on the Red Sox were cheering, "Give 'em hell, Wesley! Give 'em hell, Rick!"

The next day in a letter, Rick and Wes provided Harridge with their version of the argument: "The strike in question was an intentional pitchout play and was very questionable. It was very apparent umpire Kolls was not hustling and was entirely responsible for the affair. His attitude in the game played here is not becoming to a major league umpire." They claimed that the umpire had challenged them to a fight after the game. In concluding their telegram message the Ferrells wrote, "We would be thankful if you would give our angle of the affair every consideration."

The case against the Ferrells grew stronger when the other umpire, Harry Geisel, weighed in with testimony completely backing Kolls, saying members of the Red Sox were also unhappy with the Ferrells' actions. Geisel credited Jack Onslow with saying that he "thought the Ferrell brothers were money mad."

Punishment came swiftly, with Wes receiving a five-day suspension and his battling brother Rick getting three days off without pay. Both were ordered to pay $100 fines. Yet because they had severely embarrassed the Boston Red Sox organization, there was even a bigger penalty. The higher-ups were chagrined by Rick's behavior for he had earned a reputation as a good citizen. Wes' actions were viewed as a return to his old self. In a telegram sent the day after the game to manager Harris, the ever-professional general manager Eddie Collins wrote, "Regardless of whether players were justified in protest, their actions and conduct following banishment certainly was not warranted and will not be tolerated by the Boston Club."

This sad affair prompted several written communications between the league president and Red Sox officials. On September 19, Harridge wrote a long letter to Tom Yawkey expressing his disappointment in the Ferrell brothers:

"The actions of pitcher Ferrell did not surprise me, but after his suspension and fine just two weeks ago, I did not believe we would hear anything further from catcher Ferrell. As a matter of fact, it would appear that the association with his brother on the same club is having a bad effect on Rick Ferrell. To the best of my recollection, we have never encountered any trouble with him. We will not permit them to destroy the reputation which the League today enjoys because of years of strenuous efforts in eliminating rowdyism from the field." In a letter Collins responded, expressing his regret over this black eye and agreement with the punishment imposed. "When they both return here to Boston, I intend to talk to them personally."

Playing consistent, winning baseball is a goal of any major league team and consistency was a hallmark of the 1934 Boston Red Sox. June 17 marked the last date the team was under .500 and on that date, they had just one more loss than win. After the final game on Sunday, September 30, the Red Sox had a perfect .500 record of 76–76, to earn fourth position. That season was the first time the team had finished in the first division since 1918, having moved up three spots in the standings from 1933's seventh-place finish. Detroit captured the flag over New York by a seven game margin.

Like his team during the 1934 campaign, Rick Ferrell could be counted on for solid, consistent numbers every season. Offensively, he finished with a .297 batting average supported by 130 hits and 29 doubles. He only hit one into the seats, but accounted for 50 runs scored and batted in 48 runners. Defensively, Rick led all American League catchers (with 50 games or more) with a fielding average of .990 over 128 games. Only three other receivers caught more than 100 games: Cochrane, Dickey, and Rollie Helmsley. On page 147 of his *Ferrell Brothers of Baseball* book, Dick Thompson wrote that Rick caught in 24 of Boston's 26 doubleheaders. He started both games 12 times and caught both games in their entirety eight times.

Wesley made an impressive comeback for a sore-armed pitcher. Pitching 181 innings, he once again became a workhorse, especially considering his late season start. With a record of 14–5, he had a career tendency to allow a lot of hits while pitching tough with men on base. Wes posted a .282 batting average, hit four home runs, and drove in 17 runs in just 82 times at bat. Known as a clutch hitter, he was frequently called upon to pinch-hit. In 1934, Lefty Grove's left shoulder had been injured, his teeth removed due to abscesses, and his tonsils taken out, all of which contributed to his poor 8–8 record (5.00 ERA).[12]

The Ferrell brothers all reconvened in Guilford. Both George, a center fielder, and Marvin, a pitcher, had played the season for the Boston franchise in the Piedmont League, the Columbia (S.C.) Sandlappers. After an outstanding offensive season during which the team relocated to Asheville, North Carolina, George was runner-up for best hitter in the Piedmont League.

4

❖ ❖ ❖

1935–1937

Beantown's Brother Battery

Anxious to build a winner, Tom Yawkey again went into the market in 1935, this time securing the services of player-manager Joe Cronin. Quickly tagged for his leadership ability, the young shortstop's ascendancy to the top flight of American League players had been achieved in short order. Cronin broke in with Pittsburgh in 1926, and two years later was the Washington Nationals' (or Senators) regular shortstop. In 1930, he hit a career high .346, followed by three successive years with a batting average over .300, and was selected to play in the first All-Star Game in 1933 and again in 1934. At age 26, he became the manager of the Senators and promptly led them to the American League pennant in a 99-win season. However, his team collapsed in 1934, falling all the way to seventh place with 30 fewer wins. For Boston, acquiring Cronin meant they now had both a star shortstop and a manager who had demonstrated he could win.

The Red Sox opened the season at Yankee Stadium, the "House That Ruth Built," but the Babe was not a Yankee anymore. Obviously Boston looked different too. Writer John Drebinger, covering the opening game in the April 7, 1935, *New York Times,* observed, "A vast change has also come over the Red Sox. Once merely the party of the second part of stage-drop for Yankee inaugurals, the Sox are entering today's struggle as determined to win and with as much at stake as the New Yorkers. Close to a million dollars has been spent by the liberal-handed Tom Yawkey in the last two years to bring Boston its first American League flag winner since 1918. The latest outlay was a quarter of this sum for the circuit's outstanding shortstop, Cronin, who will be making this his championship debut as the new manager of the Boston entry. Cronin, fiery and energetic, who piloted the Senators to a pennant in 1933, is expected to give the Sox that extra lift, both physically and mentally, to carry them into the thick of the pennant fight." Drebinger only slightly exaggerated the price tag paid for Cronin—$225,000—plus Boston threw in ex–Yankees shortstop Lyn Lary.

Wes Ferrell finessed Lefty Gomez, 1–0, in the Yankees' home opener on April 16, 1935, with a sterling two-hitter on a frigid day in the Bronx. While in the East, the Red Sox visited Washington for the first time in 1935. For the season, Bucky Harris and Joe Cronin had traded residences and now faced each other in a family affair. Shirley Povich captured the dynamics of the encounter in his *Washington Post* account of the game on April 17, 1935. "The Nats accumulated their third straight defeat yesterday despite Manager Bucky Harris' attempt to disguise his club with a new batting order. The Red Sox recognized 'em as the same easy prey of the week-end and Joe Cronin's team slapped a 4–2 defeat on his father-in-law's ball club." Wes Ferrell again was the winning pitcher with a splendid day at the plate, getting four hits, including a double and a triple, which accounted for half of his team's runs. Rick was quoted in the April 18 "Daniel's Dope" column in the *Boston Globe*: "Wes had everything against those Yankees. He was faster than he had been in three years, and as you know, his control was perfect. He could put that ball anywhere he wanted to."

Though from the same bloodline, the two Ferrell brothers possessed almost opposite personalities, yet they got along well, liked each other, and were always ready to stand together. AP correspondent Dillon Graham got Wes to talk about his expectations for the upcoming season. When asked who he thought was the greatest pitcher in the league, Wes flashed his trademark grin, asking: "You mean next to me? No joking, I'm expecting to be the head man among pitchers. I've got as much stuff on the ball as I ever had. I feel great and I like the Boston setting." Ferrell specifically recognized Tom Yawkey, Eddie Collins, and Joe Cronin as great people to work for and, of course, included his catcher, Rick, in summarizing the supportive team that surrounded him. "They can't beat me," affirmed Ferrell, 25. "When I'm right, they can't beat me. Of course, I'll get my ears knocked off sometimes, as every pitcher does, but the days I'm right, I'm going to be just too right for anybody. I feel confident I'll win twenty games, and if Boston continues to hit, my tally sheet may show around thirty," exhorted Ferrell.[1]

Surprisingly, Wes had provided yeoman work in 1934, pitching 181 innings in his first season with the Red Sox. In another interview after his first-game shutout of the Yankees, Ferrell tried to provide an explanation for his revived right arm. "The only explanation I can offer is that a Carolina home remedy helped me. After I had tired of doctors and surgeons, a neighbor of mine gave me a bottle of liniment which he had cooked up himself — nothing you see advertised, but just one of those old-fashioned Southern remedies." The columnist who probed this mystery cure naturally sought out the manager's opinion. "Wes has sent down to Carolina for another batch of that liniment for me," chimed in Cronin. "You know I hurt my wrist some time ago, and Ferrell says that if it bothers me, this Tar Heel panacea will drive trouble right out of my arm. In fact, I think I'll have a few gallons of that stuff sent up. If it can

The two aces of the 1934–1936 Boston Red Sox pitching staff, Lefty Grove (left) and Wes Ferrell (right), were hunting buddies off the field. Here they strike a friendly pose leaning against a car, dressed in their civvies. (Gwenlo Ferrell Gore)

make Wes pitch the way he did on Tuesday, it seems a handy thing to have around."[2]

The Red Sox started the 1935 season with a bang, taking two out of three at Yankee Stadium, then sweeping three from Washington on the road. May brought a pattern of winning and losing every other day, yet the ever-consistent Rick Ferrell was hitting .297 on the 10th day of May. During a two-week home stand on May 20, Boston's Lefty Grove again couldn't generate much production from the club's nine hits in losing, 4–1, to Cleveland. Rick Ferrell led the offense with a home run and two singles. However, in a frustrating 5–3 loss to Detroit on May 23, the catcher flew out twice, heaved his bat to the infield in disgust, and was nailed by a foul tip on the thumb, which benched him until May 29.

On June 7, 1935, Boston nipped the Yankees, 2–1, when Rick Ferrell slugged another two-hit game and scored the winning run after belting a double. Boston played .500 baseball or better until June 17 when they lost four straight to Cleveland for a 26–28 record. In that 11–2 defeat, Rick stroked two singles and a double, going three for three. The June 18 *Globe* reported, "Rick Ferrell was the only Boston batter able to hit consistently, and it takes more than one hitter to produce runs."

One of Rick's baseball cards in 1935 was made by Diamond Stars, No. 48. The text of the card read: "Watch Rick Ferrell of the Red Sox handle high foul balls. He has the knack of a quick start and the ability to sense the direction of the foul without loss of time." Rick's catching instructions were quoted: "By experience, a catcher learns to tell the angle of a foul by the position of the batsman's club at the moment it meets the ball, a thing that young catchers will not master for years." He next admonished, "Don't make the mistake of whipping your mask off too quickly lest you lose your chance to see the foul promptly. There is ample time after spotting the foul to remove the mask while running. On high overhead fouls, throw your mask far away lest you step on it and spoil your catch or turn your ankle."[3] Rick was always willing to teach, coach, and share with other players catching tips that he had learned by himself.

In a doubleheader at Sportsman's Park on June 19, the Brownies collected 10 hits and five runs off Wes Ferrell, which wasn't good enough — Boston scored eight runs to win the first contest, 8–5. The Ferrell boys gave the Browns grief when Rick knocked a single, a double and scored a run while Wes belted out four singles and two RBIs. The Browns won the second, 6–3.

The first day of July brought hope that the Red Sox might generate some winning momentum when Boston handed Washington an 8–3 defeat, scoring eight runs on just nine hits. They scored three in the sixth, featuring a two-run homer by the manager, and in the next inning got three more runs when Rick Ferrell cleared the bases with a double. Wes earned his eleventh victory, allowing 13 hits, but pitching the opposition tough in the pinches.

On the day before the All-Star break, July 7, the Sox played two at home with Lefty Grove winning the first, 7–6. The game went 13 innings with the fleet-footed Bill Werber sprinting home for the winning run. Rick contributed strong offense, getting four hits and driving in five of Boston's seven total runs.

The third annual All-Star Game was played on July 8, 1935, in Cleveland with a crowd of 69,831 on hand, a record attendance that would hold for forty-six years, until the 1981 All-Star Game. A.L. team manager Mickey Cochrane chose catcher Rick Ferrell to represent the Red Sox in his third All-Star Game, along with pitcher Lefty Grove and shortstop Joe Cronin. However, Browns' catcher Rollie Hemsley caught the entire game, so both Cochrane and Rick sat out.

Wes Ferrell had already won 13 games in 1935, but was not selected for the team of All-Stars. A very motivated 26-year-old hurler demonstrated his skills two days later on July 10 in a 7–0 shutout against the Chicago White Sox. Ferrell allowed only two cheap hits in a performance that the July 11 *New York Times* called "brilliant." Ferrell's bat barked in a two-for-four day, which included a home run and two RBIs, as he received strong offensive support from Rick, who rapped two hits and drove in a run.

On July 14, the home team pounded the Indians, 14–3, as Rick, along with Babe Dahlgren and Oscar Melillo, each banged out four hits that resulted in nine runs. With Rick as his catcher, Wes continued to roll, winning his 14th game and looking like the 30-game winner he had predicted he would be before the season began. Following a rainout, Boston played another doubleheader against the Indians on July 17 and prevailed in both games. In the opener Rick Ferrell continued his hot hitting with a three-for-five game, knocking in three runs with two extra base hits— one a home run —for a 13–5 victory.

While Rick and Wes were enjoying great seasons, their older brother George was setting the Piedmont League afire with the Richmond (Va.) Colts, but couldn't impress the decision-makers enough to warrant a call-up to the majors. Possessing a .407 average by mid–July, he was leading all minor leaguers and had stroked 15 home runs. A writer for the *Los Angeles Times* constructed a question that surely was puzzling the young outfielder: "If Brother Wes can pitch for Boston, and Brother Rick can catch, why in the world doesn't some enterprising big-league mogul make room for that other deserving Ferrell boy, George, who can hit like nobody's business?"[4]

George Ferrell never made it to "The Show," perhaps due to an ankle injury that cut his speed in the outfield and on the bases. His circumstance was not unique, however, for in the long era before franchise expansion, there were just sixteen big league clubs and a much deeper minor league system to plough through. Also the stockpile of good-hitting outfielders was greater than at any other position. George enjoyed a long professional baseball career, earning top dollar as a minor league player from 1926 to 1945, and manager during 1941–1945, 1949, and 1951, before becoming a scout.

Boston won a thriller at Fenway Park on July 21, 1935, after Lefty Grove had fallen behind, 6–4, heading into the bottom of the ninth. With two Red Sox hitters in scoring position, Cronin called upon Wes Ferrell to pinch-hit for Grove, and Ferrell drove one over the left-field wall for a three-run blast, giving his team an exciting, come-from-behind, 7–6 victory. Rick, in a #7 uniform, had continued to swing a sizzling .318 bat in July and got a triple and a single in this ballgame. On the next day Wes matched-up with St. Louis' Dick Coffman in a pitchers' duel with the two teams deadlocked at one run apiece at the end of eight, and he deposited a long drive into the seats for a 2–1 victory.

Boston closed July with a 6–4 win over Washington in which Rick had two doubles and scored twice. Wesley pitched and batted his team to victory with a route-going performance and three hits that included a home run plus four RBIs. The Red Sox had climbed back into the first division with a record of 49–44. Surely many of the Boston faithful waited anxiously for the team to make a move in the pennant race, but the crew seemed to win and lose in equal increments, making no headway. Wes was down 6–5 in the ninth inning against the A's at home on August 4. Boston got a walk, Rick Ferrell singled, and another single tied the score. In the tenth, Wes singled and later scored for his eighteenth win, 7–6.

The team rode the trains from August 13 to September 1, taking four straight from Chicago. Clearly Manager Cronin must have believed that Wes Ferrell's Carolina potion had completely restored his star pitcher's arm strength because he left him in to absorb a 14-inning, 4–3 defeat on August 16. After permitting a White Sox 3–1 lead after five innings, Ferrell hurled eight shutout innings while his team scored two more to tie, but Wes surrendered a run in the fourteenth. His batterymate Rick contributed two hits, scoring twice, and driving in a third run, while Wes went hitless.

The next two weeks brought a slew of bodily injuries to the catcher. The August 23 *Boston Globe* reported that Rick had recently taken hits by balls to his shoulder, left arm, and thigh. However, after chasing a foul into the crowd in Detroit and colliding with a female fan, he "then gained an ovation from the throng by showing a great solicitude for his victim." Wes sprained his ankle during the next game, which sidelined him for more than a week.

Rick caught the first game of a doubleheader with Cleveland that Boston won on August 25. He slammed four hits and four RBIs, winning the game in the bottom of the ninth, 5–4, with a single that scored two runners. Despite a painful attack of lumbago on August 28, Rick wrapped his back tightly and went out and caught a Wednesday double bill, which, unfortunately, Cleveland took. The next day at Shibe Park, a recuperated Wes won his twentieth game, 6–2, vs. Johnny Marcum.

Boston played practically the entire month of September at Fenway. Wes took the mound against Chicago on September 8, after having beaten Cleveland, 6–1, on the 5th. Scoreless in the sixth with the bases loaded, Rick Ferrell socked a single for two runs, after which Wes doubled in two more for an eventual 6–2 victory. Two days later against Chicago, a foul tip snagged Ferrell's thumb, tearing off his fingernail and benching him a week, until September 17.

Each brother had his moments of glory. The September 25 *New York Times* game account began, "The Ferrell brothers performed in brilliant fashion today when the Red Sox completed their home schedule with a 7–2 victory that swept the final series with the Athletics." Wes Ferrell tossed a neat five-hitter to claim his 25th win, and Rick staked him to a three-run lead when he drove in two runs with a triple in the first inning and knocked in two more with a hit in the seventh to seal the victory." Four RBIs for Rick.

Boston ended the 1935 season on Sunday, September 29, in fourth place, 78–75, their best record since 1921. Each player received a $400 bonus for finishing in the first division. Rick sported a .301 batting average based on 138 hits and a career-best 32 doubles with seven other extra-base hits, including three that cleared the fences. His 61 RBIs would rank among his better seasons' production. Defensive stats showed a .990 fielding average, identical to 1933's, with 531 putouts. In *The Sporting News'* MVP voting, the catcher tied for tenth.

Wes enjoyed his most spectacular season yet. In voting for the American League's Most Valuable Player Award, Wesley Ferrell placed second behind Detroit Tigers first baseman Hank Greenberg. Wes topped the league in wins (25), games started (38) and completed (31), innings pitched (322.1) and hits allowed (336). Offensively in 150 plate appearances, the pitcher collected 52 hits for a .357 batting average.

Back in Guilford County, George had hit .377 for Richmond to win the Piedmont League's batting title and Most Valuable Player award and was a unanimous selection to the All-Star team. During the off-season Rick enjoyed showing his foxhound, Luck Tucker, in dog shows around North Carolina. In the All North Carolina Dog Championship Show that year, Luck won first place. Hunting deer in South Carolina with Wes and sometimes companion Lefty Grove also engaged Rick during the winter months, as he centered himself with family at the farm, training and preparing for the next campaign.

In 1936, the Red Sox were almost giddy about their chances of winning the flag, surely enhanced by the progress made the preceding season, and by the staggering player acquisitions made over the winter. Although still in an economic depression, their owner had deep pockets and insisted on trying to buy a winner. In December 1935, Tom Yawkey had again loaded up on new talent, aiming to win the elusive American League pennant. His first trade rocked the baseball world: He gave up two average players and $150,000 for perennial slugger Jimmy Foxx and pitcher Johnny Marcum. On the same day, he swapped two pretty fair hitters (Carl Reynolds and Roy Johnson) for Hall of Fame–bound outfielder Heinie Manush. On January 10, 1936, a third major trade was consummated, again capitalizing on a talent sale being conducted by A's owner Connie Mack. In this cash-induced deal Boston shipped off a couple of other second-tier players and received two frontline players in outfielder Roger "Doc" Cramer and shortstop Eric McNair.

Laurence Leonard, a writer for the *Greensboro Daily News,* contacted Rick Ferrell to ask for his appraisal of these big-time player transactions. The paper's headline, "Boston Will Take Flag, Rick Ferrell Declares," accurately described the opinion of its famed North Carolina resident. "Detroit, Cleveland, New York and possibly Chicago will be serious contenders, but our team will come home first," assured Ferrell. "How do I figure it? Simply because we've got the finest player talent obtainable. We've strengthened every weak spot. Infield, outfield, pitching and catching all have been strengthened with both defensive and offensive players capable of winning a championship." Re-affirming his prediction, he said, "1936 is going to be a good year for us. Yes sir, we're going to have a winner. Look at the roster! A pennant is inevitable!"[5]

Obscured by the excitement of a team loaded with veteran major league talent in 1936 were other acquisitions destined to shape the future of the franchise. In November 1935 of the previous year, the organization had purchased minor leaguer Bobby Doerr from Hollywood in the Pacific Coast League. In 1936, the brass would sign amateur free agent Ted Williams.

Even Rick's manager didn't hesitate to tell the press he expected to win it all. "Sure, I predict we'll win," stated Cronin. "We've put together one of the best clubs ever put together. I may as well, anyway. Everybody expects us to, don't they?"[6] Adding Jimmy Foxx to the lineup would excite any manager, and Cronin beamed when he spoke of his new star. "Foxx is the boy who has made the club. He's added a lot of power and a lot of spirit to the team. He's one of the hardest workers in camp. He showed up in the best shape in years and looks great."[7]

What players had the Boston club added to its roster that had everyone buzzing and drunk with pennant fever? First, they had filled a major hole in the team's power capacity with Jimmy Foxx, one the most fearsome sluggers in all of baseball. Then right-handed pitcher Johnny Marcum, 26, came from Philadelphia and had just enjoyed his career season winning 17 games. Heinie Manush had consistently hit for a high average, but 1935 had been a sub-par season and hindsight would demonstrate that his best years were over. He had only one comparable season left, which would come in 1937 with Brooklyn. Doc Cramer had enjoyed a huge season in 1935, getting 214 hits for a .332 batting average. Finally, shortstop Eric McNair was a slick fielder who had hit .270 the previous season, but where or when he would play was an open question. As the Sox regular shortstop, Manager Joe Cronin's .949 fielding average ranked him last at his position in 1935, while McNair's fielding ranked third among all American League shortstops.

The Red Sox opened the 1936 season on April 14 with big game winner Wes Ferrell on the mound winning, 9–4, while giving up ten walks, but striking out ten. Rick doubled, walked, and scored one run. Boston again won big on the 16th by a 10–4 count. Yawkey and company looked like geniuses in acquiring a backup shortstop because, in a collision at second base in the second inning, Cronin broke his right thumb in two places. With the manager expected to be out of the lineup for at least three weeks, enter Eric McNair.

In his first start of the new campaign on April 17, Lefty Grove pitched a gem, permitting just two Yankee hits while his mates hammered out eight runs in whitewashing the Bronx Bombers, 8–0. Rick Ferrell — who blasted two hits including a homer — spoke glowingly in the April 18 *Globe* about Grove's command in the game. "Personally I believe today's game and the 2–1 overtime game in Washington last year were the best games Grove has pitched since he's been with us. He had everything. Plenty of speed and as sharp a breaking curve as you'd want. And what's more, he had perfect control. Lefty was never in danger and on the few occasions he had three balls on a batter, he just breezed an untouchable fast one across the plate for a strike. It's a cinch to catch for a guy who was pitching the way Mose was this afternoon."

Rick Ferrell began 1936 wearing a new uniform number, 2, and hitting like a batting champ. After seven games he led the team with a .440 batting average, having garnered 11 hits in 29 times at bat. Boston won their first three games, outscoring their opponents 27 to 8. April supported the team's optimism as the Red Sox lost only four of 15 games.

In losing 12–9 to the Yankees on April 26, Foxx rifled a throw from first to home plate as Rick tagged out George Selkirk trying to score. The April 27 *Boston Globe* wrote, "However, the Yankee outfielder took a shot at knocking the ball out of Ferrell's hands and bowled into the dandy little catcher heavily, both biting the dust. Rick, who can be as fiery as any of the high-strung Hose on occasion, lost little time in delivering a few choice epithets to Selkirk when they got up. Only the act of Umpire Bill McGowan's in stepping between the antagonists prevented further activity on their part as several players, including Manager Joe Cronin of the Sox, bad thumb and all, came rushing out from the rival dugouts." Their catcher Rick continued his red-hot hitting, sporting a league-leading .438 average on May 4. He had whacked 28 hits in 17 games and scored 18 runs.

On April 28, Boston defeated Chicago, 11–8, as their catcher got three hits. In the next game, Wes lasted until the seventh inning with Boston prevailing, 6–3. With a 6–6 tie in the bottom of the ninth, Rick Ferrell banged a line drive to score the winning run for a 7–6 Boston victory. From April 29 to May 7 at home, the Sox won eight out of nine games and led the league with a 16–6 record before the "sure-bet" pennant winners began to falter. Rick's keen hitting led all batters with a .439 average in early May. On May 3, Wes faced the Tigers' Tommy Bridges, shutting him out with an incredible 6–0 two-hitter. Rick smashed a home run and a run-scoring double.

On May 7, the Red Sox had scored eight runs by the end of two innings, giving Wes Ferrell his customary strong offensive support. But after allowing 11 hits, Wes staggered to a 9–6 victory. While he was squandering the big lead, his propensity to act out his frustration reappeared. Leaving the mound at the end of the fourth inning, "Wes put on his usual display of disgust with himself and life in general by banging his glove on the ground and kicking up the turf during his walk to the dugout." *Boston Globe* writer Gerry Moore continued, "For this, he was accorded a handful of boo's and catcalls." Later, Wes put his fingers to his nose and pointed them at the crowd, in retaliation. The writer pointed out that the razing will quickly turn to cheering "when he delivers one of his inimitable pinch-hits or low-hit mound performances." Moreover, Wes didn't think anything about it after the game, calling the riding a "lot of fun."[8] Lost in the attention given to Wes was another two-hit game by his much quieter brother.

A two-week road trip lasted from May 8 to 21, starting with a series at Griffith Stadium in Washington. Despite a 12–9 drubbing in their first game, Rick pelted a homer and batted in three runs in his four at-bats.

During road trips, passing time on the long train rides could be entertaining. Rick and Wes would often play bridge on the train rides with Dusty Cooke and Bill Werber. Rick never spoke much — just played the cards of the hand that was dealt him. Most of the time when he was the "dummy," he spent time watching the play of the cards by massaging his scalp with both hands, trying to get his hair to grow.

On Sunday, May 17, Boston squeaked out an 8–7 victory over the host Chicago White Sox, as Cronin paraded out four hurlers to salvage this win. Rick Ferrell clubbed a solo home run into the left-field seats to tie the score in the eighth, and Bill Werber parked one for Boston's winning margin in the ninth. By their return to Boston, Wes had lost all three games he started.

In the final game of a series with the Senators played on May 25, Rick somehow twisted his ankle running to second on a double and was forced to sit out several games. A *Boston Globe* reporter found him at a downtown hotel and spoke to him about his injury. "There's nothing to this foot injury at all," reported Ferrell. "I guess I just turned it good. The swelling has almost all gone down, and if it were positively necessary, I know that I could get right in there and catch the ball game today." Assuring the reporter that he would soon be back in the lineup, he said: "No sir, they can't consider me in any cripple class now. I am no cripple, but am ready to go."[9] Rick sounded much like his father Rufus, tough and uncomplaining.

In June, Yawkey told the *Washington Post,* "Now watch us go after that pennant. At last we'll have all of our cripples back in the line-up this week — and we'll start going right to town."[10] The catcher that was a spy, Moe Berg, was receiving while Rick recovered from his injury. Reflective of Ferrell's key role behind the plate, a June 4 column in *The Sporting News* carried a headline stating: "Sox Hurling Sours with R. Ferrell Out."

During his absence, Rick caught up on his letter writing. On the homepages.rootsweb.com web site is a June 1, 1936, letter written to his friend Treva Wakefield in Greensboro after her mother Dallie Wakefield's death on May 12. The letterhead reads "The Sheraton Boston." "Dear Treva, We heard about your mother. Wes and I are awfully sorry and we want to extend our sincere sympathy to you and your family. Things like that just have to be and no one can help it. No one can forget those things, but it is best not to worry too much. Thanks for the card. I meant to answer sooner. Tell everybody hello around there for me. Very best of luck, and I'll see you all in October after we've won the World Series. Sincerely, Rick Ferrell"

The star catcher returned to action at Fenway on June 4, 1936, against the Indians and ripped a single in the fourth that scored Boston's first run to help Lefty Grove win his eighth game, 4–3. The Red Sox were perched in second, 2½ games out on June 11 when the Browns came to town for a single game. Rick's offense led to a 7–5 ruin of St. Louis as he clubbed a home run — his sixth of the season — over the Green Monster in the fourth inning. Then in the fifth, Ferrell launched a bases-loaded clutch double for a total of four RBIs that erased the Browns' 4–2 lead. The June 12 *Boston Globe* sports headline read, "Rick Ferrell's Bat Beats the Browns." On June 17, Wes enjoyed his ninth triumph, 9–4, over Chicago's Ted Lyons as Boston held down second place, 35–22, 3½ games out.

But all wasn't exactly peachy with the team; several players criticized the infield play and managerial practices of Joe Cronin. Pitchers disliked his habit of approaching them on the mound after each pitch with some word of obvious advice. Dissension rustled among the players as the manager became increasingly nervous and ineffectual.

At home for the traditional Fourth of July celebration in Boston, the Red Sox began a five-game winning streak by sweeping the reeling Philadelphia Athletics in back-to-back doubleheaders. On July 5, Wesley shut down the A's, 16–2, in the first contest for his eleventh victory, while Rick collected four of Boston's 19 hits and scored two runs in a strong four-for-five day at the plate.

The Boston Braves hosted the 1936 All-Star Game at Braves Field and three Red Sox were selected: Rick Ferrell, Jimmy Foxx, and Lefty Grove. Grove, 11–8, got the nod to start the mid-summer classic while his batterymate, Rick Ferrell, in his fourth All-Star Game, started behind the plate. The Nationals got to Grove for two runs in the second, building their lead to four runs—just enough to nose out a 4–3 victory and their first triumph in All-Star Game history. Ferrell had two at-bats without a hit, but Foxx got a single in two tries.

Rick had become a fan favorite since his arrival in Boston where people appreciated the many things he contributed that don't often grab headlines. He had the longest tenure on this team since Tom Yawkey had purchased the franchise in 1933. The Tuesday, July 14, edition of the *Globe* featured two action photographs of Rick under the banner: "At Least Little 'Rick' Does His Stuff." The headline for the caption read: "'Rick' Ferrell — Sox Mainstay — in Action."

The Red Sox rode the train over to Detroit, staying at the Book-Cadillac Hotel downtown, used by all visiting teams. During July 24 to 26, Boston's offense came alive, scoring a total of 35 runs in three straight Tigers' losses. In the July 24 win, Rick singled in the tenth inning with the bases loaded to break a 4–4 tie and win the game, 7–4. Two days later Wes Ferrell started the third game, a 10–3 smear that left fourteen stranded runners on base. Both Ferrells doubled, each scored, while Rick drove in another run. After a St. Louis series, the last stop of their long road trip was Chicago's Comiskey Park, minus catcher Rick Ferrell's services, who had suffered another foul-tip injury that afternoon, splitting his right thumb nail.

That afternoon, July 30, became another "first" in baseball history for Rick: He rode the first American League chartered team airplane to ever fly to a series. In an undated article from *Ledger Sports* in Rick's Guilford College file, he recalled, "As the team was dressing to leave St. Louis after the game, the traveling secretary went around the clubhouse and asked who wanted to fly and who wanted to take the train. Flying was pretty new then, and a lot of the players didn't want any part of it. I had never flown before in my life, and I said I would go. Seven others refused, but eighteen of us consented. The plane was small and was bounced to and fro by air pockets, but some 5,000 people had to be at the gate to welcome us when we landed. I told Wes, 'Heck, let's go,' but he didn't want any part of it. A.L. president Will Harridge accompanied the team while Wes safely rode the rails with the other six to get to Chicago. We needled them about it, called them a bunch of chickens, told them it was great, that they didn't know what they'd missed. It was a big story." The first major league team flight had occurred on June 8, 1934, when the Cincinnati Reds flew from Pittsburgh to Chicago to play the Cubs.

In a phenomenal individual performance, Wes willed his team to victory in the first game of the doubleheader on August 12. Philadelphia had scored four runs in two innings. But powerful Wesley stepped to the plate and blasted three hits to drive in all six Boston runs of his 6–4 victory! Among his three tallies, Wes had clobbered two home runs that included a grand slam with Rick on base. Rick had contributed a hit and a walk to the cause.

But following this incredible win, the Red Sox swirled into a terrible tailspin, losing eight games out of nine from August 16 to 23. In a 7–6 loss on August 16, Rick rapped three hits including a pair of doubles. A couple of days later, Ferrell caught Grove's fifteenth win — 6–2 vs. the A's — and contributed three hits, drove in two runs, and hit a homer off former batterymate Gordon Rhodes. Ferrell was playing well despite his team's descent into sixth place.

More trouble and misunderstanding found Wesley at Yankee Stadium in New York on Friday, August 21. Starting the second game of the four-game series, he matched Yankee Monte Pearson through the fifth, holding a 1–1 tie after Rick had averted a shutout by slamming his eighth home run. In the sixth inning, Wesley lost his command and after allowing three runs, simply left the mound in disgust. Manager Cronin motioned him back, but the pitcher continued walking into the clubhouse, something he had also done recently in a Washington game. Cronin was enraged. This time after discovering Wesley had left the ballpark, the hot Boston field boss levied punishment, announcing that Ferrell was fined $1,000 and suspended for the rest of the season. "I don't care if I never see Ferrell again," barked Cronin. "I don't care whether he obeys orders and goes back to Boston, goes home to North Carolina, or the Fiji Islands. I'm through with him."[11]

The August 23 *Boston Globe* reported that Cronin, Yawkey, and Wes all met at the hotel later that evening and the recalcitrant pitcher repented. He expressed sorrow for his behavior, recognizing that the manager was right to levy a heavy punishment. Cronin, apparently backed by the owner, softened his punishment and reduced the suspension to just ten days. The *Globe* editorialized: "All year long Ferrell has been troublesome. He was known as an individual player who carried his own interest ahead of the club. He was unpopular with the players, most of whom stated tonight that Ferrell had the fine and suspension coming."[12]

Following Cronin's announced punishment, members of the media quickly sought out the AWOL pitcher. At his hotel when Ferrell first learned of his punishment from reporters, he again exploded with anger. Asked what he intended to do about it, Ferrell allegedly said he was going to punch Cronin in the nose. Believing that Wes just might try to pick a fight with the manager, a considerable number of players staked out the lobby prepared to defend Joe Cronin.

Wes Ferrell had been ordered to return to Boston, a mild form of banishment, and the separation also served to cool off emotions and separate the volatile, verbal pitcher from the New York media frenzy. In Boston, Ferrell said the ruckus in New York was "a huge mistake, in which I probably was most to blame." He thought Cronin, by gesture, had authorized him to leave the game, which led to the huge misunderstanding. If only Wes had looked back on his way to the clubhouse, he would have realized that Cronin had not signaled him to leave the mound. "I just want it to be known that I did not leave the box of my own accord in the sixth inning. The first news I got of my fine and suspension was when a newspaper man called me up at my hotel room. I was never so stunned in my life." Apparently seeking to implicate the loose behavior and casual on-the-field execution of other players, Wes told the media: "My only criticism of Cronin is that he's too lenient."[13] When told that Ferrell claimed he had been waved out of the game, Cronin flatly denied it.

The morning after this odd encounter in New York, Shirley Povich wrote in the *Washington Post,* "The news dispatches from New York which relate that Wesley Cheek Ferrell was fined $1,000 and indefinitely suspended by Manager Joe Cronin yesterday, also quote Mr. Ferrell as being 'amazed.' If Mr. Ferrell is, indeed, amazed, then he constitutes a minority of one. Because fans throughout the circuit and all of Cronin's rival managers for several weeks had anticipated the day when Cronin would crack down on the Red Sox's mean-tempered maverick of the mound, Ferrell has been asking for it with great persistence and even the patience of Cronin was nearing its end." Povich balanced his overall assessment of this talented pitcher. "He really isn't a bad guy, this Ferrell — just temperamental," wrote Povich. "His zeal to win is exceeded by that of no other player in the big leagues, but he has never learned to temper it with reason."

Following the hullabaloo in New York on August 21, the Red Sox lost the next two to the Yankees before taking the final game, 6–3. Joe Cronin and his "Millionaires" were happy to get back to Boston, albeit with a 60–62 record and sixth place standing.

Back home Wes had an uncanny ability to land on his feet, and he carried on as though nothing had happened. Unexpectedly the heat quickly dissipated as management maintained the $1,000 fine, but reduced his suspension to a mere four days. Wesley probably apologized to Cronin, for otherwise, there would have been no reason to reduce his "jail time." On August 26, the pitcher was back in the game, as confident as ever, to shut out the Detroit cats and Tiger pitcher Elden Auker, 7–0. Batting eighth just before Wes, Rick doubled twice and drove in two runs to support his brother. According to writer Hy Hurwitz, Wes demonstrated great self-control even when teammates made what could have been damaging errors. Even more amazing was the reaction of the fans. "Ferrell was given a heart-warming reception as he walked out to pitch," wrote Hurwitz. "It was obvious from the greeting that the fans on hand at the game had forgiven Wes for his two walkouts of last week. Each time Wes came to bat he was obviously applauded, and there was no doubt Ferrell is one of the real favorites of the fans."[14]

On Sunday, August 30, there was a moment of sunshine as the Red Sox took a doubleheader from the Indians, 3–2 and 5–1. Wes was masterful in the first contest to increase his record to 17–14. After losing his heater, Wes had totally transformed his approach to pitching, relying on a generic pitch called the "nuttin' ball." Shirley Povich could identify a whole group of hurlers who relied heavily on this junk pitch. "The nothing-ball group is captained by Wes Ferrell of the Red Sox, who has won seventeen games this season despite the fact that his fast ball wouldn't, in baseball parlance, crash a window pane."[15] His faithful catcher, Rick, caught both ends of the twin bill, as Boston beat fastball pitcher Bob Feller in the second game.

In an undated *New York Times* article in Ferrell's Hall of Fame file, however, Rick described one adversarial game between the brother battery when Wes kept shaking off his signs. The catcher finally lost patience, and calling time out, stormed to the mound, screaming, "You big baboon! I'm through giving you signs. From now on, you can throw what you damn well please!" Wes countered, "Get back there, you little squirt, and keep giving me signs. I'll let you know if I want to take them!" But the catcher steadfastly maintained, "No more signs! You can't fool me anyway. I know you too well!" Back behind the plate, the catcher gave no more pitching signals while Wes tossed his trickiest curves and slowballs, trying to trip up his receiver. But Rick reached out and calmly caught every pitch without signs the entire game for a final Boston-Wesley win, and the pair enjoyed a steak dinner together after the game.

In a Sunday doubleheader a week later on September 6, Boston again won both games, 14–5 and 4–2. In the first game, both Ferrells enjoyed hot offense: Wes, on two days' rest, drove in two runs while collecting three hits, one, a home run. Rick smashed two hits, including a triple that plated two runs, and then rode home on his brother's circuit clout. In the nightcap, Lefty Grove hurled a 4–2 jewel, permitting just four hits while fanning 11. Despite this, Boston failed to win another series for the remainder of their 1936 schedule.

After dropping two games against the Browns at Sportsman's Park, Boston rode to Detroit for two games on September 13 and 14. Boston trounced the Tigers, 7–4, in the first game on Sunday, but the two-man brawl that occurred in the second inning was more memorable than the score. The *New York Times* didn't provide details, only noting that Tigers shortstop Billy Rogell and Red Sox catcher Rick Ferrell got into a fight, with both ejected and later, suspended. The spark that ignited the free-for-all was a collision at home plate. In the bottom of the second inning, Al Simmons was stationed at second and Rogell occupied first base. Tigers' catcher Frank Reiber doubled off the center-field scoreboard to score Simmons, and Rogell charged around third and bore down, heading for home. Ferrell caught the relay and had the ball waiting for the on-rushing runner. With great momentum, Rogell slammed into Ferrell, knocking him off his feet as the catcher applied the tag. Angered by Rogell's needless violent force, Rick jumped up and fired the ball at Rogell's back as he headed to the dugout. This time Ferrell's aim was deliberately off the mark; the ball whistled by Rogell's head.

The Detroit newspapers had a field day with this incident. "Tigers Lose but Rogell Gets Decision Over Rick Ferrell," reported the September 14 *Detroit Free Press*, with the banner at the top of the page reading: "Willie Rogell at Last Lands That Famous One-Two Punch." "The battle was between William George (Two Hooks) Rogell representing the Tigers, and Rick (No Punch) Ferrell, representing the Red Sox," wrote Charles Ward, the *Free Press* correspondent who described the action following the home plate collision. "As Rogell started to walk to the Tiger dugout, Ferrell picked up the ball, and aiming three times, threw it at William. It was a wild pitch, but it came close enough to Willie's noggin to put him in a belligerent mood."

Detroit News baseball writer H. G. Salsinger was even more dramatic in describing this angry encounter. After noting that Ferrell fired the ball at Rogell's head, barely missing it, he picked up the subsequent action. "The ball shot by Willie's ear and it took Willie only a second to discover what this fresh Ferrell was trying to do. As soon as he found out, he made a rush at Ferrell and gave him the one-two that he's been talking about for nine years. He landed two left hooks, the first on Ferrell's jaw and the next on Ferrell's temple. Right then, Ferrell fell into a desperate clinch. Willie tried to wiggle loose from the clinch and couldn't do it because Ferrell had a vise-like grip on him. The two citizens named Moriarty and McGowan [George and Bill — umpires] were on hand by this time, and they tried to break the combatants, but they couldn't tear Ferrell loose for several moments." They finally succeeded in separating the two aroused players and Rogell started as though heading for the dugout when he whirled and charged Ferrell again, but this time both players were corralled, and the fight finally ended.[16]

But this rough and tumble fight begs at least a couple of questions. Supposedly after Ferrell threw the ball at the Tigers' shortstop, Rogell came aggressively forward, cocking his fists and ready to hit his adversary. Given that Rick Ferrell was an experienced amateur boxer and Rogell presumably more of a street fighter, how did Willie land his punches? Second, Ferrell's explosive outburst of anger was reminiscent of his brother Wes' and seemingly uncharacteristic of the usually self-controlled older sibling. On other rare occasions too, Rick had become very excited, but the same volatility in his being usually was repressed. However, on occasion, his anger could not be contained. Third, Ferrell easily could have nailed Rogell's head after taking aim had that been his intent. He just wanted to shake him up a little bit.

In a series played at Shibe Park on September 19, Boston managed to win the opening game, 5–1, as the season began winding down. This was Wes Ferrell's last pitching assignment in 1936, for his twentieth win. Rick's last game played was on September 22, a 4–0 loss to Washington.

Boston's 5–4 victory against the A's on September 27 gave the team only 74 wins for the season against a very disappointing 80 losses. Expected by many to be a highly competitive team that would capture the flag, only St. Louis and Philadelphia finished lower than the sixth place Red Sox, who were 28 games behind the pennant-winning New York Yankees. New York won in a walk-off, besting the nearest challenger by 19½ games, with five subsequent teams, second through sixth, separated by only nine games.

A poll conducted by the *Washington Post* after the 1936 season rated the Boston Red Sox the "biggest sports disappointment of past year," predicting that the Red Sox will likely be "the biggest flop in history for the investment involved."[17] All the hoopla surrounding the acquisition of Jimmy Foxx and the outspoken optimism of team associates set Boston up for an embarrassing fizzle. Among the four new position players, all lived up to expectations, with Foxx having a superb .335 year, with 41 home runs and 143 RBIs.

Amid this great disappointment, Rick Ferrell turned in one of his best seasons. Offensively, he compiled his second-best batting average at .312 (.461 slugging average) with eight home runs. In 410 at-bats, Rick got 128 hits that included 27 doubles, 59 runs, and 65 walks. His sudden power surge that ranked him third on the team illustrated that after Foxx, the Red Sox lacked clout in its lineup. Defensively, though suffering injuries, Ferrell caught in 121 games and played his position at a high level with his .987 fielding average, ranking first among all American League catchers. His 556 putouts were the second highest of his career, and he made only eight errors. Wes Ferrell (20–15) and

Before the 1937 season began, three baseball-playing Ferrell brothers met in Richmond, Virginia, before an exhibition game between the Boston Red Sox and the Richmond Colts. Left to right: Rick Ferrell, George Ferrell and Wes Ferrell.

Lefty Grove (17–12) again anchored the starting rotation, but beyond this two-some, the proficiency fell off significantly.

The Ferrells headed back to North Carolina for the winter to see family and purchase new equipment for their parents' farm. Playing for the Richmond Colts, George Ferrell had broken up the Durham Bulls' Johnny Vander Meer's no-hitter that season. On September 1, with two outs in the bottom of the ninth, George had lined one into left field for a hit.

Entering the 1937 season, Boston's brass basically stood pat with their personnel. Bobby Doerr, kid second baseman at age 18, was creating some stir as Cronin revealed his intention to put the untested youngster into his starting lineup. Not only that, Cronin would put him in the pressurized lead-off spot where he would be up front and expected to set the table for the big hitters who followed. Doerr began as a professional at the tender age of 16 and by the spring of his debut season, had two years of seasoning in the Pacific Coast League. Playing for San Diego in 1936, he came on strong with a .342 batting average. He was ready for the challenge and said so. "Joe DiMaggio proved that Coast Leaguers can make good in the majors, so I guess I've a good chance to do the same thing with the Boston Red Sox this year."[18]

In a 2003 telephone interview, Doerr recalled his years with Rick Ferrell on the Red Sox.

BOBBY DOERR: The Boston Red Sox trained in Sarasota, Florida, in 1937, which is where I first met your dad and his brother Wes. At that time I had read about them and had pictures of these guys all over my bedroom wall when I was a kid. I was only 18 when I went to spring training that year. It was some thrill as a kid growing up and reading about these guys and then go in and see the Ferrell brothers and Cronin and Foxx and Grove and Cramer and Higgins—all those great ballplayers! I didn't play too much that first year; I got hit in the head with a ball and I was out a while. Eric McNair got in there and played pretty good ball.

[Rick} was just always one of those fellows that was a steady, class guy. There was never any controversy. You can be very, very proud of him because he was just one in a great many—one of those few, rare people—that come through and is good at what he does and has the right make-up and everything.

I always marveled—he had knuckleball pitchers over in St. Louis and then over in Washington too, and he had to catch those guys and he did it so well! It was remarkable to be able to catch those knuckleballers and not get broken fingers. He never did have a problem with too many balls getting by him.

He was a good, steady hitter, had a good arm, and NEVER any controversy. I can't recall him ever getting thrown out of a ballgame because of his even temperament. He was such a nice guy; we'd sort of visit off the field. Gosh—I always admired him so much. Then after that, I'd see him when he was with Detroit once in a while and visit with him. Then when he was at the Hall of Fame, I remember several times before they'd have the Hall of Fame banquet, he and I would go and sit at a table when they were having cocktails. We'd have a drink inside the room rather than out on the veranda there [of the Otesaga Hotel].

And I remember pumping him for information because he knew players that were back before I broke in. He broke in 1929 and played against guys—Foxx and all those guys—when he was with the St. Louis Browns. I got to ask him about players I didn't get to see and what kind of stuff the pitchers had. We'd talk for maybe an hour. He always had a sharp mind and remembered all that stuff. We did a couple of card shows together too. I got to know him better after we played than when I was with Boston, especially at the Hall of Fame.

According to the analysis of *Los Angeles Times* writer Scotty Reston in his January 13, 1937, column, quality catchers were in short supply throughout the majors in 1937. In the colorful writing style of the time, Reston wrote: "Nine major league managers, driven to desperation by an assortment of old men with social security legs, would give a right field pavilion for a good young catcher." The questionable assessment included Detroit's Mickey Cochrane, returning "after a serious illness" and long considered one of the best in the business. Bill Dickey and Rick Ferrell were the only top ranked receivers identified among the sixteen big league clubs. Though Ferrell had caught more than 120 games over the past five seasons, at age 31, management was looking for opportunities to rest him more and help him maintain his steady performance as a hitter. Moe Berg, seeming always more recognized for his ability to speak multiple languages than for his catching a pitched ball, had been Ferrell's back-up in 1936. He returned to the squad for the present season, but the Red Sox had acquired a couple of other prospects, just in case. No one imagined Rick would catch with regularity for another ten seasons.

The phenomenal renewal of spring always lifts the hopes of baseball people and manager Joe Cronin was sure that fortunes would be better in 1937. "Don't worry," he assured readers of the March 25 *Sporting News*. "It's going to be different this year." Since the team had very few changes, understanding the reason for his optimism was difficult. Exchanging third basemen with the Philadelphia Athletics represented their biggest move, Bill Werber for Pinky Higgins, who had compiled a .306 batting average over four full seasons with the club. The writer observed that Rick Ferrell was really slapping the ball around in spring training and called him "one of the best receivers in the league." But pitching would remain the biggest challenge for the Red Sox.

Just as spring training was ending, however, the Cronins met with tragedy. His wife gave birth, prematurely, to stillborn twins and almost died herself. Cronin left the team to comfort her as she tried to recover from their sad losses.

As a multi-millionaire owner anxious to produce a pennant-winning team by lavishly spending, Tom Yawkey continued to get the attention of the press. The April 28 *New York Times* carried a feature article on the business side of this franchise, claiming that Yawkey's team had experienced a $2,000,000 deficit during his four-year reign and had yet to show a season's profit.

Wes got the ball for the April 20, 1937, Red Sox opener against Harry Kelley at Shibe Park in Philadelphia. With a perfect 6–0 record as an Opening Day pitcher, Wes won again that day, 11–5, with great run support while allowing 13 hits and five runs. Rookie second baseman Bobby Doerr had a big major-league debut, knocking out three of his teams whopping 18 safeties. Rick Fer-

The 1937 Boston Red Sox catching squad strikes a squatting pose together in Sarasota, Florida, during spring training. Left to right: Moe Berg, Johnny Peacock, Rick Ferrell, Gene DeSautels. In June 1937, Rick was traded to the Washington Senators with his brother Wes. (Gwenlo Ferrell Gore)

rell chipped in with two hits and knocked in a run. As the team had grown to expect, Wes aided his own cause with a ringing double that plated another run, and he got a surprising six strikeouts.

The Red Sox immediately returned to Massachusetts to host their own season home opener against the New York Yankees on April 24. Sticking with his other major mound weapon, Cronin used Lefty Grove in this contest, which the Red Sox ultimately lost, 6–5. Rick Ferrell clobbered two singles in three trips to the plate. Wes Ferrell came right back to pitch game three on April 25, but was gone after six innings, allowing five runs on 10 hits and six walks. While Rick enjoyed his third consecutive multiple-hit game, he couldn't help his team avoid a 9–3 loss.

In a lopsided 15–5 victory over the A's on April 30, Wes poled a two-run homer and a hot-hitting Rick banged out two more safeties to cross the plate twice. On May 2, the Associated Press announced that Rick Ferrell led the

American League in batting with a sizzling .550 average based upon 11 hits in 20 at-bats, as Rick started the new campaign with a bang. In his eighth start on May 4, Wes claimed an 11–6 victory over the Browns at Sportsman's Park where Rick bashed three hits. While absorbing a 6–5 Chicago loss on May 8, Rick hit a home run in three tries while Wes went two-for-three. A May 9 *Chicago Tribune* article described Rick's blast into the seats as "Wes's peace-loving brother sailed one over the wall in the fourth."

A losing pattern was developing when on May 13, Wes took another beating — his third in a row — from Detroit, 4–0. Wes was hitless, while Rick continued his blistering attack, going three-for-four. That sparkling day allowed him to continue his league batting lead with a .536 mark. But Rick's hitting cooled off just as the Red Sox began to slide.

Detroit's May 13 shutout started a string of six losses in the next seven games that quickly dropped the team into seventh place. On May 17, double-trouble occurred as the team lost both manager Cronin and catcher Ferrell to injuries, and then Wes lost the game, 4–3, to Washington. During the pre-game warm-ups, Cronin was hit in the cheek by a throw from Higgins and forced to the sidelines. Rick took yet another foul tip off his throwing hand which fractured a bone, putting him out of action for a month to heal just when his bat was going strong. Unknown to him then, May 17 would be Rick's final game with the Red Sox. In May, with Rick on the bench, Boston piled up nine losses in eleven games to register a 9–12 season record by May 21 and a seventh place standing.

Boston played a two-week home stand during May 18 to 31. At Fenway, Wes started and won twice with the same score: 11–9 against Detroit on May 22, and St. Louis on May 26. However, he gave up 11 hits in four innings during the first win, and 12 hits in the second. His control faltered further when he lost his next two starts: on June 3, 11–4 to Chicago, and on June 7, 9–6 vs. the Browns. Rick called GM Collins to tell him his injured hand was better and that he would be back in uniform soon.

As the trading deadline drew nearer, trade winds were swirling. News leaked of a potential swap between Washington and Boston involving pitchers Ferrell and Bobo Newsom, and perhaps Rick Ferrell and a Senators outfielder. Newsom's difficult attitude was also a known characteristic. *New York World-Telegram* reporter Dan Daniel readily shared his opinion in his June 8 column. "It would be no great hardship for Cronin to let Wesley Ferrell wander to Washington. The temperamental Wes is something of a pain in the neck, even when he's winning.... Ordinarily Bucky Harris [the Nationals' manager] could not be persuaded to consider taking over the mess of trouble labeled Wesley Ferrell. But it is believed that Harris is so fed up with Newsom he would welcome a change, even to Wesley."

And then the heavy shoe dropped on June 10, 1937: Rick and Wes Ferrell were, in fact, traded to the Washington Senators for outfielder Ben Chapman and pitcher Bobo Newsom. The greater commodities were Rick Ferrell for Ben Chapman since Washington needed a quality catcher and Boston yearned for a top-flight outfielder. At 31, Rick Ferrell was still considered one of the best catchers in the circuit, and the 28-year-old Chapman brought a .308 lifetime batting average to Boston. Chapman had hit .315 in 1936 and had averaged 93 RBIs over his seven-year career. Although Rick Ferrell had been injured and had cooled off at the plate, he'd still racked up a highly respectable .308 average in 18 games with the Red Sox. As rumored, Wes Ferrell and Newsom traded uniforms. With a 3–4 record, Newsom, like Wes, hadn't gotten on track in 1937, but he was coming off a best 17–15 record in 1936.

Even though the relative value exchanged seemed fairly equal, that Boston would part with Rick Ferrell was somewhat puzzling. Several scribes observed that young catcher Gene DeSautels, who had filled in for Rick during his recuperative absence, had made a very good showing and impressed Cronin. The June 10 issue of *The Sporting News*, on the eve of the expected swap, suggested another reason for his availability. "Unfortunately for Rick, one of the steadiest and most dependable backstops who ever donned a Boston uniform, his star seems to have set locally, with the failure of his bigger brother as the principal reason for his expected departure from Fenway Park." The Fenwayfanatics.com web site noted that in Rick's Red Sox statistics during the period 1933–37, he hit .302 (#12 on the Red Sox all-time list) with 541 hits in 1791 at-bats. Baseballlibrary.com states that defensively during his Boston tenure, Rick broke team catching records for doubles (92), home runs (16) and runs-batted-in (240).

In his 2003 telephone interview Bobby Doerr lamented that the Red Sox gave up Rick and his catching expertise in 1937: "[Rick] was really such a good catcher. Boston never really did have catching until Carlton Fisk got in there. It's just too bad that Rick didn't stay there because that was one of our weak spots for a long time—catching. In '37, Boston traded the Ferrell brothers and Mel Almada to Washington and we got Ben Chapman and Bobo Newsom. When I was playing all those years after that I would think, 'Gosh dang it, I wish we had Rick Ferrell catching.' He went over to Washington and then I played *against* him all the time."

Naturally both teams enthusiastically touted the trade, believing it to be a good move for them. Cronin thought the change of venue would help each starting pitcher get back on track, inferring that the benefits would be similar. He liked Chapman, who brought both speed and a hitting prowess to his team. About giving up his catcher, he told the June 10 *Boston Globe,* "Rick Ferrell should be able to get back in the game right away, but we feel that we are not taking long chances by letting him go." Senators owner Clark Griffith's enthusiasm for the deal was laced with optimism, as Shirley Povich quoted him in the June 11 *Washington Post*, "I think Rick Ferrell is just what we need to make Washington a steady winner. He is a great catcher and a fine fellow. We haven't had a good catcher in a long time and were sorely in need of one.... When Wesley Ferrell is in shape there are few better pitchers. He has had tough going this year, but we expect him to come through for us." A couple of days later Cronin was speaking with greater sentiment. "I sure hated to lose Rick — good ball player, hard worker, easy to get along with."

Most sportswriters recognized that Wes and Bobo were equal in talent, although Ferrell's arm strength was suspect, and with Newsom, injury was no concern. Shirley Povich provided a very candid appraisal of the trade in his June 11 article, offering, along with most other sportswriters, that Rick Ferrell was the key player in the exchange. "If any particular good comes to either club in

Shortly after donning Washington Senators uniforms on June 11, 1937, newly-traded brother battery Rick Ferrell (left) and Wes Ferrell (right) are heartily greeted by Nats manager Bucky Harris (center) on the dugout steps in Chicago. In his first start, Wes helped his new club to a 6–2 win. Rick would catch for the Senators until 1941 while Wes, whose pitching arm was fading, would last until 1938. (National Baseball Hall of Fame Library, Cooperstown, N.Y.)

the deal, then the Nats are likely to be that club, and Rick Ferrell is likely to be the man around whom the advantage will revolve. For the catching end of the Ferrell battery is unquestionably the most valuable player in the lot. There never has been any doubt of his catching skill nor of his hitting talents. The Nats are gambling that his broken hand will heal." Most agreed that Rick Ferrell was best player in the recent player transaction.

Manager Bucky Harris had told Povich for the June 11 *Post* that he was going to strongly encourage pitcher Wesley to go back to his nuttin' ball and forget about trying to over-power hitters with his "want-to-be hard" stuff, which he didn't seem to command very well. Harris expressed confidence that he could manage his excitable pitcher. "I always got along well with Ferrell at Boston, and there will be no trouble with him in Washington," insisted Harris. Povich claimed: "He [Ferrell] admits he's hot-headed. He couldn't very well deny it after some of the things he's done. He averages tearing up a half dozen gloves each season and last month in Washington when Al Simmons' home run beat him in the last inning, Ferrell went back to the bench, took off his cap and tore it into a shredded-wheat affair."[19]

Over in Boston they were waiting to see how Bobo Newsom and Ben Chapman would act, Chapman because he was considered by some to be a strange character. Sooner or later, the focus would shift to the ball field and on winning and losing.

5

❖ ❖ ❖

1937–1941

Ferrells Traded to Washington Senators

At this stage of his career, adjusting to the confines of a new home field was not difficult since Rick had played road games at Griffith Stadium for eight years. The Washington Nationals (or Senators) were charter members of the American League but didn't play at the Griffith Stadium site until 1903. National Park was enlarged to hold 10,000 paying customers that season and was often called just League Park. Disaster struck during the 1911 spring training when fire consumed the entire structure.

The conflagration of ballparks during this era led to construction of steel and concrete structures that provided a new sense of safety and were built to last. The new American League Park was renamed Griffith Stadium in 1920 honoring Clark Griffith, who became manager of the team in 1911 and continued through the 1920 season when he was owner and president.

This ballpark had a stubborn personality, generally considered a graveyard for long-ball hitters. Only the 320-foot distant right-field fence was friendly, but that short field was negated by a 30-foot-high concrete wall, which kept balls in play. As originally configured, the left-field foul pole stood 407 feet from home plate, with the expansive outfield reaching 421 feet to straightaway center field. The stadium was located in an area of Washington heavily populated by people of color who were Senators fans. Griffith, anxious to add to his financial coffers, rented out his ballpark to the Negro League Homestead Grays. There were seasons in which powerful Josh Gibson hit more home runs at Griffith Stadium than the entire Washington Senators club.[1]

In the past season, 1936, under manager Bucky Harris, the Nationals, or "Nats," had placed fourth in the American League with an 82–71 record, twenty games behind the Yankees. When the Ferrells joined the club, the Senators held sixth place in the American League, 7½ games out of first, with a 19–25 record.

Manager Harris soon trotted out his new brother battery as the Ferrell brothers made their Senators debut at Comiskey Park on June 11, 1937. Wes pinch-hit and Rick, playing with a partially healed hand, caught the last three innings in a free-swinging 14–8 loss to the White Sox. Wes Ferrell got his first start the next night, June 12, with Rick calling his pitches, and shut down the White Sox, 6–2, with an efficient four-hitter. Wearing uniform number "8," Rick stroked his first hit for the Senators as he returned to duty full-time and picked off the quick Tony Piet at second base trying to steal in the seventh.

In 2003, third baseman Buddy Lewis recalled Rick and that game in a telephone interview.

BUDDY LEWIS: [Rick] was older than we were, and he had been around the league for some years prior. I went to Washington in the fall of 1935; I was less than 20. Mainly, you had fellows 19 years old and some, 35 years old. So we did not mingle. When we went out of town, it was a different situation. We all lived in the same hotel, and after the game, we would eat together in little groups.

Rick and Wesley were traded together from Boston to Washington — the team I played on — in 1937. He joined Washington in Chicago. The day that Rick caught his first game for Washington — between innings, we used to throw our glove out behind the position and just left it there — but I threw my glove down with just two outs! When they passed the ball around, Rick threw to me at third base and I wasn't looking — he hit me right on the Adam's Apple! He damn near broke my neck! (laughs) I thought the second out was the third out, and I was heading toward the dugout. That was my initiation to Rick!!

I got to know Rick the next spring, 1938, at spring training. We trained at Tinker Field in Orlando. At night, we all ate in the same dining room upstairs at the Angebilt Hotel. I would fraternize and eat with him — wherever and whenever I could get to his table. He and I got along just wonderfully. Rick and I had something in common: I liked to buy common stocks and Rick loved it! He was farther advanced in this field than I was, and I learned a lot from him. He'd been around and he'd had some money to invest, so he learned about money management. I got in on this business and made a lot more money in stocks than I did in baseball.

Most catchers back in the day were scarce. They'd put a catcher in the lineup that really wasn't qualified to be there because some of the others had gotten hurt during the season. We had collisions every day — catchers took a beating. Players back then would have metal spikes and they'd do everything they could to cut a catcher particularly. Most teams carried three catchers. It was a matter of necessity; if one got a broken finger, then you only have two left. And they can get hurt in two seconds! They can get hurt while you're lookin' at 'em!

Rick didn't pull strictly down the left-field line, but he was more like a good hit-and-run hitter. He'd hit the ball back through the box and to right-center and left-center. He was not a tremendously powerful hitter, but adequate in our game back then. He kept his arms out away from his body pretty good, and that's the only way you can hit in the major leagues— your arms have to be out and high, away from your body. And Rick did that. He was probably a better hitter than most catchers. Rick didn't hit in the first four of the lineup. The Browns were on the bottom all the time. Nobody did well over there.

But I knew Rick as well as anybody; he had the most wonderful temperament that anyone could possibly have. Rick had a real even temperament — a real wonderful fellow. [Rick and Wes] were so opposite. But the physique: Wesley was taller than Rick and had oodles of beautiful hair. And Rick had sparse hair. Sometimes opposites attract. Wes would get furious shooting in a pool game. I never did see Rick get mad. I loved your daddy and I thought the world of him."

The Senators returned home to Griffith Stadium on June 15 for a long three-week homestand through the Fourth of July holiday. After losing three straight, pitcher Ferrell took the box again on June 16, against the Detroit Tigers. He and Detroit's young pitcher, Jake Wade, had dueled for 12 methodical innings and were tied 1–1, when fleet-footed Rick Ferrell scooted home from third base on a wild pitch to give Wesley a 2–1 victory. Rick contributed three hits in five at-bats.

On June 20 with Rick catching, Wes got his third straight victory, 5–3, over the Browns, giving up three early runs but allowing only two hits in the final six innings of play. In his June 21 "This Morning" column for the *Washington Post*, Shirley Povich sang the praises of the Ferrell brothers. "It was a nearly perfect beginning for two players who were eager to show the world that the Red Sox had made a big mistake in peddling them to the Senators." Povich was particularly impressed with Rick's defensive skills. "He's cat-quick behind the plate, and during the past two days, Washington fans saw him snatch up two foul bunts that no other fellow who happened behind the batter for the club in the past four seasons would ever reach." For his part Wes had allowed only four earned runs in 30 innings of work and was batting .500 as a pinch-hitter. Rick smashed three hits in Wes' June 25 loss to Chicago.

On June 29, the Red Sox visited Washington for a three-game series, the first confrontation between the two teams since the Ferrell brothers swap June 11. The *Washington Post* called it a "three-day family quarrel given the marital relationship between the two managers [Bucky Harris and Joe Cronin]." Povich wrote that this match-up would have special meaning for Rick Ferrell. "Anything the Nats are able to contribute to the failure of the Red Sox will be particularly gratifying to Rick Ferrell, who read in the papers the other day that Manager Cronin was crediting the Red Sox rise to the improved catching of the club since it traded Ferrell. Since that utterance, Rick Ferrell has been named among the league's All-Star catchers with Cronin's present catching staff entirely ignored in the selections."[2]

Much hullabaloo arose when a Bobo Newsom vs. Wes Ferrell pitching confrontation was scheduled for June 30. Rick told the eager press, "We're ready for him. He's got six left-handed batters to face and three pretty good right-handers." Both pitchers felt they had something to prove, and one of the largest week-day crowds in years showed up at Griffith for this showdown.

In the first frame the two pitchers had a little personal fun after Newsom hit a ringing double off his adversary. "With some amazement," wrote Povich, "the 22,000 saw Wes Ferrell walk out of the pitcher's box, amble toward second base, and extend his hand to Newsom with a smile. It was the payoff on their pre-game wager that they would shake hands with the first one of 'em that made a hit yesterday. Thunderous applause greeted the demonstration. Newsom, who had been booed profusely throughout the game, held the Red Sox in check through six innings, allowing just two runs, as his mates built up a 4–2 lead." Continuing the dramatics, Wes hit a single in the eighth inning to drive home both the tying and winning runs for a 6–4 Washington win, and in Povich's words, "drove the arrogant smile from Newsom's face."[3]

Washington frosted the cake in the third game against Boston, scratching out a 3–2 victory behind the steady pitching of Jimmie DeShong and a clutch single from Rick Ferrell that drove in the winning run in the sixth. In a moment of poetic justice, Povich wrote in the July 1 *Post*, "Little Rick Ferrell blasted the decisive run — a line-drive over shortstop Cronin's glove — to score Cecil Travis from second base, beating the Boston Red Sox, 3–2." For the series, the Nats had two wins and a tie.

Rick Ferrell, Wes Ferrell, and second baseman Buddy Meyer played in the fifth Mid-Summer Classic at Griffith Stadium on July 7. American League manager Joe McCarthy had five of his Yankees in the starting lineup — battery Lefty Gomez and Bill Dickey, Lou Gehrig, Red Rolfe, and Joe DiMaggio— and he stuck with only twelve players as his Americans downed the Nationals, 8–3. No hometown favorite saw action. This game would long be remembered for the screaming line drive off the bat of Earl Averill that struck Dizzy Dean in the foot, derailing a brilliant career in the making.[4]

Still in sixth place, Washington resumed their road trip in New York on July 9 where they were promptly swept in three games by the powerful Yankees crew who tapped the Nats for 32 total runs at Yankee Stadium. Thus began a ten-game losing streak that lasted until July 20. Wes had been shutout by the Yankees, 7–0, on July 4 at home, and was trounced again July 10 at Yankee Stadium, 12–2. In his third incomplete start on July 16, Cleveland prevailed, 11–5. Then the hapless Senators put on their rally hats, and from July 24 to August 1, recorded six wins in a row, still in sixth place.

With his fractured right thumb still tender and enduring the worst batting slump of his career, Rick Ferrell was hitting just .214 when he was nailed yet again on his right thumb by another foul tip, this time off Cleveland catcher Frankie Pytalak's bat on July 30. He missed the next two weeks with another fractured bone. With a second injury to his throwing hand, coupled with having been unexpectedly traded while batting .308, Rick was experiencing a difficult period of adjustment in Washington and his game was suffering. The Senators had four regulars hitting over .300, among them shortstop Cecil Travis, the league leader at .375.

In mid–August, the Senators enjoyed an eight-game winning streak in front of the hometown fans, sweeping both the A's and Red Sox. After a 12-day absence, Rick returned to the lineup on August 12 to help snare a 5–4 victory from the Athletics. His single in the eighth inning drove in the tying run in a 4–4 game, with Buddy Lewis winning the game in the ninth. With Rick out, Wes had hurled two wins and two losses with backup catcher Wally Millies filling in. Washington took full advantage in a four-game sweep of the boys from Beantown. The first game of an August 15 doubleheader promised a match-up between ex-teammates, Lefty Grove and Wes Ferrell. Grove allowed seven runs in seven innings, while Wes went the distance for an 8–3 triumph over his old friend.

The Senators left Washington for their longest road trip of 1937, playing 17 games around the circuit from August 17 to September 2. On August 19, Wes Ferrell lost a heart-breaker when New York scored an unearned run in the bottom half of the twelfth. An unusual battle, however, ensued under the stands after the game. An insulted Rick Ferrell and Tony Lazzeri began a fist-fight following a verbal exchange at home plate when the Yankee second baseman accused Ferrell of tipping his bat. The fight ended when Wes jumped on Lazzeri. The Senators left the Big Apple swept for four more losses to retain their sixth-place standing with a 49–56 record.

After his outstanding season-start batting .308 in Boston, by the end of August Rick was closing in on a nightmarish season, sporting an even .200 batting average, the lowest in his major-league career. Although his brother was not piling up the wins he had in the past, Wes had a 7–8 record.

On September 3 the Senators defeated New York when Rick connected for two hits in four plate appearances, scoring two runs in a 4–2 victory over the Yankees. Rick caught Monte Weaver and Jimmie DeShong in both games of a doubleheader against Boston won by Washington on September 7. This marked their 11th win against three losses to the Boston Red Sox. In the first game, an 11–5 lopsided affair, Rick collected three hits while driving in two tallies.

In early September, the Nats played four back-to-back doubleheaders, two at Fenway and two at Philadelphia. The first game on September 6 brought another battle between 13-game winners Wes Ferrell and Lefty Grove. Lefty triumphed over Wes this time, 6–2, motivating Wes to tear up his glove afterward. The Nats won two doubleheaders and split two. After winning six out of seven games, the Senators were 60–67 on September 9, in sixth place. A number of rookie hurlers were introduced at this stage of a disappointing season. Given Rick's off-year at the plate and his age (32), Manager Harris had begun using him in just one game of a doubleheader and second-string catcher Wally Millies in the other.

After the long road trip, the team steamed into D.C. on September 14 for a homestand that would last until month's end. By September 15, Rick had pulled his average up to .239; Wes had an 11–11 pitching record and a .262 batting average. When Wesley's old team, the Indians, visited on the 22nd, he started the game, but lost to Johnny Allen, 6–3. On September 26 against the A's, Wesley was called in to relieve in the ninth inning with a 7–4 Senators lead, and promptly gave up three runs for a 7–7 tie game, which was thankfully called due to darkness. September 30, Wes threw his final game, setting down the Red Sox on seven hits and earning a 4–3 victory to top off a challenging season with his third big league club.

Half of the most famous brother battery in the history of baseball is Rick Ferrell, who was christened Richard Benjamin, is slight of build, and older by two years than Pitcher Wes. The little backstop started in organized baseball two years earlier than Wes, but was a year later in reaching the majors.

Rick Ferrell started with the St. Louis Cardinals in 1925, but promptly was farmed out. He made the rounds of Syracuse, Kinston and Columbus before he came back to St. Louis in 1929 as a regular. On his return, however, he played with the St. Louis Browns, who traded him to Boston in 1933. Rick served with the Red Sox until last June, when he came to Washington in trade along with Brother Wes and Outfielder Melo Almada.

Despite his slight build, Rick is tough and wiry and one of the best scrappers in the big leagues. As an undersized youngster in a family of seven strapping, ball-playing brothers, Rick was kidded about his lack of size. Determinedly, he armed himself with a pair of boxing gloves, learned the art of self-defense, and proceeded to become a boxer. He won 16 out of 18 bouts before turning ball player, professionally.

Rick always was a catcher, even as a kid. The big mitt fascinated him. "Once he dried dishes for a month because he was promised a catcher's mitt by his grandmother," recalls Brother Wes. "He was sore as all get-out when he got one of those cheap corner-store mitts, but he used it."

Ferrell is rated one of the best mechanical catchers in baseball. Despite his lack of size and power, he has a nine-year major league batting average of .291. His best year was in 1932, when he batted .315 for the Browns. Is not married. Was born October 12, 1906, at Durham, N. C.—F. E. S.

"Know the Nationals" cartoon drawing: Rick Ferrell. This cartoon drawing of catcher Rick Ferrell was in an informative series called "Know the Nationals" printed in the 1937 *Washington Star*. The article notes, "Ferrell is rated one of the best mechanical catchers in baseball. Despite his lack of size and power, he has a nine-year major league batting average of .291."

In 1937, a season from which owner Griffith had expected much more, the Washington Senators finished sixth, with a 73–80 record, 28½ games behind the pennant-winning Yankees. Ferrell managed to catch a total of 102 games for the season, collecting a .988 fielding percentage with 434 putouts and just six errors.

With a final .229 average with Washington, Rick had had his first poor season since becoming a big-leaguer nine years earlier. Between his two teams, he got a .244 average, with just 84 hits and 65 walks. Never one to offer excuses, he could have attributed the fall-off to his two significant injuries, the first forcing him to the bench when his bat was on fire. Continuing to play while hurt for the entire season, in many times at the plate, Rick could only grip his bat with one fist, trying to hit one-handed.

Wes also had a sub-par year, finishing 1937 with a 14–16 won-loss record, only his second losing record in a nine-year career. With more run support, Wes could easily have reversed the numbers for his pitching had measurably improved after being traded to Washington. *The Sporting News* in early December mentioned the possibility of the Senators trading Rick and Wes Ferrell to the Yankees for Bill Dickey at the winter meetings, but nothing developed.

Rick liked to tell the story of the off-season when he and Bill Werber were driving south on the highway for a hunting trip. Rick was driving Bill's car — a Chrysler New Yorker — and as they were talking about shooting quail and hunting with Dusty Cooke, a patrolman stopped them, saying he'd had a hard time catching the car because it was traveling over 85 m.p.h. The officer saw the name on Rick's license and asked, "You're not the ballplayer, Rick Ferrell, are you?" Ferrell said, "Yes, I play ball." The officer said, "Well, I played ball against you years ago when you were in college. Now, you go on. I'm not going to give you a ticket. But will you do me a favor and slow it down going through the rest of the state?" Rick got a break from the officer.

The ever-optimistic catcher was looking forward to regaining his true form for the 1938 season. Rick met with the owner and quickly signed his agreement, which included a $1,000 pay cut. Wes balked at the contract sent him, holding out against a $2000 pay cut to $15,000. *The Sporting News* reported that Rick had "reached an agreement with the Washington president after a short confab — exceptionally short for any ball-playing member of the temperamental North Carolina family."[5]

Like many athletes Rick put on his game face when he walked onto the playing field. He was a competitor and, being a catcher, there were plenty of collisions as he guarded home plate. Off the field, Rick Ferrell was a genuinely nice guy, well-liked, and quick to befriend others. During the pre-season, the *Washington Star* featured a series of characterized drawings entitled, "Know the Nationals." Rick was considered small for a catcher, though he stood 5'10". When he was featured in the series, the artist drew a cartoon showing a monster-sized batter and a much smaller depiction of the catcher Ferrell. Ferrell

No more promising young pitcher of modern times wore a spiked shoe and toeplate than Wesley Cheek Ferrell when the handsome, high-strung right-hander broke into the American League with Cleveland in 1930. In his first four seasons with the Indians he won well over 20 games per year.

Suddenly, in 1933, the Ferrell fast ball disappeared with the coming of a mysterious arm ailment. He was adjudged washed up. Physicians diagnosed his case as bursitis, and wagged their heads regretfully; Wesley quit baseball.

It was Bucky Harris, lacking pitching at Boston in 1934, who lured Wes back into baseball. He had no fast ball, but Ferrell had control, a good head and a fighting heart. He changed his style of pitching, spinning slow curves off his fingers and pitching to spots. His fast ball had two speeds . . . slow and slower. But he won 14 games and lost 5 in half a season in 1934, and the following year he won 25 and lost 14. In 1936 he won 20 and dropped 15, but last season, after coming to Washington in a June trade, he was plagued

by hard luck and finished with only 14 wins as against 19 defeats.

He is faster now than at any time since his arm became sore, and should be good for several more years of pitching. He takes defeat to heart more than almost any player since Ty Cobb, although Wes, in his tantrums, blames only himself. He is known to break wrist watches, tear up his glove and rip his uniform to shreds after losing ball games.

Wes was so fine a prospect that he spent next to no time in the minors. Cleveland acquired him in 1927, farmed him out to Terre Haute part of the 1928 season, and recalled him in the fall. Thereafter he was in the majors to stay, with the exception of his brief voluntary retirement.

Wes is only 30 years old, having been born in Greensboro, N. C., February 2, 1908. Stands 6 feet 1 inch and weighs 195 pounds. Is one of the best looking men in baseball and is regarded as Hollywood material. Is a stanch believer in astrology and daily hitches his wagon to the stars. He bats so well that he frequently is used to pinch hit for other pitchers. Like Brother Rick he is unmarried.   F. E. S.

Wes Ferrell's cartoon in the "Know the Nationals" series published in the *Washington Star* in 1937.

challenges the hitter stating: "Lissen, Punk! You don't look so tough to me!" And the caption read: "In spite of his size, he's a scrapper to be reckoned with." Recollections from his brother were included. "Once he dried dishes for a month because he was promised a catcher's mitt by his grandmother," recalled Wes. "He was sore as all get-out when he got one of those cheap corner-store mitts, but he had to use it."

Rick decided to try a new one-handed catching style, like Mickey Cochrane and Bill Dickey, hoping to prevent more injuries to his bare right throwing hand. With this method, the catcher holds his bare hand away from the pitch and snags the ball with one hand in the mitt, a near-revolutionary style during a time when the over-riding attitude barked out "use two hands" to catch a baseball.

The Ferrell brothers were always good businessmen. While at spring training camp an advertisement appeared in *The Sporting News* trumpeting "Ferrell Bros. 'Big League' Dog Food," referring to the thriving dog food business the pair had begun back in North Carolina.

A silly confrontation that began between Wes and a cameraman escalated into a boycott and a headline story in the March 5 *Washington Post* in 1938 during spring training. Supposedly a photographer approached Wes and asked to take his picture. Ferrell consented, but when the photographer got overly-instructive about the pose he should assume, Wes got upset and words were exchanged. Rick appeared, jumped in the middle of the verbal exchange, and announced that neither would ever pose for another shot by a Washington newspaper photographer. Wes ultimately calmed downed and agreed to do what had been called for. "This afternoon the cameramen got together and agreed not to photograph the Ferrell brothers again during the remainder of the training season."

Knuckleball pitcher Dutch Leonard had joined the rotation from Atlanta. In early April as the Nats were leaving spring training, they purchased Browns catcher Angelo Giuliani as back-up for Rick Ferrell, in case of injury. Winning in 1937 had been difficult with Ferrell out for several weeks.

Whether better or lucky, Washington broke from the gate like a champion on April 18, 1938, with President Franklin Delano Roosevelt tossing out a short first pitch before a crowd of 30,000 fans. Pitching with a sore shoulder, Wes started the Senators' opener — traditionally reserved for the squad's best hurler — against the Philadelphia A's Harry Kelley. "Wesley Ferrell pitched his typical game, giving up lots of hits, but tightening in the pinches."[6] And did he ever — sixteen hits in all, but Harris left him in to go all the way to win, 12–8, although the pitcher began to lose control in the late innings, a pattern that would repeat itself throughout the season. After one game, Ferrell had an ERA of 8.00, but a perfect 1–0 record. The Nats swept all three games from the A's, with new starter Dutch Leonard taking a 3–0 shutout with Rick as his catcher.

On April 28, Wes Ferrell picked up his third straight win of the season, 7–2, against Philadelphia's George Castor. Buddy Lewis paced the attack with three hits and six runs batted in, while the Ferrell boys, with four hits, provided the rest of the offensive support.

A short note appeared in the *Post* on May 3, an ominous foreshadowing of terrible events to come: "[Lou] Gehrig actually hit a new low yesterday when he was dropped to sixth place in the batting order as a result of his slump. Never since he joined the Yankees in 1925 has he hit below fifth place."

The Nats played at home the first two weeks of May. On May 4, Washington rookie knuckleballer Dutch Leonard faced Cleveland's emerging fastballer, Bob Feller. With Rick catching, Leonard turned in a masterful performance "fluttering his knuckleball with deadly effectiveness," wrote the *Los Angeles Times*, to edge Feller and the Indians, 1–0, in thirteen innings. Leonard allowed only six hits, retiring seventeen consecutive batters from the fifth inning through the tenth. Rick singled in three at-bats.

With that stunning victory the Senators took flight and soared, winning seven straight at Griffith. On May 9, Leonard's knuckleball whipped the Browns, 7–1, as Rick smashed a triple and singled in a run. After winning May 10, the improbable Senators were proud possessors of first place with a 15–7 record (.682). But like a hot hitter, the tables can suddenly turn.

The 1938 return to form of Rick Ferrell bode well and his consistent, strong play contributed significantly to the surging Washington ball club. In a tribute Shirley Povich devoted a long article to the Senators' catcher. "No small factor in the Nats' success this season has been the moderately-sized fellow who daily dons the catching paraphernalia and goes behind the plate," began Povich. Rick was now beginning to demonstrate that reputation after a very disappointing first season with the Senators. "Because the hits are starting to rattle from his bat — lush, productive hits with men on bases— and at this writing Rick bows only to Zeke Bonura in the important matter of runs driven in on the Washington club." Povich was very mindful of the toll that Ferrell's injuries had had on his ability to swing a bat, stating that this year the fans were seeing the real Rick Ferrell. "But Ferrell's greatest value to the Nats is probably the gilt-edge protection he is giving the club behind the plate. Bucky Harris ... appreciates Ferrell's presence and so do the Washington pitchers."

Povich noted the challenge Ferrell faced handling knuckleball starter Dutch Leonard, stating that no other catcher drew that assignment. "The knuckler can make a catcher look very awkward and inept, and Ferrell is forced to hop around, constantly trying to outguess the thing when Leonard is on the mound." Giving credit to Ferrell, Povich recognized that a knuckleball pitcher can make a catcher look bad, and a lesser receiver might be reluctant to call for it because its speed and unpredictable movement give the baserunner a big advantage. With a runner on third, calling for the knuckleball raises the risk even higher. But according to Povich, Ferrell didn't flinch. Clearly Leonard appreciated having a catcher with Ferrell's confidence and skill. "To Ferrell, Leonard gives full credit for his victories (3–2) with the Nats," wrote Povich, "declaring he has never pitched to a catcher who was so willing to take the rap. More than 50 per cent of his pitches have been knucklers ... and although Ferrell has juggled a good percentage, he has never let one get away."[7]

On May 11, the Red Sox lost to the Tigers, ending the glorious seven-game winning streak, the longest streak since 1933. In the mid–May article, Povich wrote about Rick, "There never was any complaint with Ferrell's throwing arm and he was always rated as a catcher who knew hitters."[8] Wes was hammered, 10–0, by Boston on May 13, touched for 13 hits, but he defeated Detroit, 5–1, on the 18th, allowing only six hits. Wes broke his four-game losing streak on May 18 by pitching and hitting the Nats to a 5–1 victory over Detroit. He served up his slow stuff so successfully that neither Gehringer, Greenberg, nor

After being traded together from Boston to the Washington Senators in 1937, Rick (right) and Wes (left) sit on the field to discuss pitching signs in their new uniforms. They finished the 1937 season and much of 1938 together until Wes was released during the 1938 season. (Gwenlo Ferrell Gore)

York got a hit while the Senators got ten hits, including a tenth-inning home run by Wesley himself. Ferrell's next start on May 22 in Chicago resulted in a 9–2 loss to Ted Lyons, who scored his 200th victory. Wes held the Sox hitless in four innings while Rick knocked out a single and a double and scored a run.

Although the Browns edged the Nats, 4–3, on May 25, Rick was responsible for two of his team's runs that day. He walloped three doubles, scoring on one in the second inning to tie the score, 3–3, knocking in one in the fourth, but being stranded by his pinch-hitting brother in the eighth. One of those hits missed being a homer by inches.

Once back home at Griffith Stadium the team immediately reversed direction. Starting May 28, they won six of seven games to hustle up to third place with a much-improved 25–18 record by June 3, only three games behind first. Wes Ferrell pitched two strong games, allowing only a total of four runs and chalking up a couple wins to push his victory total to seven for the season. If there is a home field advantage, these Senators were living proof: They had won 16 of 21 games played in Griffith Stadium in 1938.

A headline in the June 2 *Washington Post* most surely caused Rick Ferrell to shake his head in frustration: "Rick Ferrell's Foul in Tribe's Park Cost Him $300." The incident in question went back to a May 15, 1936, game at League Park when Rick hit a foul ball into the stands which struck a female fan. At the time Ferrell played for the Boston Red Sox. The injured woman filed suit against the Cleveland Indians and Ferrell, and a jury ruled in her favor, with damages of $300 assessed to Rick. The two lawyers settled for $250 and court costs, which were $10.04. Who was responsible for paying the damages? Rick Ferrell, Clark Griffith and Tom Yawkey all wrote letters to Baseball Commissioner Judge Kenesaw Landis basically explaining why they were not liable. On November 13, 1938, the Commissioner issued his decision in a letter addressed to the Boston Red Sox American League Club. He opened by exonerating Rick Ferrell: "My conclusion is the player is out of it for the reason that, at the time the thing occurred, he was doing only that which his contract with you required him to do...." After also excusing both Washington and Cleveland of any liability, he directed the Boston club to send a check for "$327.61, with interest on that amount from June 14, 1936 to this date, at the rate of five percent" which finally settled the claim.

When the Indians defeated Washington, 5–4, on June 5, Rick showed some of that Ferrell fire after he was called out at first on a close play. The June 6 *Washington Post* reported, "R. F., enraged when he was called out at first base on a bunt in the eighth inning, returned to the dugout and flung his bat across the first base line. Umpire George Moriarty threatened to banish the catcher from the game, but Manager Bucky Harris softened him with a sweet smile and honeyed words that caused Moriarty to change his mind." The note recorded that Rick's batting average was at .300 while Wes' was .276.

The Detroit Tigers invaded Griffith Stadium on June 10 and assaulted the Senators' pitching for thirty-two runs in a three game sweep. In the third inning on June 12, the Nats scored seven runs off Boots Poffenberger, including brother Rick's exciting inside-the-park two-run homer to the centerfield corner, giving Wes a comfortable 7–1 lead. But in the sixth, the Tigers caught fire, racking up nine runs and sending an angry Wes to the showers, before beating Washington, 18–12. The next day the team left on a road trip until July 3, and Povich wrote, "It was the worst display of Washington pitching in several seasons." In Detroit on June 17, Wes narrowly retaliated, beating Detroit, 12–10. The Nationals acquired an 11–15 record for the month.

A five-game losing streak stretched until July 3, causing the Nationals to fall below .500 for the first time with a 34–35 record. While often strong in early innings, Wes' command didn't last a complete game and he gave up too many hits and runs. As his dominance waned, Povich observed his changing fortunes. After a 12–2 smearing at Yankee Stadium, he wrote, "Wes Ferrell, who started for the Senators, had strictly nothing on his famous 'nuthin' ball.' Before he retired at the end of five innings, he gave up seven runs, three of them on homers."[9] Rick had regained his usual steady performance, batting .312 in 66 games, including three home runs. At the All-Star break, the Senators were 35–37, and held fourth place, nine games out of first.

Crosley Field in Cincinnati, Ohio, played host to the 1938 All-Star Game and three Senators were selected to represent the American League: Rick Ferrell on his sixth All-Star team, Buddy Lewis, and Cecil Travis. Only Lewis, however, saw action in a game the National League won, 4–1.

At home for most of July, the Senators played erratic baseball while Rick continued contributing with timely hits. Chicago punished them, 11–3, on July 15 when Wes quickly got the hook after allowing seven runs in three innings. Then Rick banged out a triple in the fifth frame, racing home from third on George Case's double, to score a run. The next afternoon Rick Ferrell's sixth inning single drove in Buddy Myers from third for the tying run in a tight 3–2 Senators win. On July 17 in the tenth inning, Rick doubled with a runner on for a 4–3 triumph over Detroit. Rookie catcher Tony Giuliani was summoned as back-up for Ferrell, and he got into 38 games, playing occasionally in relief.

The team steamed out of D.C. for a long road trip from July 26 to August 12. Washington finished July with a string of five straight losses to Detroit and Cleveland that dropped them to fifth place. The pitching rotation floundered, with no ready help in the Senators' farm system. Povich wrote in the July 31 *Washington Post*, "At no time has Harris' pitching situation appeared as dismal. Except for Dutch Leonard, who has not yet been given a starting role on the trip, Harris' pitchers have been pitiable failures. Ferrell, Weaver, DeShong, [Chief] Hogsett and [Ken] Chase have been pounded from the box."

The first game of an August 7 Sunday doubleheader against Chicago, in which Rick caught both games, proved disastrous for Washington and Wes Ferrell. In the first game, Chicago's offense that included a lead-off first inning, inside-the-park home run chased Wes out in the second inning; Washington was pummeled, 14–5. They returned to pound the White Sox, 12–5, in the second. This would be the last game Wes would pitch for the Washington Nationals; on August 8, he was given his unconditional release. With a 13–8 record and the third most wins in the American League, Wes had been shopped to every club by Griffith, with no takers, probably due to his high salary (about $14,000). Intimating he was ready to hang it up, Wes said he was returning home to Guilford, North Carolina, for the rest of the season.

Owner Griffith told writer Shirley Povich he was rebuilding his team and that, although Ferrell had won 13 games, he wasn't pitching well. He had completed only nine of 22 games he'd started, an uncharacteristic pattern for a hurler with a record for great endurance. An amazed Ferrell stated: "This is a new one — releasing a pitcher who has won more games than anybody else on the club. But I'm not worried."[10] Within a week's time, Wes Ferrell was back in uniform — as a New York Yankee. Oddly, at this same time in Philadelphia, Wes' dear old friend, pitcher Robert "Lefty" Grove, 38, left a game after two innings, announcing on August 11 that his famous left arm was "as dead as a board." With a 19–2 record so far with Boston, after 14 years in the majors, Grove's fabulous career was also winding down.

Wes and the Yankees called on the Nats next on August 16 when Lefty Gomez slammed the hosts in the first contest, 16–1. For the August 18 game, Wes Ferrell was designated to pitch for New York against Dutch Leonard, and old Wesley nosed out his ex-teammates with his "nuttin'" ball, 6–5, for his fourteenth win. However, Rick and Wes were never again on-field competitors.

"Naturally I'm sorry to leave Rick," said Wes in an interview. "He's the best friend I'll ever have. But you can't go much higher than Dickey when it comes to catching. I'll get along. I know I will."[11] Meanwhile Rick continued on alone in Washington, batting in the .290's and hitting line drives for the Senators.

With a 57–57 record, the Nats returned to Griffith Stadium from August 23 to September 11. On August 24, they won after the Browns scored four runs in the top of the eighth to knot the score at 6–6. But in the bottom half, the St. Louis pitcher walked the leadoff batter, and Rick Ferrell hit a long drive to right field for a triple to drive in the winning run. Ferrell, himself, scored from third base moments later with an insurance run on another safety, for a final score of 8–6. The *Washington Post* sports headline the next day announced: "Rick Ferrell Hits Triple to Win Game."[12] At August's end the Senators occupied fifth place and stood one game below .500.

The winds of fortune changed little for the Washington Senators as they continued to be a .500 club through the final month of the 1938 season, finishing in fifth place with a record of 75 wins and 76 losses. It wasn't a good month for Rick. On September 7 in an 8–5 loss to the A's, he collided with third baseman Buddy Lewis trying to catch a pop fly, allowing the runner on third base to score. He broke a finger during the game on September 9 and not until the 24th, over two weeks later, did Ferrell get back in action. Catching in two of the last five games, Rick doubled for an RBI on the final day of the season, October 2, to help with a 5–2 win.

Rebounding nicely from a painful 1937 season, Rick hit a highly respectable .292 over 135 games. In 411 times at-bat, he connected for 120 hits—among them 24 doubles—and 58 RBIs. He amassed a career-high 75 walks. Defensively, he caught 131 games for an overall fielding percentage of .981, executed a career-high fifteen double plays, and had 512 putouts. In the American League survey of fielding, Rick Ferrell topped all catchers in starting double plays with seven.

The curtain would come down with much decisiveness for his brother Wes, who picked up a couple of wins with the Yankees, giving him 15 for the year. As a team member, he received $2,000 for going to the World Series and more money afterward when they won it over the Chicago Cubs. Yankees team physician Fr. Robert Emmet Walsh had arranged for Wes to have needed elbow surgery to remove bone chips on October 10, and stay in New York for ten days to heal before returning to Guilford. Wes would play for parts of three more seasons, pitching in only eight more games. Richmond (Va.) Colts outfielder George Ferrell enjoyed a .300 season. One added historical note to the 1938 season had occurred on September 9. Seemingly invincible "Iron Man" Lou Gehrig had played first base in his 2100th consecutive game for the New York Yankees.

Spring and the warm sunshine of Orlando, Florida, did not give Washington's management good reason for confidence heading into the 1939 season, as the team played poorly in exhibition. Over the winter, they had sold Zeke Bonura and Al Simmons outright, the only legitimate home run power in the Nationals' lineup. Povich wrote in the May 28 *Post*: "The Red Sox offered Clark Griffith $25,000 for catcher Jake Early last winter and would like to have Rick Ferrell back." *The Sporting News* was extremely candid in stating the Senators "are unprepared for the opening game." *Post* writer Francis Stan summarized on April 13, "for the first time since 1924 the Senators are conceded no chance of finishing in the first division." *The Sporting News* article also reported that Rick Ferrell had come to camp armed with a Spanish dictionary after learning that a number of Nats prospects hailed from Cuba.

Not much had been done to bolster the pitching staff, though management expected "Dutch" Leonard to develop into a fine hurler. The starting rotation for the Senators consisted of "improved" left-handers Joe Krakauskas and Ken Chase, plus right-handers Leonard and rookie Joe Haynes. The bullpen was entirely made up of right-handers: Pete Appleton, Alex Carrasquel, Harry Kelley, and Walt Masterson. The outfield was a mixture of different personnel, Roberto Estalella, George Case, Taffy Wright, Sam West, and Johnny Welaj.

The infield still had Cecil Travis and Buddy Lewis at short and third base, with Jimmy Bloodworth at second.

In a 2003 interview, former first baseman Mickey Vernon recalled his rookie season with the Nats in 1939.

MICKEY VERNON: I remember Rick as one of the finest gentlemen I ever met really, or was ever associated with. He was a catcher who worked his way up to the front office. I was on the club in 1943 with all those knuckleball pitchers. He was always friendly to me.

I was a rookie with Washington in 1939 when he was a veteran, and I can recall some of the incidents in spring training when we would go on these bus trips to a Florida town to play an exhibition game. I would always try to get next to Rick on the bus and pick his mind. Anything he said, I was going to gulp it up. He was very good with me and the other young fellows on the club. I always found him to be a real gentleman and of the highest grade, very high caliber. I remember your dad telling me one time, "You know, there are two kinds of fellows they talk about in baseball. One kind is the guy who doesn't stick to his business and lives it up a little on the road and carouses. And the other guy is the guy who saves his money!" There was a lot of lobby-sitting back then. We took trains in the '40s, played cards and read to take up the time. Rick was quiet and serious, very serious when he played.

During my time, Rick and Jim Hegan (Cleveland) were the best catchers; Mickey Cochrane I saw as a kid. Bill Dickey, Mickey Cochrane, and your dad were all named to the first All-Star team in '33. I was in 10th grade. There's a difference in the catching style of today compared with that time. The catcher's mitt was different and a lot of catchers were getting broken fingers due to foul tips.

I played with one of your dad's brothers, George, the outfielder, in the minors in Greenville, South Carolina, in 1938. He was playing for the Greenville Spinners, from the mills. Times were tough then. I barnstormed up in Michigan one year with George in the '40s, before TV. The guy who was running the team, like George was, would negotiate with each guy that he asked to go on the trip. The pay varied anywhere from $75 to $200 a game. You had to wait until ten days after the season was over, and then you could barnstorm for 10 days. Then that died down when television came in.

Opening on the road in Philadelphia on April 20, the Nats suffered a 1–0 loss to begin the 1939 season in fourth place. In their home opener on Friday, April 21, Washington lost to New York, 6–3, as young Joe Krakauskas was overmatched by Yankees ace, Lefty Gomez. They recorded their first season victory the next afternoon by downing New York, 3–1, behind solid pitching from Leonard. A third-inning rally produced all of the home team's runs, and Rick Ferrell had a key single and scored during that frame.

From April 29 to May 11, the Senators went on the road, pulling into the Big Apple for games on April 29 and 30. Unbeknownst to Rick Ferrell and the rest of the baseball world, April 30, 1939, would be an historical date in the game's history: the end of Lou Gehrig's remarkable string of 2,130 consecutive games played and his final game in major league baseball. Stricken with a mystery disease that sapped his muscle strength in dramatic ways, Gehrig's illustrious iron-man career appeared to be ending. As Washington was playing the Yankees in New York, Rick vividly remembered as he watched Gehrig from close range. He later related to Wilt Browning in the July 4, 1989, *Greensboro Daily News and Record* that, prior to the game during batting practice, Rick and Lou met near the runway that led to the clubhouse. Lou leaned against the wall where Rick stood. "How ya' doin' Lou?" Rick asked. "Not so good, Rick. I don't think I'm going to be able to go today," answered the "Iron Man."

In another interview with the *Post*, Rick recalled, "The first time he came to bat that day, Lou would swing and miss balls by six inches. And he'd take pitches right down the middle of the plate. Lou never did that before. And I sat back there catching and watching him, and I said to myself, 'There's something bad wrong with Lou.'" Gehrig went hitless in four times at-bat and had a .143 batting average for the season. The Nationals beat the Yankees, 3–2, that game.

When the Yankees traveled to Detroit's Briggs Stadium for their next series, Lou pulled himself out of the lineup before the game started on May 2 due to

Washington Nationals catcher Rick Ferrell is about to drop his left leg to block the plate while looking the baseball into the mitt. His bare hand holds the ball to the leather while Rick ignores Yankee runner George Sternweiss leaping into him with a force intended to send the receiver sprawling and free the ball from him. Sternweiss was out at home. (National Baseball Hall of Fame Library, Cooperstown, N.Y.)

illness, thus ending his 2,130 consecutive-game streak. Having played the final game of his illustrious 17-year baseball career back in New York, he had racked up a .340 batting average over 2,164 total games, with 493 home runs and 1,990 RBIs. Rick Ferrell was catching the last time Lou Gehrig came to bat.

On April 27, Shirley Povich devoted his "This Morning" *Washington Post* column to engage both memory and Rick Ferrell in the discussion of dusting hitters off with the infamous bean balls. "But it's really not a bean ball I call for," assured Rick. "What I ask for is a high one, inside. We're just trying to move the batter back a bit." He explained the advantage that wild pitchers have over those with great control. "It's easy for wild pitchers to get away with it," noted Ferrell. "The umpires get suspicious when a fellow with control aims at a hitter's chin. I've had wild young pitchers, and I've told 'em that as long as they're going to be wild, they ought to be wild, inside, instead of outside. It does 'em more good. But a good pitcher like Lefty Grove scares a fellow away from there by throwing at his feet. It's no fun to get hit by Lefty's fast ball."

Rick Ferrell had a big day on May 2 against the Browns when he keyed a three-run rally in the fourth to put his team ahead with a double that drove in two runs. Then in the ninth after the Browns had closed the gap to a one-run margin, Ferrell, again, belted a hit, driving in his third RBI of the afternoon for a 9–7 Senators victory—the fourth of five straight. On May 18, the *Post* reported that Rick Ferrell was batting .273 after playing in fifteen games. Finishing off May with another six-game losing streak left the Nats in sixth place, with a 14–22 record, fifteen games out of first.

One of the team's ten wins for the month came on the 25th when they topped St. Louis, 4–1, with Ferrell deeply involved in much of the scoring. When the Browns tied the score at 1–1 in the third, it had been a throwing error by Rick that set up St. Louis' only run. However, later his two singles drove in two runs, and he scored the Nationals' last run in the seventh inning.

In the May 26 *Post*'s "News of the Capital Nightclubs," Mary Harris wrote that the roving camera at the Rainbow Room spotted "Rick Ferrell, catcher for the Senators, arrayed dazzlingly in a tan gabardine coat and light blue trousers." Rick liked dressing well.

June opened, but the ugliness persisted. The Senators continued on the road from June 1 to 11, winning only four times in 15 games. In St. Louis on June 6, they staged a big rally, scoring six runs in the ninth to capture what was becoming a rare win, 10–7. Rick stood among the heroes, coming to bat in the final frame with the bases loaded, two out, and his team trailing, 7–6. The pitch count went to 3–2 and on the next offering, he slammed a clutch double off the right-field wall, knocking in all of the baserunners.

Though they played a little better starting off their three-week homestand that began on June 14, Senators fans were not happy with their team. One irate female fan told the June 16 *Washington Post*: "Washington has had such good teams that I don't see how Mr. Griffith can keep trying to put over this bush league team on us. Why this is the Nation's Capital and everything here ought to be the best! I was so disgusted with that road trip that I sat down and wrote letters to sports editors. But I haven't sent them yet."

While the team was losing with regularity, Rick Ferrell, individually, continued to put up strong numbers. As of June 7, his batting average grew to .308. Three days later the press revealed that a proposed trade of Rick Ferrell and Cecil Travis to the Tigers in return for Rudy York and Roy Cullenbine had been turned down by Detroit.

July felt better after the Senators took four games in a row, with Buddy Lewis hitting the game-winning home run in the ninth inning for a 4–3 Washington victory. Povich wrote for the July 3 *Post*, "Rick Ferrell was the fielding hero. With the bases full of Mackmen in the eighth inning and the A's leading, 3–2, Ferrell grabbed Ambler's tap in front of the plate for a force-out and then doubled Ambler with a throw to rookie Bob Prichard [at first base]." Ferrell's fine defensive play saved the game.

The final win in the streak came in New York on an unforgettable, historic day before 61,808 fans who'd gathered to honor Lou Gehrig at Yankee Stadium. Now diagnosed with amyotrophic lateral sclerosis, the great slugger and star first baseman had been forced to quit baseball. The Fourth of July 1939 was Lou Gehrig Day with a pre-game ceremony at home plate to celebrate the man and his brilliant career. The Yankee players all lined up on the third-base side. When the visiting Senators lined up along the first-base line, Rick Ferrell by chance, stood at the head of the row fifteen feet from home plate where Gehrig would stand at the microphone. Numerous dignitaries paid tribute, and finally, it was time for the "Iron Horse" to speak. In the July 4, 1989, interview with Wilt Browning for the *Greensboro News and Record*, Rick recalled, "I stood there and watched him. Gehrig walked over to the mike and was trembling all over. I didn't know if he was trembling because of his sickness or because of the emotion of the day. I didn't think he was going to say anything, and he stood there for a long time. Then Babe Ruth walked over and put his arm around Lou's shoulder to brace him. Lou gathered his strength and started talking 'I consider myself to be the luckiest man on the face of the earth.' What a great speech. The players were stunned."

Browning further described, "The next day the Senators came out through the Yankees dugout — they both had clubhouses on the same side. Lou was sitting in the runway smoking a cigarette. Ferrell stopped to talk to the pale Gehrig. He said, 'Lou that was one of the greatest speeches I ever heard yesterday.' Gehrig had a high-pitched voice and replied, 'You think so Rick?' Ferrell said, 'Yeah, it was a hell-of-a-speech.' Rick remembered that Lou tried to light a cigarette, but was trembling so bad from the disease, he had trouble doing it. "I helped him light his cigarette before going out on the field.... Funny thing is I can't recall what Lou did in his last at-bat. Nobody can."

Lost in the overwhelming emotion of the "Lou Gehrig Day" pre-game were the two baseball games played that day. The first one went to the Senators, as Leonard throttled the Yankees, 3–2, for his third 1939 victory over New York. The Nats jumped out to a 2–0 lead in the first, adding the winning run in the fourth when Rick Ferrell tripled and rode home on Leonard's base hit. In the nightcap the Yankees had it all their way, swamping the visitors, 11–1.

During the early part of the month on July 6, the Nationals played a night game — their very first — in Philadelphia. The *Post* reported that at Shibe Park, there were "780 floodlights from eight 150-foot towers for 1,354,000 watts." Unaccustomed to the bright electrical glare, Manager Bucky Harris disliked night baseball as did several of the players, as Washington lost, 9–3. However, Rick doubled in Buddy Myer to score a run. Two days later on July 8, the team introduced highly prized first-base prospect Mickey Vernon and promptly won three straights.

Washington hammered Detroit, 10–2, at Briggs Stadium on Tuesday, July 18, but Rick Ferrell snared a foul tip off the bat of catcher Birdie Tebbetts, ripping a fingernail that forced him out of the game. Expected to be out for a least a week, management summoned minor-league catcher Jake Early to substitute, who coincidentally was on his way to Chattanooga to fill in for two other catchers disabled by injuries, and help Giulani.

The Nationals finished the rest of July's games in sixth place, with a 39–57 record, 29 games out of first. Sports editor Povich sought out owner Clark Griffith for comment, who stated, "I kept saying last winter that this 1939 team of mine would get worse before it got better. A young team always does. I knew we'd look bad for long stretches, that our young team would make a lot of mistakes that would lose ball games. And that is what has been happening. But it will be a better ball club because of those mistakes. This is the second year of my accent-on-youth policy. The next season, the fellows who have been making the mistakes this year will be the men who will take us up near the top."[13]

The Senators turned on the juice on August 1 and racked up eight straight wins by August 8. During that stretch ace right-hander Leonard notched two more victories, giving him twelve for the season. On August 3, Rick Ferrell was back behind the plate after a two-week absence, calling pitcher Joe Krakauskas in the Nationals' 9–5 victory over the Browns at Griffith Stadium. Ferrell chipped in with a single and scored a run. In their ten-inning, 6–5, win on August 4, the catcher hit a long fly ball and a single to drive home two of the Senators' six runs. Increasingly Rick was sharing catching duties with Giulani. After Washington defeated the Yankees, 8–4, on August 8 for their eighth straight win, New York halted the Nats' winning streak by taking the last two games of the series.

That game and the disastrous recent skid prompted Shirley Povich to write an extensive "editorial" in the August 28 *Washington Post* detailing the reasons for Washington's woes. There were very few players who escaped the pen of indictment. Povich began by proclaiming: "a naked truth all too apparent to

Manager Bucky Harris is: his team can't hit." He went on to charge that "the Nats are a punchless crew of slap hitters who require too many blows to produce a run." He expanded his case by writing about the catchers as a crew. "The most Harris can expect from his catchers in a hitting-way is a slap single now and then."

On September 1 came the shocking international news from England's Winston Churchill that Hitler had invaded Poland and England was at war with Germany. As the precipitating event leading to World War II, baseball and the world would begin to suffer the deleterious impact of this singular act which would reverberate for several years.

In early September, 23 minor leaguers were called up to join The Show, including catcher Al Evans and pitcher Early Wynn. Rick Ferrell alternated catching duties with Tony Giulani and had a quiet month at the plate as his team just played out a lost campaign. Dutch Leonard recorded his 20th win of the season, giving the franchise something to cheer about. He had had a remarkable season for a team lacking in run production and able to win just 65 games. Although not awarded, he was, hands-down, the most valuable player on the team.

After beginning the 1930s with several strong showings, including a pennant in 1933, the Senators had just finished their worst season of the decade in 1939, buried in sixth place with a 65–88 won/loss record, 42 games behind the winner. Aside from George Case's 51 stolen bases, a team record, no Washington hitter ranked among the offensive leaders. The team did, however, register a league best 167 double plays.

Rick Ferrell compiled a .281 batting average playing in only 87 games, his lowest game total since his 1929 rookie season with St. Louis. In 274 at-bats, he connected for 77 hits, including 13 doubles, and got 41 walks. He struck out 12 times. Catching 83 games, Rick earned a .976 defensive fielding average with 327 putouts, nine errors, and he initiated nine double plays.

He met Wesley and his family back at the Ferrell farm, his centering point, for the off-season.

Other than one off-season trade, the Nationals stood pat during the off-season. In 1940, installing lights and joining the swing to night-time baseball represented the biggest change for the Nationals. United Press staff correspondent George Kirksey announced: "Baseball begins its second century next Tuesday with the 16 major league clubs confidently looking forward to the greatest season in history."

Displeased with his 1940 contract offer, Rick Ferrell became a holdout, joining Cecil Travis, newcomer Gee Walker, Dutch Leonard, and shortstop Jimmy Pofahl. After six weeks, owner Griffith publicly aired his frustration with Ferrell, telling Povich for the February 15 *Post*: "I don't see what he did to earn his dollars last year." Surely adding fuel to the standoff was the owner's earlier statement indicating Ferrell was destined to be the back-up receiver. "I think [Jake] Early will be our regular catcher," reported Griffith. Ferrell finally signed for $8,500 on February 19, joining the team during spring training at Orlando, Florida.

On Saint Patrick's Day, March 17, 1940, an all-star game was played in Tampa, Florida, to aid President Herbert Hoover's favorite charity, the Finnish Relief Fund. Rick Ferrell was selected to play, along with Joe DiMaggio, Ted Williams, Bob Feller, Bill Dickey, and other stars. The game attracted 13,320 fans and raked in $20,000. However Griffith and Harris didn't see 34-year-old Ferrell as an All-Star catcher for the Washington Senators, with youngsters Jake Early and Al Evans getting lots of attention. Speculation grew that the veteran receiver was about to be displaced.

The Senators' 1940 pitching rotation remained basically the same with starters Leonard, Chase, Masterson and 25-year-old rookie Sid Hudson. Relievers Carrasquel, Krakauskas, Haynes, and Rene Monteagudo held down the bullpen.

On April 16, Rick got the starting assignment catching Dutch Leonard in the opener. The Nats lost to the Red Sox and 40-year-old Lefty Grove, 1–0, as the winning run was scored by Bobby Doerr on a Ferrell miscue at the plate. In response, Manager Harris announced a new arrangement of catching responsibilities: Early would catch when the opposition used a right-handed pitcher, and Ferrell would play when a southpaw took the mound. Harris emphasized, "We need power. That is apparent. Early may give us the long hits we need. In any event, he is going to get his chance." During game two, Rick Ferrell rode the pine.

After Opening Day, Nats hitters slumped, producing only five runs in four consecutive losses, the first two by shutouts. Rookie Sid Hudson, who would become a mainstay for the Senators, made his debut in the second game of the season. The Red Sox baptized him with a seven-run outburst for a 7–0 shutout.

But then fortunes turned, and the Capital City boys got it going, reeling off five victories in a row from April 24 to 28. The fans were still very appreciative of catcher Ferrell's skill behind the plate. In his column on April 28, Povich noted that they were petitioning Harris to bring back Ferrell. "The fans were shouting for Rick Ferrell, hero of the previous day's game, when Jake Early made two off-line throws in the second."

Rick Ferrell was an outstanding receiver, gifted with a great ability to cut down baserunners, yet a catcher's contributions don't often generate much ink. Yet Shirley Povich wrote about Rick in his May 23 column: "There have been occasions during the past three weeks when Rick Ferrell, throwing the ball back to the pitcher, had more on it than it had when it came to him — and more accurately too. Ferrell, incidentally, has thrown out the last five men who attempted to steal a base on him, despite the fact that careless Washington pitchers allowed them to get big leads. It required superb throwing by Ferrell and that is what he has been giving the club." Within a few days, Povich recognized the challenge of trying to corral a knuckleball. "Rick Ferrell, who has played an entire season without being charged with a passed ball, now leads the League's catchers in that aspect as a result of working with Dutch Leonard and his knuckle ball." After playing in thirty-four games, Rick was batting .257 on June 9.

June brought more tough sledding for the Washington Senators. Their June 14 road trip brought 11 losses in 12 games that dumped them into the cellar on June 20. In his June 22 *Post* column, Shirley Povich surveyed the Senator's regulars, pointing out areas of deficiency, particularly holes in the infield. "Harris has only one very flimsy excuse for butchering his infield the way he is doing and it follows: He has no first baseman, no second baseman and no third baseman. The only big league infielder on the team is Travis."

In addition to a very weak infield and only one reliable starting pitcher, the hitters were in a woeful slump. During the seven-game losing streak, the lineup Harris put on the field scored no more that one run in six of the defeats. Only a brilliant pitching performance by rookie Sid Hudson broke the losing streak. On June 21, Hudson threw a no-hitter through eight innings against the Browns at Sportsman's Park before a ninth-inning lead-off double ruined his dream game. He promptly retired the next three hitters to preserve a one-hit, 1–0, shutout. Jake Early caught this gem and explained why Hudson relied on his fast ball. "When he walked three batters at the start, I knew his curve wasn't working and made him give me his fast ball." Though he watched the game from the bench, veteran catcher Rick Ferrell took his absence from action in stride, telling the June 22 *Post* that it was "the best-pitched game I've ever seen."

In a 2003 telephone interview, Sid Hudson recalled Rick during the 1940 season: "Rick was a real nice fellow, a gentleman all the way, and he was a good catcher, a good receiver, and knew how to call a game. He developed a way of catching foul balls so that when he took his mask off, his cap would never come off because his bald head would show! Of course, nobody ever saw that bald head because his cap was still on when he caught the ball. He taught me what to pitch in different situations and I picked up most of my pitching know-how from him. Another former catcher, Benny Bengough, and Rick were like our pitching coaches in 1940."

Ferrell's superior ability as a receiver was certainly implied when Shirley Povich wrote a critical statement on July 1 about the catcher selections for the 1940 All-Star Game. "The managers who picked the American League's All-Star team muffed one when they named Dutch Leonard as one of the pitchers.... They forgot to name a catcher who could handle Leonard's knuckleball." On June 29, following a game-winning effort from Dutch Leonard, Shirley Povich wrote in the *Washington Post* about the beating Ferrell took trying to snag Leonard's unpredictable knuckleballs. "Rick Ferrell was dropping at least half of the knuckleball pitches thrown by Leonard today. He took several nasty bumps on the arms and hands from the butterfly ball." Obviously Ferrell could not anticipate what was in store for him later in his career, when being a knuckleball catcher would define his legacy.

Years later in a June 26, 1959, *Collier's* magazine interview, Ferrell described the unenviable task of trying to catch one of those baffling pitches. "How do you expect anybody to hit [it] when I can't even catch it," asked Ferrell. "It comes over the plate alright and its looks soft. But about the time I try to put a mitt on it, the damn thing jumps and socks me in the leg. The guy is about to beat me to death with this dipsy-doodler."

While no team dominated the 1940 pennant race, at the end of June the Senators were resting in seventh, just percentages points ahead of the last place Philadelphia A's, trailing the league-leading Indians by 15½ games.

On July 11 following the All-Star Game break, Washington got back into action with Sid Hudson on the hill against Detroit's Hal Newhouser. Hudson not only notched his fifth straight win, but knocked the Tigers out of the lead and lifted his club out of the basement. In the 7–3 win, Ferrell delivered a run-scoring single, a double, and later, scored. The Nats' Ken Chase won a thrilling victory on July 14, rallying for two runs with two out in the bottom of the ninth, to send the game into extra innings. Rick Ferrell drove in the first run with a single. Then in the eleventh inning, the dramatics were repeated. Buddy Lewis came to the plate with the bases loaded (Ferrell had received an intentional pass) and two out, and drove the ball into the left-field corner, knocking home the winning tally for a 6–5 victory. Ferrell compounded the big day with three hits and three RBIs.

The next day, July 15, emerging ace hurler Hudson picked up another win against the hard-charging Indians in an 8–6 affair, unseating Cleveland from the top of the league standings. Part of the July 16 *Post* sports headline carried the acclaim: "Rick Ferrell Is Star of Triumph." In a bases-loaded, third inning rally, Ferrell came to bat and lined one against the left-center-field fence for a double that scored all three runners. The Nats swept the Indians and took two from Chicago for a five-game winning streak by July 18.

Rick Ferrell's hot bat did not escape the notice of Shirley Povich. After his key hits in back-to-back games on July 14 and 15, the sports editor wrote: "Rick Ferrell, hitting in his old-time style, has suddenly blossomed into the most dangerous clutch hitter on the club." In the next day's *Washington Post*, the catcher received additional praise for his defensive skills. "Rick Ferrell is throwing to bases better than he ever threw in his life, he modestly admits. He has permitted fewer stolen bases than any regular catcher in the league."

After chalking up his sixth straight victory, Sid Hudson was also attracting attention. A pitching-starved team had summoned the 25-year-old from a Class D league and put him in the starting rotation. On July 18, Povich wrote that he was particularly impressed with the young man's poise. Sid's working with a skilled veteran catcher must have been a contributing factor when most rookie pitchers are awed by being in "The Show."

Regardless, Povich sought Ferrell's comments on Hudson. "That kid has just begun to find himself," asserted his batterymate. "He was a good pitcher the first day we ever looked at him. He could field his position and he could hit and was a big help to himself. But he found out that the same stuff that could have kept [got] him by in the Florida League would be murdered up here." Ferrell continued his insider's assessment of the developing pitching savvy and temperament of Hudson. "He had one delivery — a swell overhand fast ball. No curve, no change of pace, nothing else.... Just that fast ball that he threw from close to his neck, and they'd lay back and wait for it. Watch him now. He's a different pitcher. Notice that sidearm thing he throws. It's a beaut. Now he's got the batter guessing. They're not digging in up at the plate when they could when he was a one-pitch pitcher. Hudson's got the edge now, not the hitter. That's why he's winning. He's a pleasure to work with. No beefing, no squawking. Never says anything, in fact. But he's no dead fish out there. He can get mad. When he walked [Hal] Trosky the other day, he didn't speak a word out loud, but for anybody who can read lips, it was wonderful entertainment." Lefthander Ken Chase was the other workhorse in Manager Harris' starting rotation, and he racked up 15 wins on the season.

A Sunday doubleheader was a standard feature of baseball in the 1940s, and two-for-the-price-of-one was a fan favorite for many years. After losing the first two games in a series against the White Sox, Washington got even on Sunday, August 4, handing their hosts a double-defeat from Leonard and Chase, 4–3 and 1–0. At Griffith Stadium, Sid Hudson again flirted with his second no-hitter, pitching six innings of no-hit baseball before giving up a single to Sam Chapman, the Indians' only hit, in an 11–0 whitewash. "It was a fastball in the seventh inning," Hudson grinned. "Maybe I should've thrown him a curve."[14] Ferrell caught this masterpiece with Hudson and also bashed two hits. A couple of days later, however, Senators pitcher Monteagudo had a 4–3 lead in the ninth inning when Ferrell uncorked an errant throw down the third base line, allowing two A's runs to score. Philadelphia ultimately prevailed in a 6–4 victory over the Nats.

Baseball can be a forgiving game because of the frequency of games and the opportunities for redemption. The next day following his throwing error, #8 made the August 10 sports headline for the *Washington Post* game summary — "Ferrell Gets Winning Hit." With two strikes in the ninth of a 5–5 tie, Ferrell clobbered a clutch-single to left field to drive home the game-winning run and lift his team to a 6–5 victory as the hero.

Washington suffered through several multiple-game losing streaks closing out the month of August with an accumulative record of 52–71, still in sixth place and going nowhere in the pennant race.

First-year hurler Sid Hudson led the Senators' 1940 pitching staff with his

17 wins, followed by Chase, 15, and Leonard's 14. Dutch, the established ace, had an unusual year with a league-leading 19 defeats (3.49 ERA), career-high strikeouts and walks, and a league-high 328 hits permitted. His career in these years was inexorably linked to that of Rick Ferrell, who had 17 passed balls, the most in the league. Despite the challenge of catching Leonard's fluttering and erratic offerings, Ferrell somehow compiled a .980 fielding percentage when all fielders in the American League garnered a fielding average of .970.

The final results of the 1940 season looked much like 1939's, only slightly worse with the Senators finishing next to last. Once again, the Nats' attack had remained soft, with the exception of their speed. Three players ranked among the top five in stolen bases with George Case being the best thief in the league.

Rick Ferrell continued to ward off young guys eager to assume his job by playing in 103 games while sporting a .273 batting average. His offensive numbers shrunk, as he drove in only 28 runs and, for the second consecutive season, had less than 100 hits. Yet Ferrell had only struck out 15 times and walked 47 times. His fielding was strong with 427 putouts and 10 errors.

In his November 3 *Washington Post* column, Povich wrote, "Sid Hudson, Cecil Travis, Buddy Lewis, Rick Ferrell and dozens of other major league ball players from the South will not be affected by the military draft during the 1941 season because voluntary enlistments in most Southern states will exceed draft quotas." Rick used to comment that he was too young for the First World War, and too old for the Second. Before the calendar turned over a new leaf, rumors circulated that ownership was looking for a new main man behind the plate.

As New Year 1941 began, Rick, now 36, experienced a rite of passage in his personal life by marrying his girlfriend of three years, Ruth Virginia Wilson, on January 18, three weeks after she turned 21 years old on Christmas Day. They had met in 1937 when she worked as a secretary in the General Accounting Office of the U.S. Government. With bride and groom both dressed in dark business suits, the Reverend Lewis Havermale married them in a brief ceremony at Arlington Methodist Church, attended by only one other couple as witnesses. After a brief trip to Florida, they set up house together in a Georgetown apartment in Washington, D.C. Now both Ferrell brothers had opted out of bachelordom, for 32-year-old Wes just had married a former Miss Sarasota named Lois Johnson, 23, four months earlier on September 2, 1940.

One knew what to expect from Rick Ferrell, a team player who usually found a way to contribute. Likewise he was considered easy to get along with, except at contract time when he would hold out if he felt financially slighted. Early in 1941, Rick stalled at signing, insisting that his salary remain intact, but finally inked his new Washington Senators contract for an estimated $8,500 on February 18, just as spring training began.

However, trade winds continued to swirl around the 35-year-old Rick. *The Sporting News* reported that the St. Louis Browns were highly interested in re-acquiring his services. "We'd like to have him," stated Browns business manager Bill DeWitt. "But we're not going to go crazy to get him. Griff has our best offer, and it is a good one.... The trouble is that Griff wants too much.... We're not going overboard to get Ferrell, who, at best, has a year or two more left in him." Six years more was closer to the mark.

On the way to spring training in 1941, a young Tigers pitcher named Virgil Trucks met Rick en route. Trucks described his experience in a 2007 telephone interview.

VIRGIL TRUCKS: In 1941, I knew nothing about your dad, except for reading the papers. We had no TV or radio. There wasn't a lot written about the American or National League at that time. So I read up on Detroit, and guys like Mickey Cochrane, the catcher, and Charlie Gehringer, second baseman. Then I got to know more about your dad when I played against him the next year with the St. Louis Browns.

Rick was the first major league ballplayer that I met. In fact, I'd never seen any major league play-ers, just had pictures of them. We were going to spring training — he was with Washington then, I was with Detroit — and I had to change trains in Jacksonville to go to Lakeland. And of course, he got off at Orlando, where they were training. I was sitting in the rear car of the train and he was sitting there too. He had a bat with him, so I knew he was a ballplayer. I didn't know what caliber — whether he was a minor leaguer or what — but we got to talking. We were the only two people in that car and between Jacksonville and Orlando, I got to know a lot about Rick Ferrell. That was my first year in spring training, 1941, and then we parted com-pany. He got off in Orlando and I got off in Lakeland, which is about thirty miles down the road. We had a nice chat — talking baseball.

Rick was a good hitter, and he wasn't the type of hitter who would try to pull an outside pitch for a home run. He went with the pitch and hit it to the opposite field. Today, you don't see that very much, especially when you get two strikes on a hitter. They still try to pull the outside pitch for a homerun and all they do is hit a ground ball.

Guys today don't really appreciate what they have. They have it *great* with the salaries they make. Salaries we'd have never thought about making! We had a con-tract same as they do, but I don't think their contracts read the same as ours. We

On January 18, 1941, Rick Ferrell married the former Ruth Virginia Wilson, a secre-tary in the General Accounting Office for the United States Government in Arlington, Virginia. Shortly after setting up their new apartment in Washington, Rick was traded to the St. Louis Browns. (National Baseball Hall of Fame Library, Cooperstown, N.Y.)

couldn't do anything during the baseball season — and they watched you that you didn't do anything in the off season — that would be a detriment to the baseball team or to yourself. When we played, you'd sign a contract every year. I didn't care about doing anything except making that ballclub and working hard.

We used to go everywhere as a group by train. You had your own Pullman car and your own berth that you'd sleep in. The team was together all the time. The train pulls in, you go to the ballpark, so you didn't have time to do anything but associate with one another.

Throughout spring training before the 1941 season began, Rick Ferrell had become the senior spokesman for the team. In an Associated Press story for the *Washington Post* on March 6, Ferrell said that Washington was primed to compete for a place in the first division due to a reliable emerging pitching staff. "We have three pitchers— Ken Chase, Dutch Leonard and Sid Hudson — who are potential 20-game winners," said Ferrell. "I'm not predicting they will win twenty apiece, but I say they might and if they should, well, look out for us." Speaking of second-year pitcher Hudson, he said: "He's got poise and control, a good change of pace, and a tricky curve. Furthermore he learns fast. You tell him a batter's weakness once, and he remembers it. He ought to have a big year this season."

As he had done on other occasions, Povich used a letter received from a fan extolling Ferrell's unique ability to catch the knuckleball as the platform to comment on that tough assignment. "No doubt is there that the only catcher on the Washington club who can do a decent job with Leonard's knuckleball is Ferrell. The others are no stars at handling even fastball and curve-ball pitching."

Povich elicited from Rick his detailed analysis and strong advice: "We're kidding ourselves if we think we can come up with another Hudson this year, next year or in the next five years. That kind comes under the heading of miracles." Of Masterson, he stated, "We ought to pray that Masterson will make good for us, because if he develops, he'll be a good one. And he has shown us he has enough stuff to be a winner if he can control it. He should have learned that slow, roundhouse curve he was throwing last year is no good in this league and junk it." Then Ferrell praised Walt's fastball. "That's bunk about Ken Chase having the fastest ball on our club. Masterson's is it. It's harder and it's more alive. His fast one does more tricks coming in there than any man's I've ever caught."

For Ferrell, Sid Hudson was an ideal pupil, receptive to advice, and one who worked to master a change in delivery. "When we saw he couldn't win with what he was throwing, we asked him to try to come up with a side arm pitch.... When he did come up with his side-arm ball, it was a beaut. You don't mind working with young pitchers in a training camp when they give you a little bit to work on," claimed the catcher. "But most of 'em don't even know how to stand on the rubber, and have no idea where their pitch is going."

As a footnote to this in-depth analysis, Povich checked back with Ferrell near the end of spring camp. Apparently unimpressed by the rookie pitchers he'd seen, Ferrell said: "We'd better stop fooling with this bunch and hope that we can make a pitcher out of Walter Masterson."[15]

Spring optimism in 1941 quickly disappeared as the Washington Senators could not put it together in April. In the second contest of the young season, Rick Ferrell had a strong three-hit performance, which included rattling a couple of doubles off the fences in a 7–6 loss to Boston. The Senators ended the month with a dismal 4–10 record to occupy seventh place.

When Sid Hudson held the Browns in check for a 7–4 victory on May 2, news headlines called Rick Ferrell the game's hero. His clutch single in the twelfth inning drove home the winning run and he knocked in four of his team's runs.

And after being skunked 7–0 by the Browns at Griffith Stadium on May 15, the long-rumored trade was announced: Washington was sending Rick Ferrell back to St. Louis for pitcher Vern Kennedy, in return. Though Ferrell had recently been sidelined due to another torn fingernail inflicted by one of Dutch Leonard's ornery knuckleballs, he was hitting .281, ranked among team leaders in RBIs with 13. The Browns expressed exuberance in landing a veteran catcher that they knew. "We needed catching in the worst way, and Ferrell will fill the gap," reported an ecstatic Manager Fred Haney. "He should do us a lot of good."

Rick seemed to take the trade in stride. "I think I can help them a lot," stated "Ferrell. "I haven't made much of a study of the Browns' pitchers this year, but of what I've seen, they have enough pitching to get out of the cellar in a hurry." The article recognized that Ferrell was a fan favorite and that Dutch Leonard was the biggest loser in the trade.

In the May 16 *Post* Shirley Povich opined, "In the Ferrell-for-Kennedy deal, it's been a long time since a ball club traded its number one catcher for a pitcher who's been losing an average of 18 games a year for three seasons. The Red Sox have suffered ever since they traded Ferrell away to the Nats in 1937. All of Tom Yawkey's money couldn't buy an acceptable catcher. They are scarce. The Browns' own catching has been a headache ever since they sold Ferrell to Boston eight years ago. Ferrell's departure doesn't leave the Nats with an exactly fancy catching staff. Ferrell was behind the bat for the Nats against all kinds of pitching [and was an asset] until he caught a knuckleball on the thumb. Now, Washington has a catching problem."

The newly-wed Rick and Ruth, who was already pregnant with their first child, packed up their recently-decorated Georgetown apartment after only four months and headed west to start again for Rick's second tour of duty back in St. Louis. This sudden upheaval was one of Ruth's first introductions to the trials and demands of being a "baseball wife."

6

❖ ❖ ❖

1941–1943

Back to St. Louis as World War II Heats Up

Rick Ferrell never burned his bridges behind him, remaining on good terms with front office, teammates, fans, and press wherever he went. When Ferrell arrived in New York in 1941 to join the St. Louis Browns for his second term of service, he had strained his back, joining a growing list of infirm Brownies. First baseman George McQuinn had a pulled groin; Joe Grace, an outfielder, suffered with boils; the regular shortstop Johnny Beradino was out of the lineup with a bad knee; and third baseman Harland Clift, one of their better players, had a stiff neck. All of that led to a makeshift lineup, including the need to play a guy at shortstop who had never played that position. No wonder it was reported that Manager Fred Haney had a headache.

On May 18, the catcher was immediately brought in to pinch-hit in a game lost by a wide 12–2 margin. At the time, his new club occupied the cellar, 11 games out, with a record of 9–18. Surely the long casualty list contributed to the team's mediocre run.

The Browns used a five-man rotation featuring Elden Auker, Denny Galehouse, Bob Harris, Bob Muncrief, and Johnny Niggeling. For the most part, St. Louis had recently overhauled its starting rotation. Auker, Galehouse and Niggeling had completed their first full season with the club in 1940. Only Muncrief was a home-grown product. In the previous season, Auker had led the staff with 16 victories. Muncrief, at 13–9, was the only other winning pitcher on the staff. Harris won eleven, Galehouse, seven, and Niggeling also chalked up seven victories. All right-handers, the entire pitching staff had a combined 5.12 ERA in 1940, second highest in the circuit.

Many years later, Galehouse reminisced about Ferrell to Peter Golenbock in his book, *The Spirit of St. Louis.* The pitcher recalled the time when Ferrell became the main catcher for the Browns, recognizing what he meant to the pitching staff. "Rick Ferrell became our catcher in '41. He was a good, smart catcher, not mechanical in his pitch-calling. He wouldn't always call for a fastball when you got behind. He was a good guy, good to pitch to. It helps your confidence to know a guy will catch a ball in a tough situation when you don't want a passed ball, or [not let the ball get away] enough for a guy to go from first to second. If you can get a guy who can block the ball good, it helps your confidence."[1]

The Browns had their longest losing streaks early in the season, dropping six in a row in both April and May. Although the Browns lost 8–6 on May 21 when Boston rallied to score five runs, Rick Ferrell, wearing uniform number "11," had an opportunity to shine for his new club. In the fifth inning, the battery of Ferrell and pitcher Johnny Allen jumped on consecutive pitches and parked them in the seats for back-to-back home runs. Rick also had a single, giving him a two-RBI day. His new team won only four games out of the next fifteen to finish May.

The baseball world wept when the tragic news came on June 2, 1941, that an emaciated Lou Gehrig had died in Riverdale, New York, from ALS disease, almost two years after his retirement from baseball. The "Iron Horse" would have turned 38 years old in two weeks on June 19. The rare ALS would become popularly known as "Lou Gehrig's Disease."

Rick and his pregnant bride set up quarters at the Gatsworth Hotel Apartments in St. Louis on the Mississippi River. When the Browns began a ten-game homestand in early June, they promptly lost a twin bill to the visiting Philadelphia Athletics, 5–2 and 5–3. The owner decided to replace Haney with a new field boss. Club President Donald Barnes announced in the June 5 *St. Louis Post-Dispatch*, "We still have a high regard for Haney. Fred's a fine fellow, and I believe he has given 100 percent co-operation and effort. But when things are going bad, you know, you can't stand still; you have to make a change. We hope to have some place in the organization for Haney."

Luke Sewell, a 19-year veteran catcher who last played in 1939, would make his managerial debut with the St. Louis Browns. The 40-year-old Sewell had begun his career catching for the Cleveland Indians and had just returned as a coach. In Cleveland, he had been a teammate of his older brother Joe, who had a great career that would lead him to Cooperstown.

Typically when a new manager takes over, the club has a momentary uplift, but not this time. The Yankees were in town on June 7–8 for a three-game sweep. In a free-swinging opener against Lefty Gomez that was decided by an 11–7 score, Ferrell contributed a couple of hits to the losing cause on June 7. By the end of the series, he sported a .266 season batting average with his total 33 hits accounting for 21 runs batted in. The cross-town St. Louis Cardinals led the National League.

At this time, Joe DiMaggio was in the middle of his phenomenal 56-game hitting streak that had begun on May 15, and was extended by three games with the cooperation of the Browns' hurlers. Long after the famed streak ended on July 17, baseball correspondent Joe Falls asked Ferrell about his recollection of this series in New York. Although he didn't remember a critical last at-bat on

June 26 perfectly, he recalled the gist of it: With Rick catching, Elden Auker had pitched a strong game to silence DiMaggio in his first three times at bat. Surely, most everyone was hoping Joe would get one more crack at extending his hitting streak, now up to thirty-seven games. The first batter in the eighth went out, and Red Rolfe, the second hitter, coaxed a walk off Auker. Up stepped Tommy Henrich, and Joe D went into the on-deck circle. Henrich, worried that he might hit into a double play and forfeit DiMaggio's opportunity to hit one last time in the game, stepped out of the box and walked back to the dugout for a conversation with his manager. With the concurrence of Manager Joe McCarthy, Henrich laid down a bunt and successfully pushed Rolfe down to second. Upset with this shenanigan, the Browns' catcher started yelling at his pitcher: "Hit him! Hit him in the pants! Hit him with the ball!"[2] Instead Auker came in with his patented submarine delivery, and DiMaggio drove it into left field for a double to keep his remarkable streak alive. According to Falls, the ever-competitive Ferrell glared at his pitcher in disgust for enabling DiMaggio's hit. He didn't feel the game should be played that way.

Beginning with their 9–0 victory over Detroit on June 27, St. Louis won its first series since early June and finally broke the spell the Tigers cast over the Browns every time they played in Briggs Stadium. Detroit had mastered the Browns 15 straight times there since April 16, 1940. Rick Ferrell led the way with a three-hit game, including a two-bagger, scoring twice and driving in another run.

With the Browns still a last place ball club in mid–July, ineffective pitching was credited the most for the failure to win. The June 28 *St. Louis Post-Dispatch* criticized the past winter's decision to dole out considerable sums of money for older pitchers, hoping they would somehow rediscover an ability to win. On July 17, the *Post-Dispatch* reported that Rick Ferrell was batting .262. The next day Ray Stockton wrote in his "Extra Innings" column, "Now there's a catcher — Rick Ferrell — who can hold up his head in any company."

A *St. Louis Post-Dispatch* correspondent began entertaining the possibility of the home team finishing in the first division, arguing that despite their 34–51 record, St. Louis was 6½ games better off at this point in the season than last. "Can they do it?" asked the correspondent. "Well, 69 games remain on the Brownies' schedule, and you can make up or lose a lot of ground in that much competition. While they were knocking over the Red Sox, the Browns looked like a club good enough to beat anything in the league, except the Yankees and Indians." According to this story, a regular Boston Red Sox beat writer also spoke highly of the Browns' play. "The team can hit," said Burt Whitman. "It has a stout enough defense, and it has played intelligent ball all season. With a pickup in pitching, the Browns would rate with the pennant contenders."[3]

When Rick Ferrell joined the Browns, he paired up with another knuckleball pitcher, but one not as skilled as the Dutchman back in Washington. Iowa native Johnny Niggeling got his big league start in the National League,

On June 17, 1941, Philadelphia Athletics catcher Charlie Wagner is tagged out at home plate in the eighth inning trying to score from second on a single by A's pitcher Lemar Harris. Rick Ferrell is the St. Louis Browns catcher. On deck is A's shortstop Al Brancato. (National Baseball Hall of Fame Library, Cooperstown, N.Y.)

pitching for the Boston Bees. After one season, he was picked up by Cincinnati, and the next year saw him over in the junior circuit plying his trade with the Browns. He was destined to come into his own in St. Louis, and Ferrell's steadying influence greatly contributed to his development. For sure, Manager Luke Sewell recognized the role that Ferrell had with the 38-year-old hurler. "I can tell you one thing, though. I feel that catcher Rick Ferrell has been a big help to Niggeling. Rick is an experienced catcher and is experienced in handling knuckleball pitching. He worked with Leonard of Washington for a long time. I feel that Niggeling has a certain degree of confidence when Ferrell is handling his stuff, which unquestionably makes him a better performer," said Sewell.[4]

At the end of July 1941, after taking another series from Boston at Fenway, two games to one, the Browns' 38–57 record still had them positioned in seventh, now 28 games behind the leaders. August would turn out to be the high water-mark of winning baseball as the team won 20 games, four more than it lost, and also played in two ties. Ferrell injured his ankle on about August 12, possibly in a players' brawl, but he still continued to compete, sharing catching tasks with Bob Swift. In the 3–3 tie with Cleveland in which Niggeling battled Bob Feller on August 14, Rick belted out three hits in four at-bats. September was uneventful, though the team played better than it had the first half. Mid-month, the Browns enjoyed another modest run, clicking off four wins in a row. When the Browns topped Detroit in the second game of a double-header later in the month, Ferrell stroked his third triple of the campaign.

One of the most notorious moments of Rick's entire career occurred in the second game of a Friday doubleheader played on September 26, 1941, at Sportsman's Park. With Cleveland's Bob Feller pitching a no-hitter against St. Louis' Denny Galehouse, Rick came up to bat in the fifth inning with a runner on first. Ferrell laid down a perfect sacrifice bunt, which he beat out to break up Feller's no-hitter. Despite a 3–2 Indians win for Feller's twenty-fifth victory of the season, he missed out on his second no-hitter. In the first game, Ferrell was sent in to pinch-hit for Bob Swift in the ninth inning and delivered a single to drive in the tying run and scored on Chet Laabs' double to win the game, 6–5.

The curtain came down on the 1941 season with the Browns claiming a 5–4 victory over Cleveland for Bob Muncrief's thirteenth win, tying them with Washington for sixth place in the standings. Their 70–84 record produced a winning percentage of .455, the team's best since 1929.

Whether realistic or not, more had been expected from this team back in April, but it had gotten off to a miserable start. The *Post-Dispatch*, in a September 29, 1941, season summary, claimed it a mystery why the team had not enjoyed more success. "Barnes and DeWitt [president and vice president] have tried everything. They have fired managers, subscribed to long distance rain insurance, made modest and ambitious speeches at pep meetings of the citizens. They have built a modest farm system and scouts are abroad in the land. They have invested important money in youngsters and in veterans." The writer did recognize that all teams were searching for more talent and competition was stiff.

Rick Ferrell bounced back to play in 121 games, a high number considering he was 35 years old and 1941 had been his thirteenth season in a physically taxing position. Other than his .256 batting average, most of his numbers were higher, with 99 hits.

Meanwhile, on the domestic front, Rick's wife, Ruth, gave birth to the couple's first child, Maureen Ruth, on October 17, 1941, in Washington, D.C. Becoming parents provided another dimension to the lives of the newlyweds as they settled into family life together.

His brothers, George, player-manager of the Martinsville (Va.) Manufacturers, and Wes, player-manager of the Leaksville (Va.) Triplets near Guilford, had competed against each other all season for first place in the Bi-State League. Wesley's team ultimately nosed out George's by two games; however, George's .351 batting average topped Wesley's .332, according to the September 18, 1941, issue of *The Sporting News.*

After months of masking its attitude toward military aggression under the guise of neutrality, the United States plunged into World War II, provoked by the Japanese attack on Pearl Harbor on December 7, 1941. The future of professional baseball was uncertain but for sure, the war would dramatically impact the entire nation, baseball included.

One would not expect a club like St. Louis— with a losing tradition, coming off a sixth place finish — to have a bevy of holdouts. Yet six regulars, including Rick Ferrell, had not returned their signed contracts by March 10, 1942. Perhaps they thought they could leverage the anticipated loss of players due to the war. Among the list, only Cullenbine had experienced a strong season in 1941.

Of more concern to the players than their salary issues were the perennial financial woes of this franchise. Since Donald Barnes had purchased the club from Phil Ball five years prior, it had annually experienced red ink to the tune of $100,000. Barnes, owner of one of the largest loan companies in the country, was passionate about owning a big league club. "I'll never get back what I put into baseball and as a businessman, I guess I should get out of it, but I'm too much of a fan," Barnes told the *Washington Post.*[5]

With a yearly deficit of that magnitude, Barnes looked for various ways to reduce expenditures. As this season unfolded, he made the bold decision to eliminate the team's press agent and their three scouts, with the scouts costing $30,000. "Why we should pay that sort of money in a war year I don't know, so we got rid of them. A baseball scout in these times is simply digging up talent for Uncle Sam to grab, and it's a pure waste. We've got three farm teams and working agreements with three smaller clubs, and there are some pretty good scouts among the managers of those teams.... They'll give us just as much talent as our scouts would."

One other philosophical idea of Don Barnes stood out: He was committed to not selling any players for cash to offset his losses. He thought it unfair to the fans to sell good players to compensate for revenue shortages. Referring to the practice of the previous owner, Barnes said: "They wiped out one $100,000 deficit by selling Rick Ferrell to the Red Sox for that much money."[6]

The Browns opened the 1942 season on April 14 at Comiskey Park and, aside from the usual hype of spring hope, no bright expectations for success were predicted for the team. Four fairly dependable starters returned to pitch (Niggeling, Auker, Galehouse, Hollingsworth), though none had shown a consistent ability to dominate. The team was, however, very high on a young hurler, Bob Muncrief, who had turned in a fine 13–9 season for a rookie. Yet, nobody expected the turn of events the 1942 season would bring, thanks in large part to Rick Ferrell.

In a 2004 telephone interview, pitcher Elden Auker recalled Rick: "He was a little, sharp singles hitter — very tough up at the plate. He'd break your heart in a pinch because he was an excellent hitter. He was a good fellow to get on base and drive runs in. And, of course, he was one of the best receivers in the game. He and Mickey Cochrane were two of the best catchers plus Ray Hayworth, also. Rick had a great throwing arm. He was good with young pitchers, very knowledgeable, a guy who steadied the pitchers and brought out the best in them."

The biggest change in the lineup involved the left side of the infield where the Browns introduced rookie shortstop Vern Stephens and third baseman Don Gutteridge, a player acquired from the Cardinals' organization where he played for Sacramento in 1941. Starting together, both would become solid fixtures in the St. Louis infield.

St. Louis charged out of the gate, sweeping the first three-game series of the 1942 season from Chicago, and moved on to take the opener in Detroit. After trading games with the Tigers on April 18 and 19, the team fell into a downward slide losing nine straight, and not winning again until April 28 when Elden Auker held off the Yankees, 3–1. The Browns had quickly reversed a hopeful start and were in sixth place, 7–11, by the end of April, looking very unpromising.

On May 3, the Browns played two against the Washington Senators, losing the first, 9–8, and coming back to take the nightcap, 5–1. The 13-year veteran Ferrell went two-for-three in the second contest, scoring once and driving in another run. A six-hitter tossed by Niggeling put an end to a three-game losing streak, when the Browns topped Boston, 6–3, on May 14. Naturally his batterymate was #9, Rick Ferrell, who not only handled the darting slants of Niggeling, but also collected three of his team's ten hits.

Browns infielder Floyd Baker recalled Ferrell's offense in a 2003 telephone interview: "Mr. Ferrell was a very consistent, steady ballplayer. He was a "spray" type of hitter — he hit the ball where it was pitched. If it was pitched away from him, he'd go to the opposite field and he never struck out much. We traveled in those Pullman cars with diners. There were two extra cars for the ballplayers, but we didn't get any special treatment."

The Browns did not really perk up until the third week in May when they strung together a four-game winning streak. On May 28, St. Louis prevailed, 6–4, in the first game of a series with Chicago. As was becoming more typical, Ferrell substituted for catcher Swift in the late innings and delivered a clutch double in the eighth inning, driving in two runs during a four-run rally.

On June 1, 1942, the Browns' brass went into the market, consummating two trades and hoping to shore up deficiencies. They traded reserve catcher Bob Swift and starting pitcher Bob Harris for veteran catcher Frankie Hayes— apparently concerned that Rick Ferrell was slowing down. All receivers are vulnerable to injuries, but Ferrell was beginning to show signs of wear and tear.

Securing the 27-year-old Hayes was a significant addition, for he was highly regarded after hitting .280 in 1941 while socking twelve round trippers and knocking in 63 RBIs. That same day, the Browns also swapped outfielders and pitchers with the Washington Senators, giving up Roy Cullenbine and pitcher Bill Trotter for outfielder Mike Chartak and hurler Steve Sundra. This later trade was basically another case of reshuffling players between Washington and St. Louis.

After playing well enough to lift its record two games above .500, the Browns fell apart again, taking punch after punch, staggering to the ropes with seven straight defeats from Boston and New York. In this streak of misery, the team quickly slid five games under .500, 16½ games behind the league leader.

In June, Rick Ferrell had begun to give way to catcher Frankie Hayes for more games, but in early July, his back pain began. Diagnosed as lumbago, he was sidelined for a number of games. Soon however, Hayes also succumbed to an injury, forcing 41-year-old manager Luke Sewell to put on the tools of ignorance and go behind the plate. Ferrell's ailment came at a time when he was starting to swing the bat with greater consistency, having built up his season average to .261. On July 10 he returned to action and Hayes became a convalescent, suffering an injured leg which scratched him from the lineup until August 7.

Despite their crippled catching tandem, the Browns suddenly became dramatically hot, winning eight games with Rick behind the plate, starting with a 5–2 win over the Yankees on July 11, then sweeping the Red Sox and A's. When the Browns arrived at Griffith Stadium on July 18, Nats right-hander Alex Carrasquel throttled them in a 3–0 loss. But in a doubleheader on Sunday, July 19, St. Louis picked it right back up again, winning both games. Ferrell and Sewell shared the catching duties in the first game, but Rick caught all nine innings in the nightcap, lashing out a double and two singles for two runs to ensure Niggeling's 6–4 victory. The double victory propelled the Browns to their tenth win in the last eleven contests for a 47–44 record and a fourth place position in the first division!

Herman Wecke, staff writer for the *Post-Dispatch*, chimed in with added excitement: "And what a difference from a year ago. In 1941, after the club had played its first 91 games, the aggregation was in seventh place with a record of 36–55, .396. Thus the present club is just 11 games or .120 percentage points ahead of the 1941 entry. It's the first time since away back in 1929 that a Brownie club has been over the .500 mark at this late day of the campaign."[7]

Pitchers able to master the knuckleball—a pitch that befuddled most hitters—were often a fan delight. And the St. Louis faithful were becoming fond of Johnny Niggeling's fluttering and darting pitches, which proved to be particularly tough on Boston hitters. Although slowed by more frequent injuries and his age, now 36, Rick Ferrell continued to be respected for his unique ability to catch Niggeling's knuckleball pitch and propel the team to victory. The more they won, the tougher Ferrell hung, playing through injury and fatigue. The team came first, always.

New York swept a twin bill on August 2, 4–2 and 10–0, as weary Rick Ferrell was forced to catch both games due to the Browns' severe shortage of able-bodied receivers. He managed two hits in seven times at bat, but was charged with a passed ball in the fifth inning of the first game that contributed to two Yankee runs. Not surprisingly the pitcher was Johnny Niggeling.

Rick's recent woes were making headlines as the August 5 *St. Louis Post-Dispatch* blared: "Browns Need Relief for Catcher Ferrell." Errors receive greater attention when attributed to losing games, and the Browns had just experienced a mild interruption of their hot play, losing five of their last six games. Explaining that the team was searching for another catcher and an outfielder and recognizing that receivers were a scare commodity, a *Post-Dispatch* reporter wrote: "With Frankie Hayes out on account of an injury, Rick Ferrell has been forced to carry too much of a burden for a veteran, and his work has suffered. Sewell returned to the active list, but naturally can't run or hit up to requirements." Blessed with a couple of rainouts to rest the weary, the Browns and Indians played only one game of the scheduled series, which the Indians won, 8–5, leaving the Browns even on the season, 54–54.

"The return of Frankie Hayes undoubtedly will be helpful to the team," wrote *Post-Dispatch* correspondent James Gould. "Ferrell, during Hayes' absence, was sadly overworked and his play naturally suffered. Rick's not as young as he used to be and needs to be rested often." The empathetic choice of words reflected obvious respect for the veteran receiver.

A three-game sweep of the White Sox followed by two wins and a loss to Cleveland pushed St. Louis' record to five games over .500 and helped secure its hold on fourth place. In the Sunday twin bill with Cleveland, Ferrell caught the entire second game, smashing a single to plate a run for a Browns' 6–1 win.

In a 2003 telephone interview, Browns' infielder Don Gutteridge recalled Rick: "As to his baseball ability, it was the *best*. He made the Browns' pitching staff one of the best in the league. We had a couple of pitchers who liked to throw knuckleballs, and he was great with them.... He had an accurate arm, and he threw baserunners out trying to steal. He was a good clutch hitter — he always drove in the important runs. Time and time again, he did that. Due a lot to him, the Browns finished in the first division for the first time in a good many years."

The team played back-to-back doubleheaders on August 23 and 25, taking all four from the Tigers and Senators. Their third win lifted them into third place, a rarified position they would maintain for the rest of the season. When the Browns pulled the second game out of the fire, the sacrifice fly that drove in the deciding run flew off the bat of Rick Ferrell.

St. Louis continued their strong play in September, piling up a 14–8 record. In a scheduling aberration, the Browns played three doubleheaders against the

Indians in three days, September 4–6, and won the first five games, again with superb pitching. In the middle twin bill, Rick got in both games, nailing a single in the first, while his double in the second game drove in a run.

As long as Wes Ferrell was associated with professional baseball, he would pop-up in the press. Now player-manager for Lynchburg in the Virginia League, an undated family scrapbook article described that Ferrell led the league in batting (.361) and home runs (31), but had been suspended during a September 13 playoff game for an argument with an umpire, to be served after the playoffs ended.

For a franchise that would win only one American League crown in its history and hung out in the cellar many seasons, 1942 represented an exciting year of baseball in the "Gateway City." Finishing third with an 82–69 record, the Browns drew over a quarter million fans—their best attendance since 1922 — with their only first-division finish in fourteen years. Even at that, their attendance was surely suppressed by the hard-charging Cardinals who captured the National League flag with 106 wins.

The much-improved pitching staff had a 3.59 ERA in a season when the league's hurlers allowed 3.66 runs per nine innings. Down the stretch St. Louis' staff had pitched exceptionally well, allowing just under three runs a game in 22 contests, including five shutouts. Johnny Niggeling led the staff with 15 victories, ranking sixth in the league with 107 strikeouts.

Catcher Ferrell slumped through the worst year of his career, accumulating a paltry .223 batting average in 99 games. Though primarily a singles hitter, he continued to deliver the critical hit. Among his 61 tallies, over seven went for extra bases, and he drove in 26 runs. Despite occasional errors (6), Ferrell finished the season with a .986 fielding percentage. The Browns' first-division finish made them eligible for a piece of the World Series payout. Rick received a full share, amounting to $712.63.

The story of the three Ferrell brothers, Rick, Wes and George, all still active in professional baseball, created on-going interest for the media and baseball fans. In October 1942, *The Sporting News* reported that the Ferrell boys hustled home to North Carolina to help their father with the fall harvest, pitching hay and picking corn, and getting the crops in before the rains came.[8] Rick and his family lived with his parents at the Ferrell family farm during the winter.

Before the New Year, Rick was referenced again in the "Baseball Bible" in an article exploring the exceptional durability of big league catchers. The weekly listed nine catchers who were then ten-year veterans, including Ferrell.[9]

Although President Roosevelt had given major league baseball the green light to continue, the U.S. entry into World War II had begun to seriously disrupt the game. During 1943, 219 players listed on the rosters of major league clubs would spend all, or most, of the season in military service. Some teams, like the Yankees and Red Sox, experienced major losses of key players. However, Good Fortune smiled on the St. Louis Browns, who lost only two starters, pitcher Jack Kramer and outfielder Walt Judnick. By preserving baseball during wartime and giving Americans something to take their minds off their troubles, Rick felt he was providing service to his country.

As the United States increased its build-up of military personnel, baseball players were inducted in greater numbers, and the talent supply became a major issue, especially for the minor leagues. That new reality caused all major clubs to severely reduce their farm systems when 1943 began; Branch Rickey and the Cardinals disbanded 16 of their 22 farm clubs. Now with much greater frequency, the press reported that yet another star player was being inducted into the military. On February 17, Joe DiMaggio's enlistment in the Army was announced, noting that he traded an annual salary of $43,500 for a monthly paycheck of $50.

The World War impacted the game in various ways, including the introduction of a new baseball called the "balata ball." With a shortage of rubber, a material produced from the juice of tropical trees was used to encase ground cork in the center of the baseball. Negative comments from players resounded: "It was like hitting a piece of cement."[10]

The Office of Defense Transportation imposed significant travel restrictions on major league baseball, prohibiting spring training in the South and Southwest. Thus both St. Louis teams selected spring training camps down on the Ohio River, the Cardinals at Cairo, Illinois, and the Browns at Cape Girardeau, Missouri. The Browns, fortunately, had use of an indoor heated facility with a dirt floor ideal for taking batting practice.

Manager Luke Sewell spoke of a very uncertain future in 1943, especially disappointing after his team had experienced a fine season the previous year. "You don't know anything about this year," said Sewell. "We're never going to know where we stand from one day to the next, so we'll just have to be prepared for anything."[11]

Getting off to a very slow start, St. Louis occupied the basement at the end of May with an 11–18 record. June improved. The Browns played .500+ baseball with a 16–15 record. Ferrell and Hayes traded off catching duties, but Rick wasn't hitting much. He collected two hits in a 10–6 loss to New York early in the month, but multiple-hit games were rare.

When St. Louis edged Cleveland, 7–6, on June 12, they slipped up to inhabit seventh place. They won the next day to make it four in a row, their longest winning streak of the season. By July 1943, the team had three back-up receivers: Ferrell, Hayes and Joe Schultz. Schultz began playing more in July and Ferrell less, and when Rick did catch, he only got in for part of the game.

The Browns won on July 1 to open the new month, reviving to defeat Boston in four of five games and land back in fifth place by July 11, despite a sub-par 35–37 record. While playing Boston tough, the Browns swept a Sunday doubleheader that day, winning the opener, 8–7, in a twelve-inning affair.

Rick Ferrell enjoyed three hits in three tries and accounted for two runs, more reminiscent of his past offensive strength.

The All-Star Game always drew positive attention to major league baseball and this year caused writers to reflect on the 10-year anniversary of the original game played in 1933. The 1943 summer classic assembled in the City of Brotherly Love on July 13. Arch Ward of the *Chicago Daily Tribune* pointed out that Rick Ferrell was the only one out of the thirteen living players from the first game who was still active as a regular player.[12]

Though the recognition spoke to his longevity, Rick was not hitting like an All-Star on July 10, for his average hovered around .230. When the month closed, St. Louis had put together a 15–15 record for July. The Browns rode the train to Washington, D.C. for a long six-game series, hoping to make up some ground and return to the first division. Instead they had a horrible time at Griffith Stadium, unable to win a single game. The month's despair included an eight-game losing streak during a spell in which the Browns won only three out of 19 games. Unlike the previous year, this rapid decline left the club 15 games under .500 by August 16, gasping for air.

Then occurred another burst of energy as St. Louis returned from the dead to win the next six contests. During this stage of his career, Rick Ferrell continued to be a part-time catcher and still had his gratifying moments at the plate. When Galehouse pitched a sharp four-hit shutout for a 3–0 win on August 19, Rick was the receiver and delivered a sacrifice fly to drive in an important run in the low-scoring game. In the next series with the Nats, he caught the nightcap, and although his team lost, 4–2, he twice came through with clutch hits to tie the score. His second run-producing single sent the game into extra innings.

Washington had long been a favorite trading partner for St. Louis and on August 17, the two opponents once again swapped their players. In this transaction, the Browns surrendered an aging Johnny Niggeling. When the Browns visited Griffith Stadium on August 23, Niggeling made a statement, winning 2–1 over Nelson Potter. When the Senators won again the next day, 10–4, Rick made a costly error that allowed three Washington runs.

Infielder Ellis Clary's major league career lasted just four years and he never achieved status as a full-time regular. When he was traded to the Browns after having fought with some of them during a recent game, Clary would recall that Rick Ferrell treated him warmly, as though he were a key player on his new team. "I was scared to walk into the clubhouse.... Rick Ferrell was the catcher for the Browns then, and our dressing room in St. Louis was upstairs. I came up those steps and I dreaded it. To tell the truth, I was scared to walk in there. I walked in the door and looked around. Rick Ferrell spotted me. He jumped up and came to the door and shook my hand. This is exactly what he said: 'Welcome to our nine.' That was the greatest thing. Rick was a fine man."[13]

The Browns ran hot and cold throughout most of the final month of the season. On a short road trip to Detroit and Cleveland, they played poorly, capturing just two wins in seven games. But when they returned to St. Louis, the sleepy Browns took off, winning the next seven in a row against first Chicago, then Cleveland. Their seventh consecutive win on September 15 marked 1943's longest winning streak. Rick Ferrell caught Al Hollingsworth's 4–2 win, getting a hit while his batterymate contributed two. It must have felt good after a long season — seven games at home, all victories!

In the next ten days, the team spent lots of time packing, off first to Chicago for four games, then back home for two dates with the Senators, and finally their last road trip to finish off the 1943 season. St. Louis lost three of their four games at Comiskey Park when their offense scored a total of four runs, and the season ended bleakly in New York when the Bronx Bombers swept all three remaining games on the schedule.

After the encouraging third-place finish in 1942, this season had provided a major letdown for the Browns in a year of great uncertainty and concern. They finished in sixth place with 72 wins and 80 defeats, trailing the pennant-winning New York Yankees by 25 games.

At age 37, Rick Ferrell's playing time had been reduced to 74 games with 209 plate appearances, producing a mere .239 batting average. He had managed 50 hits and still had the ability to hit with runners in scoring position for he drove in 20 runs. His fielding average was .987 with 327 putouts.

In two years' time, 250 baseball players had been drafted by the military to fight in World War II. By mid–November 1943, Uncle Sam had already called thirty-three players from the sixteen teams, even married fathers, who had once been exempt.[14] In late December, Browns shortstop Vern Stephens and pitcher Steve Sundra were inducted.

7

❖ ❖ ❖

1944–1945

Catching Four Knuckleballers

Rick Ferrell must have smiled with deep satisfaction when he learned his old ball club, the Washington Senators, had acquired him again. When your present team has decided that you are no longer able to be an everyday catcher at age 38, being sought after is a compliment to the enduring skills that have defined one's career. On March 1, 1944, Washington traded catcher Tony Giuliani and cash to the St. Louis Browns for Rick Ferrell. The two catchers had been teammates with the Browns in 1938 and 1939, when Giuliani served as a back-up catcher to Ferrell. Following the trade announcement, however, Giuliani refused to report to the St. Louis club, and the Browns agreed to accept outfielder Gene Moore instead. Moore, too, was an aging veteran who had already celebrated his forty-fourth birthday; perhaps his ineligibility for the military draft encouraged the Browns to accept him.

Ferrell's ability to catch the knuckleball made him attractive to a team that had four knuckleballers in its starting rotation: ex-batterymates "Dutch" Leonard and Johnny Niggeling, plus Mickey Haefner and Roger Wolff. Shirley Povich was quick to recognize Rick's major influence on the success of knuckleballers Leonard and Niggeling during Ferrell's first stint with the Nats, stating that the catcher had made them both stars.

Being able to snare an unpredictable knuckleball required quick reflexes and nimbleness. Povich saw a great resemblance between Rick and former Senators' catcher Muddy Ruel, for both were slight of build, agile and stylistic. "Leonard might never have made good in the big leagues except for the help he got from Rick, who, unlike the catchers Leonard had in his trial with Brooklyn, kept calling for Leonard to throw his knuckler," wrote Povich. "Ferrell didn't care about his own catching record. In fact, in the same years when he was acknowledged to be one of the great catchers of the league, he was charged with most passed balls, due chiefly to the butterfly pitch of Leonard." Ferrell was credited with having the same transforming impact on Niggeling. "[John] couldn't win in his previous trials in the majors, but when he found a catcher who could handle his knuckler and wasn't afraid to call for it, Niggeling blossomed as one of the better pitchers in the league."[1]

Rick's return to the Nationals gave recall to his brother Wes. "The nicest of the Ferrell boys always seemed to be Brother Rick," claimed Povich. "You wouldn't exactly notice Rick in a crowd. Wes was probably the recipient of more mash notes than any player in the big leagues. Rick's a quiet guy. You could never tell by his expression or behavior after a ball game whether his team won or lost, whether he got four hits for himself or went for the collar." According to Povich, Rick played a significant role in his brother's comeback after the fireballing Wesley lost his heater and had to become a finesse pitcher.[2]

More than anything else in this third year of America's heavy involvement in the Second World War, teams were struggling to maintain the semblance of a big league ball club, stateside. National League president Ford Frick felt that despite the draft, enough replacement players would be found to complete the baseball schedule. On April 6, 1944, *The Sporting News* quoted Frick: "This season will be on a day-to day, week-to-week basis. As far as front offices are concerned, nobody has any idea of making money this year."

Many players were summoned to serve the war effort. Nats catcher Jake Early had been called to the Army in March. After 16 years as the first-string Yankees' catcher, Bill Dickey was called up by the Navy. Physical deferments and older players had become desired ways to retain an experienced baseball team. Five of Washington's regulars were classified 4-F, and several over age 38 were exempt from the draft. The presence of several Hispanic players also provided roster protection. Age and draft classification insured that all four knuckleballers would remain in the starting rotation for 1944. Venezuelan Alex Carrasquel guaranteed Washington a fifth starting pitcher.

Far from the temperate climate of the sunny South, the Senators again held spring training on the nearby University of Maryland campus, which provided both a ball field and an indoor facility. When Ferrell re-joined the Nationals, he was returning to a ball club that had finished in second place in 1943 with an 84–69 record. His new manager, Ossie Bluege, 43, had been a former teammate who had played third base for Washington most of his 18-year major league career, garnering a .272 lifetime batting average.

Based on the previous seasons' winning records, Rick was joining an accomplished pitching staff headed by emerging star Early Wynn, who had notched 18 wins with a fine ERA of 2.91. The other four starters had all won an identical 11 victories, compiling an impressive earned run average of 3.18 in a year when the league's pitchers cumulative ERA was 3.30.

Those fine statistics, however, were discounted by a general fall-off in hitting prowess, reflecting the exit of so many fine offensive players who had been drawn into the war effort. Twelve million Americans wore military uniforms, with more than 500 major leaguers serving their country. The composite American League batting average for 1943 was .243, compared to the pre-war 1940 .271 season average.

Ferrell's re-arrival demanded attention because no catcher in baseball history — before or since — had ever before been assigned to catch four knuckleballers on one team. Washington finally had a receiver who could handle this aggregation of guys who threw the wobbly and erratic off-speed pitch. In a long interview by Buck O'Neil for the April 6, 1944, issue of *The Sporting News*, with the telling sub-headline "Freak-Ball Flingers Putting Finger on Ferrell," Rick, with unhesitating confidence, stated that the catcher is the backbone of the team:

> [Catchers] handle the ball oftener than any other man on the team, except the pitcher. The catcher orders every pitch, trying to call for balls the hitter is least likely to hit safely. The catcher must cope with situations, using instantaneous judgment ... to "outguess" the other side. An important phase of a catcher's work is being able to tell when a pitcher is losing his stuff, before it is too late. When you work with a pitcher right along, you sometimes can tell an inning ahead when he is weakening. Sometimes you'll see a manager signal to the bullpen for a pitcher to start warming up. The hurler in the game may seem to be doing all right, but the catcher has tipped off the manager, and they're just getting ready for what may happen. A sort of "in time of calm, prepare for squalls" proposition.
>
> The public believes a catcher should throw out every base-runner who tries to steal, but they forget that the pitcher is often to blame.... And here's a situation that calls for careful operation. With a man on first, or perhaps on second under certain circumstances, the other side usually will bunt. Occasionally, with some bunters, you can pitch a low-ball — the good ball to bunt. With some, however, that would be suicide.

Ferrell then transitioned into defining the strike zone, saying that a real low ball "must be pitched between the level of the knees and a point about five inches above the knee. The high ball must be between the batters' letters and the shoulder. Under the rules, a pitch below the knee or about the shoulders is a ball." Roger Wolff, assembled for the interview, described the knuckleball's unpredictable path, which the catcher often must stop "with his wrist or his neck or his knee or his bare hand. If Washington comes through, you can credit Ferrell with a major share of the glory. If Washington comes through, we'd like to walk up and shake Rick's hand — if he has any hand left to shake with by that time."

Incredibly even at age 38, Rick Ferrell eagerly looked forward to the challenge, recognizing his responsibility to handle whatever they threw at him. "It will be high adventure," the veteran catcher predicted, sounding like a wet-behind-the ears rookie. "Yes, there is an element of danger in catching a knuckleball pitcher, but that's part of the job of catching for Washington this season. If we can win the pennant, I'll catch knucklers every day and night, every pitch, while my hands last."[3]

Clearly, playing at night with this unpredictable crew increased the difficulty for the receiver. In 1944, Washington had forty-four night games at

Griffith Stadium scheduled and would play at least nine more on the road. To compound the difficulty, Mickey Haefner and Bill Lefebvre were left-handers. Ferrell noted his good fortune in escaping injury in his latest stint with St. Louis.

The Nats' second-place finish the previous year fueled an even higher level of expectation for 1944. Clark Griffith was confidently talking about winning the American League flag; Al Wolf, a correspondent in the April 13 *Los Angeles Times*, stated he would be surprised if they didn't win the league crown. Some pundits had become enthralled with the uncanny dominance of knuckleball pitchers, and since the Nationals had a whole rotation of these guys, this team was going to have an edge. That assumption and the acquisition of Rick Ferrell poised the Senators to take full advantage of their special weapons.

Opening Day is always a special event across the big league scene, but especially for the home team. A packed, well-attired crowd of over 31,000 cheered lustily as their local heroes took the field at Griffith Stadium on April 18, 1944. At age 40, Johnny Niggeling was designated as opening pitcher to launch the new season. The rural Iowa native had come into his own in 1942, winning 15 games for the St. Louis Browns, where he linked up with catcher Rick Ferrell, #8. He had toiled in the minors for ten years until finally the knuckleball became appreciated in the big league ranks, and he credited two players who paved the way for him. "Dutch Leonard and Rick Ferrell are the guys," stated Niggeling in the April 18 *Washington Post*. "They made the big leagues change their minds about the knuckleball. Leonard showed that a fellow could throw the knuckleball and win. He was lucky to have a fellow like Ferrell who wasn't afraid to call for it. There were other catchers in the big leagues, supposed to be good catchers, who wouldn't risk their reputations calling for the knuckler because it was so hard to handle. But when Leonard came up from Atlanta and found out he could pitch to Ferrell and win, the whole league got knuckleball conscious."

During World War II when most teams were strapped for front-line players, being older was no longer a liability for it provided protection from the draft. When Niggeling took the mound to deliver his warm-up pitches to start the game and Ferrell crouched behind the plate, together they represented a whole lot of baseball and life experience — 79 years, 3 months and 14 days and counting![4] Though the right-hander pitched well on this day, so did the Athletics starter Lum Harris, who earned a 3–2 Philadelphia victory.

For a team expecting to be competitive, the Nats enjoyed their greatest success early before faltering badly. April was a short month with only eight games on the schedule, and Washington began sluggishly, winning just three. With a lineup of a knuckler-a-day, Ferrell was slated to carry most of the catching load, along with Cuban native Mike Guerra, a recent graduate from Chattanooga, in relief. Although the New York Yankees prevailed, 6–3, in their season opener in the Bronx, Rick had a splendid three-for-four day, including a double on which he scored one run.

Back home on the 25th, the Nationals suffered a heartbreaking 14-inning, 5–4, loss to Boston. Rick seemed destined to be the goat of this tightly fought game when he uncorked a wild throw to third base in the fourth which allowed two big runs to score. But he exonerated himself in the bottom half of the inning when, with the bases loaded, he smashed a clutch two-run single, regaining those two runs along with his pride.

The press obsession with Washington's unique pitching staff kept Rick Ferrell in the media spotlight. Shirley Povich asked him to give a rundown on each of the hurlers, writing, "Here's the way Catcher Ferrell rates the Nats' four knuckleball pitchers [Bill Lefebvre had been relegated to the bullpen]: 'Roger Wolff's knuckler has the biggest break, and that's the toughest one to catch. A knuckler doesn't have to break much to be effective. Johnny Niggeling's and Dutch Leonard's break the same, either up or down. Niggeling has other stuff, too, but when Leonard has control of his knuckler, he's the toughest pitcher in the league to beat. Mickey Haefner's knuckler is just something he throws along with his curve balls and screwballs and the hitter never knows what's coming.'"[5]

Three of four knuckleball starters for the 1945 Washington Senators demonstrate their pitching grip for the "butterfly pitch" to their catcher. From left to right, Roger Wolff, Dutch Leonard, catcher Rick Ferrell, and Mickey Haefner (the fourth knuckleballer, Johnny Niggeling, is absent from the photograph). With Ferrell as their catcher, these four hurlers achieved 60 victories in 1945, and Wolff won 20 games himself. (National Baseball Hall of Fame Library, Cooperstown, N.Y.)

Umpire Cal Hubbard recalled on page 228 of the book *Even the Browns: The Zany True Stories of Baseball in the '40s* by William Mead, that a home plate umpire had to wait before making the call on a knuckleball pitch to avoid making a mistake. Hubbard said, "I remember Rick Ferrell was catching for Washington and Roger Wolff was pitching.... This pitch, I'll never forget it, when it was right out in front of the plate, it looked like it was going to be this far inside. All of a sudden, it just went like — that — right across home plate. It was one I called too quick and called it a ball. Rick Ferrell, the catcher, missed it; it went right by him. He said to me, 'Hub, that ball was a strike.' I said, 'Why the hell didn't you catch it?' He said, 'It fooled me.' I said, 'Fooled me too.'"

May proved to be the best month of the 1944 season and the only one in which the team played above .500, winning 16, losing 15. Then the inevitable happened when Rick caught one of Niggling's knuckleball pitches on the hand, splitting his thumb nail, and was out of action for the next ten days until May 21. During his absence Mike Guerra filled in behind the plate while Rick spent more time with Ruth, now pregnant with their second child.

With World War II in progress, all teams were struggling to maintain a big league lineup, and Washington capitalized on its history of recruiting Cuban players. This squad had three: Gilberto Torres, Mike Guerra and Roberto Ortiz. Son of ex–Nationals Ricardo Torrez, Gilberto became the regular third baseman on the 1944 team. Early Wynn was called to service in the Navy while former Washington catcher Al Evans returned to the team from the Navy after his three-year enlistment ended.

Sportswriter Povich continued to be impressed with the Nats' senior catcher, as he wrote in the *Post* on May 23: "Rick Ferrell makes no mistakes behind the plate and inspires fear of his throwing arm." This appeared just before Rick made a mistake behind the plate. At Comiskey Park, the first game of a Sunday doubleheader was decided by a single run, 6–5, when Ferrell dropped a throw home on a play that should have been an out. Illustrative of the parity in the American League, the Senators were last in the circuit after being swept in four games with the White Sox, yet they were only 5½ games behind the league-leading St. Louis Browns, with a record of 20–24.

Ferrell was hitting over .350 in early June, motivating Povich to write on June 6, "With a 5–10 record so far on the road trip, the only consistent feature of the Nats' play in the West has been Rick Ferrell's hitting." Yet his offense didn't impress as much as his daunting role catching. On June 22, Arthur Daley focused on Ferrell's handling of the knucklers in a *New York Times* article. When asked how he felt about catching a knuckleball pitcher, Ferrell didn't embellish the difficulty. "I don't mind those knucklers. As long as we win with them, I'm satisfied. But I must admit that they are mighty tough to catch. They float up to you, and you never know what's going to happen.... Our flutter-ball tossers don't even hold the ball the same. Niggeling bends back one finger in order to hold his. Wolff bends back three, while both Leonard and Haefner use two." Rick was quick to point out that night games only compound the problem of snaring these crazy pitched balls. "The night air seems to make them break bigger and sharper," reported Ferrell. "Maybe it's the heavier atmosphere. Whatever it is, though, you really get a workout behind the plate."

Daley concluded his interview by asking who the best pitchers were that Ferrell had ever caught. With little hesitation he said, "Lefty Grove and my brother Wes. They were the two easiest to catch, too. You could sit in a rocking chair and handle them. Each, at his best, was absolutely untouchable."[6]

June saw the Nationals winning and losing with nearly equal frequency, with 13 victories and 14 defeats. With a 32–34 record and still only six games out, Washington remained in the race and played at a similar pace through July 19, twice pulling up to an even .500.

In early July 1944, the cast for the 12th Annual All-Star Game was announced and two Senators were among the elite chosen: catcher Rick Ferrell and outfielder Stan Spence. With tongue-in-cheek, Ferrell reacted by stating to Povich in the July 3 *Post*, "I must be improving. I was named to the squad six times up to 1938, but for the five seasons after that, I didn't make it. I guess I'm doing a come-back." Regardless of the wartime circumstance, aging veteran Rick Ferrell had maintained his status as one of the premier receivers in the league. In the classic game of baseball's best played at Forbes Field on July 9, the National League won, 7–1. Rick watched from the bench as his teammate, Stan Spence, played right field, collecting one hit.

In mid–July when the Senators learned that their Cuban players were now subject to the military draft, the contingent of Guerra (Rick's backup), Ortiz, and Torres got out of Dodge. Given ten days to register for the draft, the threesome returned to Cuba, with Torres announcing he would seek a new U.S. passport.

War relief games were a common occurrence, as baseball produced a considerable amount of money to aid various causes. Before a large crowd of over 30,000 fans on July 26, the host Senators and their rival Chicago White Sox staged a number of skill competitions to entertain the attendees. The White Sox won the game that mattered, but the Nats dominated the pre-game running and throwing competition. Four-player teams competed to see how quickly they could relay the ball in from deep center field, with Rick Ferrell on the receiving end for the Nationals. The home team won, by an eyelash. Each team used two catchers who were to throw a ball into a barrel at second base. Only Ferrell achieved the goal, and he did it twice. Another event saw one player running from home to second base pitted against an opposing player running from second to home. In this dash, Washington shortstop Johnny Sullivan won, giving the home team a clean sweep and receiving war bonds for their championship wins. Even the coaches were good sports, subjecting themselves to laughter as they competed, blindfolded, in a wheelbarrow race from second base to home plate. Nats coach Nick Altrock, a very funny man and later well-known baseball clown, was the first coach to find home plate.[7]

Rick sported an average over .280 deep into July, but he made two glaring mistakes that resulted in game losses. On July 19, Washington lost to Detroit, 2–1, when the catcher dropped a throw that permitted the winning run to score. In another game shortly thereafter, the Nationals started a promising rally in which Ferrell and Sullivan opened an inning with consecutive singles, but Rick, the lead runner, fell down racing to second base. Later Povich observed in his August 1 column, "It was 10,000 to one that Ferrell could keep his feet, but he didn't." Washington was beaten, 9–6, for its fourth consecutive loss en route to a disastrous eleven-game losing streak that ended on August 4. Still Rick continued hitting the ball quite well considering his age and the catching load he was carrying. By July 26, he was batting .282 with 81 hits in 61 games.

The Senators finally halted an extended 11-game losing streak with 7–5 victory over the Red Sox on August 14, but shortly afterward, their bad baseball resumed with four straight losses—18 defeats in the last 20 games!

"Rick Ferrell is sadly overworked, with Mickey Guerra no longer around to relieve him and give the club timely hits," wrote Shirley Povich in his August 18 *Post* column. "The club's only other catcher is Al Evans, who's lately out of the Navy and hasn't played big league ball since 1942." The team got two of its Cuban exiles back in late summer, including catcher Guerra, who took a pitch off his bare hand during the first week of August, damaging his thumb soon after he returned.

In another War Bond benefit game, Rick competed in his specialty — throwing into a barrel at second base — and again nailed it to win the event. Winning three out of four games from the Cleveland Indians represented one of the few high points in August for this faltering team. Ferrell had a dandy three-for-three day at the plate on August 26, despite a 10–3 drubbing by the Yankees.

Entering September, the Senators' primary motivation was to sneak out of the cellar, but they were never able to string together more than one three-game winning streak, piling up six losses in a row late in the month. Much has been written above the lower level of individual performance during the war years, and Povich sounded an appropriate benediction when he stated: "There are fellows now playing regularly in the majors who are there by default."

The schedule-makers and a very close race at the top cast the Senators in a potential spoiler's role. At the very end of the season, the Detroit Tigers and the St. Louis Browns were locked in a near dead heat for first place, and the schedule seemed to favor the Tigers. For their final series, the Tigers would face off against the last place Nationals, while St. Louis would square off against the much more formidable New York Yankees. In an unexpected twist, St. Louis played like champions, whipping the Bronx Bombers four straight.

Meanwhile, Washington met Detroit at Briggs Stadium in a do-or-die series for the Bengals. Detroit had dominated Washington the entire 1944 season, winning 15 out of 18 games, but this series would be different. Detroit started off with a must win, but after the two teams traded victories on each succeeding day, the Tigers were left one game short of the pennant-winning St. Louis Browns. How unfortunate for Rick Ferrell that by being traded from the Browns before the 1944 season began, he was denied the opportunity to play in a World Series, a goal that eluded him throughout his stellar catching career.

Most baseball people had expected the Senators team to be competitive in 1944, but the club landed in eighth — and last — place, 25 games behind the Browns with a 64–90 record. Playing in a relatively weak league, they were only eight games out of fifth. Ferrell finished with a decent .277 batting average (.377 OBP) in 339 at-bats with 13 strikeouts and 46 walks. In catching 96 games, Rick had amassed 20 passed balls for a final .981 fielding percentage.

Once the 1944 season ended, Rick and his wife suffered an unexpected and intense personal disappointment of their own. On December 11, 1944, Ruth delivered their second child, another daughter whom they named Janet Louise. But while still in the hospital, their daughter was attacked by a contagious virus which she could not survive. After sixteen days of life, Janet died on December 27, two days after Ruth's 24th birthday on Christmas Day, and was buried in New Garden Cemetery across from Guilford College before the New Year began.

Though the war momentum had swung toward the Allies, the mobilization of forces continued to severely tax baseball in 1945. The Senators, among others, were concerned whether they would have enough warm bodies. "We're going to play even if we have to use nine old men," proclaimed 75-year-old Washington owner Clark Griffith. "There will be no hesitancy about going ahead." In a situation where the pickings were slim, owner Griffith would look like a genius for drafting pitcher Marino Pieretti from Portland in the Pacific Coast League. The little right-hander surprisingly emerged as the fourth man in the starting rotation and racked up 14 big wins in his only flash of real success in the majors. The team would continue to count on Hispanics to bolster its depleted roster, with nine Cubans reporting to spring camp at College Park, Maryland, as baseball began its fourth war-time spring training program close to home.

Always his best representative when it came to compensation, the 39-year-old catcher again held out, demanding a higher salary. When the first six Senators assembled on March 6 to begin the spring tune up, Rick Ferrell was absent. Because of a critical player shortage in general, Griffith verbally took a hard stance in dealing with Ferrell. "He is ridiculous in his demands," asserted the owner. "I understand he has some business interests that are good. Be that as it may, he will play with us or not at all. I never make a deal involving an unsigned player."[8] Ferrell continued to hold his ground until the two parties reached an undisclosed agreement on April 2, and Rick reported to camp five days later, missing nearly a month of spring training.

As the beginning of the 1945 season neared, two subjects again cast Rick

Ferrell into the headlines: his close pursuit of the record for most games caught in American League history and his critical responsibility with a knuckleball rotation. Ray Schalk, the famed catcher who did not join in with the Black Sox conspirators in 1919, held the American League record at 1,721 games caught. Ferrell would enter the season needing just 106 games to surpass his record. Other receivers, Al Lopez, Spud Davis and Frank Hayes, had the major-league-record-holder Gabby Hartnett in their sights, for he had caught the most games of all catchers: 1,790.

In a feature article published in *The Sporting News*, Frank "Buck" O'Neil recapped an extensive interview with Ferrell, focusing first on the approach to catching a knuckleball. The interview began with the forthright Ferrell expressing his regret at letting a pitch get by him that cost his team a win, and he readily noted that the circumstance had happened before. The most recent pitch he had missed snaring was a super-duper knuckler that he just couldn't catch up to, as Bob Uecker was fond of saying, until it stopped rolling. Asked a question with an obvious answer, what is the hardest pitch to catch, Ferrell immediately said: "The knuckler. The knuckleball is the No. 1 enemy of catchers. I've caught spitball pitchers and batted against them.... But going out there day after day to catch knuckleball pitchers is like going out looking for an accident to befall you. Sooner or later, you find one. Sooner or later, you help a knuckleball pitcher beat himself by being unable to stop the sort of stuff he throws at you."

When O'Neill asked what made catching a knuckleball so difficult, Ferrell explained, "You don't know where it is going to break. Some of them break in, some drop to the outside, and others just take off as if they had wings. It not only is harder to catch than any other style, but it's harder to hit." Reflecting back on those times when he just couldn't come up with a wicked, breaking knuckler that got past him to the screen — and in the process, allowing the runner to score easily from third — Ferrell said: "Now, let's look at this knuckleball business for a minute. You sign for a knuckler in a pinch because it's the best pitch the hurler has. You're asking for trouble on winning or losing on one ball. So, up the ball comes. You can see the stitches, and it looks very easy. But you can't make a move to meet the pitch. You don't know how it's going to break. Maybe in, or down, or maybe it will jump up 45 degrees and go to the stand." Given Ferrell's intimate description of the irregular flight of the ball, one can easily empathize with the concentration and pressure a knuckleball pitcher imposed on the catcher. No wonder many referred to this erratic toss as a "butterfly pitch."

The threat of a runner stealing second is the most common concern for a catcher, represents his longest throw, and sets up a cat-and-mouse-game between the pitcher, the catcher, and the baserunner and coaches that are directing traffic. Rick continued, "On a fast ball, a receiver can jump up or out and throw the daylights out of the ball. Not on a knuckleball. You have to wait and snatch it as it breaks and then make your peg. Maybe you'll be off balance. Perhaps you'll barely be able to catch the ball. All these elements favor the runner and reduce your chances of throwing him out stealing."

But when the reporter asked which hitters were likely to have the greatest success against a knuckleball pitcher, the trio of hurlers, Dutch Leonard, Johnny Niggeling and Roger Wolfe, chimed in with one accord: "The weaker ones." All agreed, including Ferrell, if you didn't try to kill it, one's chances of getting the bat on the ball and serving it beyond the infielders' reach represented the best approach for getting a hit.

For Ferrell, the classic example of their joint conclusion was Ted Williams. "Teddy Williams is a fine hitter. I consider him one of the best, if not the very best. He has rhythm, timing, and everything that goes to make up a fine batsman. But he has all kinds of trouble with a well-pitched knuckleball. He overswings." After being asked about the damage inflicted to the catcher's throwing hand by knuckleballs and the challenge of catching them, Ferrell concluded: "I say that the best way to approach a day with a knuckleball pitcher is to resolve to yourself: 'Those I can't catch, I'll run down.' You'll save yourself a lot of grief." His instructions to his pitchers were basic: "Let's just don't walk anybody."[9]

Record-wise, Rick wanted to overtake Schalk's American League record, but also had his sights on Hartnett's all-time record and beyond. Before the season got underway, he publicly stated his ambition to play four more years. Always a competitor and a man with great pride, Rick Ferrell was conscious of the legacy he wanted to establish.

The Nats opened in Philadelphia on April 7, 1945, and in a free-for-all, won, 14–8. By month's end, they were one game over .500, with a 6–5 record. Third baseman Hillis Layne recalled his teammate, Rick, in a 2003 telephone interview.

HILLIS LAYNE: He was the best, best thing. He was quiet; he was smart. In all my years, the players were so kind to each other. They roasted a pig outside of Maryland. We didn't have very much agitation or drinking or anything. Back then, we didn't know about dope or any of the drugs much. That was a good thing.

We were playing the Yankees in Yankee Stadium and I was playing third, of course, your dad was catching. This player—(George) Sternweiss with the Yankees, good basestealer, comes into third base and so Rick flipped that ball to me. So, I reached out to get it, and [the runner] was almost sliding in safe, and I put that ball on him, and you know what? I think I broke my index finger on my left hand. I told Rick later, 'We got THAT guy out, didn't we?' And we just laughed.

When he managed, Ted Williams said, "Washington had the best four pitchers that he had ever faced: Johnny Niggeling, Roger Wolff, Mickey Haeffner, and the main one: Dutch Leonard, all knuckleballers. And your daddy was the ONLY one who could go out and catch them without his masks and his chest protector. He didn't have to wear his equipment. He could catch Leonard and those knuckleballs, just dancing like butterflies. I just can't say enough about him. I can't believe he was as nice as he was. I was blessed. Now they have to have steroids. I can't believe

The 1945 Washington Senators team enjoys a pig roast in Baltimore, Maryland, during an off-day during the season. Encircling the pig, from left to right: A fan, Fred Vaughn (second base), Rick Ferrell (catcher), unknown man in white hat, Harlan Clift (third base), unknown man in shadow, George Myatt (second base), Hillis Layne, behind pig (third base), George Binks (right field), Al Evans (catcher), Joe Kuhel (first base), and Mickey Haefner (pitcher).

the difference in the game. We didn't make much money — but the love of the game was there. We set the stage for the guys today — kept baseball alive during the war.

The sun shone much brighter on the Capitol City boys in June, as they compiled an impressive 16–10 mark for the month, moving into the first division. In one of his best offensive games of the season on June 2, Rick Ferrell knocked in four runs with a double and a triple to help propel the Nationals to an 8–1 triumph over Chicago. Next, the Yankees came calling and Washington took two of three as a sharp Dutch Leonard limited the New Yorkers to four hits in a 4–0 shutout victory on June 6. Of course, Ferrell was behind the plate to call and catch this masterpiece, and he contributed an important hit that kept a two-run rally alive. As the 1945 season would soon prove, the real strength of the Washington Senators was their four starting pitchers.

As he closed in on Ray Schalk's record, the media attention again focused on Rick's great career. A July 5 article by Shirley Povich in *The Sporting News* revealed that Ferrell heard a lot of foul language as he crouched behind the plate. "I guess I've had to listen to more profanity than any other man in baseball," suggested Ferrell. "Not that I minded, particularly. When you've got the hitters cussin', your club is in pretty good shape. They don't say anything when they're hitting." After that quite astute observation, Ferrell continued by illustrating the nature and reasons for this kind of venting. "Some of those guys are squawking at the umpires, and some of 'em just stand up there and cuss themselves out. You should a heard Bob Johnson the other day when he came to bat after dropping a fly ball that let in two runs.... What he said about himself was a caution: He told his left hand he ought to cut it off."

Ferrell estimated that he had caught about 400 pitchers in his seventeen-year career, citing Lefty Grove as the fastest pitcher he had ever caught, and the toughest hurler to catch as wild, fast southpaw Jack Krakaukas. During the 1938 through 1940 seasons, Krakaukas gave up an average of 92 walks a year, strong evidence of Ferrell's statement.

He thought Wes had the best control, who "even after he lost his stuff, he won 20 games with the Red Sox." Then perhaps for the first time, Rick revealed the jostling that went on between the pair when they were batterymates. "But sometimes we'd fuss," revealed Rick. "I had to tell him one day to stop shaking off my signs so much. He said 'I'm doing all right, you tend to your catching.' I said 'Okay, I'll catch you without signs.' I caught the rest of the game standing up, without crouching at all because I didn't have any signs to give, and we stayed mad for the rest of the day, but Wes won the game."

If Rick caught 400 hurlers, imagine how many hitters he tried to cross-up by calling for an unexpected pitch or location. Ferrell's most admired hitters included Charlie Gehringer (best batting stroke and the best eye), Ruth (most power), and Ted Williams (almost as fast as Ruth). Joe DiMaggio, Cecil Travis and Buddy Meyers also rated as artists up there. "But the toughest guy to pitch to was Al Simmons. Every time we got him out, it surprised me."

On July 5, Rick Ferrell attained his goal and caught his 1,721st game in Chicago to tie the American League "Most Games Caught" record that Ray Schalk set following the 1929 season. Schalk had spent seventeen of his eighteen-year career in the White Sox uniform and was in the stands for the predictable event. The two All-Star record-holders posed for photos before the game. Ferrell also delivered a hit during a three-run rally in the fifth inning, and when Eddie Lopat threw a pickoff attempt into the stands, Rick trotted home from third. The Senators had lots to celebrate; eight victories in the last nine games had moved them into second place.

The more important personal milestone was reached the next day, July 6, 1945, in St. Louis where his illustrious career had begun: Rick Ferrell established a new league record for most games caught. The 39-year-old receiver had made history in impressive fashion while demonstrating remarkable durability. The hotter-than-hot Senators made it five straight wins, whipping the

In a historic milestone, two future Hall of Fame catchers pose on July 5, 1945, the day Rick tied Ray Schalk's American League record for "most games caught." In this game against the Chicago White Sox, Ferrell caught his 1,721st game to tie the record, and in the next game played at his home ball park in St. Louis, Rick became sole holder of this coveted record for the next 43 years. (National Baseball Hall of Fame Library, Cooperstown, N.Y.)

Brownies, 6–3, in the opener of a twin bill; 13,801 fans witnessed this historic 1 hour and 45 minute game.

The next issue of *The Sporting News* designated Rick as "Player of the Week," with an article predicting he would likely also surpass Gabby Hartnett's major league record of 1,793 games caught. Ferrell was credited for his important role in the resurgence of the Washington Senators and his skillful handling of the knuckleball gang. The author noted that Rick seemed to be "improving with age." With typical modesty, Ferrell recognized his ageless endurance as the key factor in his ability to capture the American League record.[10]

In the Friday, July 13, 1945, edition of the *Washington Post*, Shirley Povich reported that star player and serviceman Buddy Lewis would soon be returning to action on the home front. In 2003, Buddy recalled Rick in a telephone interview.

BUDDY LEWIS: I was in Washington in '45 and we had five knuckleball pitchers: Wolff, Haeffner, Niggeling, Leonard, and another one — Pieretti. The knuckleball broke so irrationally — it would move from left to right, and up and down. So, the right idea was to wait for the ball to get there. Rick could catch 'em one-handed, and most of the time, he *did* catch one-handed. The sign for a knuckleball was just a fist — no fingers down. If there's a runner on second base, you have to do your signs differently because he could possibly get the signs. There were many, many times when I was at-bat that people would offer to holler and tell me what pitches were coming. But I didn't want to know — because you have to get prepared. If you're looking for one pitch and you get another one, well, it upsets your timing so bad. So, I never did prefer to have anyone tell me. The signs were: One finger equals fastball; Two fingers equals curve ball; Three fingers equals spit ball/changeup. If you wanted a change-of-pace on a fast ball, you'd put one finger down, but you'd work your finger back-and-forth. That could change everything. So, generally, if you want just a plain changeup, you'd probably put down three fingers and then, shake 'em, and that would be a change-of-pace. On a 0–2 count — you'd call a bean ball! Most managers in the majors back when I was playing coached on the baselines. Now the managers are on the bench. So the runner can't see into the dugout, so he flashes some signs to the third-base coach. Our system was almost infallible. We had three signs: you'd touch your cap; you'd touch your shirt; and you'd touch your trousers. Harris was a master at that.

August 1945 must rank among the most intense number of games played in any month in major league baseball history. Washington played thirty-nine games, made possible by thirteen doubleheaders, which is almost half of the days in the month! After eking out a 2–1 win on August 1, they moved back up to second place and came blazing out of the blocks. Winning doubleheaders on three consecutive days, the team also racked up a seventh straight win in the first game of a fourth consecutive twin bill! In this game, ex-serviceman Bert Shepard courageously hurled five-and-one-third innings in relief, permitting only three Red Sox hits. This was Shepard's only major-league appearance on the mound, following a severe combat wound that resulted in the amputation of a leg. Having been hit by one of Shepard's batting practice balls, Rick did not catch this game.

Sweeping the Cleveland Indians for five straight over three days and only a half-game behind, Washington won its 68th game on August 28 in Philadelphia, 6–5. Rick Ferrell pounded the winning blow, a line drive home run into the left-field stands. As the future would determine, this would be Ferrell's last trot around the bases, giving him 28 career home runs.

In the critical stretch drive that began on September 1, the 1945 Senators readied to overtake the first-place Detroit Tigers, and Rick Ferrell played his heart out. In the first game of a Wednesday doubleheader played on August 10, Washington won an eleven-inning, 2–1, victory on a clutch single by Ferrell. In a nip-and-tuck race where every game was critical, Washington and Niggeling dropped a painful loss on September 11 when, after hanging on to a 1–0 lead through eight innings, mental errors gave Chicago two runs in the ninth for a 2–1 victory. Rick had driven in the Nationals' only score in the seventh inning. Next the Nats swept three from Cleveland.

Beginning with back-to-back twin bills on September 15 and 16, sold-out crowds at Griffith Stadium were set for a five-game showdown between the second-place Washington Senators and the league-leading Detroit Tigers. The September 15 column, "This Morning with Shirley Povich," captured the tension: "For the Washington ball club, this is it"— meaning the home team had to win at least three games. If the Senators had an edge, claimed Povich, it rested with their fine pitching staff. "The Nats' pitchers have been carrying the club on their collective backs all season, and that's why the Nats have any chance to win the pennant."

This series—a do-or-die moment in a torrid race—began poorly for the home team, when the Tigers took both September 15 games against Leonard, 7–4, and Haefner, 7–3, while widening its lead over the Senators to 2½ games. Rick caught Leonard, getting two hits. A primed Rick caught two close games

On September 15, 1945, in Washington, Bob Maier, Detroit third baseman, is out at home plate in the fourth inning of the opener during a pennant race between the second-place Washington Senators and the first-place Detroit Tigers. Washington catcher Rick Ferrell makes the out as the Tigers win, 7–4. Notice the flimsy chest protector and small mitt, which provided his body little protection, used by Ferrell in 1945 when he caught four knuckleball starters. (William M. Anderson)

the next day on September 16, his first twin bill all season. Roger Wolff got one back, 3–2, from Newhouser. But Detroit countered with a 5–4 win against Niggeling. In each, Rick got a hit and a run scored. On September 18, a desperate Nats offense came alive, knocking out Dizzy Trout in the first round and walloping the Tigers, 12–5. Rick Ferrell enjoyed a two-for-four-day, driving in two runs and cracking a double. When Detroit left town, they were leading the race by 1½ lengths.

This stretch represented Rick's last run for the elusive league pennant, and he continued putting on the steam. Though the Senators lost 5–3 on September 21, they scored twice in the second frame, with Rick driving in the first run and scoring the second. In the third frame, he delivered one of three two-out singles which knotted the score at 3–3.

The schedule-makers determined that the Nationals would finish their season on September 23, a week ahead of the rest of the league, so that the Washington football team could use Griffith Stadium to practice. The rest of the American League played until September 30. As the 1945 season ended, the American League champion would be determined by the winner of a final game between Steve O'Neill's Detroit Tigers and Luke Sewell's St. Louis Browns. Either the Washington Senators would be number one if the Tigers lost, or the Tigers would win the game and the crown. Nats players could only wait through the endless week, hoping that fortune would crown their fine effort.

On Saturday, September 29, Nationals manager Bluege sent his four starting pitchers by train to Detroit, site of the potential one-game championship playoff between Washington and Detroit, if the Tigers lost in St. Louis. The four hurlers checked into two rooms at the Book Cadillac Hotel on Sunday afternoon, just as the critical Tigers-Browns game began at Sportsman's Park. They turned on the radio and huddled together to listen to the broadcast of the game.[11]

Since rain had fallen for three days in St. Louis, the final Sunday game was delayed fifty minutes. Virgil Trucks started for the Tigers, Nelson Potter for the Browns. In the sixth inning, Detroit's Hal Newhouser came in to relieve Trucks. Going into the ninth, the Browns led the Tigers by a run, 3–2, but a tiring Potter loaded up the bases with Tigers. As the rain continued falling, up to the plate stepped Tigers' slugger Hank Greenberg. On a one-one pitch, Greenberg connected, powering the ball into the left-field stands for a grand-slam home run to beat the Browns, 6–3. Washington's hopes for a playoff evaporated along with that hit. Detroit won the American League pennant, narrowly nosing out the Senators by 1½ games for a season record of 88–65 compared to the Nats' 87–67.

Hillis Layne who played third base in 33 games for the Nats in 1945, described the last hours of that season in a 2005 telephone interview: "In 1945, we almost won the pennant. We were at the stadium, and we had our gear and bags packed to go either to Detroit or home. When Hank Greenberg hit the home run — well, that was a devastating blow! It really was. I remember going back and saying, 'Oh — if we could only get into the World Series, it'll be great.' So, that was the last game ... we were some sad players. But we got so close — 1½ games." It was the closest Rick Ferrell ever came to winning a pennant during his 18-year playing career.

Washington finished 20 games above .500, winning at a .565 clip. The Washington express rode on the rails of a fine pitching staff. Together, the group compiled an efficient 2.92 ERA, best in the majors. They were tied for first in the American League with 19 shutouts, and remarkably, considering the knuckleballers, led the league with the fewest walks. Roger Wolff led the staff with 20 wins and an incredible 2.12 ERA. Leonard had 17 wins; Haefner, 16; Pieretti, 14; and Niggeling and Carrasquel gained seven victories each to round out the highly effective mound corps.

Rick acquired a .266 batting average (.325 slugging average), with 76 hits (12 doubles) and 38 RBIs in 286 at-bats. He caught 83 games for a .990 fielding average, with 331 putouts, 21 passed balls, and four errors. At age 39-going-on-40, he figured 1945 would be his last year behind the plate. An undated clipping from Ferrell's Hall of Fame file noted, "In the 1945 season, Ferrell was charged with 21 passed balls, the equivalent of a catcher's error when the missed throw permits a runner to advance a base. What made this particularly embarrassing for Rick was that he had the reputation of being one of the slickest glove men in the business."

The end of World War II in both Europe and the Far East in 1945 brought a flood of quality players back home to rejoin their pro baseball teams. A few hundred players had kept "America's favorite pastime" alive in the United States for the four years, 1942 through 1945, during their absence. Bill Gilbert, in his book about wartime baseball, *They Also Served*, wrote: "Rick Ferrell said he felt that the baseball players during that war were doing their part to help the war effort by giving fans something to take their minds off the suffering and hardships that surrounded them. 'I felt I was making a contribution in my own way.'" Rick said the other players who were overage or had physical deferments felt the same way. "It was the best thing you could do."[12]

8

❖ ❖ ❖

1946–1949

From Catcher to Coach

After their second place finish in an exceptional 1945 season, the Senators' optimism remained strong, as they anticipated being in the 1946 pennant race as well. Winning the pennant became an attainable goal, and they made only one player transaction of any note, swapping George Case to Cleveland for outfielder Jeff Heath. Perhaps added optimism in Washington came from the return of a number of talented players from the military.

In late December, Wes Ferrell was back in the sports pages. He had been hired to manage the Lynchburg (Va.) Cardinals of the Piedmont League for the 1946 season.

With war restrictions off, teams returned to warmer sites for their 1946 spring training camps. The Nationals opened camp in Orlando, Florida, on February 16 at Tinker Field, named for the famous Cubs infielder, Joe Tinker. For the first time in seventeen years, since 1926, Rick Ferrell would not report to his team as an active player. He told the press he would have retired following the 1944 season, except he wanted to break the record for the most games caught.

Manager Ossie Bluege returned for his fourth season at the helm of the Nationals, joined by six coaches: Rick Ferrell, Joe Judge, Clyde Milan, Nick Altrock, Joe Fitzgerald and Bert Shepard. When Ferrell signed on as a coach, a sportswriter in the January 27, 1946, *Washington Post* was hardly ready to concede that he shouldn't continue behind the plate, stating, "Rick Ferrell has been signed by Griffith as a coach, but may still be the Nats' best catcher." Ferrell, however, was hired to work with catchers and pitchers. Catchers Al Evans, back from last season, and ex-serviceman Jake Early, former first-string receiver, were the top candidates to replace Ferrell as backstop.

The overhaul of the team, caused in large part by the return of players from the armed services, was regulated by an act passed by Congress requiring businesses to offer servicemen their regular pre-war jobs. Owner Clark Griffith publicly announced, "We're obliged to put our returned veterans back on the same job they held before they went into the service, and that's how we're going to start out. If they fail, we'll have to make changes, of course, but those boys are going to get a good shot at their old jobs."[1] Thus, Griffith projected that Mickey Vernon would start at first base, Gerry Priddy at second, Cecil Travis at short, Sherry Robertson at third, Steve Spence in the center field, Buddy Lewis in right, and Jake Early behind the plate. All of these position players were ex-servicemen.

Suffering with a sore back made Rick a temporary casualty. With his usual good humor, he joked with the February 22 *Post*: "It looks like this coaching profession is too strenuous for me." Later he must have felt snake-bit, for when catching batting practice, a foul ball ricocheted off his mask, cutting his ear.

Rick Ferrell was the kind of person that the media liked to engage, knowing he would consistently share his honest opinions. The practice of knocking batters down or driving them off the plate had always been a subject of interest. When asked about whether he ever called for a knockdown pitch, writer Shirley Povich wrote, "Rick Ferrell, now a coach after nearly 20 years as a big league catcher, never would admit that he called for a bean ball. When somebody suggested that you'd ask for a dust-off pitch if your grandmother was up there at the plate, Ferrell would only say, 'No, I wouldn't, but I might brush her back a bit.'"[2]

Washington opened at home on April 16, 1946, with 30,372 ebullient fans in attendance. A smiling President Harry Truman threw out the first pitch, but the excitement subsided after the ninth inning when the Red Sox recorded the final out in a 6–3 victory. The Nats started poorly, losing four straight and six of the first seven. By month's end, they had sunk to sixth place, having won only five of thirteen games.

June saw the team experience its longest losing and winning streaks, six in number. After winning its sixth consecutive victory, Washington stood at 28–19, the high-water mark for the season. All season long the Nats hung around .500, never deviating more than two or three games on either side of a breakeven record.

In late April, the press reported that charges had been filed by the American Baseball Guild against Clark Griffith "for allegedly engaging in unfair labor practices." According to a story in the April 30 *Washington Post*, Griffith had been discouraging players from joining the union, spoken disparagingly about the guild, and used intimidation to quell union organizers. Calling the charges "ridiculous," Griffith stated: "I have never talked to my players about joining a baseball union, and I don't intend to. I did defend the reserve clause that prevents players from jumping from one team to another, and I always shall defend it as the only method baseball can operate successfully."

Evidence of the emergence of a union involving Washington's players again surfaced when the July 24 *Post* reported that Bobo Newsom had been elected their player representative. "I have my own ideas what adjustments the players should ask for, including minimum pay, particularly for first year men, and pensions," stated Newsom. "But I want the players to submit their ideas." The next day, July 25, Newsom released the details of the player demands to the *Washington Post*. The list of so-called grievances included a $5,000 minimum salary for first-year players, thirty days' severance pay for released players, expense reimbursement and per-diem allowances during spring training, a rent subsidy if traded to another city, and a cut of the sale price paid for a minor league player. Thus was the beginning of the players union in baseball.

Winning and losing streaks were of relatively short duration in September, making for an unexciting finish in a pennant race in which the Nats never participated. One happy note included Nats first baseman Mickey Vernon's leading the A.L. in batting with a .354 average, just ahead of Ted Williams' .343.

The 1946 season ended on Sunday, September 29, in Boston, following five victories in the final six games, to net the Nationals a season record of 76–78 and a fourth place berth, 28 games behind the champion Boston Red Sox. The Nats finished with the worst fielding average in the league at .966, and they had missed Rick Ferrell being their catcher. His two replacements, Early and Evans, ranked first and second in the league for committing the most errors.

Rick returned to Greensboro for the off-season, living in a house on Walker Avenue where Ruth would again become pregnant. He enjoyed regrouping back in Guilford County, the smell of the pines, and reconnecting again with his beloved parents, brothers, and their families close by.

Rick returned as a coach for the Senators to start the 1947 season. But after their two chief knuckleballers, Dutch Leonard and Roger Wolff, were dispatched to other clubs, he made known his desire to return as a player-coach. Although he had turned 41 the past October, Washington's management figured Rick was still primed to play and re-activated him as a catcher. However, he was not only gifted with strong genes, but also had maintained his constant playing weight (160 lbs.) and strong stamina by staying physically active during the off-season. Also during the winter, Rick was prospering as a "partner in North Carolina's largest juke box distributing agency which nets him many times more money than his baseball contract."[3]

By late March as spring training was winding down, Manager Ossie Bluege was ready to announce his starting lineup. Bluege expected Al Evans to continue as his number one catcher, but a bum knee put him out of action. Thus the catcher's job went to the ever-reliable Rick Ferrell.

Rick's fellow coaches on the 1947 Senators were Clyde Milan, Sammy West, John Fitzgerald, and Nick Altrock. The pitching corps that Ferrell would help to handle did not appear particularly strong, and some of the slots were not yet assured. Even before he had been activated, Shirley Povich was promoting Ferrell's value to the club. "At least when Rick Ferrell is in there, we'll be rid of one weakness: every club in the league was stealing our signs last season," wrote Povich in the March 22 *Post*.

Washington visited Fenway Park to open the season in Boston on April 15, losing 7–6. They proceeded to lose the first three games, before reversing their fortunes with a three-game winning streak. By the end of April the Nats had built up a 16–19 record and occupied the sixth rung in the standings. For the first time, Rick Ferrell acquired a nickname, "B.B.," which meant in the parlance of his teammates "Big Brain." Known as intelligent, Ferrell had always been a "coach on the field" type of guy that people listened to since he had something meaningful to say.

Early Wynn quickly re-established himself as the ace of the pitching staff, racking up his seventh victory on June 11 on a nifty six-hitter as Washington bested the Browns, 4–2, at Sportsman's Park. With the score tied, 2–2, the Senators scratched out what would prove to be the winning run in the fourth on a walk. Ferrell's perfectly executed hit-and-run single got the runner over to third, and a fly ball off the bat of Wynn drove home the winning tally.

Before the end of June, owner Griffith announced that all of the remaining home games in their schedule would be televised. Many teams were concerned that televising games would hurt attendance, but presumably the contract Griffith signed was worth the risk.[4]

After a successful June, one game over .500, with a 14–13 record, the Senators began their descent. Opening July, they suffered through six straight losses on the road, as the pitching staff allowed an average of seven runs per game, and the seeds of dissension began to sprout.

In the first game of a doubleheader at Fenway Park on July 6, the Nationals committed six errors, allowing several unearned runs in a 7–4 loss. Starting pitcher Bobo Newsom left after five innings and entered the clubhouse, raging mad. He ripped off his uniform, castigating outfielder Stan Spence for an errant throw. The Senators had three errors in the first three innings and added three more before this horrible fielding exhibition ended. Ferrell was included among the guilty, as one of his throws ended up in center field, but he escaped Newsom's wrath, probably because of a blockbuster day at plate, going four-for-four with three doubles. "What's the sense of hustling when the whole team isn't?" barked Newsom. Apparently, Newsom's outburst reflected a growing feeling of team frustration beneath the surface.

After that drubbing, a New York sportswriter reported that Griffith was contemplating replacing Manager Bluege with Rick Ferrell. Upon hearing that statement, owner Griffith emphatically stated: "Nonsense! I'm not going to change managers, never do in mid-season. This talk of a new manager is a consequence of our six-game losing streak, and I haven't given a thought to making a change. Ferrell hasn't entered into my plans, anyway."[5]

The Nationals resumed play with a Thursday doubleheader on July 10 in Chicago and reversed the downward spiral by winning both contests. Ferrell caught the second game and was a big contributor offensively, collecting two safeties in three at-bats and driving in two runs.

The announcement was made that a special day of recognition would be held August 13 at Griffith Stadium to honor the great career of Cecil Travis. With that, a fan from Virginia wrote a letter advocating that Rick Ferrell also deserved similar recognition. She began by asking: "Do you know of one player on the Washington Senators who deserves to have a day set aside for him more than Rick Ferrell? He is certainly one of the best catchers in the American League, and I'd like to say now would be an ideal time to have a Rick Ferrell Day for a great catcher."[6] No Rick Ferrell Day ever resulted, however.

Things got ugly in August, for starting with a tough 1–0 loss to Boston on August 11, the overwhelmed Senators were defeated 11 games in a row, falling 20 games below .500. The rumblings of player discontent grew louder. On August 20, the *Washington Post* reported an allegation that eight players would quit the team if manager Bluege was not replaced. Apparently Bruce Hawkins of the *Evening Star* had written of the pending player revolt. Calling the story a "malicious bit of propaganda," Bluege threw down the gauntlet. "The time has come for a showdown," raged Bluege. "We are going to have a team meeting in Detroit tomorrow, I'll read the players the newspaper article, and if any or all eight of them admit that they made that statement, they are through." With that threat made, one wonders why Bluege would expect any player to own up to any criticism unless an aggregate of players thought their grievances were so severe, they could pressure the owner into firing the field boss.

"This whole business started in Chicago at the All-Star game when someone printed a story that I would be succeeded by Rick Ferrell next year," continued Bluege. "We held a meeting then, I read the team the story and pointed out that I was manager of the team and would continue so. That story was very embarrassing to Rick, and he told me so. He knew nothing about it, and I was in the same boat." Bluege believed the extending losing streak was a major factor in the supposition that his job was in jeopardy. "I must confess that I don't know what to do to bring us a victory. I can't hit for the boys." Admitting that you don't know what to do is usually the wrong thing to say, but Griffith stuck with him.

Though the denials would be strong, Morris Siegel, this article's author, editorialized and stated that there were problems in the Senators' clubhouse. "From this reporter's observations, however, everything is not exactly lovey-dovey with the Nats. The protracted losing streak has a lot to do with their downcast spirits. They are a lifeless outfit who appear to have lost all zest for their profession and are merely playing out the schedule."

Bluege, and presumably Griffith, set out to dispel the adage that "where there's smoke, there's fire." As promised, Bluege held a team meeting while in Detroit for their four-game series. He read aloud the now infamous story and asked who had made the accusations. No one came forth. He then summoned reporter Hawkins into the clubhouse and told him that all but one player had denied making any criticism and had reaffirmed their loyalty to their manager.

He stated that Jerry Priddy's communication with Hawkins about a tiff he had with Bleuge set this whole thing off. Both "conspirators" denied having had such a conversation. A heated manager then accused Hawkins of snooping in his waste basket in search of information, stating that the club house boys had observed him rifling the trash basket. In a loud voice, Hawkins called Bluege a liar, and the verbal exchange heated up to a point where Bluege threw a couple of punches that missed the mark. Hawkins did not retaliate. Surprisingly, Bluege cooled off and offered a general apology, stating he didn't have any grievances with newspapermen.

However, the above happened after he had gotten "sworn" and signed statements from all of his players, although it is unclear whether Priddy cooperated. The statements, obviously prepared by an attorney, read: "I, being duly sworn, dispose and say, that the undersigned player of the Washington baseball club, of my own free will and accord, do hereby denounce the derogatory and malicious statements written about our manager, Ossie Bluege, in an article appearing in the Washington Evening Star, in the issue of August 20, 1947. I, as a member of the Washington club, deny having made any of the statements as published in the article by Mr. Burton Hawkins in said issue. I, furthermore, deny the existence to my knowledge of any dissension on our club, nor do I hold any grievance, ill feeling, or malice toward Mr. Bluege personally, or as manager." This amazing transaction vividly illustrates how the balance power heavily tilted toward management before the emergence of a stronger players union.

That summer another baby presented herself to Rick and Ruth in Washington, D.C. On August 21, 1947, a third daughter, Kerrie Carpenter, was born. Rick was with the team in Detroit to play a five-game series and caught a quick flight back to Washington to be with Ruth during her A.M. delivery, arriving after-the-fact. The couple now had two daughters, six years apart in age.

With some fight left in them, the Nats took both four-game series with Philadelphia and New York for a combined record of six wins and just two defeats. In their Labor Day doubleheader against the A's, Washington first shut down the home team, 4–0. The Nats' bats came alive in the second game for an exhilarating 7–4 victory. Rick Ferrell led the way with four hits, evenly divided between singles and doubles, in five tries. Philadelphia landed a heavy blow in the final contest when Bill McCahan hurled an absolute gem — a no-hitter — in which he faced only 28 batters.

Needing re-enforcements from all sources, the Nationals had elevated an unknown rookie pitcher to the front line. Scott Carey, 23, in just his second year of pro ball, had pitched in Class D the preceding summer, and now found himself on the hill in a game against Philadelphia. After he'd recorded three straight victories, the press seemed enamored by the success of such a raw-boned kid. Bluege expressed great exuberance in assessing the youngster. "He's got the courage of a lion," stated the manager. But the old pro behind the plate was a little more reserved. He, too, liked Carey's confidence, but he didn't sugarcoat his personal appraisal. "He hasn't got too much, but whatever it is, he's winning with it, and that's what counts," said Ferrell.[7] Reality soon struck: the young hurler never won another game and was soon gone from "The Show" after appearing in just 23 games.

The team played a little better the final month of the season, winning 12 and losing 16. Their sixth consecutive loss on September 15 would be Rick Ferrell's final game as an active player in a big league uniform. He left without fanfare or curtain calls, and fortune did not provide one last moment of glory. He went quietly. Only the visiting Tigers were roaring, as they pounded Senators' pitchers for 20 hits.

For the Washington ball club, the 1947 season mercifully ended on September 28 with a meaningless victory, only their 64th in a season that must have felt infinitely long. Their seventh place finish and 90-loss season left them 33 games behind the World Series–bound Yankees. Hard feelings extended into the winter when the Nationals did a little housecleaning by dispatching Jerry Priddy to St. Louis in a straight cash deal, after "being charged with leading a player revolt against Manager Ossie Bluege," stated the December 8 *Washington Post*.

Though he played in a career-low 37 games, Rick bowed out with admirable numbers: a .303 batting average, 11 doubles among his 30 hits, and a fielding average of .994 with just one error. On December 29, 1947, the Washington Senators released Rick Ferrell as a player. In his long 18-year career, he had played in 1,884 total games, catching 1,806. (Due to a disputed game back in 1933 when Ferrell caught for both the Browns and the Red Sox, some thought his number of games caught totaled 1,805. *The Sporting News* and Elias Sports Bureau determined that Ferrell caught 137 games in 1933, but the *Baseball Encyclopedia* differed, stating he'd caught only 136 games that season. Rick maintained that the game counted and that his record was 1,806.)

Rick recorded a lifetime batting average of .281 with 1,692 hits, 321 doubles, and 734 runs batted in. In 6,028 at-bats, he struck out a mere 277 times and acquired 931 walks for an on-base percentage of .378. While always a steady clutch hitter, Ferrell's outstanding fielding prowess had attracted the most attention. With a sparkling overall fielding average of .984, the catcher amassed 7,248 putouts, second only to Dickey, and 1,127 assists while committing only 135 errors.

Ferrell had retired as an active player after 18 seasons behind the plate. However both the Washington Nationals and Rick wanted to continue the relationship, so Ferrell returned for the 1948 season exclusively as a coach. When pitchers and catchers assembled in Orlando for spring training on February 28, 1948, Ferrell drew permission to report a week later.

After a dismal 1947 season of 90 losses, Ossie Bluege departed as skipper while ownership brought in rookie manager Joe Kuhel. Kuhel, 41, had ended his playing career in 1947, getting into just three games as a member of the Chicago White Sox. An 18-year veteran, Kuhel was well known in the Capital

City, having spent ten-plus seasons as their stellar-fielding first baseman, compiling a .277 lifetime batting average.

Manager Kuhel probably allowed his excitement to mask reality, because, fortunately, he didn't completely comprehend the challenges that waited. His managerial career would be over after just two seasons at the helm of these struggling Senators, and his losing record would rank among the worst.

After dropping their home opener on April 19, 1948, to the visiting New York Yankees, the losses began to pile up, with no breaks for losers. Kuhel got a real taste of how unfair baseball could be when he became certain that the umpires were in conspiracy against his ball club well into the 1948 season. The ten-day suspension of umpire Bill McGowan on July 20 for allegedly swearing and abusing Washington's players seemed to be catalyst for retaliation. Kuhel was ejected for the first time in his career on July 20 and was chased again later in the week. Sid Hudson and Rick Ferrell were the next to be banished in separate games, following the skipper's second ejection.

Manager Kuhel wanted to appeal his concerns to the American League President Will Harridge, but wasn't supported by the team's owner. "Our umpires are not the kind of men who would rub it in on a ball club," said Clark Griffith. The manager continued to have a decidedly different opinion. "We can't remain quiet and peaceful if we think we have been wronged, yet at the same time, we can't protest without having the threat of being chased hung over us," stated Kuhel. "What must we do?"[8] Unfortunately, he and the players received neither support nor sympathy from their owner.

The team lost 19 games out of 29, ending July in sixth place with a 40–52 record, 16 games out. The wreck of a season escalated in the final two months as a battered team stumbled toward the end. This season of misery produced only 56 wins against 97 defeats for a .366 winning percentage.

During the 1948 off-season, Rick purchased an enormous English Tudor mansion at 1602 West Market Street in Greensboro for Ruth and his two daughters. Since busy West Market was the main street leading downtown, the enormity of this house clarified to passers-by that their local farm boy had made good. The extra space was necessary when Ruth gave birth to their first son on St. Patrick's Day, March 17, 1949. Named Richard Benjamin Ferrell, Jr., after his father, he joined his two older sisters, who were 18 months and seven years old.

In 1949, Rick returned to coach for the Senators, with particular responsibility for working with the catchers. The club had two aging veterans, Evans and Early, and undoubtedly was anticipating a transition to younger receivers. The Washington Senators began their 1949 season on the right foot, edging the Athletics, 3–2, on April 18, before hustling off for the Yankees' opener the next day at Yankee Stadium. One win was quickly followed by a seven-game losing streak, as the squad won only two of nine encounters to finish the month in seventh place.

However the Nats bounced back on the road from May 3 to 11, winning

The Ferrells lived in this English Tudor home on West Market Street in Greensboro, North Carolina, from 1948 to 1951. Located on the central downtown thoroughfare, its stately grandeur displayed the major league success attained by the town's local farm boy.

nine straight games against Chicago, St. Louis, Cleveland, and Detroit. They finally lost — a tough one on May 12 to the Tigers, 2–1 — but nonetheless, returned home to a euphoric welcome. Enthusiastic over their winning Senators, 10,000 exuberant fans greeted the team's arrival. Writing for the May 16 *Washington Post*, Herb Heft sounded the trumpet. "Washington's conquerors of the West, Those Wondrous Nats, received a hero's welcome yesterday from 10,000 hungry citizens, who greeted them at Union Station and watched them receive the key to the city at the District Building."

This epitomized the excitement that baseball could generate, but these hopeful fans had no conception of the collapse that would eventually wreck their hopeful dreams. Following a convincing 9–3 victory over the White Sox on June 21, a slow slippage began to occur. On a road trip during July 16–26, the floodgates opened and the Nats were washed downstream by an eleven-game losing streak that left them, somehow, still in seventh place.

August 1–7 brought a string of seven consecutive defeats. Winning two of the next three, the team then racked up another twelve straight losses from August 12 through 21. By the end of August, the Nationals had 26 beatings for the month and an 84-loss total for the season.

September 1–9 was more painful as the Nationals lost seven-of-eight games to the White Sox, Red Sox, and Athletics. Washington completed the 1949 schedule at home on October 2 by winning only their 50th game, this one against the Philadelphia A's, who they had defeated back in the season opener. In between, the Nats lost 104 times, finishing three games behind the perennial doormats, the St. Louis Browns, and 47 games back of the pennant-winning Yankees.

Rick Ferrell bowed out gracefully in late November 1949. "I talked to Griff from Baltimore Thursday night," reported Ferrell in an undated scrapbook article from the *Greensboro News and Record*. "The resignation was agreeable to all concerned. I have enjoyed my stay at Washington, but believe a change will be best for me and the club. My plans for the future are indefinite. But I think I will remain in the American League, probably as a coach again. I won't know anything definite until after the major league meetings next week."

Caught in the back-and-forth of the St. Louis–Washington player express, Rick had had his longest tenure with the Washington organization — eight plus seasons of losing. In his most recent stint over the past six years, the Nationals had averaged 87 losses a season. Fortune had not been especially generous to Rick Ferrell. In all his years, he had never gotten to a World Series, having been traded from St. Louis to Washington just before the Browns' pennant-winning 1944 season. While with the Senators the second time, his team made a valiant run for the flag in 1945, yet was nosed out by Detroit, losing by just 1½ games. Rick had been selected to American League All-Star teams eight times and the "dandy catcher" retired from his playing days in possession of the American League record for most games caught.

PART II

Front Office

9

❖ ❖ ❖

1950–1958

The Detroit Tigers' Coach and Scout

Joining the Detroit Tigers again brought Rick's baseball career full-circle: he was returning to the club that had originally signed him back in 1925. This time, however, Detroit wouldn't let him get away. For the next forty-two years, Rick would work his way up to—and stay in—the Tigers' front office. The Detroit Tigers' story would directly interweave with Rick Ferrell's story.

The year 1950 saw the United States engaged in another war—the Korean War—with concern heightened by the spread of communism. Baseball again provided a balm for the American public's anxiety. In February Boston Red Sox slugger Ted Williams signed the largest contract in major league history: $125,000.

In 1949, former Yankees third baseman Red Rolfe, a ten-year veteran with six World Series under his belt, had begun managing the Tigers, taking them to a fourth-place finish behind the Yankees, with an 87–67 record. All-Star third baseman George Kell had barely nosed out Ted Williams for the American League batting title on the last day of the season, .3429 to .3427. Pitcher Virgil Trucks had garnered a 19–11 record, with the second lowest ERA in the American League, 2.81; southpaw Hal Newhouser went 18–11.

On February 27, 1950, Rick left his family at the West Market Street house to report for coaching duties at the Tigers' spring training camp in Lakeland, Florida. While Rolfe encouraged wives to accompany their ball-playing husbands to spring training, Rick abstained. Ruth and his three young children remained home in Greensboro for the entire seven-month, March-through-September baseball season while Rick coached up north in Detroit.

In Lakeland, Rick joined Ted Lyons and Dick Bartell on Red Rolfe's talented coaching staff in 1950. A Chicago White Sox pitcher for 21 years (260–230, ERA of 3.67), Ted Lyons had been on the first A.L. All-Star team with Rick and would be enshrined in the Baseball Hall of Fame in 1955. Former 18-year National League shortstop Dick Bartell had a .284 lifetime batting average with 2,165 hits. Rolfe told the *Detroit Free Press* in April, "I am most fortunate in

After joining the Tigers coaching staff in 1950, one of Rick's special assignments was tutoring catching prospect Frank House (left). Detroit had been searching for an accomplished receiver who could hit since Birdie Tebbetts left the team after the 1946 season. (William M. Anderson)

having so competent a coaching staff as Dick Bartell, Ted Lyons, and Rick Ferrell. There is no better combination in the league."[1]

During the off-season Tigers general manager Billy Evans had acquired Browns second baseman Jerry Priddy, Senators relief pitcher Paul Calvert, and Yankees first baseman Dick Kryhoski. Catchers in camp included $70,000-bonus-baby Frank House, 20, whom Rick was hired to develop, but who would only play five games in 1950. The *Washington Post* reported on May 7: "The Detroit Tigers are five deep in catchers. In addition to Aaron Robinson and Bob Swift, their regulars, Joe Ginsberg and Frank House, are on the active list, and there's Rick Ferrell to do the receiving in the bullpen."[2] Catchers Rick and Bob Swift had been St. Louis Browns' teammates back in the early 1940s, alternating games behind the plate.

In his journal, Red Rolfe described the camp's opening: "Pitchers start throwing the first day. Bartell led conditioning and running. For infield drills, coaches hit grounders and fungos to infielders and outfielders, and the squad played pepper games. Pitchers were to master the fundamentals of covering first base, running to third base on a squeeze play, and the skill of bunting."[3] Under no circumstance did Rolfe fraternize with his ballplayers.

Pitcher Virgil Trucks in camp that season, recalled in a 2007 telephone interview seeing Rick.

VIRGIL TRUCKS: Rick was a player-coach, you might say. He worked with me. Knowing him like I did — since I first came into baseball — I put my trust in him, and he was a person you *could* trust. I know — I assume — that *all* pitchers felt that way about Rick: they knew they could trust him.

One of the nicest people I ever met was Rick Ferrell. He was a good person, an easy-going person — even after he became a coach with Detroit, and then moving up into the front office after he finished coaching. That's exactly why he progressed like that — he was a man that you wanted to stick around. Detroit kept him and I was glad that they did. Rick was a good catcher and helped me in some things since we didn't have coaches in the minor leagues.

Back in Detroit Rick arranged his living quarters at a downtown hotel near Briggs Stadium, the historic double-decker ballpark where the Tigers played, named for the club's current owners, the Walter O. Briggs family. As a player on opposing teams, Ferrell had caught dozens of games there against Mickey Cochrane, Hank Greenberg, and Charlie Gehringer. An opera-house style ballpark, the upper deck rose straight up on all sides, enveloping the fans, blocking the city views, and creating an intimacy for spectators to focus solely on the game in a singular, baseball reality. Its dimensions measured 467' to center field where the 125-foot flagpole stood, 370' to right field, and 345' to left field, with a seating capacity of 53,000.

The 1950 season began on the road April 18 with Detroit pitcher Freddie Hutchinson edging out Cleveland's Bob Lemon, 7–6. The celebratory Opening Day, April 21, awoke Briggs Stadium in downtown Detroit, with Rick coaching third base. Virgil Trucks started for Detroit against Rick's ex-batterymate, White Sox knuckleballer Mickey Haefner, winning 4–1.

Leading the American League with a 13–6 record until May 16, the crew fell to second place and veteran Virgil Trucks (3–1) developed a sore pitching arm that would disable him for the season. The Tigers won seven straight during June 1–6; third baseman George Kell hit for the cycle in game one of a doubleheader at Shibe Park on June 2. By June 10 after sweeping a Red Sox series, they regained first place where they remained most of the summer and by August 30, were 77–46.

On the long train rides, Red Rolfe used to play gin rummy with his coaches, always partnering with Rick. The two would play Lyons and Bartell and win for their "meal money."

Trouble began on August 30 when the team dropped to second place (for only the second time all season) and ricocheted between second and first place the remaining weeks. The Cleveland Indians proved the Tigers' nemesis. Bob Lemon pummeled them, 12–2, on September 29 in Detroit—a victory that clinched the American League pennant for the Yankees.

With a 95–59 won-loss record in 1950, Red Rolfe's Detroit Tigers placed second in the American League, three games out. *The Sporting News* named Rolfe the Manager of the Year. George Kell's .340 batting average was second in the American League, and he led all A.L. third basemen in fielding (.982). The celebrated season represented another new beginning with the Detroit Tigers for Rick Ferrell.

That fall Rick returned to Greensboro and his grand English Tudor mansion on busy West Market Street to spend the off-season with Ruth and their three children, Rick Jr., 1½; Kerrie, 3; and Maureen, 9. Rick's parents, Mother and Daddy Ferrell, and brothers, particularly Wes and George, and their children lived nearby. Brother George and wife Kate had a girl and boy, Bonnie and George Jr., as did Wes and wife Lois, with Gwenlo and Wesley Jr., adding another generation to the Ferrell lineage.

In early 1951 after a near-accident with Rick Jr. on busy West Market Street, the Ferrells sold that house, moving to a quieter neighborhood on the less-traveled Madison Avenue near Starmount Forest Golf and Country Club. In February, Rick's brother George, a five-year St. Louis Cardinals scout, was hired to manage the Goldsboro, North Carolina, minor league team in the Coastal Plain League.

For the 1951 season, Red Rolfe served another year as manager at an estimated $40,000 salary, retaining his coaching staff of Ferrell, Lyons, and Bartell. Reportedly the entire Detroit Tigers payroll of players, manager, and coaches amounted to $600,000.

On March 1, 1951, spring training began promptly at 10:00 A.M. in Lakeland, Florida. Rolfe, always a stickler for fundamentals and structure, established the following rules: "Stay out of the clubhouse; no poker (gin rummy and hearts were OK at low stakes); midnight curfew." Spring training drills emphasized team hitting and power, pitchers' bunting skills, and baserunning.[4]

The pitching staff returned with Virgil Trucks, Fred Hutchinson, Dizzy Trout, Ted Gray, and Hal Newhouser. Left-handed rookie pitcher Billy Hoeft, just out of high school, threw in camp. Coach Ferrell observed to *The Sporting News*: "He doesn't act like a Southpaw. He's always around the plate. He's not real fast. He's just starting to work on a good curve, but he has great control, a good change-up, and a very deceptive motion."[5]

Pitcher Ted Gray remembered Ferrell in a 2007 telephone interview: "It's hard to say anything bad about Rick because he was such a great guy — a good, good guy. He was a coach of the team when I was there and the other coach was Ted Lyons, also a super guy. We called them the Brute and the Beast. Rick was the Brute."

But the Tigers' spring training team displayed mediocre hitting and pitching that foreshadowed the dismal upcoming season. George Kell optimistically wrote in his column, "The Tigers are not as bad as spring training games would have us look."[6]

As a coach, not much was written about Rick during the 1951 season. He was at third base on Opening Day, April 17, 1951, with 43,000 fans at Briggs Stadium to see Detroit pitcher Hal Newhouser lose to Cleveland's Bob Lemon, 2–1. For another season the Cleveland Indians would prove the Tigers' undoing, winning 10 games and losing only one — the last — against Detroit. A boon to the team was the return of injured George Kell to the lineup.

In a May 27 victory, Virgil Trucks, in his first start, beat the St. Louis Browns' Stubby Overmire, 3–2. Everybody hoped this signified the return of his pitching arm since Trucks had not won a game in almost a year — since May 13, 1950.

By May 30, 1951, Detroit was lodged in fifth, 17–20, which became the team's permanent residence for much of the season. From June through August, the Tigers couldn't gain any ground. On July 1, Cleveland fastballer Bob Feller pitched a brilliant 1–0 no-hitter against Detroit's Bob Cain.

Rick and 52,000 fans welcomed baseball greats to Briggs Stadium when the Detroit Tigers hosted the 18th Annual All-Star Game on July 10, 1951, during Detroit's 250th anniversary celebration. Tigers George Kell and Vic Wertz both hit home runs, although the National League prevailed, 8–3.

On August 10 of a mediocre season, the Tigers announced sweeping front office changes. Former Tigers second baseman Charlie Gehringer became vice president/general manager, replacing Billy Evans. Former catcher Muddy Ruel was named director of minor league clubs. Changes in player personnel included catcher Aaron Robinson's release, which left Bob Swift and rookie Joe Ginsberg to do the receiving, both of whom Rick had coached.

Rick used to tell the story of a memorable moment on August 19, 1951, when the Tigers met the Browns at Sportsman's Park for a doubleheader. In

Coach Rick Ferrell (right) talks with Detroit Tigers manager Red Rolfe (left) on the dugout steps after joining the Tigers coaching staff in 1950. Coaches Ferrell and Ted Lyons were retained by new Detroit skipper Fred Hutchinson following Rolfe's dismissal in July 1952. (William M. Anderson)

game two, Browns president Bill Veeck pulled a public relations stunt by sending in Eddie Gaedel, a 3'7" midget, to pinch-hit. Detroit's Bob Cain walked him on four pitches, but Gaedel never had another major league at-bat. The Tigers won that doubleheader, 5–2 and 6–2. When Gaedel died in 1962, the only baseball player to attend his funeral was Bob Cain.[7]

By September, Virgil Trucks had won his last six starts, including his 100th career victory on September 13. On September 30, the final game of the season, he won a pitcher's duel with Cleveland rookie Sam "Red" Jones. Having been defeated ten times by the Indians, Trucks finally edged Cleveland, 2–1, driving-in both Tiger runs in the seventh inning, himself!

In 1951, Red Rolfe's Detroit Tigers fell to the second division and fifth place in the American League with a final record of 73–81, 25 games out of first. George Kell's batting average reached .319; his .960 fielding average topped the league for all infielders. Slumping Hoot Evers' batting average dropped dramatically from .323 the previous year to .224 in 1951. Virgil Trucks recorded the best won-loss record at 13–8. Aging star Hal Newhouser recorded a 6–6 season, his first sub-par performance in eight years.

At season's end Rick hastened to North Carolina to be with Ruth, now eight months pregnant, and their three kids. The next three months would bring both ecstasy and anguish. On November 11, Ruth, 31, delivered her baby — a second son, Thomas Lyon Ferrell, making four children, two girls and two boys. But soon after, sorrow struck when "Mother Ferrell" (Alice), 72, who had lost her left eye to glaucoma, became gravely ill and, following a brief hospital stay, succumbed to stomach cancer on December 1. Alice had been the very heartbeat of the family, the gentle touch, the kind word. Married for fifty-three years, the seemingly invincible Rufus felt bereft without her. A somber Daddy Ferrell and his six sons buried Mother Ferrell in the family plot at New Garden Friends Cemetery, leaving them to deeply mourn her passing.

Sorrow flooded the Tiger organization, as well, when team president and principal owner Walter O. Briggs died on January 17, 1952. His son Walter O. Briggs, Jr., known as "Spike," took over the reins of the baseball corporation.

Like a blessing, Ferrell's third Opening Day as a Detroit coach came on April 15, 1952, but the Tigers stalled, losing their first eight games. Houtteman finally walloped the Indians in a 13–0 shutout April 26 for Detroit's first win, but the team had already plunged to eighth place — dead last.

A note in the May 15 *Washington Post* humorously referenced Coach Ferrell: "With Ted Lyons ailing, former Nats coach Rick Ferrell took over the first base coaching assignment for the Tigers today and looked extremely sharp, telling Mullin and Wertz to continue around the bases after they unloaded their home runs."[8]

A bright moment occurred on May 15, 1952, when at Briggs Stadium Virgil Trucks pitched the first of two no-hitters of this season. With Joe Ginsberg catching, no hits, no score, and two outs in the bottom of the ninth, Vic Wertz pounded a homer off Washington pitcher Bob Porterfield for a Tigers 1–0 win to preserve Trucks' no-hitter. The fans rollicked and rejoiced! Not since 1912, forty years earlier, had a Tigers pitcher hurled a no-hitter.

The May 28, 1952, issue of *The Sporting News* noted that catcher Joe Ginsberg caught Trucks' no-hitter in fewer than 200 games, a rare feat. Rick Ferrell had caught 1,806 games without getting a no-hitter. Former 19-year A.L. catcher and then–Tigers farm director, Muddy Ruel, who caught 1,413 games without a no-hitter, remarked with a sly grin: "Ginsberg caught a no-hitter early in his career. This must be evidence that catching has improved tremendously since old fellows like Rick and myself were around."[9]

In 2007, Joe Ginsberg reminisced from his Florida home about Rick in a telephone interview.

> JOE GINSBERG: My recollection of Rick is that he was a very mild-mannered man and he was just a nice guy. Being a catcher, we had a lot in common and we talked a lot about the position. He really was a very kind man. He was a coach. He didn't come right out and tell you what he thought you should do. He'd wait until you asked him, and then he'd give you suggestions, and he really helped me, I know that.
>
> He gave me some good tips and some good advice that helped me through my career. I sort of bugged him; he might not have liked it. But I always sought him out and said, "Now Rick, what about this?" about blocking the plate and blocking the ball. There's a lot to learn in the catching position ... calling signals and signs, and handling pitchers. There's a lot to learn and Rick knew a lot about it, I'll tell you.
>
> In my opinion, he was a gentleman. In every sense of the word, he was a gentleman, no doubt about it. He was a very quiet man, especially when he put the uniform on. What he said was interesting and everybody listened to him, but he wasn't outgoing; he was very mild. He was a quiet sort of a man, but whatever he said, everyone listened. When he spoke, he was speaking with some wisdom and he knew what he was talking about.
>
> I keep thinking about Rick and how he looked. We were about the same size; neither one of us were real big, like some of the catchers. But we were both pretty agile. He had a good arm and his eyes were good. We were alike. What a great career he had in baseball. I remember his brother, Wes, the pitcher. It was really something to have a pitcher and catcher in the same family.

On June 3, desperate to improve his last-place squad, GM Gehringer made an enormous nine-player trade with Boston, giving up Detroit's pride, George Kell, plus outfielder Hoot Evers, shortstop Johnny Lipon, and pitcher Dizzy Trout for infielders Johnny Pesky, Walt Dropo, Fred Hatfield, outfielder Don Lenhardt, and pitcher Bill Wright.

But these personnel changes failed to ignite the team, and on July 5, an exasperated Spike Briggs fired manager Red Rolfe and coach Dick Bartell, while retaining coaches Ferrell and Lyons. Rick coached third base, vacated by Bartell, and pitcher Freddie Hutchinson was hired as the fourteenth Detroit manager in 52 years, replacing Rolfe.

During the All-Star break, Rick flew home to Greensboro to visit his father,

79, who lay critically ill in bed. However, during the recess on July 12, 1952, only six months after his beloved Alice's death, Rufus himself died, perhaps partly due to a broken heart. Daddy Ferrell — who had educated himself, become a train engineer, started and maintained a successful dairy farm for his family, and raised seven strong sons— had been the driving force behind the Ferrell clan. His orphaned sons buried him beside Alice at New Garden Cemetery, but the death of both beloved parents within a half-year devastated Rick and his brothers, unlike anything before. Though too stoic to show his emotions, baseball, again, became the distraction from Rick's deep sorrow.

On July 15, the coach re-joined his team in Washington but from July 30 to August 14, Detroit lost 14 out of their 16 games. At Sportsman's Park on August 6, Browns pitcher Satchel Paige, 46, the oldest major leaguer ever to throw a complete game or a shutout, defeated the Tigers' Virgil Trucks, 1–0, in a twelve-inning pitchers' duel.

Rick was with the team on August 25 at Yankee Stadium to watch as Trucks became the third pitcher in major league history to pitch a second no-hitter in a single season. His 1–0 score matched that of his first no-hitter three months earlier. Ironically, Trucks' 1952 pitching record was 5–19.

Despite front office maneuvers, for the first time in their entire history, the Tigers finished last in the American League in 1952, 50–104, 45 games behind the Yankees. However, one bright hope for future seasons had presented itself in a University of Wisconsin rookie shortstop, Harvey Kuenn, 21, who played in 19 games and hit .325 in 80 at-bats.

Rick, 45, of course, returned home to North Carolina once the disastrous season ended, but life had changed there. With both parents now gone, the Ferrell brothers assembled often with their families. Rufus B. Ferrell and Sons Dairy Farm had been dismantled and divided among the six sons, and they often gathered on Sundays to fish at Wes and Lois' place, "Weslo Willows," with its five fishing lakes, their part of the Ferrell family farm.

In an early December baseball trade, again with the St. Louis Browns, three Tigers veterans— outfielder Johnny Groth and ten-year pitchers Virgil Trucks and Hal White — were sent west for outfielder Bob Nieman, infielder Owen Friend, and rookie J. W. Porter in return. In January, nine-year Tiger catcher Bob Swift, 34, left the player ranks to join the Ferrell-Lyons coaching staff.

The Tigers organization paid $120,000 for three young bonus players: southpaw Bob Miller, 17, ($60,000); outfielder from Baltimore Al Kaline, 18, ($35,000); and Canadian infielder Reno Bertoia ($25,000). All three saw limited action in 1953. They also obtained infielder Billy Hitchcock from Philadelphia and brought up outfielder Don Lund from Toledo.

When the Tigers opened 1953 against the Browns at St. Louis' Sportsman's Park, the opposing lineup resembled another intra-squad game: Ten former Tigers had been traded to the Browns over the past winter. On April 14, Opening Day, now–Browns pitcher Virgil Trucks started against the Tigers' Ned Garver, and the St. Louis "Revenge Club" of ex–Tigers proceeded to pound Detroit in a 10-run shutout. Trucks would beat his ex-team four times during the 1953 season, with no defeats.

Losing frequently in the first half recalled to fans the Tigers' painful previous year. May 31 found them seventh in the standings (10–31) midway through a 13-game losing streak that eventually dropped them to the bottom. On June 25, two new Tigers rookies debuted at Shibe Park against the A's: Al Kaline and Bob Miller. Kaline played right field for the first time ever. Conversely on July 5, veteran pitcher Hal Newhouser was released due to chronic shoulder pain after 15 years and 200 games with the Detroit Tigers.

Disproportionate losing continued for the rest of the season for a final sixth place finish, 60–94, 40½ games behind the Yankees. The lowly St. Louis Browns finished last again (54–100) and in 1954, club ownership moved the Browns to Baltimore. Thanks largely to Harvey Kuenn's hitting (.308; led the majors with 209 hits), the grim 1953 Tigers season had improved in the second half, and the shortstop was voted Rookie of the Year by the Baseball Writers' Association.

After releasing several veteran players, the Tigers also guillotined two veteran coaches at season's end: Ted Lyons and Rick Ferrell. Former players Bob Swift, Johnny Hopp, and pitcher "Schoolboy" Rowe would become the Tigers' coaches for 1954.

Rick, especially, was shocked by his sudden release, saying: "They told me I was doing good work, and the next thing, I was out. I can't understand it."[11] Detroit sportswriter Walt Spoelstra wrote in the October 14, 1953, issue of *The Sporting News* that both Rick, 48, and Ted Lyons, 53, were well-liked coaches in Detroit, but were pitching-catching specialists at a time when Detroit's youth movement required infield-outfield specialists to train the newcomers— an odd observation given that only one of the new coaches was an infielder and the other two, a former catcher and pitcher.

Ferrell packed up and returned to his family in Greensboro, uncertain of his direction or of where future paychecks would come from. Baseball was all the slender Southerner knew — all he'd ever done for twenty-seven years. Offers came in to manage minor league and college baseball teams, but Rick never wanted the pressure of managing, preferring to teach and coach, and so he waited.

When Tigers Director of Minor League Clubs John McHale called Rick in North Carolina with the opportunity to rejoin the Tigers as a minor league scout, a thrilled Ferrell eagerly accepted. The December 9 issue of *The Sporting News* reported that Tigers General Manager Muddy Ruel was "happy to have Rick Ferrell return to the club," adding that Rick would scout the Southeastern Region, consisting of North and South Carolina, and parts of Virginia and Tennessee, from his home in Greensboro. Teams generally regretted losing a fine baseball man like Rick, often wanting him back after the fact.

Rick as a family man in 1952 at home in Greensboro, N.C., with, from left to right, Kerrie, 4, Rick Jr., 3, and holding infant Thomas. Rick was a coach for the Detroit Tigers from 1950 to 1954, spending those seasons in Detroit.

On Rick and Ruth's thirteenth wedding anniversary, January 18, 1954, "Spike" Briggs hosted the annual pre-season Detroit Tigers party in Detroit. General manager Muddy Ruel and vice president Charlie Gehringer, both ex-players, welcomed their two new scouts, Rick Ferrell and Jack Tighe. Rick told sportswriter Walt Spoelstra during the occasion: "The Tigers will be much stronger this year. I'm optimistic about them. I think Detroit will be fighting for fourth place and could finish as high as second. Frank House, coming back from the Army, will help. So will several others."[12]

In 1954, the Detroit Tigers' six-tier farm system consisted of eight teams:

AAA	Buffalo Bisons (International League)
AA	Little Rock Travelers (Southern Association)
A	Wilkes-Barre Barons (Eastern League)
B	Durham Bulls (Carolina League)
C	Greenville Tigers (Cotton States League)
C	Idaho Falls Russets (Pioneer League)
D	Valdosta Tigers (Georgia-Florida League)
D	Jamestown Falcons (Pony League)

That season Rick established an office in his Madison Avenue home in Greensboro to begin the solitary job of scouting the Southeastern territory. After observing a player at least three times, Ferrell hand-wrote scouting reports in pencil, ranking abilities in hitting, throwing, catching, fielding, running speed, power and more on a rating scale, 1 to 5, with 5 being the best. In a hitter, he observed the swing, power, number of strikeouts, how the player reacted under different counts, adjusted to pitchers and a variety of pitches. Reports, with comments, were then forwarded to Briggs Stadium in Detroit and placed in their headquarter files. His first signing was 17-year-old, six-footer John Tsitouris, an American Legion high school pitcher from Monroe, North Carolina.

If Ruth expected her husband to be home more as a local scout, she was only partly correct, but at least he wasn't away for seven months! Rick would map out his master schedule for scouting trips — sometimes two weeks long — driving around North and South Carolina, stopwatch in hand, to observe prospects. Once he took Kerrie, 5, with him "scouting" a day game; they drove down long, dusty gravel roads through country pastures and shady forests for hours before finally reaching a baseball field in a backwoods clearing to "go see a kid pitch."

Scouts all knew each other and socialized at games, but scouting was highly competitive and each wanted to beat the other to prospects. They maintained secrecy about who they were scouting and where they were. If someone called Rick at home, he was told Rick was gone — but never where.

In March Rick re-joined the Tigers in Lakeland for spring training, instructing both major and minor league players. However, the third week of camp, he suffered a broken nose when hit in the face by a thrown ball. In September, Rick traveled to Georgia to watch the Army baseball tournament, reporting that Bubba Phillips was the best player he saw there. Phillips was signed by the Tigers, playing 95 games in 1955 before being traded to the White Sox for pitcher Virgil Trucks.

Rick's prediction expressed at the Tigers' pre-season party turned out to be prophetic in 1954. The Tigers did fight for fourth place, but lost, finishing fifth — a distant 43 games behind the A.L. champion Cleveland Indians — going 68–86 under Manager Freddie Hutchinson.

After a slow start, shortstop Harvey Kuenn powered a .306 average, stroking 201 hits, to tie with Nellie Fox for most in the American League. Another bright spot for the Tigers emerged in right fielder Al Kaline, 19, who finished 1954 with a .276 batting average, 43 RBIs, and four home runs. Did anyone imagine that the slender rookie would win the American League batting title the following season and become one of the greatest players in Detroit Tigers' history? Tigers scout Ed Katalinas did. On his scouting report he'd rated Kaline, at age 15, the best player he'd ever seen, immediately signing him to a contract at age 18 following his graduation from Baltimore's Southern High School, Kaline had gone straight to "The Show," by-passing the minors.

Following another season of futility, Hutchinson resigned as manager. Rick's former, and favorite, manager, Stanley "Bucky" Harris, just released from the Washington Senators after finishing in sixth place, accepted the challenge, returning to the team he had managed from 1929 to 1933, always for a second division finish.

In the 1950s, baseball men often carried two jobs during the year to earn their annual income — one playing baseball during the season, and a second job doing something else during the off-season. Rick had never worked at anything other than playing baseball, but on his scouting salary with a wife and four children, he decided to try selling new Ford automobiles. Another ex–major leaguer and current Red Sox scout, Mace Brown, lived nearby, and he and Rick became salesmen for Ingram Ford Motor Company downtown on North Elm Street during that winter. An ad — accompanied by photographs of Mace and Rick — in the November 14, 1954, *Greensboro Daily News* read:

> "Best in Any League" — Says Big League Scouts
> See It NOW — 1955 Ford
> Major League Scouts Mace Brown and Rick Ferrell say they have scouted
> the whole country and are convinced the new 1955 Fords with the
> THUNDERBIRD styling are the best prospects for this season.
> See Us Now — We're on the Ball Ready to Serve You!

That job lasted one winter. "Buyers" came into the dealership under the pretext of wanting a car while really seeking introductions to, and autographs from, the former ballplayers. The other car salesmen felt resentment because their income depended solely on car sales. To assist his co-workers, Rick frequently directed his own paying customers over to another salesman so that the other guy could "write up" the sale and collect the commission. "Heck, I didn't need the money," Rick would say later to cover his generosity.

During 1955, Rick continued to scout the Southern minor league teams from his Greensboro home, covering the Carolinas and Virginia. The Tigers' minor league affiliates had expanded to ten teams in ten different leagues.

In a 2008 interview, longtime Detroit Tigers announcer and Hall of Famer

Ernie Harwell described the importance of good scouting to an organization: "Developing through the farm system is the way you really develop a franchise; it's the only way to do it on a solid basis. You can't go out and buy guys because sometimes they don't work out. That's the basis really. The backbone of a franchise is scouting, developing players and bringing them up, then trading the excess for other players that you're looking for. But you can never judge a trade until about two or three years later. That's what makes baseball great!"

When Rick was home, family life operated at a mid–1950s "semi-normal" pace. He played golf at Starmount Forest Country Club, site of the Greater Greensboro Open (GGO) annual golf tournament, teaming with golf legend Sam Snead when he came through town. The Ferrell kids swam competitively on the Starmount Forest Country Club AAU swim teams. On Sunday afternoons in summer, the family went to lavish outdoor country picnics with Wes and George and their families, tables spread with Southern home-cooked food. On autumn evenings everyone, including Sparkle the fox terrier, would all pile into the "Green Hornet," their pale green Ford sedan, to go see John Wayne westerns at the drive-in movies.

Up in Michigan, manager Bucky Harris' 1955 Detroit Tigers team stayed in contention all season, however, ultimately finished in fifth place, 79–75, 17 games behind the perennial pennant-winning New York Yankees. Outfielder Al Kaline, 20, had burst onto the big league stage like a meteor, blasting a .340 batting average to become the youngest player ever to win the American League batting title. He was the only major leaguer to get 200 hits, 27 of which were homers.

The instructional school for players opened on February 14, 1956, in Lakeland with fifty athletes attending the two-week session, the largest group ever. Tigers' GM Muddy Ruel and farm director John McHale had chosen scouts Rick Ferrell, Don Lund, Willis Hudlin, and Bernie DiViveros as special instructors for the young players, especially Roger Sheppard, (27–1), a UNC pitcher that Rick had signed. Manager Bucky Harris returned with coaches Billy Hitchcock, Jack Tighe, and Joe Gordon. In a Lakeland golf tournament, Rick won the Detroit Tigers' plaque as the champion player.

Under John McHale, the Tigers modified their farm system. Buffalo was replaced by the Charleston (W. Va.) Senators (American Association), the Syracuse Chiefs were added as a second class A team (Eastern League), Greenville was dropped in the Class C Cotton States circuit, and Hazlehurst-Baxley (Georgia State League) and Palatka (Florida State League) were picked up, bringing the minor league team total to eleven clubs.

On July 16, 1956, the Briggs family sold the Tigers to an eleven-man syndicate for $5.5 million dollars. "Spike" Briggs remained as the vice president/ general manager of the club. Members of the syndicate included broadcasting magnate John Fetzer, Fred Knorr, Harvey Hansen, William McCoy, and Kenyon Brown.

Off-the-field concerns plus a 10-game losing streak at home in mid–June affected the team's play as it finished in fifth place again in 1956 with an 82–72 record, 15 games behind the Yankees. Shortstop Harvey Kuenn (.332) and outfielders Charlie Maxwell (.326) and Al Kaline (.314) all provided strong offense, with Kaline hitting a career-high 128 RBIs. In a break-out season, Frank Lary led the pitching staff (and the league) with 21 wins, while hurler Jim Bunning debuted.

On October 1, 1956, Board Chairman John Fetzer and President Harvey Hansen took over the Detroit Tigers from the Briggs family, making John McHale, Sr., the director of player personnel and promoting Ohio State University alum Jim Campbell to minor league business manager. Rick Ferrell was given new stature as the Tigers' scouting supervisor for the Southeastern states, assisted by scout George McDonald. Other scouts in the system were Marv Owen, Ed Katalinas, Bill Norman, Jack Tighe, and Billy Hitchcock.

In early 1957, *The Sporting News* printed several items revealing Rick's activities. On January 19, Rick played in the 2nd Annual March of Dimes benefit game in Tampa, Florida, with several former major leaguers like Heine Manush and Freddie Hutchinson in an effort to raise money to fight the polio epidemic in the United States.[13] On March 5, he attended the Governor's Dinner for Florida governor LeRoy Collins at the Palm Room of the Tampa Terrace Hotel with 350 other baseball people.[14] Also at age 52, Rick was eligible to collect a baseball pension after thirty years in baseball.[15]

In late March during spring training, Rick's expertise was summoned by St. Louis Cardinals GM Frank Lane and manager Freddie Hutchinson to present a seminar on catching the knuckleball to their catchers Hal Smith, Hobie Landrith, and Gene Green. The Cards now had three knuckleballers in their rotation — Hoyt Wilhelm, Murray Dickson, and Jim Davis. Rick presented tips to the St. Louis receivers on how to manage the pitch Stan Musial called "mercury in a bottle." "The key word Ferrell used was 'relax.' Rick advised 'em to give with the pitch, not challenge or fight it." Ferrell, of course, had learned his skills the hard way, through trial and error, injury and insult, with little instruction or assistance. Yet in the April 10 issue of *The Sporting News*, he generously shared what he knew about catching the knuckler: "1. Keep your elbows away from your sides. Carry the glove well in front of your body with your elbows free to swing laterally without hitting your ribs or stomach. 2. Don't take your eye off the ball until the ball is inside your mitt. It may break at the last second and you will be out of position to take it. You can't trust a knuckler like a fastball; you never know where it will break. 3. Keep the fingers on your throwing hand loose and relaxed at all times. There is less danger of breaking a finger. 4. Lean forward just slightly while waiting for the pitch; never back on your heels. With the forward balance you can go out to meet the pitch."[16]

The Detroit Tigers' front office changes continued on April 19, as Harvey Hansen replaced Fred Knorr as president. In May, director of player personnel

John McHale was promoted to general manager of the Tigers, with Tigers great Charlie Gehringer as his advisor. John McHale had known the Ferrell brothers — Rick, Wes, and George — from his days as a minor leaguer playing baseball in the Carolinas and valued Rick's expertise in evaluating player talent. In mid–May, McHale invited Rick to Detroit to watch the Tigers play several games.

Manager Jack Tighe's Tigers played .500 baseball for most of 1957, managing a first division finish for the first time in seven years, despite winning four fewer games than in 1956. Al Kaline again led team offense with a .295 average. Pitcher Jim Bunning (20–8, 2.70 ERA) tied Chicago's Billy Pierce for most A.L. wins.

On November 6, Rick's older brother, George Ferrell, a former St. Louis Cardinals scout, joined the Detroit Tigers' scouting staff for the Southeastern Region. John McHale told *The Sporting News*: "George will work with his brother Rick, who has become one of the best scouts in the major leagues."[17]

To raise funds to fight the polio epidemic that had gripped America, the 3rd Annual March of Dimes Game between American and National League old-timers was held at Al Lang Field in Tampa, Florida, on January 25, 1958. Both Rick and Wes appeared in the game. The brother battery also appeared in the third annual Old Timers Baseball Game on February 1 in St. Petersburg, Florida. Two days later, Rick was in Tigertown for the Tigers Baseball School, held from January 27 to February 10, to instruct some of the one hundred young players, ages 18–24, that attended camp.

While still in Florida for spring training, Rick competed in the 1st Bill Cody Golf Tournament in St. Petersburg, Florida. He tied for sixth place, scoring an 80, while former outfielder Roy Cullenbine won with a 74, and Heinie Manush came in second with a 77.

For the 1958 season, the Major League Rules Committee passed a new rule requiring all hitters to wear batting helmets at the plate. Rick prepared to scout the East Coast American League teams with Frank Skaff, in addition to scouting the Southeastern Region minor leagues.

The Tigers got off to a slow start in 1958 with injuries and slumps under manager Jack Tighe, enduring a nine-game losing streak that left them in last place. On June 10, McHale hurriedly replaced manager Tighe with AAA Charleston (West Virginia) minor league manager Bill Norman.

A few days prior, on June 6, at Washington's Griffith Stadium with the Tigers in seventh place, minor leaguer Ozzie Virgil had been summoned to play third base for big league club. This date proved historical in Tigers history because Virgil, a Dominican Republic native, was considered a "player of color." Since Brooklyn's Jackie Robinson had smashed the color barrier in 1947, the Tigers had been continually criticized for not signing minority players, although nineteen were serving in their minor league system. Virgil was the first to see "The Show" at Briggs Stadium on June 17 against the Washington

Senators. Going five-for-five at the plate in that game, he hit a double and four singles for a 9–2 win. By the All-Star break, Norman's Tigers were in third place, 37–37.

In 1958, the 25th anniversary of the first All-Star Game, Baltimore held festivities honoring the original 1933 players. With thirty-four All-Stars from the original two teams invited, twenty-nine actually attended. Among them were Rick and Wes Ferrell enjoying the celebration.

The sixth-place Tigers were experiencing a six-game winning streak in early August when John McHale announced the promotion of supervising scout Rick Ferrell, 53, to direct the Tigers' entire farm system. Ferrell's new title was "Director of Minor League Personnel," with a new office located on the second floor of Briggs Stadium in Detroit rather than in his North Carolina home. Rick eagerly planned the departure to his elevated position in Detroit.

In Rick's new stadium office hung a wall-sized, black felt board listing all

Rick (right) stands in front of the Detroit Tigers' big board of minor league teams and players on the wall of his Briggs Stadium office after being promoted to farm director of the Detroit Tigers in 1958. Talking with him is secretary of minor league operations, Ralph Snyder. (Ilitch Enterprises; Detroit Tigers Baseball Archives)

of the Tigers' farm teams and minor league players in white push-in metal letters that could be moved around as the names changed. In 1958, the Tigers' farm system consisted of about twenty scouts over eight regions in the U.S. The minor league territories and scouting staff (*supervisor-scout) were comprised of:

Region	Scout
Midwestern States	*George Moriarty
Eastern States	"Rabbit" Jacobson, Cy Williams, Lew Cassell, Pete Haley
Southeastern States	George McDonald, George Ferrell
Southern States	*William Pierre
Michigan-Ohio	*Pat Mullin, Wayne Blackburn, Ray Meyers, D. Lectka
Central States	NA
Southwestern States	*"Schoolboy" Rowe, Jess Landrum
Western States	*Marv Owen, Harrison Wickel, Bernie de Viveiros

Rick's job gave him the responsibility of presiding over all scouts in all regions, receiving and reading their scouting reports, and making determinations about player development and trades for both the major and minor leagues. Additionally, within the regions, the Tigers had ten minor league teams for which Rick was responsible:

Rank	Team	League
AAA	Charleston Senators	American Association
AA	Birmingham Barons	Southern Association
A	Augusta Tigers	South Atlantic League
A	Lancaster Red Roses	Eastern League
B	Durham Bulls	Carolina League
C	Idaho Falls Russets	Pioneer League
D	Erie Sailors	New York–Pennsylvania League
D	Decatur Commodores	Midwest League
D	Montgomery Rebels	Alabama-Florida League
D	Valdosta Tigers	Georgia-Florida League

Four of Detroit's ten minor league affiliates won pennants in 1958: Charleston, Birmingham, Augusta, and Valdosta. Additionally, Ferrell personally scouted certain major league prospects.

After making other promotions from within, by mid–September new Chairman and President John Fetzer's Detroit Tigers' front office consisted of General Manager John McHale, Executive Vice President Harry Sisson, Secretary-Treasurer Jim Campbell, Director of Minor League Personnel Rick Ferrell, Traveling Secretary Charlie Creedon, and Publicity Director "Doc" Fenkell.

John McHale recalled Ferrell in a 2007 telephone interview shortly before he died.

JOHN MCHALE: In those days, it just seems like there was more [pause] *thought* given to how to win or lose and how to handle people. And Rick was a great third base coach! You'd think he'd have been a pitching coach or a bullpen coach, but he was a third base coach. That's when I got to know him really, and that's why when Red was fired, I think the only one of those guys that we really wanted to retain as an organization member was your father. He and Jim Campbell got to be really good friends. [Rick] fit in everywhere. And he brought with him so much. He was a man for all seasons! If I remember, he had a sideline of music ... lifting weights— he was doing all kinds of interesting things—fishing, golf.

When I was a ballplayer, we would drive up to your father's home between Winston-Salem and Greensboro and, of course, I knew Wesley and I knew George — and I loved your father.

I thought he was so wonderful. I was just sitting here thinking of all the wonderful things about him and the dignity he brought to the uniform, and how different it is today ... the respect, the dignity, all of those nice terms—integrity, knowledge, and all of those things that you can think of that are good — Rick had.

He was a phrase-maker, too—quietly. Jim Campbell, who had gone to Ohio State, had a player he was very interested in who was going to Ohio State at that time, and I said, "Well, we can't let him get away, if he's pretty good." And so your dad went to see him play and he made one of the great reports of all time: he said, "He hit four ground balls to the four corners of the infield." (laughs) I've used that so many times and have never heard anybody make that kind of a comment before. Nobody knows there are four corners to the infield.

He had a great sense of humor, quietly, and just sort of let it slip out. I would say that if there was ever anyone I would want next to me in a decision-making capacity, it would be your father. And all those years in Detroit after I left was a wonderful group of farmhands and people on the staff. He brought to it a wonderful sense of integrity and judgment — all those things that make you feel good about knowing him.

I saw Rick play. He was always difficult to play first base against because he could hit and run ... and if you ever had a man on base, he could almost direct the ball when you were leaving the base to cover the player running to second base. Of course, he was a very, very tough competitor. He was such a pleasant, quiet guy, but on the field, you don't treat him roughly. As I remember, Ben Chapman slid into him very aggressively and not too cleanly, and he jumped up and had it out. And Rogell — I remember *that* incident (laughs). He fired the ball at him as he walked away.

Rick and I served on the Major League Rules Committee together for many years. I was on the Hall of Fame Board of Directors when he was voted into the Hall of Fame in 1984. I joined the Veterans Committee in 1991. The Veterans Committee at the time was made up of some very outstanding talent: Ted Williams, Joe Cronin, Yogi Berra, Bob Broeg. I succeeded Buzzi Bavasi, who'd been on it for a long time.

But I think everybody was sort of dazzled by offensive players. Defensive players were sort of sidetracked, and who's more important than a great defensive catcher? He could catch the knuckleball and caught all the knuckleball pitchers in Washington in 1945: Niggeling, Haefner, Wolff, Leonard. He always said, "Don't reach for the knuckleball, just let it come to you."

I wouldn't have the Veterans Committee quite like it is now. I think we gave in to the media a little too quickly on changing the Veterans Committee. They're thinking of changing it again, now. After Rick came to the Tigers in 1959, I was gone, but he was Jim Campbell's right-hand man and confidante. He was really in on all the decisions. Probably every decision that was made that was good, he was in on it and recommended it. We met at a lot at banquets and major league meetings. Those were wonderful days."

That September, Rick's nephew, outfielder George Wesley Ferrell, Jr., visited Briggs Stadium from North Carolina for a pre-arranged tryout with the

Tigers. Dick Thompson's book, *The Ferrell Brothers of Baseball*, states that the younger Ferrell impressed the front office brass with his long-ball, power hitting during batting practice, and Rick helped George negotiate a minor league contract with John McHale, plus obtain other paid endorsements.

By season's end the Detroit Tigers were locked in fifth place —for the seventh time in eight seasons— with a record of 76–78, 15 games out. Right fielder Al Kaline hit .313 and won the Gold Glove vote by a landslide. "Yankee-Killer" Frank Lary went 16–16.

On November 14, tragedy struck when Tigers broadcaster Mel Ott was suddenly killed in an automobile accident. Owner John Fetzer hired former Detroit star George Kell to replace Ott in the broadcast booth with Van Patrick, where Kell would become a fixture, calling Tigers games for thirty-seven years. Ferrell had scouted Cleveland Indians pitchers Ray Narleski and Don Mossi, and on November 20, the club traded for them, giving up Tigers infielder Billy Martin and pitcher Al Cicotte.

10

❖ ❖ ❖

1959–1965

The Tigers' Front Office/General Manager

The evening of January 26, 1959, brought a huge and unexpected surprise to the Tigers' 54-year old farm director. At home in Greensboro, Rick and Ruth were enjoying a dinner party with friends before his departure for the instructional league in Lakeland, Florida, the next day. A long-distance phone call from Harry Sisson, executive vice president of the Tigers, interrupted the festivities. Sisson told Rick to immediately catch a plane to Detroit at 8:30 A.M. the next morning rather than report to Lakeland. Why? General Manager John McHale had resigned from the Tigers.

When Rick arrived at Briggs Stadium in Detroit the next day, he joined an hour-long meeting with the Tigers' brass: Chairman of the Board John Fetzer, President Harvey Hansen, and Executive Vice President Harry Sisson. John McHale had accepted a generous offer from the Braves' vice President "Birdie" Tebbetts that was "too good to refuse" as vice president/general manager with a salary increase from $30,000 to $50,000.[1] After considering replacements within the organization, including Jim Campbell, Rick was selected as "acting" general manager of the Tigers.

Fetzer's public announcement stated that Ferrell would "assume all duties of the general manager as acting executive until such time as we name a general manager.... The Detroit Club is fortunate to have a man like Ferrell in the organization to step into an emergency situation like this." Jim Campbell assumed Rick's duties as farm director. The February 4 issue of *The Sporting News* reported the promotion, "Rick Ferrell, as nice a guy as one encounters in baseball, has spent ten years in the Detroit organization since finishing his iron-man catching career at Washington in 1949."[2]

A *Greensboro Daily News* reporter interviewed Rick, writing that "his friendly eyes penetrate deep into the invisible future" as Ferrell stated, "My aim is to do such a good job as acting general manager that they will want to keep me permanently."[3] A new vision for a front-office future had formed.

Ferrell's baseball uniform was gone, along with the casual attire of a scout.

His executive position placed Rick in a large third-floor office at Briggs Stadium with a secretary, requiring a new uniform for work every day: a dark business man's suit with white handkerchief in the coat pocket, starched white shirt, conservative tie, and dark, polished shoes.

The acting GM immediately began the task of signing players to 1959 contracts, since general managers still negotiated directly with players on salary for annual contracts, without agents or lawyers involved. On January 29, Al Kaline called for an appointment to discuss his 1959 contract. The outfielder had hit .313 with 85 RBIs and 16 home runs in 1958, his sixth season with the team. After about an hour's discussion, Al signed his '59 contract, estimated at about $32,000. Rick was the fourth general manager in four years that Kaline had signed with, following Muddy Ruel, Spike Briggs, and John McHale.

In early February first baseman Gail Harris signed with Rick, as did minor league first baseman Larry Osbourne and pitcher Jerry Davie. The "Yankee-killer" pitcher Frank Lary was sealed, along with starter Jim Bunning. Short-stop-turned-outfielder Harvey Kuenn (.319) inked for $40,000. Ferrell contracted the new players, pitchers Ray Narleski and Don Mossi, plus third baseman Eddie Yost, who as a rookie had played with Rick on the Washington Nationals team in the mid–1940s.

On February 20, spring training began at Lakeland, with a new, larger clubhouse at Henley Field offering special training rooms for the players. Ferrell told the *Greensboro Daily News*: "It's going to take a lot of hard work and money to catch the Yankees. But that's my objective, and I don't intend to slacken the pace in the slightest. I want to be around to render what help may be needed in making trades, judging new talent, looking for new talent among our minor league teams, and so forth. I'll have daily conferences with our manager Bill Norman. I'll also have to keep a close watch on our minor league operations."[4]

In spring training Rick accurately predicted to a reporter: "Al Kaline has matured. I'd say he has a fine chance to earn a place among the best outfielders Detroit has had. Kaline will keep improving. He has too much ability to tail off in his development."[5]

Nephew George Ferrell, Jr., an outfielder, came to Tigertown with high hopes for a minor league career with the Tigers. However while chasing a fly ball during a game, he unluckily slammed into the concrete left-field wall at Henley Field and was knocked unconscious for four and a half hours. The impact resulted in a brain concussion and many injuries to the left side of his body which mended slowly. Shortly after returning to play, another ball to his face smashed George's teeth out, requiring extensive surgery to replace. With damaged reflexes, his baseball career ended prematurely.

Eleven players brought their families with them to spring training, while most, including Rick, did not. Due to Florida's segregation laws, players of color Ossie Virgil, Ossie Alvarez, and Maury Wills were forced to live separately at Tigertown rather than at the team hotel. Ferrell and Fetzer opposed this arrangement, wanting the entire team lodged together under the same roof, a goal that eventually was accomplished through the Holiday Inn–North in Lakeland.

April 10, 1959, Opening Day, brought the announcement from the club's eleven-man Board of Directors that, due to his outstanding leadership and strong business sense, Rick Ferrell was officially named "vice president and general manager" of the Detroit Tigers, with the word "acting" removed from his title. At this executive pinnacle, he joined several former major league players who had worked their way into baseball's front office, including Charlie Gehringer, Hank Greenberg, Ralph Kiner, and Birdie Tebbets. Jim Campbell was promoted to vice president from farm director.

The Tigers lost their opener, 9–7, enduring a dreadful 1–12 start. By April 26, the team had scored only 42 runs and left 122 runners stranded on base. No Tigers' team had begun so poorly since 1939 when manager Del Baker started at 0–13.

Receiving the finger of blame, the press criticized Ferrell as an inexperienced Southerner who knew little about running a ball club, but the new GM remained cool and calm during the losing spell, seeking a trade to improve the club. He told Bob Addie of the *Washington Post*, "I got accustomed to slumps when I played with and coached Washington," perhaps referring to the 18 straight Nats' losses in 1949 under manager Joe Kuhel when Rick was their third base coach.[6]

By May 2, the Tigers had lost 15 of their first 17 outings and were in seventh place. Fetzer consulted with Rick regarding a replacement for manager Bill Norman. As a fan and friend of Norman's, Rick reluctantly recommended Jimmy Dykes, 64, who was being released as a coach from the Pittsburgh Pirates. After another Tigers loss, Ferrell put a telephone call through to Dykes at the Pirates' locker room, who was taking a shower. Manager Danny Murtaugh called him to the phone and on the spot, the veteran Dykes accepted Rick's offer to manage the Detroit Tigers. "I was the first manager ever hired in his birthday suit!" Dykes remarked.[7] Dykes became the third Tigers manager in less than three seasons. Firing Bill Norman was "the hardest decision I've had to make in baseball," Ferrell responded after announcing the managerial change. The 40-minute hiring-firing process had left both Ferrell and Norman emotionally deflated.

The Tigers played well above .500 after their horrible start to climb to a 15–22 record on May 24. "I still think we can move up despite the bad start," was Rick's optimistic observation.[8] With the help of Kuenn's bat, the team reached fifth place by early June, and some mention was made of Harvey's winning the batting title. Ferrell told *The Sporting News*: "It's a little early to think about that. But why shouldn't Harvey win it? Kuenn is a line-drive hitter. He lifts one up occasionally. He doesn't strike out much. I think right field suits him better."[9] In the six weeks since Jimmy Dykes had become manager, the Tigers had a 21–10 record and had reached .500.

By mid–June 1959, the Ferrell children had finished their school terms back in Greensboro, and Rick returned South to pack his family into two cars and finally relocate them to the Detroit area, seven hundred miles north. Rick rented out his Carolina home for that summer, knowing the tenuous nature of the baseball business. In February 1960, the local Woolworth's would become the site of the first lunch counter "sit-in" for Black civil rights.

Detroit in 1959 stood out as a modern, cosmopolitan city with a vibrant, thriving downtown area filled with movie theaters, restaurants, fountains, and fashionable shopping, stage plays, art museums and a symphony. The children had never seen such a large downtown. Not knowing how long his front office job might last, Rick had leased a home on Berkshire Road in stately Grosse Pointe Park, a twenty-minute drive down Jefferson Avenue to Briggs Stadium. Seven front-row box seats in section 115 on the third-base line had been generously provided the family, positioned right beside the Tigers' dugout. Rick's family and friends spent almost every summer day out at the ball games, where the smell of hot ballpark franks filled the air. Rick's only rules to his kids were "Act like you're somebody" and "Stay away from those ballplayers!" Interacting with the players was strictly verboten, despite sitting beside the dugout.

Oddly, Ferrell rarely sat in his own box. The rest of the Tigers brass watched the games from a special enclosed box off the second deck above the first base-right field line, but Ferrell preferred viewing games from somewhere behind home plate. In fact, the *New York Times* John Drebinger wrote in the June 14, 1959, issue, "Rick Ferrell is one general manager who doesn't believe his job calls for a sumptuous office equipped with a polished desk, clerks, yesmen, and all the other luxuries of life. He is still every inch a baseball man and insists on getting information about his ball club first hand. The Detroit GM is watching the series from the press box."[10]

During a June 18 game in his hometown Baltimore, star outfielder Al Kaline suffered a fractured cheekbone that disabled him for 33 games. During the five-week period without Kaline, the Tigers lost 23 games. Below .500 and in sixth, the ever-positive Ferrell stated: "We've got to pull ourselves up to the .500 mark again. We did it once before. I still think this club can finish in the first division."[11]

Rick still enjoyed suiting up in his baseball uniform. On August 9, he flew to Washington to play in an Old Timer's Game before the Tigers–White Sox doubleheader, where he met up with his brother Wes. Two days later at Briggs Stadium, a rehabilitated Al Kaline got his 1000th hit — a seventh inning single off Chicago pitcher Ken McBride — helping Jim Bunning win, 8–1.

On August 26, a resolute Ferrell told Walt Spoelstra, Detroit sportswriter: "We can't use injuries as an alibi. All our guys were hurt at once. We want to finish as high as we can. We have a real good chance for third place — maybe higher. We won't give up. It's been a strange season. It may keep on being strange."[12]

But the team finished the 1959 season in fourth with a 76–78 record, the worst in five years, 18 games behind the White Sox. Pitchers Bunning, Lary, and Mossi racked up 17 victories each, with Bunning leading the league with 201 strikeouts. Harvey Kuenn did win the American League batting championship with a .353 average and led the league for the fourth time with 198 hits. Teammate Al Kaline came in second with a .327 average, 27 home runs and 94 RBIs, while also winning a third Gold Glove as a center fielder. Third baseman Eddie Yost, "The Walking Man," led the American League in walks (135), runs scored (115), while slugging 21 homers. The Detroit Baseball Writers voted Kuenn the Most Valuable Player for 1959, with Eddie Yost second.

In a 2008 telephone interview, Eddie Yost recalled Rick.

EDDIE YOST: When I signed in 1944, it was in mid-season. I was only there for a half a year, so I didn't get friendly with many of those players. However, I remember I came to the ballpark for my first game and Rick came over to me and said, "Hi, young man. It's nice having you here. Welcome to the Washington Senators, and I wish you a lot of luck." I'll never forget that. I was seventeen at the time.

In 1944, Rick was the main catcher. What was interesting was that he caught four knuckleball pitchers. It was incredible! He was good at it too. He was a quiet, unassuming guy, very professional, and he was an excellent player. Not only could he catch, but he hit well and scored runs, knocked runs in. He's at the top of the list for the number of games that a catcher caught. I looked up his record as a player. It was fantastic! That was as a player, then he becomes an executive and he did a great job there, too. So he was a wonderful man ... and a gentleman. To me, that was very important, too. He was a wonderful gentleman.

As a coach, he worked with the pitchers. He wasn't one of these guys who was flashy. He was very, very intent on what he was doing. He was a wonderful professional player, a very good one. He had everything going for him! One of the things I admired about him was he didn't blow his own horn. A lot of guys who had the stats that he had, everybody in the world would have heard about it. He wasn't that type of a man. The other players liked him a lot.

I was in a trade to the Detroit Tigers and Rick was responsible for the trade. It was one of the best things that ever happened to me. That's another reason I adored the guy. I think the best year I ever had in my career was in 1959, and I scored 115 runs. It was a terrific year. Now it comes time to sign my contract the next spring training and Rick, of course, is the general manager now. So, he sent me a contract that I didn't have to dispute at all. He gave me a one-third increase in my pay. I had been making with the Washington Senators about $20,000, and he took me up to $30,000. At that time it was pretty good, but compared to today, it's not much. One reason I did so well was because I hit first, and Harvey Kuenn hit second. Bill Norman was part of the organization; he'd come up through the minor leagues.

It might have been a little bit more than he could handle and that's why they didn't continue with him for the rest of the year. But Dykes has many years of experience as a manager, and it was a good move. We should have been better than the fourth place finish. In 1960, they traded managers— Gordon for Dykes. That was a first. Rick wanted to make a change and so he did. The two managers were similar in temperament and how they ran the team, and I enjoyed both of them. Then the Tigers came in sixth. In December, I went to Los Angeles with the expansion. Reno Bertoia played third base after me.

Rick wasn't the type of guy to get into a fight or to raise hell or anything like that. He was a very even-tempered man and concentrated 100 percent on everything that he was doing. I never saw him get into an argument unless he was protecting his brother. I went to the last game at Tiger Stadium and a lot of the players were invited back. I went and saw a lot of the players there — Jim Bunning, Al Kaline.

On the eve of the World Series, the Tigers Board of Directors enacted an executive shake-up when the St. Louis Cardinals' Bill DeWitt, 57, was hired as president of the Detroit Tigers and given a three-year contract. Rick was retained as general manager, and Jim Campbell was named as vice president and farm director. Bill DeWitt had known Rick since he caught for the St. Louis Browns when DeWitt was their president. Now, ironically, the ex-catcher would work with his former boss as two equals rebuilding the Detroit Tigers.

DeWitt told *The Sporting News*, "Rick Ferrell is in charge of all players in the Detroit Tigers organization from top to bottom." In November 1959, Rick launched a two-week scouting tour of the Latin American winter leagues in Havana, Cuba, and San Juan, Puerto Rico. While there, Ferrell hired two full-time scouts to permanently cover the area: Mike Guerra, former catcher with Rick on the Senators' team, for Cuba; and Babel Perez for Puerto Rico. In a *Chicago Tribune* article, Rick asserted, "We don't want to overlook any bets. We must compete with other clubs that have scouts in Cuba and Puerto Rico. We figure territory that has produced the likes of Minnie Minoso, Vic Power, and Orlando Cepeda is worth checking."[13] Ferrell compared Puerto Rican baseball to AAA caliber in the United States.

On December 5 after being scouted in Puerto Rico by Ferrell, shortstop Chico Fernandez was obtained in the new inter-league trade from the National League Philadelphia Phillies and promptly named Detroit's new shortstop for 1960. "He looks good to me," commented Rick. "We're hoping a change of scenery will snap him out of whatever doldrums he was in with the Phillies."[14]

After his first year as general manager, Rick found out that there was no such thing as the off-season he had enjoyed as a player, coach, and scout. His executive job operated round-the-clock, year round, and the team's off-season was spent traveling to observe players in the instructional leagues, scouting, making deals, attending meetings, and signing players. Spring training began in mid–February, the season ran for six months from April to September before the championships were played in October and winter meetings transpired in December. Baseball really never stopped.

President DeWitt determined that Rick, 55, would negotiate major league player contracts for the 1960 season, just as he had in 1959. Due to Tiger owners' tight pursestrings, DeWitt wanted no part of it. With Jim Campbell's promotion, Rick no longer had responsibility over the eight minor league affiliates.

On February 8, Ferrell had signed fifteen out of forty players, dealing pay cuts to several. "I expected a cut, but not an amputation!" complained one player. Ferrell wrote in a letter to the team that he personally considered Detroit's fourth-place finish in 1959 "a disappointing season." By month's end, Rick had signed 28 Tigers, but Kuenn, Kaline, Maxwell, and Yost still held out. After refusing five contract offers, Al Kaline, 25, came to terms with Ferrell in early March, saying that Rick was "a tough man to deal with. What I got was close enough to what I had in mind from the beginning that it wasn't any use to argue any more."[15]

Batting champ Harvey Kuenn had refused six contract offers from Ferrell during twice as many meetings, but finally signed for an estimated $44,500. Harvey said, "We both gave a little." After a ten-day holdout, left fielder Maxwell met with Ferrell on March 11 and signed. Ernie Harwell and George Kell were designated as radio broadcasters for the 1960 season.

Once Rick had completed the final contract negotiations for players and spring training was over, DeWitt promptly assumed his general manager duties for trade negotiations and transfers and withdrew Ferrell's title as general manager. Instead, Rick's new assignation was "Special Assistant to the President" with no salary cut.

President DeWitt and Special Assistant Ferrell made a series of three long-remembered trades in 1960. In the first one on April 12, third baseman Steve Demeter was traded to Cleveland for the young outfielder/first-baseman named Norm Cash, who would become a valuable fixture for the Tigers, hitting 373 home runs over 15 seasons. After playing in only four games for the Indians, Demeter went to the minors. Some have rated this trade as one of the best ever made.

The second move came less than a week later on April 17 just before Opening Day, when Cleveland general manager Frank Lane called DeWitt about trading Harvey Kuenn for Rocky Colavito—the league batting champ for the league home-run king. DeWitt, not as familiar with the American League players as Rick, consulted with his assistant, who gave the idea a "thumbs up." Recalling that Colavito had hit four consecutive home runs in 1959 games and 42 for the season, Ferrell later said, "I felt we needed more power to go with Al Kaline and Norm Cash. Kuenn was a singles hitter."[16]

The announcement shocked the baseball world! In a 2008 telephone interview, longtime Tiger broadcaster Ernie Harwell recalled the day the trade was announced: "I remember Rick coming into the press box in Lakeland, Florida. George Kell and I were broadcasting the final game of spring training, and he came in and made the announcement that they'd made that super trade of Kuenn-for-Colavito. We thought it was a joke at first! But it was a great trade because you had two big stars traded for each other. The trade was a big one because Rocky had so many fans in Cleveland, and Harvey had a lot of fans in Detroit. I think in the long run, the Tigers got the better of that trade. Rocky lasted a lot longer and did a little bit more on the field than Harvey, but Harvey made it up as a manager."

Truthfully, the historic exchange took its toll on both players involved. In fact Harvey Kuenn, 29, was completely shaken by the sudden trade and did not last in Cleveland. His 1960 batting average dropped 45 points—from .353 to .308 — and Lane traded him to the San Francisco Giants after the season ended. Likewise, Colavito said in a 2000 interview with the *Detroit Free Press*, "I was in total shock! I really was. I'll admit that more now than I ever did then because I didn't want anybody to think I couldn't handle it.... We weren't too happy about it, but it's one of those things— you have to accept it."[17] Rocky, 26, played well with the Tigers for four seasons, becoming a local fan favorite.

Manager Jimmy Dykes, with coaches Billy Hitchcock and Luke Appling, opened the Detroit Tigers' 1960 season at Briggs Stadium on a chilly April 19 by winning five straight games. But by June 30 after 66 games, they were below .500, in fifth place. Unhappy outfielders Maxwell, Colavito, and Kaline were all batting below .230, helping drop the Bengals to sixth, 44–49, 11 games out of first by the end of July.

August 10 brought the third memorable trade by Ferrell and DeWitt in 1960, executed during a meeting with Cleveland general manager Frank Lane. Later, Rick described the trade: "DeWitt was throwing ball players' names around with Lane, but couldn't agree on anything. I was sitting there with DeWitt and slipped him a note that said, 'Ask Frank if he wants to trade managers.' DeWitt did, and damned if Lane didn't jump at it. DeWitt and Lane both loved it! The reason I'd suggested it was because Dykes was a good friend of mine, and I knew he was through in Detroit at the end of the season. I knew his contract wouldn't be renewed. I told Dykes to go to Cleveland. That way he'd get another year or two in the big leagues. But I'd always liked Gordon, thought he'd be a good manager, and — hell, neither we nor the Indians were going anywhere that season."[18]

But the managerial trade — the first ever in baseball — did little for the Tigers, who still finished in sixth place under Gordon, 71–83, 26 games behind the pennant-winning Yankees. Jimmy Dykes' Indians finished in fourth.

On October 11, after the dismal 1960 season finally ended, an exasperated Fetzer bought out Kenyon Brown's one-third ownership of the Tigers for $900,000, bringing Fetzer's total club ownership to two-thirds. With majority control, Fetzer named himself president of the Tigers and offered DeWitt an assistant title, but DeWitt resigned. Short-lived manager Joe Gordon also resigned in frustration.

Distinguished gentleman-president John Fetzer's standards for running a baseball team were traditional, conservative, and business-oriented, his first concern always being what was best for the game. He expected the highest moral standards of loyalty, honesty, and hard work from his employees. Rick and other department heads were responsible for submitting weekly activity reports to

President Fetzer every Friday. An "Operations Committee" composed of Rick, Harry Sisson, Jim Campbell, and Hal Middlesworth met weekly together to discuss their activities. Fetzer's philosophy for rebuilding the Tigers focused on developing players from within the Tigers system: scouting and signing players, then bringing them up through the Tigers' minor leagues. By the end of 1960, Fetzer had shelled out the price of his ball club ($5,500,000) in signing and developing new ballplayers.

Ferrell and Jim Campbell selected former catcher and ex–Cubs manager Bob Scheffing, 45, as the Tigers' eighth manager in eight years, who signed a two-year contract, with Don Heffner and Phil Cavarretta as first and third base coaches. In an early December, six-player trade with general manager John McHale's Milwaukee Braves, Ferrell acquired agile center fielder Billy Bruton, 31, who became the first African-American player ever to play as a regular in Detroit's lineup.

Changes in baseball upended the Tigers for the 1961 season. The American League, which had consisted of eight teams for decades, opted to expand to ten teams. To create two new expansion teams— the Los Angeles Angels and a replacement Washington Senators— each American League team had to name seven active players available to be drafted by August 31, 1960. The expansion clubs would then pay $75,000 for each of twenty-eight players drafted from existing clubs. The Angels claimed five Tigers, among them third baseman Eddie Yost. The Senators claimed three — pitchers Dave Sisler and Pete Burnside, plus shortstop Coot Veal — as the entire Washington organization relocated to Minneapolis to become the Minnesota Twins. On December 29, 1960, the ballpark's name, Briggs Stadium, was changed to Tiger Stadium, just two days after Fred Knorr, final one-third owner of the Tigers, died from suffering a scalding bathtub injury.

Rick's weekly reports to Fetzer demonstrated attempts to inform and educate the new president. Rick's January 20, 1961, report read, in part: "On my recent twelve-day trip, I thoroughly scouted the Puerto Rican Winter League. Every club in the Majors is represented in this league, and it is very important that we should become more active in Winter League play. These Winter Leagues are especially beneficial to young pitchers. We have experienced great success with the development of Jim Bunning, Bob Shaw, Bob Bruce, and now Regan…. I plan to have Mickey Cochrane report to our training camp to scout all Major League clubs training in Florida. I regard Cochrane's judgment on the major league level as being very valuable."

Rick began 1961 signing major leaguers to contracts. Outfielders Colavito and Bruton plus pitcher Bunning were signed early and by January 18, twelve of the 36-man roster were on-board. In his January 27 report to Fetzer, Rick wrote: "Discussed player trades with Kansas City, Cincinnati, Houston, and Chicago Cubs. I am concerned with lack of depth in our infield and would like to acquire another good utility infielder who can play short and second." His

February 17 report from spring training accurately predicted: "Our policy of fielding a young club is definitely going in the right direction.... Everyone is working well together and with one purpose in mind — organizational improvement. We could surprise."

By February 24, Al Kaline, Frank Lary, and Charlie Maxwell had signed contracts. Ferrell noted to Fetzer: "The 1961 season has been extended eight days and eight games longer than the previous season ... definitely a factor in contract negotiations...."

The slender outfielder Billy Bruton was joined by another African-American regular, second baseman Jake Wood, who would play for the Tigers until 1967. The slow process of integration was taking hold within the Tigers' organization.

In 1961 the Tigers had a new stadium name, a new manager, a new electronic scoreboard, and several new amateur free agents. Two Michigan free agents, big catcher Bill Freehan from the University of Michigan and outfielder Mickey Stanley, signed, who would become members of the 1968 Tigers' championship team. Eight rookies filled the roster on Opening Day, April 11, 1961, (including infielders Jake Wood, Steve Boros, and pitcher Jim Donahue) as Jim Bunning and three relievers were roughed up by the Indians, 9–5. When the players complained the glare from the new electronic scoreboard's lights made plays harder, Ferrell promptly had the very expensive electronic scoreboard removed.

During April 14 to 24, the team held first place after winning eight straight before losing to New York's Whitey Ford, 13–10. In this game, Roger Maris slugged the first of his 61 season home run. Then the mighty Mickey Mantle slugged two home runs, with one breaking a 10–10 tie in the tenth inning. Yankees' manager Ralph Houk may have sensed his two power-hitters would provide many thrills throughout 1961.

If anyone was shocked at the Tigers' phenomenal start, the sage Rick was not, telling *The Sporting News* on April 15: "We're going down the line with young players. I've never felt so good about a club coming out of spring training as this one. We'll be an aggressive club. And if these young players start believing in themselves, we could be a dangerous club."[19]

Manager Scheffing's Tigers went 17–5 to start the season. Rocky Colavito's first at-bat in Detroit was a two-run homer. Rick's reports indicated "our main concern at the moment is our pitching staff ... and cutting three players by May 10." The team stayed in first until after the All-Star break.

Rick's wife, Ruth, had been ill in Henry Ford Hospital and underwent internal surgery on May 10. Rick constantly traveled the three miles between Tiger Stadium and Ford Hospital to visit her, but as the summer wore on, her health would be fragile.

In his June 2, 1961, report, Rick wrote: "We are still in search of a relief pitcher to help with the load of doubleheaders in June.... Thomas is working out every day at shortstop, just in case.... We asked waivers on Bruce, Foytack, and Aguirre..." His June 23 report read, "Due to injuries to Boros, Cash, and Fernandez on the infield, it became necessary to add an infielder for insurance.... McAuliffe is the logical one to bring up." On July 25, the Tigers lost to the Los Angeles Angels, 5–4, and fell back to second place, giving the Yankees the lead.

For Fetzer's rebuilding program, the Tigers re-acquired infielder Reno Bertoia and pitcher Gerry Staley on August 2 from the Kansas City Athletics for Ozzie Virgil, pitcher Bill Fischer, and cash. One week later on August 7, 18-year-old outfielder Willie Horton from Detroit Northwestern High was signed as an amateur free agent; Horton would become an outfield mainstay for Detroit for 14 years and much later, a front-office member. Rick's August 25 report informed, "I am making every effort to get Vic Wertz from the Boston Red Sox to add to our left-hand power and bench strength." On August 27, slugger Rocky Colavito hit three homers for the afternoon, helping the Tigers win a doubleheader against the Washington Senators, 7–4 and 10–1.

The most critical series of 1961 came over Labor Day weekend against the league-leading Yankees at Yankee Stadium: winning one game could move the Tigers into first place. The largest New York crowd of the year — 65,560 fans — packed the ballpark for the first game, as New York won all three for a series sweep, surging ahead of the Tigers by 4½ games.

Rick's September 15 report stated, "The race is about over, but we still want to win every game possible and finish at least second. Most of our plans materialized from last winter.... The trades we made were good. Our farm system produced and the young players came through to give us a nucleus for a good ball club for years to come."

During the final two weeks, the team burned, winning twelve of their last fifteen games. They ended the season on October 1 by beating the Twins, 8–3, for their 101st win. On the same day over in New York, after a grueling season competing with teammate Mickey Mantle, Roger Maris hit his 61st homer to break Babe Ruth's season home run record.

For the 1961 season under Manager Bob Scheffing, the Tigers had improved from sixth to second place, finishing eight games out with a 101–61 record. For the first time since 1934, Detroit won more than a hundred games. Norm Cash (.361) won the American League batting title, getting 193 hits, 41 homers, and 132 RBIs. Al Kaline (.324) accumulated 190 hits, while Rocky Colavito (.290) blasted 45 home runs and 140 RBIs. Pitcher Frank Lary won 23 games (3.24 ERA). The Tigers' front office was beginning to reap rewards.

Convinced that his job with the Tigers was secure, Rick finally sold the North Carolina home, much to his brother George's dismay. They bought another grand English Tudor home at 1003 Berkshire Road in Grosse Pointe Park, a twenty-minute drive to the ballpark down Jefferson Avenue.

On November 14, 1961, John Fetzer paid $2 million for the final one-third portion of the Detroit Tigers from Fred Knorr's estate, giving him almost total control over the organization. Fetzer owned 10,000 shares of the ballclub with an additional four hundred shares jointly owned by vice presidents Rick Ferrell, Jim Campbell, and treasurer Harry Sisson. Fetzer would own the Tigers ballclub for 21 years until 1983, when he sold it to Domino's Pizza magnate Tom Monaghan. The front office would be run by a loyal, reliable, and expert executive staff, most of whom would remain with the club until retirement.

Rick's September 15 report informed Fetzer, "Joe Cronin elected me as a member of the Playing Rules Committee, an opening that occurred when Hank Greenburg resigned. Our first meeting is at Tampa on Sunday, November 26. One of the first questions to be decided is the return of the spitball. I have noticed that Frick, Cronin and others have come out in favor of the spitball; however, I cannot agree to such thinking. Baseball has done quite well without the spitball for some 40 years and I do not feel that it should be returned. It will only encourage every kid in semi-pro, high school, and college to spit all over the ball. I certainly cannot see where this rule will benefit baseball in the least."

His December 22 report revealed, "I again made an offer to Minneapolis—Maxwell and Wert for Pedro Ramos.... They won't say no but hesitate to deal ... I have mailed out 22 contracts but no replies."

Rick, with Jim Campbell, signed the Tigers to their annual 1962 contracts with Jim Bunning signing his thirteenth contract with Detroit. In early January 1962, Rick, 57, announced that Tiger Stadium's left-field fence would be lowered from eleven feet to nine feet to conform to other outfield fences. That higher left-field screen had cost the Tigers at least seven homers in 1961. The 1962 schedule added three twi-night doubleheaders, six daytime doubleheaders, and twenty-four night games.

On February 7, the Tigers' pre–spring training camp opened in Lakeland, with young prospects like outfielder Mickey Stanley, catcher Bill Freehan, and pitcher Mickey Lolich. Norm Cash reached a salary agreement by February 27. By March 5, holdout Rocky Colavito and Ferrell had agreed to terms.

Generally the easy-going Rick had little difficulty signing even the most demanding players. As a holdout himself several times during his 18-year catching career, he knew how players thought, what their motivations were and could be flexible, but firm. Once before the 1961 season began, a self-promoting, young relief pitcher came into his office requesting a higher salary offer. Rick recalled the incident to *Sport* magazine in May 1962: "I think you should know, Mr. Ferrell, that I appeared in quite a few games last season and saved several of those," said the pitcher. "You know, it isn't easy to be a relief pitcher."

"I think I know your problems quite well, young man," replied Ferrell. "I must have caught about 1,000 relief pitchers in my day!" The surprised pitcher replied, "By gosh, that's right! You *were* a catcher, weren't you?" and immediately signed his contract."[20] Fred Katz, author of that *Sport* magazine article,

"Rick Ferrell: Free Thinking Front-Office Man," asserted that Rick was largely responsible for elevating "the Tigers from mediocrity to pennant contention" against the imperious New York Yankees.

The Tigers opened on the road at RFK Stadium in Washington on April 9, 1962, with the identical batting lineup as in 1961. Losing to the Senators, 4–1, they were in third place after their first game, a harbinger of the coming season. Until the All-Star break, Scheffing's team ricocheted in the standings from second to last place, rarely staying in one position for long.

In late April, word reached the Tigers that one of their scouts, Mickey Cochrane, was seriously ill in Lake Forest, Illinois, and unable to work. Two months later — on June 28 — the great Hall of Fame Tigers catcher passed away.

Just when May 20–26 brought a five-game winning streak — the Tigers' longest of the season — outfielder Al Kaline sustained a broken collarbone making a ninth-inning, game-saving catch at Yankee Stadium, disabling him until July 23. Rick's June 4 report to Fetzer read, "Injuries continue to plague us.... Kaline feels optimistic and expects to play before the estimated two-month period.... Bunning pulled a muscle in his leg and had to leave the game in the third inning. Dick Brown received a foul-tip on the bad finger of last year. Neither is too serious." But by mid–June, Detroit had dropped to seventh. Meanwhile the Tigers signed young Canadian pitcher John Hiller as an amateur free agent and traded outfielder Charlie Maxwell to the Chicago White Sox.

On July 28, Rick flew to New York to participate in a celebratory fifty-player "Old Timer's Day" at Yankee Stadium. Sixteen Hall of Famers attended, including Jackie Robinson, Joe DiMaggio, Hank Greenberg, Lefty Grove, and Bob Feller. Former All-Stars included Wes Ferrell, Luke Sewell, Lefty Gomez, and Dick Bartell. Being together provided the guys an excuse to swap fishing tales, replay by-gone games, and be ballplayers again.

After winning twelve of their last fifteen games, the end of the season found the team fighting Chicago for fourth place. In their final season series against Kansas City at Tiger Stadium, Detroit swept the Athletics to nose-out the White Sox for fourth by a mere half-game. Detroit's season record was 85–76, 10½ games out; Chicago's record was 85–77, 11 games out, for a finish that was too close for comfort.

Hank Aguirre (16–8) became the 1962 American League ERA champ (2.21). The Tigers led the A.L. in home runs, setting a team record at 209. While Norm Cash did hit 39 homers, his batting average dropped a dramatic 118 points from his championship 1961 year —from .361 to .243.— the largest single-season decline ever for a batting title winner. Frank Lary's sore pitching arm resulted in a 2–6 record over 80 innings, a disappointing follow-up to his outstanding 22–9 previous season.

The rumor mill spun into high gear when some speculated that Ferrell would be out as general manager of the Tigers. Fetzer strongly denied the whispers to the September 8, 1962, issue of *The Sporting News*: "Rick Ferrell is the fall guy for a lot of the things that have happened to the Tigers. Ferrell is a sound baseball man, and he's doing a good job in Detroit. Nobody's taking over for him."[21]

But despite his previous words, on September 27, Fetzer did, in fact, rearrange front office assignments. With his new "accent on youth," he promoted minor league director Jim Campbell, 38, to replace Rick as the new Tigers general manager in charge of making trades and negotiating player contracts. Fetzer gave Campbell "total authority to run the entire organization." Ferrell's new title would be "Vice President in Charge of Player Evaluations." Campbell stated then, "Rick Ferrell is the best man at that job of anyone I know."[22] In the September 28 *Detroit Free Press*, Jim said, "[Rick]'ll be the eyes and ears of our talent staff." Ex-Tiger Don Lund, 39, took over Campbell's position as minor league director. As usual, the front office changes were fine with Rick and actually made his focus on scouting and acquiring major league baseball talent easier.

The combo of Jim Campbell, general manager, and Rick Ferrell, vice president, would form a primary Detroit Tigers executive team for the next thirty years under owners John Fetzer and Tom Monaghan, only ending in 1992 when Little Caesar's Pizza owner Mike Ilitch bought the team. Detroit's organizational brass shared a vision, with each member totally devoted to building the Tigers into a championship team via integrity and hard work, while maintaining fiscal strength. Scouting young players to develop through their minor league system represented the primary means of reaching their common goal of winning an American League pennant. Rick and Jim were as loyal and dedicated to each other for the decades to come as they were to Fetzer, the Detroit Tigers organization, and to the grand tradition of baseball, itself.

On Rick's 57th birthday, October 12, 1962, with members of the Tigers' front office and team, he and Ruth left on a six-week, goodwill tour of Hawaii and Japan. Leaving from San Francisco, the group flew to Hawaii for a few days, then on to Japan and Korea where on October 27, they began a seventeen-game tour playing baseball games against various Japanese teams.

Upon their return from the Far East, Campbell and Ferrell made three major league transactions at the end of November 1962. First-string catcher Dick Brown was traded to the Baltimore Orioles for catcher Gus Triandos and outfielder Whitey Herzog. Then pitchers Ron Nischwitz and Gordon Seyfried were shipped to Cleveland for third baseman–outfielder Bubba Phillips. Finally, third baseman Steve Boros went to the Chicago Cubs for pitcher Bob Anderson.

At the December 15 winter meetings, Rick was again appointed to the Major League Rules Committee, along with Calvin Griffith (Minnesota Twins) and Cal Hubbard (American League Umpire Supervisor) of the American League. National League members were Chub Feeney (New York Giants), Joe L. Brown (Pittsburgh Pirates), Fresco Thompson (Los Angeles Dodgers), and other baseball associates. Afterwards Ferrell and Campbell spent a week in

Dunedin, Florida, looking at prospects together at the Florida Instructional League.

As 1963 began the Tigers signed several free agents, among them pitcher Joe Sparma. Before Rick traveled south to Puerto Rico in mid–January to scout the Winter Leagues, he commented to sportswriter Walt Spoelstra, "I like the scouting end of it. It gets me out on the field and away from the paper work. This is what I like." Jim Campbell told Spoelstra, "Rick can talk trades with anyone he meets." Rick and Bob Scheffing offered their opinions on Tigers' trades at the winter meetings, with Campbell making the final decisions.

In the early 1960s, Lakeland, Florida's, racial prejudices resembled those of the Deep South. To finally eliminate segregation against any Tiger player, lodging arrangements were made for 1963 spring training to house all team members in one location, the Holiday Inn–North, a new motel in Lakeland, regardless of race. Additionally, all local restaurants were to be integrated and available to all Tiger players.

On April 8, the Tigers claimed pitcher Denny McLain from the Chicago White Sox on first-year waivers, an acquisition that would prove both a blessing and a curse for the club. The next day was Opening Day at Tiger Stadium, which the Tigers lost, 7–5, to the White Sox. By the end of April, the team had fallen to seventh place, 8–10. The front office made quick changes. Vic Wertz was released on May 5 and shortstop Chico Fernandez went to the Milwaukee Braves for outfielder Lou Johnson and cash. Pitcher Paul Foytack and infielder Frank Kostro were traded to Los Angeles for outfielder George Thomas, while outfielder Gates Brown, 24, was summoned from the minors.

But slumps and injuries dropped the Tigers down to ninth place. By June 16, they'd won only 24 of 60 games played. To shake-up the team, Campbell fired manager Bob Scheffing and his coaches and hired ex-third baseman Charlie Dressen, 64, who'd been scouting for the Dodgers, as manager. Developing the Tigers' upcoming youth underscored Dressen's priorities.

Dressen joined the team at Boston's Fenway Park on June 18 after a humiliating double-loss at Yankee Stadium. His much stricter management style brought no response as Detroit held ninth place until mid–August, when they were 52–64. But suddenly in late August, the Tigers enjoyed an eight-game winning streak that raised them to fifth place. On September 10, 1963, in a 4–1 win vs. the Senators at Robert Kennedy Stadium, new Detroit outfielder Willie Horton debuted. Soon after a young catcher named Jim Leyland signed a minor league contract.

Dressen's Tigers finished the 1963 season in an exact tie for fifth place with the Cleveland Indians. Both teams had identical 79–83 records and finished 25½ games behind Ralph Houk's New York Yankees, winner of 104 games. The Tigers' best hitter, outfielder Al Kaline, hit .312 with 172 hits, 101 RBIs, and 27 homers to come in second in American League batting behind Carl Yastrzemski, .321.

In November Rick spent a week observing the Arizona Instructional League before joining Jim Campbell for the Florida Instructional League. An excited Rick reported to Spoelstra, "The Arizona League is a good one. We want all the information on first year players we can get. We might be able to pick up another Denny McLain."[23]

In the final two months of the year, Detroit made two major trades. First, slugging outfielder Rocky Colavito was traded with pitcher Bob Anderson and $50,000 to Kansas City for second baseman Jerry Lumpe and pitchers Ed Rakow and Dave Wickersham. Then Detroit sent pitcher Jim Bunning (12–13) and catcher Gus Triandos to the Philadelphia Phillies in exchange for center fielder Don Demeter and pitcher Jack Hamilton. Bunning had won 118 games with Detroit, hurled a no-hitter on July 20, 1958, and his great career was far from over. As a National Leaguer, Bunning would rack up 108 more wins and pitch another no-hitter before being selected to Baseball's Hall of Fame in 1998. Many did not understand trading away a talented pitcher like Bunning.

Charlie Dressen returned in 1964 to manage Detroit, along with coaches Wayne Blackburn, Pat Mullin, "Stubby" Overmire, and Bob Swift. The club was pinning future hopes on the young players: second-year catcher Bill Freehan, young slugger Willie Horton, and a southpaw named Mickey Lolich.

Rick's nickname "Big Brain" served the Tigers' organization well for decades. Before the advent of computerization, Ferrell maintained his own mental database of statistics for every player in the both major leagues. Someone could ask him a question about any obscure player in either league — American or National — and, with his steel-trap memory, Rick would rattle off vast information about the guy on the spot. During spring training Jim Campbell's longtime executive secretary Alice Sloane was interviewed for a *Sporting News* article March 21, 1964, about the Tigers. When asked who had been the "most knowledgeable" general manager she'd known for the Tigers, she immediately said, "Mr. Ferrell. He can answer questions about baseball in 1–2–3 order."[24]

The Tigers celebrated their 1964 season opener on April 14 with a 7–3 victory over Kansas City and played .500 ball for the rest of the month. This brief period of success was, however, followed by a long siege of inept performance.

When the Baseball Rules Committee met in mid–April, Ferrell recommended that the low right field wall at Yankee Stadium be raised to nine feet. He maintained that increasing the height would prevent fans from interfering with the plays by outfielders and would keep players from falling into the stands as they chased fly balls.

A May 9 clip in *The Sporting News* reported that Rick Ferrell had made his first visit to the dugout in ten years before a White Sox game. "Former catcher [and current Sox manager] Al Lopez warmly greeted him. Both catchers hold iron-man records. Lopez holds the most games caught ever, 1918, while Rick hold most games caught in the American League, 1806. The two old catchers made a show of hands, pointing out where breaks and bruises had occurred."

Rick Ferrell commented humorously, 'Remember, Al, when the old timers would tell us to spit on a split finger and rub it in the dirt? Somehow I never could make that work!'"[25]

In mid–May 1964, the North Carolina Sports Hall of Fame in Raleigh inducted Rick Ferrell as a member along with four other second-year inductees, including baseball player Enos "Country" Slaughter. Brother Wes had been selected as an inaugural member the year before in 1963 when it first opened. Future members would include Buck Leonard, Gaylord Perry, Catfish Hunter, Arnold Palmer, and Lee and Richard Petty.

By July 1, the crew occupied the league basement. The whole team was scuffling, with star player Al Kaline's foot injury taking him out of the lineup. Dressen publicly criticized his players; Tigers fans stayed away from the ball-park.

August brought some relief as the Tigers won enough to move into fifth. By mid–August they even overtook fourth and managed to finish the 1964 season there with an 85–77 record, 14 games behind the Yankees. Season attendance fell to an uncharacteristic low of 816,139. The only Tiger to hit .300 or better was second-year catcher Bill Freehan (.301), the first Tiger catcher in almost thirty years— since Mickey Cochrane in 1935 — to do so, while also collecting 80 RBIs and 18 homers.

Newly-acquired Dave Wickersham led the starting rotation with 19 victories; young Mickey Lolich garnered an 18–9 record. Rick told *The Sporting News* in November, "That young Lolich is all business out there. I like his good breaking stuff."[26] Meanwhile departed pitcher Jim Bunning was experiencing a Renaissance with the Philadelphia Phillies with a 19–8 record for the season (2.63 ERA).

After the 1964 season ended, the player shuffle began again. The Tigers released catcher Mike Roarke and outfielder Billy Bruton, who retired from baseball to work for Chrysler Corporation. "Bruton is the best player I've ever seen retire," stated Rick Ferrell. "Usually, you have to cut the uniform off a guy to make him quit. Billy can still run, throw, and hit the ball."[27] But Gates Brown and Willie Horton were expected to fill the void.

In 1965, Rick began his fifteenth year with the Detroit Tigers, his eighth in the front office. President John Fetzer had created a family-type organization where members essentially worked until they retired. His executive team at Tiger Stadium was comprised of VP and GM Jim Campbell, Vice President Rick Ferrell, Secretary-Treasurer Harry Sisson, Director of Public Relations Hal Middlesworth, Director of Minor League Operations and Scouting Don Lund, Business Manager Alex Callum, Chief Scout Ed Katalinas, and Traveling Secretary Charlie Creedon. Fetzer did not interfere with Campbell and Ferrell's management of the Tigers' roster, giving them total control over player contracts and transactions.

Since 1963, broadcasting millionaire John Fetzer had served as chairper-

The Detroit Tigers' brass discuss operational matters during a meeting held in the executive offices at Tiger Stadium during the early 1960s. Sitting at the head of the table, Detroit Tigers owner John Fetzer (left) makes a point while Jim Campbell (in front, profile) talks with Hal Middlesworth (back to camera). On the other side of the table are stadium manager Ralph Snyder (obscured) and vice president Rick Ferrell, listening (unidentified man standing). (Patricia Kenney)

son of the Major League Baseball Television Committee. For the 1965 season he made a pioneering arrangement with ABC that guaranteed all major league teams would share revenue from televised games at $300,000 per team for the season. He wanted televised baseball to reap profits for all the clubs and help teams that were struggling financially.

At the March meeting of the Official Playing Rules Committee, Ferrell again endorsed standard heights for outfield fences in major league ballparks: "Every fence or wall in fair territory should be at least nine feet high. That goes for Yankee Stadium, where it is less than four feet, and for a couple of other parks, including Cleveland. There are two dangers to the lower fences: outfielders can topple over them in pursuit of fly balls and seriously injure themselves, and the fans are able to interfere with such pursuing players."[28]

Spring training 1965 had no sooner started in March — with soaring spirits and optimistic fervor — than disaster struck. On March 8, manager Charlie

Dressen, 68, unexpectedly left camp to fly home to Los Angeles for a family emergency, which turned out to be his own heart attack. Charlie was ordered to remain in the hospital to recuperate. Third base coach Bob Swift stepped in as Tigers manager to finish spring training and open the new season.

The Tigers began the 1965 season April 12 on the road with Mickey Lolich pitching against Kansas City at Municipal Stadium and swept the series. When Dressen returned to manage on May 31, his boys inhabited third place, 24–18 under Swift, only three games out. The Tigers alternated between third and fifth place in the standings; by the July 11 All-Star break, they were seven games out, with a 46–36 record. Al Kaline, Willie Horton, and Dick McAuliffe represented the Tigers at the Mid-Summer Classic.

The First Year Player's Amateur Draft of high school and college players originally began in 1965 for the "Rule 4" draft. Major league teams picked prospects in reverse order of the previous year's standings, with the American and National Leagues alternating picks. On June 8, the Tigers selected catcher Gene Lamont (thirteenth) who forty years later, would be their third base coach under manager Jim Leyland.

LaMont recalled Rick in a 2008 phone interview, saying "When Rick was general manager of the Tigers, he'd come to games in Toledo unannounced and just sit up in the stands and watch the game.... He didn't want to cause any commotion.... The players respected him and his baseball knowledge. Then the buzz would get around, 'Rick Ferrell is here!' Another thing I remember is he always dressed well and he carried himself well."

On July 24, 1965, Rick participated in a twenty-year retrospective of the 1945 All-Star Game in Baltimore — a game for which players had been chosen, but which was never actually played due to World War II travel restrictions. The All-Stars had been invited to a "Shrine of Immortals Night" to play two innings of the missed game. American Leaguer Hal Newhouser was shut out by National League pitcher Paul Derringer, 2–0. Rick struck out in his at-bat, but immensely enjoyed the players' reunion.

Back in Detroit, Dressen's Tigers ping-ponged in the standings until September 10 when they clinched a fourth place finish. In 1965, the Tigers went 89–73, their best record since 1961, finishing 13 games behind the Minnesota Twins. Outgoing American League champion New York Yankees fell to sixth.

With a first-division finish, several newcomers had shown promise as future Tiger stars. Slugger Willie Horton got 140 hits in 143 games with a team-high 104 RBIs. Denny McLain, 21, went 16–6 (2.62 ERA) and Lolich, 15–9. Norm Cash slammed 30 homers and won "American League Comeback Player of the Year."

Front office transactions began on October 4, the day after the 1965 season ended. Campbell and Ferrell traded outfielder George Thomas (.213) and infielder George Smith (Syracuse) to Boston for eight-year veteran right-hander Bill Monbouquette (10–18, 3.70 ERA). Red Sox manager Billy Herman gave up a starting pitcher to strengthen Boston's defense. In Minneapolis–St. Paul for the World Series between Minnesota and Los Angeles, Rick was mentioned in an article by Bill Veeck: "Detroit Tigers V.P. Rick Ferrell was standing around the lobby with a Cheshire-cat grin, a fat Cheshire cat, I might mention, taking bows as he mouthed the usual platitudes about how the trade was 'a good thing for both clubs (especially us).'"[29]

On December 15, the front office traded six-year Tigers pitcher Phil Regan (1–5) to the Los Angeles Dodgers for infielder Dick Tracewski (.215). Regan, known as "The Vulture," chewed up hitters in relief of starters in trouble while Tracewski established a long tenure as a Tigers coach.

11

❖ ❖ ❖

1966–1973

The Winning Years

When spring training opened in Lakeland in 1966, the Tigers played in a brand new ballpark at Tigertown named Joker Marchant Field. A recovered Charlie Dressen had returned to manage, assisted by coaches Bob Swift, Frank Skaff, Stubby Overmire, Mike Roarke, and Pat Mullin. Their young pitching staff included Denny McLain, Mickey Lolich, and Joe Sparma, all products of the farm system. The outfield—comprised of Al Kaline, Willie Horton, Jim Northrup, and Gates Brown—was considered one of the best in the American League.

On April 12, the Tigers opened on the road at Yankee Stadium and swept three from New York before opening at Tiger Stadium and winning two out of three games from the Washington Senators. By May 15, Detroit cruised in third place—a mere three games out of first—when history repeated itself: Manager Charlie Dressen suffered his second heart attack in just over a year and was admitted to the hospital. Again, third base coach Bob Swift astutely filled in. Although stunned, the Tigers fought to hold on to third place through May and pulled into second on June 21 with a 39–23 record, only three games behind.

On June 14, the Tigers traded expendable outfielder Don Demeter (.212) to the Boston Red Sox for pitcher Earl Wilson (5–5) and Joe Christopher. The next day, outfielder Al Kaline got his 2000th hit in a Tigers' 11–7 win at Fenway Park. By the All-Star break on July 10, the Tigers still held second place, eight games out with a 48–35 record. Five Detroit Tigers appeared on the All-Star team roster: Norm Cash, Bill Freehan, Al Kaline, Denny McLain, and Dick McAuliffe—the most in many years.

In a 2008 handwritten note, Bill Freehan recalled the help Rick gave him.

BILL FREEHAN: When I think of your father, Rick Ferrell, I remember him as a very quiet man. He was a fine catcher, and when I was young, he helped me when I would struggle behind the plate. He would always be there for any questions about defense and was a resource for me. Rick was always very positive with me because he knew that I was very hard on myself when I made a mistake. Having a Hall of Fame catcher as an instructor — what could have been better?

After the All-Star break, unexpected tragedy hit the Tigers: Subbing manager Bob Swift had been hospitalized during the time off. Another Tigers third base coach, Frank Skaff, was called to fill in and direct the young Tigers. When Swift was diagnosed with malignant lung cancer, Rick was saddened that the Tigers were losing their second manager to illness in as many months. Player injuries, ineffective hitting, sloppy defense, and a general lethargy negatively affected the team's play. Then, three weeks later on August 5, Charlie Dressen was readmitted to Henry Ford Hospital in Detroit with a severe kidney infection. Within five days, on August 10, he died.

Ferrell and the organization were reeling from the sudden passing of one manager and the terminal illness of another. Determined Tiger players persevered in their fight for second place in the A.L. against the encroaching Twins. Pitcher Earl Wilson strung together several wins with a simpler pitching windup. Ferrell told the *Chicago Daily Defender*, "I remember seeing him several years ago when he had that big kick and exaggerated windup. He couldn't get the ball near the plate. Now Wilson has a simple windup and he's throwing strikes." Acting-manager Frank Skaff said, "Wilson should be a big man in Detroit for the next four or five years. I like the deal with Wilson better every day!"[1]

After maintaining their second-place standing through trials and tribulations since June 21, another blow staggered the team in late September, just before playing the last, vital series: Hospitalized Bob Swift had fallen into a coma and was in critical condition from malignant lung cancer. From September 30 to October 2, Kansas City swept the fighting Tigers in a season-ending series as Detroit fell to third place on October 1, where they finished the season the next day after almost three months of occupying the runner-up position.

For the unnerving 1966 season, the Tigers went 88–74 (.543), finishing 10 games behind the first place Baltimore Orioles. But with an 89–73 (.549) record, the Minnesota Twins nosed Detroit out of second place by one game, another disappointing season end for Rick and the club.

The highest batting average belonged to Mickey Stanley (.289). The pitching staff starred pitcher Denny McLain, 22, who'd won 20 games (including two one-hitters) and Earl Wilson, obtained from Boston in June, who went 18–11 for the season, and 13–6 for the Tigers, including nine straight wins.

In late September Rick was faced with the task of finding a new manager. During a golf game he approached his first choice, former catcher Al Lopez, 58, about managing Detroit; Lopez declined, as did Bill Rigney of the California Angels. The club finally announced that Mayo Smith, former manager for the Phillies and Reds, had accepted the offer to become the new Tigers' skipper. Rick chose not to arrange a golf game with Smith, who had a ten handicap. The year's final epilogue occurred on October 17, when Bob Swift died in

Henry Ford Hospital of lung cancer at age 52. Two managers gone in one season was a first for the baseball history books and a sad season's end.

But the next season always beckoned. During January 1967, Rick and Jim Campbell went first to Puerto Rico to scout the Winter Leagues and from there on to Dunedin, Florida, to observe youngsters in the Instructional League. On February 11 for the twelfth year in a row, Rick competed in the 12th Annual March of Dimes Old Timers Game at St. Pete Beach, along with his participating brother Wes. Golf continued as a hobby that both brothers enjoyed.

Spring training percolated with hot, young players— Bill Freehan, Willie Horton, Mickey Stanley, Jim Northrup, Gates Brown, Dick McAuliffe, and Mickey Lolich — who had all been scouted and developed through the Tigers' farm system, in accordance with Fetzer and Ferrell's traditional philosophy. But during 1967 spring training, initial rumors of Denny McLain's gambling first surfaced. A *Flint Journal* sports reporter, Doug Mintline, informed Jim Campbell that while in the Tigertown clubhouse, he'd actually heard McLain on the telephone placing a bet on a college basketball game.[2] Campbell, with Rick Ferrell, called for an immediate meeting with Denny and manager Mayo Smith. During the private huddle, McLain confessed that he'd bet on the horses and college basketball games, but never bet on a baseball game. Befuddled, Jim and Rick accepted McLain's version, but Campbell told Smith to keep a careful eye on his pitcher off the field.[3]

Before the season began on April 7, the front office purchased catcher Jim Price from the Pittsburgh Pirates as a backup catcher to Bill Freehan. Tiger regulars for 1967 included first baseman Norm Cash, second sacker Dick McAuliffe, shortstop Ray Oyler, third baseman Don Wert, outfielders Jim Northrup, Al Kaline, and Mickey Stanley, and catcher Bill Freehan. Earl Wilson, Denny McLain, Mickey Lolich, and Joe Sparma comprised the slated staff of starting pitchers. Reliever John Hiller would rejoin the team in July, after recuperating at his Canadian home from a heart attack.

Detroit opened on the road April 11 against the California Angels at Anaheim Stadium and were pinned with a loss, then opened in Detroit on April 18. Opening Day in Detroit was always a festive celebration for a sellout crowd with high hopes for the season, and the Tigers prevailed, 4–1. On April 30, the team was in first place.

Rick, meanwhile, continued monitoring the development of minor league prospects. From May through June the Tigers seesawed between first and second; from July to the beginning of September, between third and fourth place.

During the baseball season, the disciplined Ferrell usually worked all day, every day at his stadium office or traveled on the road, but never missed seeing a Tigers home game if he was in town. When the team played night games, he didn't arrive home until after midnight, but was up at 7:00 A.M. the next morning, heading back to the stadium, regular as a clock. As the number of night games increased, he would leave home at 7:30 A.M., return after midnight, only to get up and repeat the day-into-night schedule again. Like the Energizer bunny, he just kept on ticking, year after year.

An historic event in Detroit's history occurred in the city on July 23, 1967, often referred to as "Black Day in July." Following a Sunday doubleheader against the Yankees downtown at Tiger Stadium, the Ferrell family walked to their car in the players' parking lot. An unusual smell of smoke pervaded the air and the sky held an eerie, orange glow. Chaos engulfed the city streets around Tiger Stadium, as Detroit's inner-city residences were burning up in flames. In the simmering July heat, racial riots had suddenly, violently erupted throughout the city.

A nervous Rick drove his family safely to their east-side home, but the "Detroit Riots" lasted through four days of burning, looting, and destruction that left forty-three people dead. After that, downtown Detroit never fully returned to being the fashionable, energetic metropolitan city it had been in the 1950s and 1960s, and residents began a "flight to suburbia."

The Tigers didn't play again until July 27 in Baltimore where the indomitable Denny McLain shut out the Orioles, 4–0. By July 30, the fighting Tigers had gained third place, 53–45, and finished August 1½ games out. September brought more musical chairs among Boston, Minnesota, Detroit, and Chicago, with all moving between first and fourth place in the standings. Before the September 30 season-ending games, Mayo Smith's Tigers were lodged in fourth place, yet only 1½ games out, bunched together with the other three. The 1967 American League pennant race wound up being one of the tightest pennant races in all of baseball history.

Rick was at Tiger Stadium Saturday and Sunday, September 30 and October 1, for the season's final four games: two doubleheaders, back-to-back, with the California Angels. In order to tie and force a one-game playoff, Detroit had to win all four. In the end, the Tigers managed two splits.

As luck would have it, the other competitors—Boston and Minnesota—were battling each other at Fenway Park. On October 1, Red Sox ace Jim Lonborg won his twenty-second game, 5–3, to clinch the 1967 A.L. pennant for Boston with a 92–70 record. The Tigers tied the Twins for second place, each with a 91–71 record, one game behind Boston.

Detroit had given the season their all. Despite injury, outfielder Al Kaline finished with a team-high .308 batting average. Bill Freehan played a career-high 155 games (147 as catcher), hitting .282 with 20 home runs, a team-high 146 hits, and 74 RBIs, the highest for all A.L. catchers. Baseball writers voted him "Tiger of the Year."

On November 4, 1967, Rick and GM Jim Campbell were in Boston the morning after the World Series ended, when Jim suffered an agonizing kidney stone attack that required his hospitalization. When Rick returned to Detroit, Fetzer appointed him to fill in as acting general manager for the Tigers until Jim could return to work. Tigers representatives Ferrell and Fetzer attended an American League meeting together in Chicago, as Jim recuperated. Rick's hopeful year-end mantra — "We'll get 'em next year!" — would finally prove prophetic.

In January 1968, Ferrell again traveled to Puerto Rico for two weeks to scout before spring training began in mid–February. At Tigertown, watching pitcher Tom Timmerman four out of five days impressed Rick. "He threw hard and had a fine sinker," reported Ferrell.[4] Of new backup catcher Jim Price, purchased from Pittsburgh, Ferrell said, "I don't know where you'd find a better number-two catcher. Jim is coming along well. He did a pretty good job for us last year."[5]

The year 1968 was one of the most politically and socially volatile years the United States has ever known, which, of course, affected baseball, the national pastime. Detroit was still recovering from the trauma and destruction of the 1967 race riots. This year, due to Martin Luther King, Jr.'s, murder and funeral, the Tigers' home opener was postponed from April 9 to the 10th.

The lineup for Detroit remained essentially unchanged from last year's. After losing the home opener to Boston, the Tigers staged a nine-game winning streak that vaulted them into first place on April 18. During May 3 to 8, they fell back to second place. But on May 10, the Tigers regained the lead where they remained all season long, pursued by the Baltimore Orioles.

A devastating personal tragedy struck Rick Ferrell out of the blue in 1968. On April 20, his wife Ruth drove him to the airport for a flight to Minnesota to scout the Yankees. The next night, Rick received a call to return home to Michigan at once. After twenty-eight years of marriage, his wife, 48, had died suddenly of a heart attack on April 21. A shocked Ferrell flew home to Michigan to absorb his loss. With his children, he flew Ruth's body back to Greensboro, North Carolina, where she was buried in the Ferrell family plot at New Garden Cemetery beside their infant daughter, Janet. A numb, bereft Rick would now grapple with suddenly becoming a widower at age 62 and a single parent to his four children, whose ages now ranged from sixteen to twenty-six years old.

For the rest of that year, the Tigers' games became — again — distractions from Rick's grief. Thankfully, the team won consistently, with much drama and tension highlighting the games. The Tigers proved to be a strong offensive team, while not hitting for high average. Outfielder Jim Northrup, single-handedly, astounded Detroit fans with his dramatic baseball flair. On May 17 in the ninth inning of a 3–2 deficit, Jim hit his first grand slam home run to beat the Senators, 7–3. In a June 24 game against the Chicago White Sox, Northrup slugged a record-tying two grand slam home runs, back-to-back, in the fifth and sixth innings for a 14–3 victory and eight RBIs. Then five days later on June 29 against the White Sox, the unbelievable slugger hit his fourth grand slam of the year, helping McLain to a fourteenth win, 5–2. Two days later with Detroit leading 2–0 in the ninth inning over Baltimore, Northrup leapt high, reaching over the left-field wall to snare Davey Johnson's long drive, then threw it to the infielder for a double play to preserve the Tigers' victory. With Northrup on fire at the All-Star break, the Tigers staked out first place with a 9½ game lead.

A couple of Tiger players hit two homers in a game during the season. On July 5, Bill Freehan connected twice for an 8–5 win over Oakland. In a game against the second-place Baltimore Orioles on July 27, Willie Horton blasted two homers to propel McLain's twentieth victory, a three-hit, 9–0 shutout. And again on August 8, Bill Freehan hit two long round-trippers in a 14–1 win over the Cleveland Indians for McLain's twenty-third victory.

From September 9 to 21, Detroit steamrolled through an eleven-game winning streak to sweep the Angels, Athletics, and Yankees. Denny McLain won his 30th game on September 14 to become the first pitcher to win 30 games since the Cardinals' Dizzy Dean in 1934. On September 15, catcher Bill Freehan, for the third time, hit two homers in a game against the A's in which the incredible Jim Northrup also hit two homers to support Lolich's, 13–0, shutout.

A monumentally exciting day came on September 17, before a crowd of 46,500, when the Tigers defeated the Yankees, 2–1, and Boston beat Baltimore, 2–0, which clinched the American League pennant for the Bengals. At Tiger Stadium, fans leapt over the walls onto the field in a wild frenzy! They had not won a pennant for 23 years—since 1945 when they beat out Ferrell's Washington Senators team. For a change, Rick was not at Tiger Stadium that day, but was in San Francisco advance-scouting the Cardinals, in case the Tigers played them in the post-season. He gulped watching the Giants' Gaylord Perry and the Cards' Ray Washburn pitch two no-hitters, back-to back, on September 17 and 18.

The jubilant Tigers concluded the 1968 season with a 103–59 record, as Baltimore followed in second place, 12 games behind. Now the team charged on to the World Series against the St. Louis Cardinals. Finally one of Rick Ferrell's teams would play in the World Series. He'd been close in 1945 when catching for the Washington Senators, but they'd lost out to Detroit in the final week that year. Now twenty-three years later in 1968, the Detroit Tigers were taking a thrilled Ferrell to the fall classic for the first time in his forty-two-year baseball career!

Manager Mayo Smith's most fortunate dilemma was that his team had four fine-hitting outfielders: Al Kaline, Willie Horton, Mickey Stanley, and Jim Northrup. To get a healed Kaline into the lineup, the veteran manager replaced weak-hitting shortstop Ray Oyler with center fielder Mickey Stanley so the other three fly hawks could get into the World Series. The obvious problem with Smith's plan was that Mickey Stanley, an outfielder, would play a very difficult, unfamiliar infield position during an intense World Series championship.

Rick and the front office contingent traveled to the 1968 championship games when they opened on Wednesday, October 2, at St. Louis' Busch Stadium. Offensively, both teams boasted a strong lineup that collectively included several future Hall of Famers. The Detroit Tigers' batting order for the first game was comprised of Dick McAuliffe (2B), Mickey Stanley (SS), Al Kaline (RF), Norm Cash (1B), Willie Horton (LF), Jim Northrup (CF), Bill Freehan (C), Dick Wert (3B), and Denny McLain (P). On the bench was power pinch-hitter Gates Brown.

The St. Louis Cardinals had a 97–65 record for the season. Manager Red Schoendienst's lineup card put speedster Lou Brock (LF) at the top of the order, followed by Curt Flood (CF), Roger Maris (RF), Orlando Cepeda (1B), Tim McCarver (C), Mike Shannon (3B), Julian Javier (2B), Dal Maxvill (SS), and Bob Gibson (P).

Both teams led with their ace pitchers, Denny McLain and Bob Gibson, 29. The Cards' Gibson (22–9, 1.12 ERA, 268 strikeouts) KO'd seventeen batters by the end of the game for a 4–0 St. Louis win, breaking Sandy Koufax's World Series record for most strikeouts in a game (15). In game two the next afternoon, October 3, Detroit roared back behind ace Mickey Lolich, who fanned nine Cardinals and hit his first — and final — career home run for a convincing 8–1 victory, evening the series at one game apiece.

Ferrell returned for games three through five, which began Saturday afternoon, October 5, at Tiger Stadium in Detroit. St. Louis won both by lopsided scores of 7–3 and 10–1.

Knowing that only two teams had ever come back from a 3–1 deficit to win the World Series made game five at Tiger Stadium a must-win for Detroit. On Monday, October 7, Mayo Smith called on his lefthander Lolich, who, after giving up a three-run homer to Cepeda in the first inning, pitched nine perfect, scoreless innings. The Series' turning point occurred when Brock failed to slide on a bang-bang play at home in the fifth inning. Catcher Bill Freehan caught Horton's perfect throw from left field and body-blocked the Cardinals' runner off the plate from scoring! Kaline and Cash delivered key hits for a thrilling, 5–3, come-from-behind Tigers win.

Rick and the Tigers flew back to St. Louis with the Tigers in a deep hole, three games to two. On October 9, McLain snuffed Cardinals starter Ray Washburn and his relievers in a runaway 10–1 victory. Jim Northrup connected for yet another dramatic grand slam home run, and the World Series was tied at three games a piece.

McLain's first Series win had forced a game seven showdown in St. Louis, and Kerrie drove to St. Louis to join Rick for the final game. Lolich and Gibson battled through seven and two-thirds scoreless innings, retiring hitters with great efficiency. But with two out and two on, Detroit's hero, Jim Northrup, nailed a line drive triple past center fielder Curt Flood that scored the winning runs in a thrilling, 4–1, victory!

Afterwards in the clubhouse champagne exploded and popped out of bottles onto the Tigers players, manager, coaches — even drenching the properly-suited president, Mr. Fetzer—in uproarious, victorious mayhem.[6] Rick was filled with exhilaration. The Tigers returned to Detroit amid cheering fanfare, wild celebration, welcoming crowds, and a festive parade that united the city in victory as it momentarily forgot the turmoil and destruction of the previous year's city riots.

Three-game winner Mickey Lolich (1.67 ERA) became the Series MVP. Norm Cash had hit .385 with 10 hits; Kaline, in his first World Series, went .379, with eight RBIs on 11 hits, including two homers. Horton and Northrup collected seven hits a piece, with the latter slamming two home runs for eight RBIs. The seven-game Series drew nearly 380,000 eager spectators. Each Tiger player's share of the proceeds was $10,937.[7] After working and waiting for a lifetime, Rick Ferrell would finally get a World Series ring—the perfect surprise for his sixty-third birthday on October 12.

But amid the Tigers' euphoria, trouble brewed behind the scenes. On November 29, Tom McKeon, attorney with the U.S. Department of Justice, met with Jim Campbell and Denny McLain to allow the FBI to further question McLain about his suspected gambling. Apparently McLain convinced his interrogators that he was innocent of all speculative crimes, and the matter seemed closed.

Also at season's end, after ten years of marriage, GM Jim Campbell's lovely, yet lonely, red-haired wife, Helene, issued an ultimatum to her workaholic husband to make a decision: "It's either me or baseball!" she declared.[8] Traveling and baseball kept him away continually. Jim chose baseball. The childless couple divorced, with Helene returning to home-state Ohio while Jim remained married to baseball for the rest of his days, living a mile from the ballpark.

Detroit's front office faced new issues during October 1968, when professional baseball expanded again, adding two teams to each league for the 1969 season. The Kansas City Royals and the Seattle Pilots joined the American League, while the San Diego Padres and the Montreal Expos were added to the National League. The two twelve-team leagues were split into two six-team divisions—East and West — with the pennant winner determined by post-season playoffs. The new teams required thirty players each for their rosters, to be drafted from existing teams. Existing clubs could protect fifteen players from being drafted during the first round, the so-called "untouchables," but could expect to lose at least one player to expansion, with compensation of $175,000 each. Kansas City drafted three Detroit pitchers. The Seattle Pilots took shortstop Ray Oyler, outfielder Wayne Comer, and pitcher Mike Marshall. Meanwhile, Fetzer broadened his broadcasting interests to include television of expansion team games and created his own channel, PASS, to exclusively broadcast Tiger games.

During the 1969 season, baseball celebrated its Centennial complete with an All-Time Great baseball game and a new major league logo. Following expansion in Kansas City and Seattle, the Detroit Tigers were now part of the six-team AL East Division, along with Baltimore, Boston, Cleveland, New York, and Washington. The AL West division was comprised of the California, Chicago, Kansas City, Minnesota, Oakland, and Seattle clubs.

The nine-member Major League Rules Committee consisted of American League representatives Rick Ferrell, Cal Griffith, and umpire Cal Hubbard; National League reps John McHale (Montreal), Chub Feeney (San Francisco), and Joe L. Brown (Pittsburgh), plus three minor league reps. Meeting on January 29, discussion centered on a possible new "designated hitter" rule in baseball that would allow a pre-designated pinch-hitter to bat for the pitcher while still keeping the pitcher in the game. The committee voted that the rule would be tried — experimentally — in four minor leagues. Soon afterward Bowie Kuhn was elected as the new baseball commissioner.

Major leaguers finally reported to spring training in 1969 — two weeks late — after resolving demands that management increase their baseball pensions. While scouting in Florida, Rick became wracked with severe lower back pain, forcing him to fly back to Detroit to see his Henry Ford Hospital doctors. On March 29, Ferrell was promptly hospitalized to undergo a spinal disc operation which sidelined him temporarily. Scout Wayne Blackburn filled in for him while Ferrell recuperated.

Mayo Smith, 54, returned to manage the Tigers, hoping to repeat the 1968 success. Tigers' radio announcers Ernie Harwell and Ray Lane returned to the booth while TV broadcasts were delivered by Tigers third-base great George Kell and Larry Osterman.

The Champs opened their 1969 season on April 8 at Tiger Stadium by winning a doubleheader against Cleveland, but by April's end, had sunk to fifth place with a 10–10 record, 4½ games out. The players began pressing as fans were losing patience, but managed to improve to third place for all of May and June. Following a five-game winning streak in mid–July, Detroit assumed second place in the standings, where they remained for the rest of the season, failing in their attempts to catch the first-place Baltimore Orioles for another pennant win.

The Tigers went 90–72, finishing 19 games behind Earl Weaver's unstoppable Baltimore Orioles' 109–53. Willie Horton had hit three grand slam home runs during the season, leading the Tigers with 91 RBIs. Jim Northrup had led the team with a .295 batting average. Gold Gloves were awarded to Bill Freehan and Mickey Stanley.

Mickey Lolich compiled a 19–11 record, missing his twentieth win with a 2–1 loss to Baltimore in the final game of the season. Pitcher Denny McLain led the league in victories (24–9, 2.80 ERA), tying for the Cy Young Award with Mike Cuellar. The problem with Denny all season long, however, had been his self-absorbed egotism and total disregard for team rules and fellow players. He had left the All-Star Game early in his plane, stranding Mickey Lolich and his wife in the city, who'd planned to fly back to Detroit with him.[9] McLain had personal financial difficulties off the field, plus the FBI was still investigating suspicions of his booking and gambling.

On December 2, 1969, the Tigers traded pitcher Joe Sparma to the Montreal Expos for pitcher Jerry Robertson. Then pitcher Pat Dobson and infielder Dave Campbell were swapped to the San Diego Padres for pitcher Joe Niekro. Rick had scouted Niekro in the National League and thought he was a better pitcher without using his knuckleball pitch.

Detroit's front office looked forward with optimism to the 1970 season ... until February 19, 1970. That day they received word from Commissioner Bowie Kuhn that Denny McLain would be suspended from baseball while the Commissioner's Office continued its own investigation into rumors of gambling, bookmaking, and mafia relationships.

On March 31, McLain was suspended from playing baseball for three months, until July 1, 1970. When the season began a week later, the Tigers had to open with a three-man rotation: Mickey Lolich, Earl Wilson, and Joe Niekro. Lolich shut out the Washington Senators, 5–0, in their home opener on April 6. When the Tigers finally opened at Tiger Stadium on April 14, they were in second place with a 4–3 record. Lolich stopped the Indians, 12–4, as his team began an eight-game winning streak through April 24 that took them to first place before falling to fourth. Minor league pitchers Tom Timmerman and Les Cain joined the starting rotation to bolster the three mainstays.

The Tigers rose to third place on June 9, 1970 — the same day Willie Horton slugged three homers to defeat the Brewers, 8–3. When McLain was reinstated on July 1, the Tigers were 38–33. But the fallen hurler lasted only into the sixth inning, while the team beat the Yankees, 6–5. By July 8, the Tigers occupied second place for a month, then until September 10, dropped back into third.

Off the field, 26-year-old Denny McLain's brazen attitude brought more migraines to Rick and the Tigers' front office. In late August the unruly pitcher poured retaliatory buckets of ice water over the heads of two different sportswriters who'd written unfavorably about him, and on August 28, the Tigers, dismayed themselves, suspended McLain, temporarily.

On September 9, following a three-hour discussion, Bowie Kuhn suspended McLain for the rest of the season for gun possession.[10] As events developed, the final game he'd ever pitch for Detroit had been on August 26, 1970, a 6–3 loss to the Angels. Since his return, he had compiled a 3–5 record (4.65 ERA), completing one game in fourteen starts, hardly the twenty-four-game winner of the previous year.

Detroit's reeling team dropped into fourth place on September 17, where they finished the season on October 1. John Hiller pitched a two-hit shutout against Cleveland, his first complete game since June 1969, and tied the A.L. record for seven consecutive strikeouts. The Tigers' record was 79–83, below .500 for the first time in seven years, 29 games behind the first-place Orioles who finished 108–54. Lolich led the pitching staff with 14–19 record. Disappointed manager Mayo Smith resigned when his contract expired on October 1. On October 2, the Tigers announced that temperamental ex–Yankee, 42-year-old Billy Martin, would be the new Tigers manager for the next two years, a spitfire choice that delighted Ferrell.

On October 8, the clever Campbell and Ferrell engineered a masterful eight-player deal with the Washington Senators. They got rid of Denny McLain, who was traded to the Senators with Don Wert, Norm McRae, and Elliott Maddux for pitchers Joe Coleman and Jim Hannan plus infielders Eddie Brinkman and Aurelio Roderiguez. Many argued that this was one of the greatest transactions ever dealt in Tigers history. Not only was their troublesome pitcher gone, but McLain's skills were so diminished that he would compile a losing record of 10–22 in 1971 for Washington, winning only 18 more games in his career, while losing 36. Joe Coleman would blossom for the Tigers, winning 20 games in 1971, 19 in '72, and 23 games in 1973. Brinkman and Rodriguez would anchor the left side of the infield for several years, helping lead Detroit to the 1972 American League East Division championship.

In the 1970 draft Campbell, Ferrell, and company had selected forty-nine players for the Tigers. Their best pick was pitcher Fernando Arroyo, 18, from Sacramento, California.

Rick's personal life had changed dramatically since the death of his wife in 1968. By 1970, his four children had completed high school and left home for college. The large six-bedroom Grosse Pointe home on Berkshire Road was too large and empty for Rick to remain there alone. He sold the home along with half of his furnishings, and relocated to a smaller, rented two-bedroom apartment in Harper Woods where his children often visited.

Having to develop a social life for himself at age 65, Rick had begun getting together with friends after work during the off-season. One such friend, Patricia Kenney from the Detroit Tigers' accounting department, introduced Rick to her circle, who welcomed him. The group enjoyed sports, holidays, and parties together in a supportive network that brought new enjoyment to Rick's solitary personal life and he blossomed considerably in his middle age.

Lew Matlin joined the club's executive team in January 1971, as the Tigers' new Director of Special Events, Speakers Bureau and Group Sales. Lew would be a member of the Tigers' executive team for the next nineteen years. The Rules Committee passed a rule requiring mandatory protective helmets be worn by all batters.

Early injuries plagued the 1971 Tigers. In January pitcher John Hiller, 27, suffered a sudden heart attack —followed by abdominal surgery— that put him out for the season to recuperate. In spring training, pitcher Les Cain developed a sore shoulder. Then in spring training, right-hander Joe Coleman, McLain's replacement in the rotation, was struck in the head by a line drive, suffering a fractured skull. Nobody knew how long he'd be on the disabled list.

New manager Billy Martin's 1971 Tigers starting lineup was comprised primarily of the core players from the 1968 World Champs, plus newcomers Aurelio Rodriguez and Eddie Brinkman. The pitching rotation, compromised by injuries, had Lolich and Niekro as primary starters, with help from Pat Dobson and Mike Kilkenney. The Tigers added 10-year veteran right-hander Dean Chance, acquired from the New York Mets.

Some people thought the hard-drinking, hot-tempered Billy Martin would prove an ill-fit with Fetzer's conservative, straight-laced Tigers organization. But the players had been disillusioned by Denny McLain's bizarre behavior and suspensions during 1970, and Fetzer, Campbell, and Ferrell were hoping that Martin's aggressive leadership would light a fire and bring new life to their ex–World Champs.

On April 6, Detroit opened at Tiger Stadium for one game with Cleveland, which Lolich won, 8–2, followed by a long road trip to Baltimore and New York. Miraculously Joe Coleman's head injury had healed sufficiently for him to start against Oakland on April 24, but he lost, 5–4. By June 30, Detroit was in third with a 43–24 record.

Detroit hosted the 1971 All-Star Game on July 13 with four Tigers selected: Mickey Lolich, Bill Freehan, Al Kaline, and Norm Cash. Ferrell and his family watched the American League win, 6–4.

As hoped by the Tiger brass, Billy Martin's flamboyant style motivated the Tigers all year. On August 12, they moved into second place in the American League East where they finished the 1971 season, 91–71, (.562) 12 games behind the Baltimore Orioles, a major improvement over the previous season.

Southpaw Mickey Lolich won a league-leading 25 games (2.92 ERA), completing 29 games out of 45 starts. In over 376 innings pitched, Lolich amassed 308 strikeouts, the highest number in the majors since Grover Cleveland Alexander in 1917, giving him "Tiger of the Year" honors. Joe Coleman won 20 games (3.15 ERA). Detroit led the majors in home runs: 179, and Billy Martin's two-year contract was extended by another year, until 1973.

GM Jim Campbell had refused to negotiate contracts with lawyers who represented players, preferring to negotiate directly with the player himself, as he'd always done. Mickey Lolich's lawyer, Bob Fenton, who'd represented the pitcher in contract negotiations since 1968, wound up talking with Rick Ferrell rather than Campbell. Even when Lolich showed up to talk without his lawyer, he saw Ferrell. Finally Lolich signed with Rick in spring training. Seeking talent, the Tigers had drafted fifty players during 1971. The January 18, 1972, *Chicago Tribune* stated that ex–Tiger Denny McLain owed $137,000, with only $3,300 to his name.

As spring training was humming along, Rick and others feared a players strike might be inevitable. Sure enough, on April 1, the Major League Players Association voted for the first-ever players' strike. Executive union director Marvin Miller wanted the players' pension fund increased by $850,000. At

Tigertown, a stunned Jim Campbell announced, "We're closing down. The players were told to clean out their lockers and take their equipment. The clubhouse is locked and the facilities are closed."[11] Owners and many players, alike, were shocked that the disagreement had shut down baseball just as the season was to begin.

After 86 games were cancelled — six by the Tigers — the 1972 season began on April 15. Winning the home opener, the Tigers launched a ten-day road trip, returning in late April in first place with a 5–3 record. Rick's team remained in first through May, June and most of July. On June 27 at Tiger Stadium on only two days' rest, Lolich won his twelfth, 5–2, against the Yankees. In the first inning, Rodriguez, Kaline and Horton hit consecutive, back-to-back home runs, providing memorable thrills for the fans. In early July, southpaw and fan favorite John Hiller, 29, was reactivated — 18 months after his heart attack — to pitch batting practice. Four Tigers went to the 1972 All Star Game on July 25 in Atlanta: Mickey Lolich, Joe Coleman, Bill Freehan, and Norm Cash, which was won by the National League.

Eager to strengthen their staff for the stretch, the front office made two important transactions in August. They claimed Phillies left-hander Woody Fryman, 32, and Dodgers catcher Duke Sims on waivers, who would hit .316 during the last two months. In 16 games, Fryman would register a 10–3 record (2.06 ERA). The Tigers swung between first and third until mid–September. The pennant race intensified as Detroit, Boston, Baltimore, and New York all jockeyed for top position in the Eastern Division. The Tigers turned on the steam. Joe Coleman pitched the Tigers to five of their 14 wins as they lost only five games.

When the Red Sox visited Tiger Stadium for the final series, October 2–4, they were a half game ahead of the second-place Tigers. These last three games of the season would determine the 1972 division winner. For the first game on Friday, October 2, an excited Ferrell and 51,518 fans swarmed into Tiger Stadium to see Mickey Lolich strike out 15 Boston batters for a 4–1 win, to reclaim the lead. On Saturday with new Tiger hurler Woody Fryman starting, Al Kaline cut loose a clutch blast in the seventh that won the game for the Tigers, 3–1, as well as the 1972 divisional championship! The crowd exploded! Despite Sunday's 4–1 loss, first place was Detroit's, with an 86–70 record to Boston's 85–70 record. Rick felt on top of the world.

The 1972 division playoffs between Detroit and the Oakland A's were conducted October 7–12, with the victors needing to win three of a possible five games. The Tigers' executives traveled to game one in Oakland, California, on Saturday, October 7. Mickey Lolich faced Oakland's Catfish Hunter and stopper Rollie Fingers into the eleventh inning with a 1–1 tie score. Kaline homered, but the A's scored two in the eleventh to win, 3–2. In game two, the Tigers struggled against veteran "Blue Moon" Odom, who pitched a 5–0 shutout while allowing just three safeties. Oakland: 2 games; Tigers: 0.

Ferrell traveled back to Detroit with the team for the third contest. Every battle became a must-win for the Tigers, who faced early elimination. In a clutch performance on Tuesday, October 10, Coleman stopped the Oakland train, 3–0, striking out 14 batters. On Wednesday, Detroit rallied for three runs in the bottom of the tenth to snare a 4–3 desperation victory and tie Oakland for the series, two games to two.

Thursday, October 12, was Rick Ferrell's sixty-seventh birthday, as well as the final game of the American League Championship Series. His family and friends excitedly gathered in their box seats to watch, along with over 50,000 screaming fans at Tiger Stadium. "Blue Moon" Odom took on Woody Fryman, as the Tigers scored in the first. But the A's scored twice, winning 2–1, on just four hits. There was no final American League pennant for a disappointed Ferrell or the Tigers in 1972. With Jim Campbell, he attended the World Series, which Oakland won over Cincinnati, 4–3.

During the 1972 season, pitching had been Detroit's strength. Mickey Lolich compiled a 22–14 record (2.50 ERA), while Coleman won 19. The Tigers produced a combined batting average of .237, two percentage points below the league average. Kaline's .313 average was highest among regulars. Attendance at Tiger Stadium was first in the A.L. at 1,892,386 for the season.[12]

Shortly after the World Series ended, brother Wes telephoned Rick bearing sad personal news: His wife, Lois, a former Miss Sarasota, had died on October 21 in Sarasota, Florida. Rick hurried to her funeral in Guilford. Now that both Ferrell brothers were widowed bachelors, Wes would need to adjust to his single status as Rick had. "He'll learn," Rick surmised, speaking from experience.

Rick took his two daughters to Waikiki Beach, Hawaii, for baseball's winter meetings in December 1972 where one matter of discussion was passage of the designated hitter rule. Five of the nine members on the Rules Committee had voted against the new rule, including Rick, and its pros and cons were intensely debated.

On January 11, 1973, in Chicago, Commissioner Kuhn called a special meeting of the Rules Committee during which the rule change was re-introduced and approved, one of the most historic changes ever made to the game of baseball. The DH rule would be used in the A.L. only, on an experimental basis, for three years and would not be applied to World Series or inter-league games.[13]

In an article in *The Sporting News*, Rick discussed the Tigers' catchers for 1973. "Bill Freehan will be there for an awful lot of games before he quits.... Bill stands a good chance of breaking my record. The thing in Freehan's favor is an early start.... I've aways liked [Duke] Sims and now he's a steadier catcher than ever. Martin might carry a third receiver. Gene Lamont is great defensively. I'd say he was the most valuable player with the pennant winner at Montgomery (Southern League), catching every day. He really handled the Montgomery pitching."[14]

In February, Rick again negotiated with Mickey Lolich's lawyer, Mr. Fenton, with whom GM Campbell refused to talk. Lolich signed a $100,000 contract after his excellent 1972 season — the highest salary ever paid a pitcher in Tigers history — but he would only win 16 games in 1973. In February, the players' union called another strike over salary arbitration and other issues, with baseball losing twelve work days and spring training opening late. Rick couldn't believe it. A three-year collective bargaining agreement raised owners' contribution to the players' pension fund and increased the minimum salary from $13,500 to $15,000 for first-year players.

Once spring training opened in Lakeland, more problems followed manager Billy Martin. On March 27, Martin and a minor leaguer were arrested together outside a restaurant-bar for using profanity and making racial comments. Each paid the $32 fine and went back to his hotel.[15] Then the volatile Martin had a disagreement with outfielder Willie Horton, which resulted in a three-man conference with Jim Campbell on March 30. Martin became upset, left, claiming he was quitting. The next morning, a repentant Billy knocked on Campbell's hotel room door and asked to return, which Campbell agreed to. However Martin's hot temper would shorten his tenure with Detroit.

The Tigers opened on April 7 at Cleveland Stadium with practically the same lineup used since 1968. Mickey Lolich faced Cleveland's Gaylord Perry, winning, 2–1. Ironically, Perry would be there at season's end, as well. Detroit began the 1973 season in third place, but following an eight-game losing streak, slid to fifth on June 25. During July the team bounced between fourth and third place. The front office signed a young outfielder named Ron LeFlore, 22, who'd served three years in Southern Michigan Prison for robbery. The young outfielder's hitting, throwing ability, and speed had impressed Martin and LeFlore was assigned to the Clinton, Iowa, farm club.[16]

Since 1973 was the fortieth anniversary of the first 1933 All-Star Game, festivities were planned around the Mid-Summer Classic. On July 22, two days before the actual All-Star Game at Busch Stadium in St Louis, an All-Star reunion game was played with forty American and National League All-Stars gathered, including Rick Ferrell, Lefty Grove, Joe Cronin, and Lefty Gomez. They swapped old memories, which Rick thoroughly enjoyed, as the National League shut out the junior circuit All-Stars, 7–0.

During the actual July 24th All-Star Game ceremonies in Kansas City, Commissioner Bowie Kuhn gave All-Star rings to both the 1973 All-Stars and the nineteen original All-Star players in attendance from the first game. Rick and Wes Ferrell, along with Joe Cronin, Sam West, and Ben Chapman, received fortieth anniversary, claret-red Linde Star rings to commemorate the first All-Star Game.[17]

By mid-season players and fans, alike, were adapting to the new designated hitter rule. American League games had gained excitement due to greater offense, more frequent homers, and critical RBIs. Aging power sluggers could lengthen their careers and still contribute as designated hitters.

By August 30, with his team in third place, seven games out, Billy Martin's temper erupted again — this time at Cleveland Indians spitball pitcher Gaylord Perry. After ordering two Tiger pitchers to throw spitballs in retaliation, an irate A.L. President Joe Cronin suspended Martin for three days. The infuriated manager criticized Kuhn to the press, which sealed his fate with the Detroit Tigers. Despite having another year on his $65,000 contract, Martin was fired on September 2 during his suspension "for the good of the organization," and was promptly hired to manage the Texas Rangers.

Third base coach Joe Schultz managed the Tigers for September, finishing in third place, 85–77, 12 games behind Baltimore. Pitcher Joe Coleman led the staff with a 23–15 record; John Hiller went 10–5 (1.44 ERA) and was voted "American League Comeback Player of the Year." Mickey Stanley earned a Gold Glove Award. Attendance remained strong throughout the 1973, totaling 1,724,146.

As soon as the 1973 World Series ended, Campbell and Ferrell urgently sought a new manager to help rebuild their aging roster. On October 11, Ralph Houk, who had just resigned from the Yankees, accepted the managerial job of rebuilding the Tigers by signing a three-year contract — and was a plum pick for the organization.[18]

In rebuilding for 1974, the Tigers drafted thirty-five total players, with twenty-eight coming during the June draft, but none made it to the big club. In October, veteran infielder Dick McAuliffe went to the Boston Red Sox for outfielder Ben Oglivie and Frank Howard was released. Minor leaguer Larry Elliott was traded to the St. Louis Cardinals for 24-year-old rookie catcher John Wockenfuss.

At a meeting of the American League owners in Chicago on October 23, former Yankees' general manager Lee MacPhail, Jr., was selected to replace American League president Joe Cronin, 55, starting January 1, 1974. Also, the league decided that the year-old designated-hitter experiment would become a permanent rule. Attendance and interest in baseball had markedly improved since its implementation. On the Major League Playing Rules Committee, Chicago White Sox owner John Allyn replaced Dick Butler, American League umpire supervisor, to join the Tigers' Rick Ferrell and the Twins' Cal Griffith as American League representatives.

12

❖ ❖ ❖

1974–1983

Rebuilding with Ralph Houk and Sparky Anderson

In spring training 1974, manager Ralph Houk knew his job for the next three years would be rebuilding the Tigers. In a 2008 telephone interview, he explained: "When Jim Campbell talked me into coming to Detroit, he said they didn't expect to win, but they wanted me to develop ballplayers, and they were very honest about it. That's how I came to know Rick so well, and of course, Rick gave me good information."[1]

Houk's responsibility was to help develop the young players into regulars as they replaced the aging 1968 World Series veterans. The transition included having catcher Bill Freehan play half his games at first base and veteran Al Kaline become the designated hitter.

On April 5 at Memorial Stadium, the Baltimore Orioles edged Detroit, 3–2, as Detroit stayed in third place through May, with a 22–24 record, only three games out. Losing streaks drove the Tigers into fifth place as they closed out July.

In the Amateur Free-Agent Draft, front office members had selected Tempe, Arizona, catcher Lance Parrish, 17, (first), pitcher Mark Fidrych, 19, from Massachusetts, plus hurler Bob Sykes. With a forward focus on developing youth, the club continued eliminating the older players. In August, 14-year Tigers first baseman Norm Cash was released while outfielder Jim Northrup was sent to Montreal.

Through the month of September the Tigers went 10–20, finishing the 1974 season in sixth place — last in the A.L. East — 19 games behind Baltimore. After twenty-two seasons, outfielder Al Kaline, 39, retired with ten Gold Gloves after bashing his 3000th career hit in September. Reliever John Hiller pitched 17 wins (2.64 ERA), but perennial mainstay Lolich went 16–21 and the team performed at a mediocre level. A Detroit championship appeared very far way.

Vice President Rick Ferrell, Frank Skaff, and Jack Tighe comprised the Tigers' major league scouting staff in 1974. However, down in Guilford County,

213

N.C., Rick's brother, George Ferrell, retired from his position as a Tigers scout after seventeen years.

In that 2008 interview, Ralph Houk discussed Rick and the Detroit Tigers.

RALPH HOUK: Rick was so close to Jim (Campbell), you know, who hired me. If we were going to make a trade, why we'd sit down and [Rick] would be the one who would pull the string — one way or the other. If we were going to try to make a deal, he was really the one behind it all ... even over Campbell. Campbell had to OK it. But I don't think we were ever going to make a trade if Rick didn't want to. And we did improve when we got guys like Trammell and Whittaker, and that big first baseman, Jason Thompson. They were very young and made a lot of mistakes, but they became good players. The other thing I remember is that Rick was a great scout, too, and when we wanted to get information on certain players, he'd be the guy who'd bring me the information. He had a great mind and knew baseball very well. Rick was a good judge of talent ... and everybody liked him, you know.

So after I came to Detroit, the three of us always had dinner together — very, very often when I was in Detroit. Rick was a fellow who enjoyed his food, and we usually ordered what he did because he knew how to order.... We couldn't believe that he never did gain any weight! (laughs) We couldn't eat what he did; he was a bigger eater than we were! Unbelievable! He never gained an ounce and always looked in shape.

He was a likeable person, and he knew his business. I would take his word over any scout's or anything. His information was always top information — on how to pitch certain hitters — that we didn't know. He was just a very close friend of mine. He was a fun-loving guy who was very serious about his work. You knew that he knew what he was talking about. You'd take anything he said for the good and use that information.

I saw him play, and the thing I remember about him the most was he was so good at blocking balls. Nothing could get by him — balls in the dirt and all that kind of stuff. He was very fast with his hands. He was just a great catcher and a great student of the game. I was sort of the guy who broke in Yogi's glove. [Laughs] That's right.

He had a great sense of humor. He was just a good guy. He was a "Man's Man" is the way to put it. He was really a good man for me when I was with Detroit, and I knew him for quite some time, no question about it. We used to talk about him having been a boxer. I had forgotten about that. We'd kid him about it — tell him we were going to get him a bout and all that. The funny things men talk about sometimes. Everything was good about him. He was a very deserving Hall of Famer.[2]

New prospects were discovered and signed, providing hope for the future. In the January 1975 Free-Agent Draft, Detroit selected infielder Tom Brookens, 21 (first), and two right-handers, Dave Tobik and Dave Rozema.

The Tigers' 1975 roster blended the old with the new in a motley stew. Familiar fan favorites still on the team included Mickey Lolich, Bill Freehan, Willie Horton, Mickey Stanley, and John Hiller. But gone from the lineup were beloved 1968 champs like Al Kaline, Norm Cash, Jim Northrup, and Dick McAuliffe. Their replacements appeared as untested rookies and newcomers with names unfamiliar to most fans: Ron LeFlore, Leon Roberts, Danny Myers, Vern Ruhl, and Nate Colbert. Manager Houk had his work cut out for him.

The 1975 season began well with the Tigers in first place at the end of April, with a 10–6 record. At Fetzer's suggestion, several players and their wives, the manager, and members of the front office were learning Transcendental Meditation to improve the team's concentration and ability to handle stress.[3] Rick did not learn meditation, although Campbell and Houk did.

On May 22, word reached Rick that Lefty Grove had died at age 75 in Norwalk, Ohio — one of the greatest pitchers that had ever lived or that Rick had ever caught. According to the Society for American Baseball Research website, in 64 starts with Ferrell as Lefty's catcher with Boston in the mid–1930s, seven had been shutouts.

At the Amateur Draft, Jim, Rick, and others selected two players, infielder Jason Thompson and second baseman Lou Whittaker, 18, who both signed. However, an unfortunate June brought nothing but losses, leaving Houk's team in last place by June 30, 27–45, 14 games out. Detroit endured an almost record-breaking 19-game losing streak from July 29 to August 15 that solidified their place in the cellar. September went no better, as the Tigers ended the 1975 season 37½ games behind first-place Boston, with a final 57–102 record — the worst record in both leagues and the second-worst season in Detroit Tigers' history at that time (after 1952's 50–104).[4] With 173 team errors for the season, no pitcher carried a winning record, and the lineup was saturated with weak hitters.

On his October 12, 1975, birthday, Rick turned seventy years old — a time when most guys consider retiring. Instead Fetzer retained Ferrell, changing his title from "vice president" to "executive consultant" for the Detroit Tigers organization, a position he would retain for yet another seventeen years. Rick was healthy and still kept his same office on the third floor of Tiger Stadium, adjacent to Jim Campbell's, who claimed never to have made a decision without first consulting Rick. Ferrell's duties remained scouting the majors and minor leagues for new players, advising Campbell in all front office baseball trades and transactions, and evaluating prospects.

Pat Kenney, Rick's friend and co-worker at the Tigers, had introduced him to the game of tennis, and after hours, they would play singles matches at the Franklin Racquet Club. New to the game, the first time he played, Rick insisted on wearing long, athletic pants out on the tennis courts, unable to imagine himself wearing shorts in public. But after Rick saw all the men playing tennis in athletic shorts with tennis shoes, the next time he took to the courts with his racquet, he, too, had on bright green tennis shorts!

In off-season changes, the Tigers' front office transacted a seven-player deal with the Houston Astros on December 6 that sent Leon Roberts, Terry Humphrey, and two other players to Houston for catcher Milt May and left-handed pitchers Dave Roberts and Jim Crawford. At baseball's winter meetings in Hollywood, Florida, in December, pitcher Mickey Lolich (12–18) was traded to the New York Mets for outfielder Rusty Staub and pitcher Bill Laxton. Initially Lolich refused the trade under the "seniority veto," but accepted once he felt assured he would receive more than his current $90,000 salary. Gone from the Tigers was yet another from the '68 champs.

At the winter meetings, the Rules Committee decided the baseball could be covered with cowhide due to a shortage of horses. Also a three-day mandatory suspension would go to any batter caught using a filled, doctored, flat surface bat to hit a fair ball during a game. The save rule was modified again. A 6–3 vote kept the designated-hitter rule optional for the National League, which opposed leaving the use of the DH rule up to the manager.

The independent Seitz Decision made on December 23, 1975, forever changed player-management negotiations in baseball. Dodgers pitcher Andy

Messersmith, Expos Dave McNally, and players union director Marvin Miller had challenged baseball's reserve clause, which bound a player to his team after his contract expired, prohibiting negotiation with another club. Arbitrator Peter Seitz sided with the players union, striking down the reserve clause and granting Messersmith and McNally free agency to negotiate with any team. Following this decision all future negotiations between players and management would be conducted by players' agents, who essentially auctioned their client to the highest team bidder, allowing players to jump from team to team with greater regularity. These operational changes created a difficult adjustment for the traditional Detroit Tigers' front office.

After playing his first tennis game at age 70 in long pants at the Franklin Racquet Club, Rick donned a pair of fashionable green tennis shorts for a subsequent outdoor game. (Patricia Kenney)

January 1, 1976, began another seven-year term for Baseball Commissioner Bowie Kuhn, who had been re-elected the past July. The National League owners fully supported him, but certain American League owners, particularly Charlie Finley and George Steinbrenner, had locked horns with him on free agency and other issues.

Due to challenges by Miller to the reserve clause, the Players Relations Committee cancelled spring training "indefinitely" on February 23, which caused another baseball strike that lasted seventeen days during March 1 to 17. Ultimately, a federal judge upheld the free-agent ruling of Messersmith and McNally by Seitz, and Commissioner Kuhn had to negotiate an entirely new basic agreement with the Players Union.[5]

The new season brought an infusion of new Detroit players acquired through several trades. Dave Roberts, Alex Johnson and Rusty Staub were among the newcomers joining the Tigers' aging roster of veterans like Bill Freehan, Willie Horton, Mickey Stanley and John Hiller.

Rookie Mark Fidrych had made the team in April as the last player on the Tigers' 25-man roster, getting his first start on May 15, 1976, pitching a beautifully efficient 2–1 win over the Indians. What a character he was! A curly-headed mop of dirty-blond hair covered his intense eyes as he actually talked out-loud to himself and the baseball on the mound. On his hands and knees, he'd sweep the dirt from the pitcher's rubber, and standing up, circle nervously before settling into his windup. The antics, his innocence, and his ability to win captivated Detroit baseball fans, who would turn out in capacity crowds whenever Mark "The Bird" (nicknamed after *Sesame Street*'s Big Bird character, which Fidrych resembled) pitched. His popularity even spread nationally as he attracted fans wherever he went.

The Tigers played like a second division team, finishing May in sixth place. In June, Detroit sold pitcher Joe Coleman to the Chicago Cubs, and then purchased Cubs pitcher Milt Wilcox. In the June draft, the Tigers selected pitcher Pat Underwood (first) from Kokomo, Indiana. California shortstop Alan Trammell, 18, was chosen second. By the July 11 All-Star break, the Tigers were in fourth place, 38–41, 11 games out.

A new basic agreement with the players union announced in July declared that after six full seasons of service, a player could become a free agent and negotiate with up to twelve different teams. Players with between two and six years of service could request salary arbitration, if not satisfied with the team's offer.[6] Signing players to contracts would become a whole new ballgame for the Tigers' front office.

The Bengals ended 1976 in fifth place with a 74–87 record, 24 games out. Avoiding the cellar, Ralph Houk's Tigers had improved their 1975 win-record by 17 victories. Mark Fidrych enjoyed a phenomenal 19–9 (2.34 ERA) first season to win the A.L. Rookie of the Year Award. Houk's three-year contract was extended indefinitely, set to automatically renew itself every year until either he or the Tigers wanted out. An optimistic Houk told *The Sporting News*: "This is a great organization to work for. They're all baseball people, so they understand what we have to go through in order to build a winner. I'm fortunate in that respect."[7]

The American League expansion draft held on November 5, 1976, formed two new teams— the Seattle Mariners (A.L. West) and the Toronto Blue Jays (A.L. East)— by claiming sixty players from existing clubs. Each division would now consist of seven teams.[8] Seattle claimed first baseman Dan Meyers and left-handed pitchers Frank MacCormack and Bill Laxton. Toronto claimed pitchers Dennis DeBarr and Dave Lemanczyck. On December 12, veteran 1968 catcher Bill Freehan was released from the Tigers, ending an outstanding fifteen years with the club.

On December 8, Rick spoke on the phone with his 68-year-old brother Wes, who was in a Sarasota, Florida, hospital preparing for a routine appendectomy the next day. They promised to talk again once the procedure was over. However on December 9, 1976, Rick was notified that Wesley had unexpectedly died on the operating table from surgical complications. Devastated, Rick immediately flew to his brother's funeral in Greensboro. Wes Ferrell's obituary recounted that as baseball's greatest hitting-pitcher with 38 career home runs, Wes had won 20 games or more six times and had a lifetime record of 193–128. Grief-stricken beyond words at the loss of his younger brother and batterymate, now Rick, George, and Basil were the last three survivors of the seven Ferrell brothers. Rick continued to pour himself into baseball.

Beneath owner John Fetzer, the Tigers' executive chain-of-command in 1977 listed Executive Vice President and General Manager, Jim Campbell; Director of Player Procurement, Bill Lajoie; Executive Consultant, Rick Ferrell; Business Manager, William Haase; and Lew Matlin, Assistant Director of Special Events. Opposed to free agency, John Fetzer objected to the long-term, multi–million dollar contracts being offered free agents by other teams, who essentially outbid Detroit. Fetzer believed free agency encouraged disloyal "team-hopping" by a player in search of the highest bidder.[9]

Regardless, ballplayers like John Hiller, Mark Fidrych, Ben Oglivie, and Ron LeFLore were signed to multi-year contracts in order to retain them. On February 23, the Tigers front office actually signed minor league free agent infielder Tito Fuentes, 32, for $90,000. Fuentes would play in 151 games at second base in 1977, batting .309 with 190 hits.

High hopes pinned on Mark Fidrych to pitch as he had in 1976 were dashed in spring training when "The Bird" tore his right knee cartilage and went on the sixty-day disabled list. Also in camp were new players Lou Whittaker and Alan Trammell.

The Tigers opened their season on April 7 with highly-prized rookie Steve Kemp in left field. The pitching rotation of Roberts, Ray Bare, Ruhl, and Hiller lost its first four games of the new season. By the end of April the team was in sixth place. With Steve Kemp now playing left field, the front office traded fan-favorite, fourteen-year veteran outfielder Willie Horton — one of the last 1968 team members — to Texas for pitcher Steve Foucault. Fidrych returned to the Tigers at May's end, but lost his game.

At the Free Agent Draft, the Tigers selected outfielders Darrell Brown, Rick Peters, Gary Champagne, and pitcher Bruce Robbins. GM Jim Campbell said he had signed the final two Tigers players — catcher Milt May and third baseman Aurelio Rodriguez — to contracts so that "No one can walk!" once the season ended. In a July 13 game against Toronto, Fidrych developed a sore shoulder after fifteen pitches and left the game.[10] However, another rookie debuted in July — pitcher Jack Morris.

By the 31st of July, Houk had his team in fourth place. In September Detroit called up several highly-regarded minor league prospects: catcher Lance Parrish and double-play combination Lou Whittaker (second base) and Alan Trammell (shortstop).

The Tigers finished 1977 in fourth place with a 74–88 record (.457), 26 games behind New York. Tigers free-agent second-baseman Tito Fuentes led the team with his .309 average. "Tiger of the Year" recipient Ron LeFlore hit .325.

During off-hours, Rick had been searching Detroit's periphery for a new apartment. After the 1977 World Series ended, he packed up and moved to the modern Somerset Park Apartment community in Troy, Michigan, a well-to-do northern suburb of Detroit. Home became a spacious 2,200-square-foot, second-floor apartment with a balcony overlooking a par-three, nine-hole golf-course near the upscale Somerset Shopping Mall. The vibrant activity of the north side appealed to Rick, who wound up living there for the next eighteen years.

In his article published in the October 8 issue of *The Sporting News*, Bob Broeg quoted Cubs scout Joe Mathes in a discussion about catchers: "Hall of Famer Al Lopez was Ray Schalk's equal behind the plate, and Rick Ferrell was even better. Ferrell could out-hit Schalk, and he ought to have been given the Congressional Medal of Honor at Washington for catching those four knuckleballers at the same time!"[11]

Two deaths hit Rick in November. First, Bucky Harris, his favorite manager, died on November 8, 1977, at age 82. American League President Lee McPhail paid tribute to Bucky at a Touchdown Club luncheon in Washington, D.C., on November 17 which Rick attended, along with former Senators Mickey Vernon, Eddie Yost, Sid Hudson, George Case, and others. Next Mayo Smith, manager of the 1968 Championship Tigers team, died from a stroke in Boyton Beach, Florida, at age 62.

During the off-season Tigers brass were hoping to find another deal. Campbell had told *The Sporting News* in early December, "We'll draft guys we're interested in and make what we consider a fair offer. But we're not going to make anyone a big millionaire."[12] But all the players and agents the GM spoke with wanted huge contracts with seven-figure deals. Campbell opposed the skyrocketing free-agent bidding, as did Ferrell. Yet ironically, Rick had begun his major league career as a free agent. Now he found himself on the other side of the bargaining table.

With Whitaker ready to assume second base, infielder Tito Fuentos was sold to the Montreal Expos in January 1978. In early March the front office obtained veteran National League pitcher Jack Billingham from Cincinnati for two Tigers.

The Tigers 1978 lineup was comprised primarily of newer, young players in their early twenties: first baseman Jason Thompson, 23, infielders Lou Whittaker and Alan Trammell, both 20, and Mark Wagner, 24, plus catcher Lance Parrish, 23. The pitching staff also reflected the Tigers' youth movement in Dave Rozema, Mark Fidrych, Jack Morris, and Bob Sykes.

Fidrych opened up on April 7, 1978, with a 6–2 win against Toronto. But ten days later, he was pulled from a game after again suffering bursitis in his pitching arm, a condition which sidelined him for most of the season. Unfortunately he would never regain his outstanding form of 1976. The Tigers remained in first place through April, then fell to third, then primarily into fifth from mid–June through July.

The June Amateur Free Agent Draft was ripe with talent for the Tigers' front office. Their first-round selection was outfielder Kirk Gibson from Michigan State University, along with pitcher Jerry Ujdur (fourth), catcher Marty Castillo (fifth), and outfielder Bruce Fields (seventh).[13] Ferrell attended the 49th All-Star Game in San Diego, California, with first baseman Jason Thompson as the sole Tiger on the A.L. team managed by Billy Martin.

The Detroit Tigers ping-ponged between third and fifth place through August and September, finally finishing 1978 in fifth on October 1, 86–76, 13½ games behind the Yankees. Despite finishing one rung lower in the standings, Houk had improved his previous year's record by 12 victories, with this season being the first in five years to finish with a winning record. Pitchers obtained through trades greatly bolstered the starting rotation, with Jim Slaton going 17–11. Lou Whittaker won the "Rookie of the Year Award" with a .285 average and 138 hits. Detroit Baseball Writers gave Ron LeFlore the "Tiger of the Year Award."

In September, Ralph Houk, 59, announced his decision to retire from baseball at the end of the season, saying, "We have a fine club after four tough years."[14] Meanwhile in Detroit, the front office tapped AAA Evansville manager Les Moss, a former major league catcher, to be the 1979 field leader of the Tigers.

Following the season, the Tigers' executive branch underwent changes. Fetzer promoted Jim Campbell to president after sixteen years as general manager. Rick remained on as Campbell's executive consultant and right-hand man behind-the-scenes. In an August 12, 1984, *Detroit News* interview with Ferrell, Joe Falls wrote, "[Rick] has been Jim Campbell's adviser in all Campbell's years in Detroit. He has never made a player move — not one — without first talking it over with his good friend, Rick. He keeps Ferrell at his side at all times and says, 'I've talked to Rick until the final moments before we did anything. He has been a tremendous help to me through all of these years.'"

In terms of player personnel, Jim Slaton declared himself a free agent and was gone. At the mid–November Instructional League in St. Petersburg, Jim Campbell, digging in his heels, reiterated that Detroit was not going to enter the free-agent bidding wars, that the Tigers preferred developing their own players through the minor league system. "Yes— we can win developing players the traditional way. And that's best for baseball and for the players, in the long run."[15] His approach elicited both praise and criticism.

In December, the Tigers obtained pitcher Aurelio Lopez, 23, and outfielder Jerry Morales, 22, from the St. Louis Cardinals, then made two unexpected announcements. Mark Fidrych's doctors confirmed that the pitcher would be unable to pitch for the entire 1979 season. Also, fifteen-year veteran and four-time Gold Glove winner Mickey Stanley, 36, was given his unconditional release. Jim Campbell praised him, saying, "Mickey is one of the finest all-round athletes to ever wear a Tigers uniform." Although offered a job with the Tigers' organization, the much-loved Stanley embarked on a business career outside of baseball, another great from the 1968 World Series team gone, with only John Hiller remaining.

At the 1979 January draft, the Tigers' staff chose infielder Howard Johnson, 18 (first). But making trades was becoming tougher under the labor-management baseball practices of 1979 and excessive demands of the players. In an article in *The Sporting News*, Rick Ferrell related a trade that Detroit had almost cinched: "All it needed was a handshake," said the Detroit Tigers' super-scout. "Then Jim Campbell and I found out that the guy we were getting had a clause that pays him $25,000 for 25 years *after* he's finished playing! We almost threw up!"[16]

Another example of what was considered unreasonable player demands occurred when designated hitter Rusty Staub, 35, demanded that the Tigers renegotiate his $200,000 annual contract by adding a three-year extension to the two years he had yet to play, or else he would quit baseball. Campbell dismissed the ridiculous demands, saying, "This business had become unglued. It's gotten completely out of hand. Somebody has to take a stand and make up his mind what is good for the game.... We're taking a stand on the renegotiation of contracts. I'm not going to back down."[17]

The Tigers' season opener was played on April 7 — without Rusty Staub — as Dave Rozema lost, 8–2, to Texas. The Tigers' pitching rotation also consisted of Jack Morris, Milt Wilcox, John Hiller, and Jack Billingham, plus rookie Dan Petry. By their third game Detroit was in fifth place, where the team would spend most of the 1979 season. The rebuilding process had resulted in a lineup comprised of a youthful Tiger nucleus: Jason Thompson, Lou Whittaker, Alan Trammell, Lance Parrish, and Steve Kemp.

On April 28, the suspended DH Rusty Staub—who had not yet reported to the Tigers and was losing $1,099 a day plus benefits—agreed to abandon his excessive contract re-negotiation demands with the front office and join the team in Chicago. Resolute Jim Campbell hadn't given an inch.[18]

Despite prior reports, a supposedly-rehabbed Fidrych took the mound in Minnesota on May 5. After throwing twenty strikes in fifty pitches, manager Les Moss pulled him in the fourth. Fidrych made two other starts in May, but his season ended with a 0–3 record (10.43 ERA). His doctors had been correct in their initial predictions. Fortunately, when pitcher Jack Morris was recalled from the Tigers' AAA club at Evansville in May, he began chalking up wins. Detroit obtained outfielder Champ Summers from the Cincinnati Reds on May 25, who provided some immediate punch. During the Free Agent Draft on June 5, the brass selected outfielder Rick Leach.

Their young team was entrenched in fifth place, eight games out of first. Despite having won 13 of their last 18 games, manager Les Moss got the ax on June 12 when coveted, ex–National League manager George "Sparky" Anderson became available. While managing the Cincinnati Reds, Anderson had led his team to five divisional championships and two World Series championships, yet had been fired by Reds owner Marge Schott. Commenting on Sparky's hiring, Jim Campbell stated, "We feel the team is capable of playing more aggressively and with more emotion."[19]

When Anderson landed in Detroit with friend and coach, Billy Consolo, he expressed excitement about managing a crop of young players in a new league and made two promises: (1) The Tigers would become a world champion team within five years, and (2) he would not get fired. Sparky kept them both.

An appreciative crowd of 22,000 fans welcomed him to Tiger Stadium to manage his first Tigers game on June 14, 1979—which the Mariners won, 3–2. Sparky's rules weren't questioned: No moustaches or facial hair allowed on players, no jeans or corduroy pants in the clubhouse. By the All-Star break on July 15, despite the new manager's presence, the Tigers still lingered in fifth place, at 44–45. Immediately following the All-Star break on July 19, Rusty Staub was dispatched to the Montreal Expos for cash and a player to-be-named-later.

Sparky Anderson's 1979 Tigers finished fifth in the American League East with a record of 84–76, 18½ games behind Baltimore. Under their new manager, Detroit had a 56–50 won-loss record. Pitcher Jack Morris pitched an outstanding 17–7 season (3.27 ERA). Steve Kemp hit .318. Rookie outfielder Kirk Gibson broke in playing ten games.

Off-season duties began when the World Series ended. Rick visited the Florida Instructional League in October where pitcher Fidrych was trying to regain his ninety-mph fastball, but he was shelled by Texas Rangers minor-leaguers on October 29. Then Detroit traded for New York Mets first baseman–DH Richie Hebner, 31.

On the final day of the December winter meetings in 1979, the Tigers made two more player transactions. Aurelio Rodriguez, an eight-year Tigers veteran, was sold to the San Diego Padres for $200,000. Ron LeFlore joined Staub with the Montreal Expos after being traded for left-handed pitcher Dan Schatzader. The Tigers had parted with one of their better hitters for a young pitcher from whom much was expected.

Players' salary demands due to free agency dominated contract signings in early 1980, with television revenue factoring in increasing salaries. Ticket prices continued to be raised to help cover rapidly rising costs of player personnel. Outfielder Dave Winfield wanted a $20 million salary to be guaranteed over a ten-year period. Ex-Dodger Duke Snider echoed the sentiments of most former ballplayers, stating, "It's out of whack. It's incongruous for me to visualize anyone making $1,000,000 a year. If the owners are crazy enough to pay, I'll tell you, I'm first in line."[20]

Increasingly, unionized baseball players sought binding third-party arbitration to settle contract disputes with team owners, which usually went in the player's favor. Players seldom negotiated with management directly any more, but rather used agents who were often lawyers to represent them in contract deals. In mid–February, the Tigers' double-play combo, Lou Whittaker and Alan Trammell, each sought third-party arbitration via their agent Rick Brode and won. Shortly afterward outfielder Steve Kemp was awarded the highest salary ever by an arbitrator: $210,000, up from an $80,000 salary in 1979. The Tigers front office was 0–3 in winning arbitrations.[21]

Led by Marvin Miller, the players union staged an eight-day baseball strike during the period April 1 to 8, 1979, that challenged owners to again negotiate a new contract and salary structure. But the owners disagreed among themselves and were not at all united on the issue of free agency. Fiscally-liberal ball clubs that spent big money for free agents (Yankees, Angels, Red Sox, and others) disagreed with the conservative, traditional clubs that did not (Tigers, Cubs, and Blue Jays). The latter feared free agency would destroy the foundations of baseball. An agreement was mediated between the players and management so that, luckily, the strike did not affect the schedule or the fans.

Sparky Anderson and his young team began the season on April 10, 1980, with Jack Morris defeating Kansas City, 5–1, but ended the month in fifth with a 7–11 record. The pitching rotation included Morris, Wilcox, Schatzeder, Rozema, and farm product Pat Underwood, with Lopez in the bullpen.

Player personnel required further streamlining and improvement. In May, pitcher Jack Billingham went to the Red Sox. First baseman Jason Thompson was traded to the California Angels for outfielder Al Cowans, 28 — a right-handed hitter desperately needed. Still the Tigers ended the month in seventh place, nine games out.

During the June 6 draft, Detroit brass signed utility player Barbaro Garbey. Despite player injuries to Kirk Gibson and Al Cowans, the team went on a nine-game winning streak during June 20–28 — their longest in five years — that moved them into fourth place by July 1. Going into the All-Star break on July 6, Detroit had played well enough to move up to second place.

Rick traveled with the Tigers contingent to the 51st All-Star festivities in Los Angeles where he enjoyed a celebratory dinner at Universal Studios, along with Tigers All-Stars Lance Parrish and Alan Trammell. After the break Rick returned to see his team play .500 ball so that by August 10, it held third place. In early August, Rick went with Campbell and Fetzer to Cooperstown for Al Kaline's induction into the National Baseball Hall of Fame, along with Duke Snider. Ferrell's ex-boss, Red Sox owner Tom Yawkey, was also inducted posthumously by the Veterans Committee.

After spending the season in AAA Evansville, Mark Fidrych would again try to pitch on August 12 — his fourth comeback attempt in as many years. Before 50,000 loyal Tigers fans packed into Tiger Stadium to watch him pitch eight innings, he gave up 11 hits, and lost to Boston, 5–4. Going 2–3 over nine starts, Mark Fidrych was pulled from the rotation on September 16, ending his last attempted comeback with the Tigers.

Sparky Anderson's Tigers finished the 1980 season in fifth place, 84–78 record, 19 games out of first. Despite scoring more runs than any team in the majors (830), the pitchers produced a 4.25 ERA. Failing to get out left-handed hitters in late innings and clutch situations had lost too many games during a disappointing year.

Off-season signings had become anathema for the Tigers, who still opposed long-term player contracts, believing annual, year-to-year deals were best for both player and management. Though trying to operate with fiscal conservatism, the Tigers were fighting a losing battle. Yankees owner George Steinbrenner had signed eight free agents to contracts totaling over $14,500,000 in guaranteed salaries, bonuses, and deferred compensation. He gave outfielder Winfield, alone, $13,000,000 for ten years with an 8–10 percent cost-of-living increase each year.[22] At the winter meetings in Dallas, the front office obtained southpaw Kevin Saucier to pitch short relief with Lopez.

There was little that Jim Campbell, John Fetzer, Rick Ferrell or anyone else could do about the escalating salary barrage that kept hitting the Tigers' payroll. Catcher Lance Parrish sought a five-year/$2,000,000 contract, rejecting an offer for seven years at $2,660,000. For a second year, outfielder Steve Kemp, with his agent Dick Moss, took the Tigers to binding arbitration. A Rutgers professor of economics acted as the impartial arbitrator and awarded Kemp his demanded $600,000 salary rather than the Tigers' $360,000 offer. Kemp would then be a free agent at the end of 1982. The result sat poorly with Campbell, who publicly declared that Kemp had tried for too much cash too early in his career. The working-class fans of Detroit frequently expressed their displeasure with Kemp's on-going salary demands.

Baseball was undergoing severe economic challenges in determining how to divide baseball and television revenues between the owners and the players. Commissioner Kuhn was concerned that certain underfunded franchises like the Philadelphia Phillies would fold altogether, while several teams had been sold (Mets, Mariners, A's). Campbell and Ferrell worried that paying the players huge salaries would mean that peripheral baseball employees— office staff, scouts, minor league managers— would forego pay hikes. Rumblings of a players strike kept everyone on edge throughout spring training, as Milt Wilcox acted as the Tiger players' representative.

Manager Sparky Anderson (left) and Rick Ferrell (right) enjoy a laugh at a Detroit Tigers social function during the early 1980s. Sparky managed the Tigers for seventeen years, from 1979 to 1995, winning the World Series in 1984.

The pitching rotation for 1981 returned with Morris, Wilcox, and Rozema and one new starter, Howard Bailey. In the April 9 opener, the Tigers topped Toronto, 6–2, but a week later, lost ten straight, which deposited them in sixth place. With his wrist healed, Kirk Gibson was hitting so well, he became Detroit's regular outfielder.

The Tigers selected outfielder Nelson Simmons in the Amateur Free Agent Draft on June 8, three days before Marvin Miller and the Players Association halted the 1981 playing season by calling another players strike on June 11, 1981. At the time, the Tigers were in fourth place, at 31–26, 3½ games out of first, when they vacated the clubhouse for an unforeseen length of time

For the first time in history, the baseball season had been interrupted. The National Labor Relations Board charged unfair labor practices by the club owners over free agent compensation. Tigers president John Fetzer favored unity among the disparate owners in confronting the Player Relations Committee. Rick, having been a free agent himself, did not blame the players, but felt that certain free-spending owners had created baseball's turmoil by yielding so readily to players' contract demands, which made things tougher on all the other teams trying to maintain fiscal responsibility in negotiations. Long-term guaranteed contracts put management at considerable risk, especially if a player became injured. Rick maintained that the owners couldn't "let the tail wag the dog" by letting the players control baseball. "These unions are going to ruin this country," he observed.

But tradition was fighting the future. Major league baseball was undergoing a fundamental transformation in which ownership was being forced to surrender more of its power and control to agents, arbitration, and the players union. Contentious relations, exorbitant salaries, and work stoppages began to erode fan interest in the "Great American Pastime."

For 650 major league ballplayers, the 1981 players strike lasted seven weeks and a day —fifty days total —from June 12 to July 31, with 712 games lost. Both teams and players were losing money the longer the strike continued, some players did not feel duly represented by the players union, and the owners' strike insurance policy was to expire on August 6. The strike ended in time for a minimal 100-game season and determined that clubs could not be compensated for the loss of free agents. Players could be retained for six years, but only be compensated with other players and draftees if they became free agents. At the strike's finale, the players voted to have a split-season for 1981, literally, with one part occurring before, and one after, the labor stoppage — another first in baseball history.[23]

At the August 2 Hall of Fame ceremonies in Cooperstown, beloved Tigers radio announcer Ernie Harwell was given the Ford C. Frick broadcasting award for service to baseball. Now Harwell was enshrined in the Baseball Hall of Fame. He gave his recollection of Rick in a 2007 telephone interview.

ERNIE HARWELL: I didn't have the opportunity to see Rick play baseball. He was with Washington in 1945–46; I was in the Marines then. I was allowed to go out and cover spring training, and in '45, it was in Bethesda, somewhere outside of Washington. I might have met Rick at that time, but I don't remember.... I was with the Marines' magazine, *The Leatherneck*.

Of course I met him after I came here to the Tigers in 1960. That was the year that Harvey Kuenn and Rocky Colavito were traded for each other. I remember him coming into the press box at Lakeland. George Kell and I were broadcasting the final game of spring training, and your dad came in and made the announcement that they'd made that super trade. We thought it was a joke at first! But it was a great trade because you had two big stars traded for each other rather than the usual scrubinis traded for each other.

Then strangely enough, they played against each other the first game of the season on Opening Day in Cleveland. George and I broadcast that. It went fifteen innings and we were so cold — it was a terrible day with the wind coming in off the lake — and it went fifteen innings and the Tigers won it! That trade was a big one too because Rocky had so many fans in Cleveland and Harvey had a lot of fans in Detroit. I think in the long run, the Tigers got the better of that trade. Rocky lasted a lot longer and did a little bit more on the field than Harvey did. But Harvey made it up as a manager later on.

John Fetzer analyzed the jobs that Rick and Jim were doing and decided that one would be better here and the other one better there. When I came here, the club was owned by the thirteen partners, then Fetzer decided he'd buy everybody out — that happened in late 1960 after Fred Knorr burned himself in the bathtub. He'd been drinking too much, and he was in the shower or tub and he burned himself over about 90 percent of his body. He lingered a little while, and then he died.

[Rick] was so well-respected in baseball and had a good eye for talent. He could sort-out a guy. He was a great advisor for Jim Campbell — he helped Jim immensely, and Jim was very proud of the fact that they could work together. As an executive, Rick's strengths were in scouting and appraisal of a talent because he had a good eye for who could do it and who couldn't do it.

Rick was a good businessman, a solid man. He had a great precept of life; he had high morals. I think people looked up to him. He was modest and self-effacing, a fellow who had played major league ball, made the Hall of Fame, but he certainly didn't insert himself into any conversation when he didn't think he was needed. I just admired him a lot because of his level-headedness and his attitude about things. He didn't get too excited, one way or the other. I never did see him riled up. I doubt if anybody ever did, but they might have.

The Smoltz-Alexander trade in 1987—I think that the Tigers did very well because they never would have gotten into the playoffs without Alexander. He was fantastic ... and later on, Smoltz developed into a great star for Atlanta. But I'm a great believer that "a bird in the hand is worth two in the bush," and you just can't count on prospects because so many things can happen before they make it.

I remember one anecdote: When you lived in Grosse Pointe, you got to meet some society people, and some of them were not too interested in baseball. The Tigers had lost the game on Opening Day that year, and one of Rick's Grosse Pointe friends came up to him and said, 'Don't worry about it, Rick. We'll get 'em next year!' [Laughs] He probably didn't even know that they played every day!

I remember after he semi-retired, he would come back to the Annex where he had that big office there. We used to kid him about coming in at 11:00, having lunch, taking a nap, and going home! (laughs) My kind of hours.... Originally the Annex was a Detroit Lions office and when the Lions moved, the Tigers moved there. I think it was after Monaghan took over the club. I had an office there too. In a way, it was good to be over there, away from the central offices.

One great story was when he challenged the Commissioner—I wrote an article for the *Free Press* about that. Rick was a very modest guy, coming off the farm, didn't have a lot of experience in the big city or in big business, and he had the guts enough and courage enough to challenge this thing and go in and talk to the Commissioner, himself, and make his case. He stood up against the baseball commissioner, who, at that time, had such tremendous power. Nobody ever challenged Judge Landis! Here's a guy from down in North Carolina without a whole lot of experience who would stand up and challenge the old, big Wizard! I thought that was one of the most interesting things about your dad's career. Another article I wrote about him was when he caught the first All-Star Game.

I've wondered about Wes not being in the Hall of Fame. I was on the Veterans Committee for two or three different terms and his name would come up, but—I don't know, it's a strange thing—that some really great players deserving of the Hall of Fame have never been elected. I don't know, that's the way it goes. But he certainly had a fantastic record, there's no question about that! For the most part, he didn't pitch for very good teams and still had good records.

Rick had a great record, especially the longevity record. There's no reason he shouldn't be in the Hall. I certainly thought he deserved to be there. Some of the catchers have caught a little bit longer now since Rick retired. But, at that time, he was at the top of the list as far as longevity was concerned. Probably one of the true requisites for being in the Hall of Fame is "How long did the guy last?" He caught the first All-Star Game which was really an honor. Good choice, I'd say.

He never did appear in a World Series and sometimes that's held against people. I think it's a great showcase—the World Series—and that's why you see so many Yankees in the Hall of Fame. They had a run of World Series appearances, and people get to know them and the writers absorb that along the way.

The 1984 team was developed through the farm system and I think the '68 team was, in a sense. Some of those guys like Horton, Northrup came up that way, too. That's the way you really develop a franchise; it's the only way to do it on a solid basis. You can't go out and buy guys because sometimes they don't work out. That's the basis really. The backbone of a franchise is scouting, developing players and bringing them up, then trading the excess for other players that you're looking for. But you can never judge a trade until about two or three years later. That's what makes baseball great!

In the second half of the 1981 season, divisional competition was so fierce that the Tigers fluctuated between first and fourth place. By October 1, the Tigers had rallied to tie for first place with the Milwaukee Brewers, but Milwaukee clinched the division title on October 3. Detroit tied with Boston for second place with a 29–23 record during the shortened second phase of the season, and a 60–49 record overall to finish in fourth for the entire season. Timely hitting and clutch pitching primarily accounted for the team's success. Outfielder Kirk Gibson had a career-best batting average of .328.

The 1981 split-season added to fan discontent, and increasing numbers began to physically and emotionally boycott the game. Detroit's off-season transactions included finally releasing Mark Fidrych and trading Steve Kemp to the Chicago White Sox for outfielder Chet Lemon, a seven-year veteran. Kemp's salary history was illustrative of the increased bargaining power that major league baseball players had wrestled from management. In five seasons with Detroit, Kemp's salary had increased from $19,000 in 1977, to $50,000 in 1978, to $75,000 in 1979, then jumping to $210,000 after arbitration in 1980, and to $600,000 following arbitration in 1981.[24] Of course, Kemp's improving performance was also a significant factor in his improved compensation, but his salary increases represented the soaring fiscal trends in baseball contracts.

At baseball's winter meetings in Hollywood, Florida, in December, there were aftershocks from the season's strike and talk of expanding the leagues into three divisions. Now 80 years old, Tigers owner John Fetzer was presented the August Busch, Jr., Award for "meritorious service to baseball" in running one of the finest major league franchises while remaining financially solvent (the Tigers' estimated worth: $36.2 million). However, a disillusioned Fetzer withdrew from the American League Executive Council and began gradually divesting himself of his duties as Tigers owner.

On December 9, the Tigers' brass traded pitcher Dan Schatzeder to the San Francisco Giants for outfielder Larry Herndon, 28, the 1976 *Sporting News* Rookie of the Year. Kirk Gibson wanted $500,000 for his 1982 salary — up from $60,000, which Ferrell found extreme.

The Tigers had lost several arbitration cases involving players like Whitaker, Trammell, and Kemp. To strengthen their defense, in early January 1982, Tigers GM Jim Campbell hired ex–Astros general manager Talbot Smith to represent Detroit at arbitration hearings over salary disputes. Saying he was not seeking arbitration, Gibson signed a one-year contract thought to be four times higher than his estimated $65,000 the previous year.

In late January, Rick's close friend and business partner, the now-rotund bachelor Jim Campbell, 57, began suffering chest pains and was quickly admitted to Henry Ford Hospital. On February 2, he was diagnosed with angina that required immediate emergency surgery: five by-pass grafts. Almost dying, Jim incredibly survived the surgery, recuperating during the winter, and keeping in close touch by phone with a concerned Ferrell at the stadium.

In March 1982, Talbot Smith helped the Tigers actually win an arbitration case filed by Jack Morris, who was seeking a $650,000 annual contract to replace his $112,000 deal for 1981. The Tigers had offered $450,000, which the arbitrator had ruled fair, deciding in Detroit's favor. The front office was stupefied that it had finally won a case against a player's demands! They obtained first baseman Enos Cabell from San Francisco for Champ Summers; pitcher Juan Berenguer signed as a free agent.

The Tigers' lineup for the 1982 season boasted two strong defensive outfielders: newly-acquired Chet Lemon in right field, and Larry Herndon in left. Coming out of the gate in April, the team ran hot with an eight-game winning streak in mid–April that put it in first place. On April 20, pitcher Milt Wilcox, on his thirty-second birthday, threw an 8–0, one-hitter against Kansas City with his split-fingered forkball. By May 31, the Tigers led their division, 24–12, staying in first place until June 11.

However, suddenly Rick, a restored Jim, and the rest of Detroit watched as their team collapsed from mid-to-late June, losing 14 of 15 games. On June 20, ex–Tiger Ben Oglivie slammed three homers against his old team, driving in five runs for Milwaukee. Sparky accurately predicted, "If Milwaukee plays the way they did against us, they might run away with it."[25] Meanwhile the Tigers ended June in fourth place, 5½ games behind Ralph Houk's first-place Boston Red Sox. In two weeks' time, Detroit had dropped from first to fourth.

After the All-Star break, fourth place became the Tigers home for the rest of the season, despite playing better than .500 ball, as they ended 1982 with an 83–79 record (.512), 12 games out, in fourth place. Unforeseen injuries had plagued the Tigers all year long. Ace Jack Morris went 17–16. True to Sparky's prophecy, Harvey Kuenn's Milwaukee Brewers won both the A.L. East crown and the American League championship.

In the June draft, the front office selected Rick Monteleone (first), Chris Pittaro (sixth), and Doug Baker (ninth). Infielder Richie Hebner had been sold to the Pittsburgh Pirates in mid–August. In early November, two outfielders, Chet Lemon and Larry Herndon, agreed to long-term contracts. Even Jim Campbell conceded, "If you want to stay in the game, you have to pay market prices. We haven't lost that many (free agents). We've traded a couple the year before they became free agents. But we've lost fewer players to free agency than any club in baseball."[26] Lou Whitaker, who could have been a free agent in 1983, signed a five-year deal. Next year Jack Morris would also be eligible for free agency.

In early December 1982, Rick attended the 81st annual winter meetings in Honolulu, Hawaii, taking his daughters. A central topic concerned the strife and disunity among baseball owners over Commissioner Bowie Kuhn's leadership, with some, like George Steinbrenner, opposing his re-election. Tigers owner John Fetzer strongly supported Kuhn. During the meetings, Rick heard Bowie give an impassioned speech, telling the owners that baseball needed a strong commissioner and a high quality of ownership to preserve the integrity of the game, especially since the 1981 strike had left so many fans embittered. Kuhn stressed the need to keep baseball as a focused, family event rather than turning it into a carnival packed with gimmicks that distracted fans from the game, itself — the primary attraction. Rick, along with Fetzer and Kuhn, felt the owners should work together in a unified stance to preserve baseball's grand tradition. Tumult and dissension pervaded the owners, themselves, as well as their relations with the Players Association.

The 1983 season began with the divided baseball owners trying to find a suitable successor to Commissioner Bowie Kuhn, with little luck. Pro-Bowie John Fetzer said in a *Los Angeles Times* article, "Anyone who would want that job must be out of his mind. Bowie is the best commissioner we've ever had. He's been very effective, but in doing so, he's had to step on some toes. That eventually cost him his job. Finances in baseball are not improving. Eighteen to twenty baseball franchises operated in the red. We are in danger of pricing ourselves right out of the market."

On February 11, 1983, after several losses, the Tigers' front office finally won another arbitration ruling. Reliever Aurelio Lopez, after spending much of 1992 in AAA making $285,000, had requested $315,000 for the 1983 season. But the arbitrator gave him a salary cut to about $250,000. Still declining to participate much in the free agent market, vice president Bill LaJoie was primarily responsible for signing players. The core players — Morris, Herndon, Lemon, Parrish, Whittaker, and Trammell — had been signed to long-term contracts to keep them from becoming free agents. At about $6,600,000, the Detroit Tigers placed seventeenth in payroll expenditures among major league clubs. The average Tiger player was making about $263,900 a year in 1983, up from about $87,000 in 1980, a hefty increase of about $176,900.

Manager Sparky Anderson was in the fourth year of a five-year contract. Each year under his guidance, the Tigers had played better than .500 ball, but the American League East was so strong, the team had not placed higher than fourth in the standings. Among other things, Detroit needed stronger late-inning relief pitching.

The Tigers opened the 1983 season on the road in Minnesota, and by the time they opened in Detroit on April 8, they were 2–2, in third place. By the July 3 All-Star break, the team was still in third, at 41–35, just two games out of first. Pitcher Jeff Robinson was third-round draft choice in the June draft.

Meanwhile, Rick was witnessing another huge transition occurring in major league baseball: commercially televised games were giving way to pay TV. On June 13, 1983, John Fetzer, along with the Chicago White Sox and Milwaukee Brewers' owners, announced the fall debut of a national pay-for-satellite-cable Sports Network which would show over 500 sporting events yearly. The three had put up an estimated $16 million in start-up funds. Detroit's network would be called Pro-AM Sports and would begin broadcasting baseball games for the 1984 season. With five million subscribers, the owners could provide $300 million in proceeds for all the clubs to evenly divide.

The 1983 season marked the 50th anniversary of the first All-Star Game, and White Sox president Eddie Einhorn was determined to put on a memorable entertainment extravaganza in Chicago to celebrate this historic event. As one of the original All-Stars from the first 1933 game, Rick, 77, was invited to participate in an Old Timer's Game during the celebration, which he attended with daughter Kerrie. On July 5 at Comiskey Park, he suited up in a Boston Red Sox uniform and cap that duplicated the one he'd worn as a catcher, with his name "FERRELL" emblazoned in red across the back. Fourteen of the original fifteen living All-Stars from the 1933 game participated, plus 42 Hall of

Famers, 19 MVP's, 17 batting champions, and 17 home run champions, representing the largest gathering of baseball greats ever assembled in history. In addition to Rick Ferrell, the team members from the first twenty-five years of All-Stars included Charlie Gehringer, Lefty Gomez, Bill Dickey, Joe Cronin, and Ben Chapman. A Babe Ruth commemorative stamp was issued. Before the 1:15 P.M. game, a "Parade of Stars" was given. A private Golden Anniversary Gala Banquet seating 2,500 people was held at Navy Pier where current All-Stars mingled with past All-Star greats and musician Chubby Checker sang "The Twist" on stage. The actual Golden Anniversary All-Star Game was played the next afternoon, which the A.L. team won, 13–3.

Two weeks later, Rick, with Kerrie, attended the Second Annual Cracker Jack Old Timer's

Rick appeared in Old Timers Games held around the country well into his 80s. Suited up in his Boston uniform at age 77, this photograph was taken before the 1983 Cracker Jack Classic in Washington, D.C., in which he coached third base.

Classic at RFK Stadium in Washington, D.C., to benefit the Association for Professional Ball Players of America. Rick suited up with 31 other former American League stars, including Joe DiMaggio, Al Kaline, George Kell, Bobby Doerr, Mickey Vernon, Sid Hudson, Bob Feller, and Rocky Colavito. The 32-member National League roster consisted of heroes like Ernie Banks, Pee Wee Reese, Stan Musial, Monte Irvin, and Hank Aaron, who won the five-inning competition, 5–3.

The ex-players discussed new changes in baseball: drug use, the players union, labor management disputes, long-term contracts, rising salaries and jet travel that had replaced the long train rides when the players had eaten, slept, and played baseball together for an entire season. The former group camaraderie had given way to some individual players jetting in and out of town to play games, concerned more for themselves than the team.

Following the All-Star break, Ferrell returned to watch the Tigers go 17–7 for the rest of July. On the 25th, the Tigers, Yankees, Blue Jays, and Orioles converged in a four-way tie for first place in the East Division, with identical records of 54–40.

On July 31, 1983, in Cooperstown, the Tigers' play-by-play announcer, former third baseman George Kell was inducted into the Baseball Hall of Fame, along with Brooks Robinson, Juan Marichal, and manager Walt Alston. Kell recalled Rick in a 2007 interview.

GEORGE KELL: I met Rick when I came to the major leagues my first full season in 1944. I did not get to know him for a long time. He did not say much, and I was too scared to talk to genuine major leaguers. He was one of the nicest men — calm, quiet, said very little, but it all came from the heart. Rick and I were good friends and I treasured his friendship very much. I played cards with him on the long train rides and we played golf together.

Rick was a solid baseball man with good judgment. Jim Campbell leaned on him for advice. He was Campbell's right-hand man. My impression of the Kuenn-for-Colavito trade at the time was that neither club was doing much, and Frank Lane of Cleveland was known as a "trader." It turned out to be a great trade for Detroit — Colavito hit 45 home runs his first year in Detroit. Trading managers — Jimmy Dykes for Joe Gordon — was more of a publicity stunt than a trade. It did not affect either club too much.

He, Jim Campbell, and I had dinner together almost every night, especially after I left the playing field and started broadcasting. It was always a good time for us to relax and talk, mostly about the old days and the old ball players that we played with and against. I always considered Rick one of my closest friends. He was a perfect gentleman. I don't ever remember him being mad. If so, he kept it to himself. The loss of his wife with young children had to hurt him a lot.

Not too many ball players play a whole career without making some enemies for one reason or another. But if Rick had an enemy, I did not know. If I could copy my life after any man I knew in baseball, it would be Rick. He was a good husband, father, and a perfect gentleman in every respect.

Kell added in a handwritten note from January 2008: "Kerrie — Your father was one of my most trusted friends. His word was as true as the Bible. I admired

Rick so much. He was my friend as a player when he was with Washington and later, as my boss as General Manger. When I was telecasting for the Tigers, we all wanted to be like Rick Ferrell — so calm, so soft-spoken, a real gentleman!"

Embattled Baseball Commissioner Bowie Kuhn attended the Hall of Fame induction, and four days later on August 4, after having served two seven-year terms since 1969, announced his resignation from baseball. During his tenure, Kuhn — a strong traditionalist like Judge Landis — had suspended both Denny McLain and George Steinbrenner, sued owner Charlie Finley, seen the designated rule implemented by the American League, and the reserve clause give way to free agency. He had endured the strike of 1981, observed major league expansion from twenty to twenty-six teams, helped negotiate the billion-dollar TV contract for owners, and had helped preserve the integrity of baseball. Bowie Kuhn left office on December 31, 1983, much to the dismay of staunch supporter John Fetzer and his front office team.

By mid–August, five teams battled for the division flag with only 1½ games separating the contenders: Baltimore, Milwaukee, Detroit, Toronto, and New York. By the final week, Detroit held second place, pursuing Baltimore for first. However, the Bengals finished the season on October 2 still on the second rung, six games behind the Orioles (98–62). Sparky's 92–70 record was Detroit's best in fifteen years, and his contract was promptly extended for two more years through 1986.

Jack Morris won 20 games, lost 13, and led the league in strikeouts (232). Gold Gloves were awarded to Parrish, Whitaker, and Trammell, the first and only time in Tigers history there were three winners. Four Tigers hit over .300.

With the owners' banishment of Bowie Kuhn and free-agent salaries skyrocketing, 82-year-old John Fetzer's enthusiasm for owning the Tigers had diminished considerably. After twenty-one years as sole owner, on October 10, he announced his decision to sell his club to Domino's Pizza magnate Tom Monaghan for an estimated $53 million.

Fetzer wanted stable ownership and would remain with the Tigers for two more years to advise Monaghan. The new owner intended to retain the same members of the Tigers' front office, including executive consultant Ferrell and newly-appointed general manager Bill LaJoie. Jim Campbell was promoted to President and CEO. During the period 1963 to 1983 under Fetzer's ownership, the Detroit Tigers had won the World Series once (1968), the divisional championship twice (1968, 1972), and come in second place three times (1969, '71, '83). But John quit one year too soon.

In December, Rick, Jim, Bill and the Tigers contingent went to the winter meetings in Nashville, Tennessee. Several cities were lobbying for their own major league baseball teams in case expansion was passed again: Tampa Bay, St. Petersburg, Indianapolis, Denver, Vancouver, and Buffalo. In order to have two sixteen-team leagues, the American League needed to add two teams to their fourteen team total, and the National League had to expand its twelve-team league by four. Another item of consideration was the big new TV package for 1984 that would give each team between $6 million and $7 million per season. Tigers' president Jim Campbell succeeded Oakland A's president Roy Eisenhardt on the Player Relations Committee, baseball's labor negotiation group.

Post-season executive transactions included granting free agency to Lynn Jones, Enos Cabell, Milt Wilcox, and Doug Bair, with the latter two players resigning with Detroit. After years of opposing free agency under owner John Fetzer, the Tigers and LaJoie signed their first top-flight free agent under Tom Monaghan: slugger Darrell Evans, 37, a 17-year infielder from the San Francisco Giants.

Settled comfortably in his Troy, Michigan, apartment, Rick's health was strong as he turned 79 and he played tennis and golf with his friends during his free time. His children visited frequently — son Tom had married and produced Ferrell's first grandson, Joshua — and he dined out often with friends. Autograph requests arrived which he promptly signed with his evenly spaced signature and returned.

13

❖ ❖ ❖

1984–1992

The 1984 World Series, Baseball
Hall of Fame, and Changing Times

In mid–February 1984, Ferrell reported to Lakeland for the opening of the Tigers' spring training camp. When the Grapefruit League games began on March 3, he drove up to Jack Russell Field at Clearwater Beach to scout pitcher Willie Hernandez in the Phillies–Blue Jays game. At about noon, while talking with Toronto manager Bobby Cox, an usher told Rick to call Tigers president Jim Campbell in Lakeland immediately.

Alarmed that a family emergency had occurred, Rick hurried to call Jim, who announced that Ferrell had been elected to the Baseball Hall of Fame by the Veterans Committee! Campbell later said that Rick's first words were, "Oh, my children will be so proud!" The 78-year-old ex-catcher would be inducted into the Baseball Hall of Fame at Cooperstown on August 12, along with the other Veterans Committee selection, shortstop Pee Wee Reese, and regular inductees, pitchers Don Drysdale and Harmon Killebrew, plus shortstop Luis Aparicio. The thirteen-member Hall of Fame Veterans Committee in 1984 included such baseball luminaries as Chairman Joe Cronin, Charlie Gehringer, Monte Irvin, Roy Campanella, Al Lopez, Stan Musial, and Burleigh Grimes, who had reviewed thirty nominated candidates.[1]

One of the first congratulatory calls Ferrell received was from ex–Tiger great George Kell, who later said in a telephone interview from his Arkansas home, "I couldn't be happier for him. Rick is such a quietly efficient person that he didn't make a whole lot of headlines in his career. But he was one of the best catchers I've seen. You couldn't strike him out." He added, "I played against him. I don't know how they kept him out for so long."[2] *Detroit News* sportswriter Jerry Greene observed, "Among Hall of Fame catchers, he ranks third in years of service, third in total games played but first in games caught, third in hits with 1,692, and sixth with a .281 career batting average."[3]

In a 2007 telephone interview, Tigers executive Lew Matlin recalled Rick Ferrell.

LEW MATLIN: Rick had integrity, he was soft-spoken, and he was easy to be around. In 1946 when they started organizing the Players Association, the forerunner of the players union, the Senators met and had to put $250 down to join. Some of the players groused about it and Rick said, "Well, you should do it, and if you can't afford it, I'll loan you the money." It turned out that if you had been on the major league roster by some date of the 1946 season, you were eligible for the pension. Some of them did it and some didn't. He thought the pension was a good idea. Mickey and I were together in Vancouver for three years. Bobby Doerr and Mickey Vernon are exceptional.

[Rick] was with the Tigers as a coach from 1950 to 1953, then he started scouting, and he scouted for about four years. He was general manager in late 1958, '59, and, despite big changes, he was still general manager in 1960. In 1961, they reorganized. Jim Campbell became general manager and your dad became more-or-less the advance man. He set up the deals and he did, primarily, the major-league scouting. He was Jim's "eyes in the field" and a vice president of the club.

Jim was his campaign manager for the Hall of Fame. In the winter of 1983, Jim called me one day. He said, "I want you to do a little research. Find out who the four knuckleball pitchers were that Rick caught in Washington." I sort of surmised that he was starting a campaign to get your dad elected to the Hall of Fame, and he was successful. It was a subtle campaign. He didn't run it in the newspapers. He got his facts sheet and sent it to the members on the Veterans Committee.

In 1984, Bill LaJoie was the general manager and Rick was the advance scout. They made a tentative deal that if Hernandez "passed the mustard" with Rick Ferrell, then they would make the deal. I think I told you about how Bill LaJoie had sent Rick out to scout Hernandez of the Phillies. Jim Campbell got the word that Rick had been elected to the Hall of Fame by the Veterans Committee, so he left word for your dad to report back to Lakeland. I was running Marchant Stadium at the time. The day Rick was supposed to see Hernandez pitch, he was called back to Lakeland and told he'd been elected to the Hall of Fame. Rick later checked Willie out, and they made the deal. Hernandez made significant contributions to the 1984 pennant and World Series.

About Ferrell's Hall of Fame selection, *Detroit News* sportswriter Joe Falls wrote, "Rick Ferrell: He still knows more baseball than anyone in the [Tigers'] organization. He's the happiest bachelor I know, a man who doesn't ask much of life and enjoys everything that's given him. I'll be in Cooperstown partner, for the big day in August."[4] *Detroit Free Press* sportswriter Mike Downey wrote, "I think few men deserved the Hall of Fame more than Rick Ferrell."[5] Taking the honor in stride, Rick looked forward to the coming baseball season, as he'd done for the past fifty-seven years.

In other baseball news, Peter Ueberroth, chairman of the Los Angeles Olympic Organizing Committee for the Summer Games, was elected to a five-year term as baseball commissioner in early March 1984, to assume the new position in October. Additionally in mid–March, former Tigers ace Denny McLain was indicted on racketeering charges, as well as extortion, loan-sharking, and possession of cocaine.

The Tigers front office strengthened the team for another pennant run by making a key trade with the National League Philadelphia Phillies on March

24. They obtained a couple of veterans, pitcher Guillermo "Willie" Hernandez, 29, and first baseman Dave Bergman, 30, for catcher John Wockenfuss and outfielder Glenn Wilson. Hernandez was a former MVP and Cy Young Award winner, while Bergman was a smart, defensive first baseman and strong clutch-hitter. Outfielder Rick Leach was released.

After barely losing the 1983 pennant, the Detroit Tigers were ready to win it all in 1984. Trades had improved the lineup. Dave Bergman replaced Enos Cabell at first base; Evans became designated hitter for Gibson and also played first. Regulars Whittaker and Trammell comprised a quick second base/short-stop combo, while Johnson and Brookens together manned third base. Lemon, Gibson, and Herdon patrolled the outfield while Lance Parrish was catcher. Starters Morris, Petry, and Wilcox received help from relievers Hernandez and Aurelio Lopez.

Rick Ferrell did not imagine the magical season of thrills and victories the 1984 Tigers would provide, from beginning to end. Opening up on the road against the Minnesota Twins on April 3, Morris pitched an 8–1 win, and on April 7, he pitched an historical 4–0 no-hitter to defeat Chicago's Floyd Bannister.

A *Chicago Tribune* article by Jerome Holtzman referred to the visiting Tigers' excellent team and said of Rick: "Election to the Hall of Fame does make a difference. Rick Ferrell, the old catcher who will be enshrined in August, has accepted eight speaking engagements in the last two weeks and gets stacks of mail every morning. Most of the letters ask for autographs, but there was one worth framing—from Ronald Reagan. Whether you like the president or not, you've got to admit one thing: he knows his baseball!"[6]

On April 10, an exhilarated crowd at Tiger Stadium welcomed the undefeated Tigers (6–0) to Detroit's home opener against the visiting Texas Rangers, won by Petry, 5–1. On April 18, the still-undefeated Tigers lost one to the Rangers, then proceeded to win seven straight through April 26. By the end of the month, Detroit was 18–2, dominating first place since the beginning of the season. The boys of summer were playing baseball like champions.

The Tigers lost two to the Red Sox in early May before going on another seven-game winning streak through May 11, mostly on the road. After losing a single game to the Angels at Tiger Stadium on May 12, the team embarked on a nine-game winning streak, primarily at home.

Unfortunately during this jubilant period, sorrow befell manager Sparky Anderson when he learned his father had passed away. From May 17 to 21, the captain went to California for the funeral rejoining his team in Anaheim on May 22 to watch a three-game sweep of the Angels. Through May 24, the Tigers had an amazing 35–5 record—a record-breaking start—winning 17 straight road games to tie the major league record. Oddly, the fired-up Tigers were swept three games by the Mariners at the Seattle Kingdome.

Increasingly, late-inning victories provided intense excitement for Tiger fans. Still in first place on June 4, Detroit was tied, 3–3, with Toronto in the bottom of the tenth. With two outs and two on, first baseman Dave Bergman fouled-off the three-two pitch from Toronto's Roy Howell a suspenseful seven times in seven minutes. Finally Bergman belted the eighth pitch into the right-field upper deck for a three-run homer and an exhilarating 6–3 victory.

On July 5, the Tigers were tied 4–4 against the Rangers at Arlington Stadium. With two outs and two men on in the ninth, Kirk Gibson smashed a three-run homer over the right-field fence for a thrilling 7–4 Tigers victory. Sparky Anderson wrote in his diary of the 1984 season, *Bless You Boys*, "But if this wasn't a miracle tonight, then my hair isn't white."[7]

Anyone who watched the execution of that 1984 team marveled at its excellence. When the players launched in unison from the dugout onto the playing field to start each game, a raw power and unbridled confidence propelled them. On the diamond, dramatic pitching and astounding defense characterized the entire season. The critical hit, the late-inning rally, the walk-off home-run all became hallmarks of the Tigers' offense in games throughout 1984.

At the All-Star break on July 8, the Detroit Tigers had exceeded everyone's expectations with a 57–27 record. Five players were voted to the American League All-Star team: Whittaker, Parrish, Lemon, Morris, and Hernandez.

In a year in which the "boys were blessed," the team charged on to the finish line after the All-Star break, providing memorable highlights for baseball fans. In extra innings on July 13, Lou Whittaker hit an inside-the-park home run to defeat Minnesota, 5–3, at the Metrodome.

The annual Baseball Hall of Fame weekend in 1984 stretched from Thursday, August 9, through Sunday, Induction Day, August 12, in the little hamlet of Cooperstown, New York. Rick and three children checked-in at the stately, historic Otesaga Hotel situated on Lake Otsego which lodged Hall of Famers and their families. Jane Forbes Clark, II, legacy bearer for Hall of Fame founder Stephen Clark, threw a magnificent tent gala with sumptuous food and music; Stan Musial entertained by playing his harmonica. Some players and their guests competed in a golf tournament amid much story-telling and reminiscing. Seeing so many great baseball players assembled on the hotel's grand veranda was unforgettable.

For six weeks, Rick had diligently rehearsed his induction speech behind closed doors. On Sunday, the induction ceremony was to be held outdoors at the Clark Sports Arena with Hall of Famers seated on stage behind the speaker's podium, facing the crowd.

As the crowd settled in their seats, Commissioner Bowie Kuhn stepped up to the podium and began to speak:

> Let us turn now to the new members of the Hall of Fame. The first new member is a guy for whom I rooted as a little Washington Senators kid —fan — when he came to Washington in 1937. He began his major league career, however, in 1929 and he continues it — only changed in form — to this very day. He caught 1,805 games in

the American League, a total surpassed by no one in the entire history of the American League and surpassed by only one man — fellow Hall of Famer Al Lopez. Outstanding defensively, he had the incredible task of catching not one — but four — knuckleball pitchers on the Washington Senators team that came, in 1945, to within one game of winning the American League pennant. Happily, I'm sure, he formed from time-to-time, a battery with his brother Wes, a great pitcher and a really outstanding hitter, and for five seasons — from 1934 to 1937 and for one more with Washington — they were a brother-battery together.

Rick was also a fine offensive player and compiled a career batting average of .281, topping the .300 mark four times. And remember that when the first All-Star Game was played in 1933, remember that Rick Ferrell caught that game for the American League that entire game — and there were a couple of guys on the bench named Cochrane and Dickey. Today, at the youthful age of 78 — and in his case, it is very youthful, indeed — Rick is still an active and important part of the Detroit Tigers organization. Here is the official language on this very fine man:

Kuhn then read the text on Rick Ferrell's Hall of Fame plaque:

RICHARD BENJAMIN FERRELL
St. Louis A.L. 1929–1933, 1941–1943
Boston A.L. 1933–1937
Washington A.L. 1937–1941, 1944–1947
CAUGHT MORE GAMES (1,806) THAN ANY OTHER
AMERICAN LEAGUER. DURABLE DEFENSIVE STAND-OUT
WITH FINE ARM. EXPERT AT HANDLING PTICHERS.
MET CHALLENGE FOR 4 KNUCKLEBALLERS IN SENATORS'
STARTING ROTATION. OFTEN FORMED BATTERY WITH
BROTHER, WES. HIT OVER .300 5 TIMES. SECOND
ONLY TO DICKEY IN A.L. CAREER PUTOUTS AT
RETIREMENT.

After Kuhn concluded by saying, "Rick Ferrell!" the crowd clapped. Rick stood at the podium to slowly and deliberately deliver his Hall of Fame acceptance speech:

Commissioner, Members of the Hall of Fame, Ladies and Gentlemen,

First, I would like to congratulate the other new members of the Hall of Fame. I am sure they feel as I do that this is a great honor and a very special day for all of us. I have been to Cooperstown a number of times for the Hall of Fame ceremonies, but only as a spectator. I would get a nice seat out there in the audience and relax and enjoy the program, and pull for my friends and fellow players who were *being* inducted. This year, however, it is an entirely different feeling. It was on March 4 last spring that I was in Clearwater, Florida, just before game time when I first learned I had been elected to the Hall of Fame by the Veterans Committee. Jim Campbell called me that day from Lakeland to tell me about it, and it came as such a surprise, I hardly knew how to answer. Then shock set in for a while, and then you're on Cloud Nine. But through it all, I was very happy about the whole thing.

As a kid growing up on this farm down in Greensboro, North Carolina, my whole family consisted of my mother, dad, and seven boys. So I began to play ball at a very early age. My brothers and I would play at every opportunity. I still remember this kid game we had going when we held batting practice out in this field. The one who hit the farthest ball, we would stick a stick up at that point. If

In Cooperstown, New York, on August 12, 1984, the newest inductees to the National Baseball Hall of Fame pose happily for a portrait while holding their Hall of Fame plaques. Standing, left to right, Harmon Killebrew and Don Drysdale. Seated, left to right, Pee Wee Reese, Rick Ferrell, and Luis Aparicio. (National Baseball Hall of Fame Library, Cooperstown, N.Y.)

someone hit one further back, we would take the stick and place it where *that* ball had landed. So one day many years later, I was catching for the Boston Red Sox and my brother Wes Ferrell was pitching for the Cleveland Indians. So I hit a home run off Wes that day and in circling the bases, I said, "Stick a stick up on *that* one!" [laughter from crowd] I don't think he liked the remark — it didn't go over too well. He kicked the mound a little bit. So the next inning, Wes came up and hit a home run also. In crossing the plate, he said, "Stick a stick up on *that* one!" [crowd laughs again] So to this day, we don't know which home run went the farthest.

As I mentioned before, I've been to Cooperstown a number of times, and I've always enjoyed my trips here. But of course this one tops them all. I have my family here. We've enjoyed meeting baseball people, meeting fans, seeing the museum, the city, and we just hope we can come back again many more times. [The crowd claps, but Kuhn tells Rick to introduce his family, so Rick continues.] I'd like to introduce my family. I have three kids here. Would you please stand up? [The kids stand up.] This is Maureen on the left. [Pause] I think I can get 'em right ... and this is Kerrie in the center, my daughter, and this is Tommy, my son. We're very proud of them. [clapping from the crowd]

Announcer: "The most durable catcher in major league history and Rick Ferrell is now a member of the Hall of Fame ... and you can stick a stick up on *that* one."

After the induction was all over, Rick told sportswriter Gene Guidi, "Now that I think about it, maybe catching all those knuckleballs wasn't as tough as getting up there and speaking in front of those people."[8]

Back at Tiger Stadium, the division-leading Tigers were playing at a .652 clip with a 77–41 record. With a winning, first-place team, every game brought in a packed house of enthusiastic fans. In the August 28 game against the Angels in Anaheim, the Tigers' offense exploded for a 12–6 victory: Lemon hit a grand slam home run, Gibson belted two homers, and Castillo unleashed one homer and had three RBIs.[9] Another late-inning thriller occurred in Toronto on September 7, thanks again to Dave Bergman, who with a 4–4 tie in the tenth inning, slammed another clutch three-run homer to win the game, 7–4.

The Detroit Tigers officially clinched the American League East title on Tuesday, September 18, at Tiger Stadium after a 3–0 shutout of the Milwaukee Brewers. Then the team's record stood at 97–54, 13 games ahead. Only the third twentieth century team to hold first place for the entire season, the Tigers joined the 1927 Yankees and the 1955 Dodgers. After an 11–3 win at Yankee Stadium on September 29, the Tigers won their 104th game, setting a new club record.

Rick, Jim, and the Tigers contingent sat in the stands at Royals Stadium when the American League divisional playoffs between Detroit and the champs of the West, Dick Howser's Kansas City Royals, began on Tuesday, October 2, 1984. To win, the Tigers needed three victories in the best-of-five-games series. The first game displayed a shining Jack Morris, who allowed one run in seven innings for an 8–1 Detroit victory. The next day, in extra innings with a 3–3 tie in the eleventh inning, Detroit outfielder Johnny Grubb hit a game-winning double with two men on for a 5–3 Tigers win. With timely offense by Gibson, Parrish, Herndon, Trammell, and Grubb, the Tigers looked more and more like champs. Plans were made for the return series in Detroit, with Rick slated to throw out the first pitch for Friday's game, George Kell on Saturday, and Charlie Gehringer for Sunday's game. But pitching rather than offense dominated the third game in Kansas City, as Detroit's Milt Wilcox battled Kansas City pitcher Charlie Leibrandt. Wilcox pitched a two-hitter through the eighth; Leibrandt threw a complete-game three-hitter, but allowed the critical run for a 1–0 Tiger victory. In three games, the Tigers swept Kansas City to become the East Division champs and continue on to the World Series against the San Diego Padres.

The Tigers brass traveled to California as the World Series began at Jack Murphy Stadium in San Diego on October 9. The Tigers' Jack Morris trimmed the Padres the first game, 3–2, winning on Herdon's fifth-inning home run. The next day, a fifth-inning, three-run Royals homer defeated the Tigers in the second game, 5–3. Returning to Detroit's Tiger Stadium for an October 12 third game (Rick's seventy-ninth birthday), Wilcox and Hernandez out-dueled Padres hurlers for a 5–2 win. Starting game four, Jack Morris pitched the complete nine the next day for a 5–2 Detroit victory and a three-to-one Series lead.

On October 14 at Tiger Stadium for a suspenseful fifth game, Tiger Kirk Gibson hit two home runs— one in the first and one dramatic game-winner in the eighth inning —for an 8–4 Detroit win over San Diego! The Detroit Tigers had won the World Series in five games! Not in sixteen years had the Tigers won the World Series, and the jubilation of cheers and high spirits rang out in Tiger Stadium and throughout Michigan. Former owner John Fetzer, who had actually built the winning team, rushed to the players' locker room to congratulate everyone. The championship players sprayed celebratory champagne all over each other, soaking the well-dressed Mr. Fetzer to the skin, as well, as he enjoyed the festivities like a kid, himself.[10] Along with Fetzer, Ferrell, Campbell, LaJoie, Anderson, and Monaghan, the entire Tigers organization felt the rare exhilaration of being part of a world championship team — something everyone had worked toward since their last World Series in 1968.

Individual Tiger players won various awards with Detroit's left-handed stopper Willie Hernandez (9–2, 1.92 ERA, 32 saves) voted the A.L.'s Most Valuable Player. "Senor Smoke" (Willie's nickname) also won the American League Cy Young Award and *The Sporting News* Pitcher of the Year Award. Kirk Gibson won American League Championship Series MVP. Gold Gloves went to Parrish, Whittaker, and Trammell. Jack Morris won 19 games (second best in the A.L.) and Dan Petry 18. Through the Tiger Stadium turnstiles had passed 2,704,794 happy fans— the highest number in Tigers history.[11]

However, despite all the awards, no single Detroit position player stood out above the others. Team batting averaged only .271; the only hitter above .300 was shortstop Trammell (.314), with Whittaker next at .289. Yet every player on that 1984 team had contributed to the winning outcome in his own way. The team's nucleus was a brother-like fraternity of players who had developed through the minors together, and the entire group possessed a cohesive chemistry strong enough to win the world championship in 1984 — the second one for Rick Ferrell.

Once the World Series had ended, exiting baseball commissioner Bowie Kuhn was replaced by Peter Ueberroth, who favored a more-commercial, less-traditional approach to baseball, with gimmicks, diversions, and giveaways to entertain fans in addition to the main attraction: the old ball game. Tigers general manager Bill LaJoie traded third baseman Howard Johnson to the New York Mets for right-handed pitcher Walt Terrell.

What had been a well-deserved year in 1984 closed on an almost miraculous note for Rick Ferrell. In early December just before leaving for the baseball's winter meetings in Houston, he was proceeding to turn left on a green arrow light near his Troy apartment when an oncoming car slammed into the passenger side of his metallic-beige Cadillac. "I was only two blocks from my [Troy] home, making a left turn at Coolidge and Maple, when I got broadsided," Ferrell later told a local newspaper.[12] His crumpled Cadillac had been totaled by a speeding, sixteen-year-old, newly-licensed driver who escaped injury. Incredibly, Rick, who easily could have been killed or paralyzed, was treated for minor cuts at Beaumont Hospital in Royal Oak and released. Under doctor's orders, however, Ferrell did not attend the winter meetings for the first time in twenty-five years, saying, "I'm going to ache all week, so I'll have to consult [for the meetings] over the phone this year instead of in person."[13] Rick's family was both tremendously relieved and eternally grateful for his safety.

Life after his Hall of Fame induction and the World Series became increasingly busy for Rick in 1985. His alma mater, Guilford College, wanted him to attend Alumni Weekend that spring in Greensboro, which he declined in a letter of January 4, 1985: "Dear Mrs. Hines, I have enclosed a few pictures and write-up's which I hope will be of some use. The form which was sent me has been misplaced. I appreciate your telephone call for my mail has been extremely heavy since the Hall of Fame thing. I have hundreds of letters which have not been opened. My schedule for April has not been determined yet, so I cannot give you an answer as to a trip to North Carolina. I have received letters from George Ralls and Mr. Fulton in regards to Alumni Weekend. Best regards to them and you and all my friends at Guilford. Sincerely, Rick Ferrell."

In Raleigh, North Carolina, Rick was honored with the North Carolina Governor's Award by Governor Jim Martin in late February, but was unable to attend the ceremony. Spring training had already opened for the Tigers in Lakeland.

In early April as the 1985 season was beginning, Rick and fifty-six other members of the Detroit Tigers' organization were presented with their 1984 World Series rings. Three versions of the ring were distributed to individuals according to their share, ranging in cost from a $1,500 diamond-studded heavyweight style to a $250 glass replica.[14] Rick's diamond-studded model rarely left his finger.

Sparky opened his seventh season managing the team on April 10, 1985. As World Series champions, media exposure for the team was at an all-time high. Ernie Harwell and Paul Carey had returned to announce the Tigers' games on radio. Al Kaline and George Kell called games on commercial TV while on PASS, the pay-for-cable sports channel implemented by John Fetzer, ex–Tiger stars Bill Freehan and Jim Northrup joined Larry Osterman in the play-by-play.

But the World Champions didn't fly out the gate as fast in 1985 as they had the prior year. The Tigers remained in first place through April, but in May, began bouncing between second and third. Rowdy crowds in the outfield bleachers began loudly chanting obscenities, motivating a disgusted Jim Campbell to close 11,000 center-field bleacher seats for a month. When they reopened, the alcohol content in the Tiger Stadium beer had been diluted. By June 1, Detroit was in third place, with a 25–20 record, 5½ games out.

In June, Detroit drafted Randy Nosek (first), southpaw Steve Searcy, and infielders Scott Lusader (sixth) and Doug Strange (seventh). In the twenty-second round, a cousin of Tigers great Charlie Gehringer was selected: pitcher John Smoltz, 18, whom Detroit signed on September 3, 1985. Rangers' pitcher Frank Tanana, 31, was obtained in trade, who had been voted *The Sporting News* Rookie of the Year in 1975.

At the All-Star break, Detroit still clung to third place, 48–37, and was just 3½ games behind the front runner. Rick returned to Cooperstown for Hall of Fame induction weekend, his second visit as a Hall of Famer himself. Lou Brock, Hoyt Wilhelm, Enos Slaughter, and Arkey Vaughan joined the 193 bronze plaques in the museum. The headline of a *Sporting News* article by Joe Durso read, "4 Specialists Set to Step into the Hall." Durso noted that "The arrival of the specialists was probably signaled a year ago with the election of Luis Aparicio, Pee Wee Reese, and Rick Ferrell, who made it with Harmon Killebrew, an old-fashioned specialist in hitting home runs."[15] Rick's specialty had been his unique ability as the only catcher in major league history to catch four knuckleball starters in 1944–1945 like he was "sitting in a rocking chair."

Another baseball strike, however, loomed with salary arbitration and owners' contributions to the players pension plan as key bargaining points. Executive director of the Player's Association Donald Fehr was determined to win for his team. Darrell Evans represented the Tiger players at the union table. A work stoppage occurred in baseball for only two days—August 6–7—with no games lost on the schedule. The final labor agreement required that the baseball owners give $33,000,000 dollars to the players pension fund from 1986 to 1988. For 1989, the amount would be increased to $39,000,000.

Drug testing gathered momentum as another hot-button issue. Commissioner Ueberroth had already implemented a mandatory drug-testing policy for all baseball employees (except the players), and now wanted drug testing in the Winter Leagues in Latin America. Donald Fehr maintained that drug use had declined considerably, while Jim Campbell said drug use on the Tigers was less than on other major league teams, although he admitted that some Tiger players, past and present, had used illegal drugs.[16] The topic of steroids had not yet developed.

The Tigers had spent August in third place, but dropped to fourth by September's end with an 80–75 record while competing for third with Baltimore and Boston. Toronto led the division, with New York in second place. From October 1 to 6, Detroit won four of six, playing well enough to claim third place for the 1985 season, 15 games out of first, with an 84–77 record.

Compared with the prior year's championship season, the Tigers lost 20 more games. Sparky felt this team had played mediocre baseball. The team fielding average (.977) had dropped only two points from the previous year, but their 143 errors ranked second-highest in the division. One bright spot was the slugging DH Darrell Evans, who led the American League in homers with 40.

The *Chicago Tribune* had printed an article in late August about vintage catchers who played after reaching age 36, which began: "An old catcher, like an old hunting dog, has an endearing quality about him, worn and scarred with an odd walk from squatting 150 times a day for 20 years. There's something comforting about all that experience behind the plate, never mind if his hitting power may have declined to warning-track range...."[17] The article focused on 37-year-old Carlton Fisk's longevity and his high number of games caught. Accompanying the article was a graph of twelve catchers in major league history who had caught regularly beyond age thirty-six. Having caught 381 games in his final five years, Rick was listed third of the twelve catchers, bested only by Wally Schang (448 games caught) and Chief Zimmer (403). Al Lopez placed seventh with 323 games caught after age 36, Ernie Lombardi (10), and

Commissioner Peter Ueberroth (1984 to 1989), left, stands with Rick Ferrell in the mid–1980s at Tiger Stadium before the start of a Detroit Tigers game.

Birdie Tebbetts (11). At the time, Rick's durability as a major league catcher had rarely been matched.

From late September 1985 through the year's end, the 26 owners met several times to discuss long-range planning in baseball and the high costs of player development. Rick's lament was that a team could find and sign a young prospect, spend years, money, and time developing him into a major league player, and then once the player's career gets going, he can simply walk away from his home team to the highest bidder. The Commissioner and certain owners — the Tigers included — felt that long-term contracts were undesirable and "not smart" because if players didn't perform or became injured, they were paid their salaries, regardless. Like-minded owners felt they needed to be more "self-disciplined" against unreasonable contract demands by players.

GM Bill LaJoie traded with the San Francisco Giants in early October which brought catcher Matt Nokes and pitchers Eric King and Dave LaPoint to Detroit for Juan Berenguer and Bob Melvin. In late November, Detroit outfielder Kirk Gibson, who wanted a contract longer than the three-year Tigers offer — obtained free agency, along with Tom Brookens and Aurelio Lopez. On December 20, Milt Wilcox was given his release. However, two former Tigers, Willie Horton and John Hiller, returned to the organization as minor league coaches.

Ferrell attended the winter meetings in San Diego where topics of debate included limiting the free agent market and National League expansion. The National League had last expanded in 1977. With at least twelve cities seeking major league franchises, opposition centered on current clubs that were losing money annually. Jim Campbell, a member of the Expansion Committee, favored expansion in the future at the appropriate time.

With the free agent market slow and the owners not bidding, both Kirk Gibson and Tom Brookens were forced to re-sign with the Tigers in early January 1986, for three-year and two-year contracts, respectively. Gibson had sought a five-year, $8,000,000 deal. For the first time since 1976, the twenty-six club owners had agreed to try to control escalating salaries by not competing with each other in bidding wars for free agents. The average player's salary had mushroomed from $74,000 in 1977 to $363,000 in 1985. With a payroll of between $15 and $16 million, the Tigers wanted players to submit to drug tests, but the players union objected. On February 1, 1986, the Players Association filed a grievance against the club owners for collusion in not signing free agents over the winter, in violation of the union agreement.

Rick was eagerly beginning his thirty-sixth season with the Detroit Tigers on Opening Day, April 7, 1986, as Detroit pitcher Jack Morris edged Boston, 6–5. While in third place at the end of April, the team slid back into fifth by June 1. By the July 15th All-Star break, the Tigers were in sixth, 14 games out. Following the All-Star break, Detroit obtained catcher Mike Heath from the St. Louis Cards. At the Hall of Fame ceremonies, Ferrell welcomed first baseman Willie McCovey into the esteemed shrine at Cooperstown.

An article in the August 16 *Los Angeles Times* featured Chris Bando, who was catching two knuckleball pitchers, Phil Niekro and Tom Candiotti, for the Cleveland Indians then. When someone told him that Rick Ferrell used to catch four knuckleballers, he responded, "That's a lot of sleepless nights!"[18]

In late September, 38-year-old Bob Boone, son of Ray Boone, caught his 1800th career game, a milestone achieved by only two other catchers in major league history, thus far: Al Lopez, who caught 1,918 games between 1928 and 1947, and Rick Ferrell, who caught 1,806 games between 1929 and 1947. In early October 1986, Boone passed Ferrell by catching 1,808 total games to take second place on the all-time list, moving Rick down to third after forty-one years.[19]

On the very last day of the 1986 season, the Tigers beat Baltimore, 6–3, winning all five games to edge out the Toronto Blue Jays for third place by one game with a final record of 87–75. Offensively, there were no .300 hitters on this team. Darrell Evans led the Bengals again with 29 homers. Jack Morris won a league-leading 21 victories.

Ferrell, with the Tigers' contingent, saw the New York Mets beat the Boston Red Sox in the World Series, four games to three. As Rick was celebrating his 81st birthday on October 12, 1986, the tragic announcement came that former Tigers first baseman Norm Cash, 51, had drowned suddenly in a Lake Michigan accident near upper Michigan.

The Tigers' front office had worked on improving player rosters all year. In the June draft, they had claimed Phil Clark (first), Milt Cuyler (second), outfielder Billy Bean (fourth), and Scott Aldred (sixteenth). In October, when pitcher Jack Morris was offered a two-year contract despite wanting a four-year deal, he filed for free agency, along with nine-year Tigers catcher Lance Parrish.

Ferrell attended the 85th annual baseball winter meetings for three days in Hollywood, Florida, in early December, where most owners reiterated their desire to hold down salaries. The 1985 average player salary had been $368,000; in 1986, it was $410,000 — an eleven per cent increase. The owners confirmed their earlier commitment to stick together on a player's price rather than "blind bidding" and competing with each other.[20] This was made apparent when free-agent Jack Morris traveled to meet with four other clubs, but none bested the Tigers' two-year salary offer, forcing the ace to finally re-sign with the Tigers.

In February 1987, Morris won his arbitration case against the Tigers for colluding to control player salaries. The club owed him $1.85 million — the highest award in twelve years of arbitration decisions — which almost doubled his 1986 salary. The Players Association filed another grievance charging owners with restricting free agent salaries in 1987 and those who filed for arbitration. Lance Parrish still hadn't signed, having received no competitive offers, but eventually got a contract from the Philadelphia Phillies for $50,000 less than Detroit had offered him. Several arbitration cases were heard during the winter, with players usually winning over the owners.

Rick's thirty-seventh season with Detroit began at Tiger Stadium on April 6, 1987, when Morris opened and lost against the Yankees, 2–1. The starting lineup consisted of Darrell Evans, Dave Bergman, Lou Whitaker, Alan Trammell, Tom Brookens in the infield and Chet Lemon, Pat Sheridan, Kirk Gibson in the outfield, with Matt Nokes catching. The pitching rotation featured Jack Morris, Walt Terrell, Frank Tanana, and Mike Henneman. For the first thirty games through May 11, the Tigers went 11–19, and settled into fifth place in the standings, 9½ games behind. Even playing well and going 14–4 from May 12 to month's end couldn't improve their fifth-place standing, despite being out only six games then.

The June Draft proved fruitful for the Tigers when they selected infielders Travis Fryman (second) and Torey Lovullo. Four-time National League batting champion Bill Madlock signed as a free agent. By the 1987 All-Star break, Detroit was in third place, 48–37, five games out. Rick attended the 58th All-Star Game in the Oakland-Alameda County Coliseum and later, the Hall of Fame ceremonies with his daughters for the induction of Catfish Hunter, Billy Williams, and Ray Dandridge.

Post All-Star break, Detroit flip-flopped between third and second place, swapping with Toronto and Milwaukee. By August, the crew found themselves only two games out of first place and in the middle of a pennant drive. For the stretch, on August 12 they acquired veteran Braves pitcher Doyle Alexander in a trade for a single, highly-regarded pitching prospect: John Smoltz. No one then could have predicted the success of Smoltz' long major league career. And Doyle did exactly what he was hired to do: win. From August 12 on, the Tigers went 33–18 for the rest of the season, with Alexander pitching like a laser beam to achieve a perfect 9–0 record. The 1987 season came down to a final series against Toronto which the Tigers swept in three one-run games (4–3, 3–2, 1–0) to clinch the eastern division title on the very last day of the season, October 4. The Blue Jays finished two games behind Detroit with a 96–66 record.

After finishing third the past two years, Sparky's 1987 team had gone 98–64 for the tenth best season record in Tigers' history. The Baseball Writers voted Anderson "The American League Manager of the Year" again. Evans hit 34 homers, Morris won 18 games, and Trammell experienced a sudden, spectacular finish.

The divisional playoffs pitted Detroit against the Minnesota Twins during October 7 to 12. Ferrell traveled to Minnesota where the home team took the first two games from Detroit, then the Tigers won one back once they returned to Tiger Stadium. But Minnesota defeated Detroit twice to win the American League championship, four games to one. In the World Series, the Twins also defeated the St. Louis Cardinals, four games to three.

Just as the divisional playoffs were to begin, Rick was called to Greensboro with the sad news of the death of his brother, George Ferrell, 83, on October 6, 1987. George had spent fifty years in professional baseball as a minor league outfielder and manager and as scout for the St. Louis Cardinals and Detroit Tigers. Almost two years older than Rick, these two brothers had very similar personalities, mild temperaments, easy-going dispositions, and positive outlooks. Now of the seven Ferrell brothers, only Rick and the reclusive Basil remained. Basil would pass away in January 1991.

Long-time local *Greensboro New and Record* reporter and author Wilt Browning provided his memories of Rick in a 2003 telephone interview from North Carolina.

WILT BROWNING: I met Rick in the late 1970s, early '80s. His memory was so good that I would call him frequently after that first meeting. I would always read the AP every day moves—"This Day in Baseball"—and occasionally I'd see something I wanted to write a column about, and I'd almost always call Rick and say "What is your take on this?" and it was incredible how much of all that he remembered and with what detail. It was just unbelievable.

The one that always sticks in my mind is the date of the anniversary of Lou Gehrig's streak of appearances that stood until Cal Ripken broke the record. I called Rick and asked him about that. He remembered, "Well, they were playing us that day." Down to the point that he remembered lighting the cigarette for Lou because Lou's hands were shaking so much. That's just incredible. He said it was down under the stands and it was real dusty, but out of sight of the fans. I couldn't come close to recalling the detail in my life that he could recall in his.

He'd come down to Greensboro and check into the Hilton there on West Market, but he would always call me to meet him for breakfast or dinner — always very delightful. We stayed in touch on the phone and when he would come to town.

St Louis is the hottest place in the world in August catching those doubleheaders. He never put on weight. He always looked like he was very fit.

Six days after George's death, Rick turned 82, and was still driving the highway to Tiger Stadium every day. That autumn arbitrators ruled in favor of Kirk Gibson and the Players Association and against club owners, who were found guilty of colluding to stifle free agency, in violation of the labor agreement. When asked about the collusion matter, Rick remained tight-lipped, but he felt that players should be paid for one or two years based on performance rather than with long-term, guaranteed salaries. Two free agents re-signed: catcher Mike Heath and pitcher Jack Morris. Morris accepted a two-year deal worth an estimated $4,000,000. Pitcher Dan Petry was traded to the California Angels for Gary Pettis at the end of December.

During January 1988, the Players Association filed a third grievance against the club owners for withholding competitive offers from 1987 free agents. An arbitrator ruled that Gibson and other Tiger free agents could negotiate with other teams or return to their original team by March 1. Brookens, Tanana, and Luis Salazar re-signed with the Tigers as free agents. Kirk Gibson signed a three-year deal with the L.A. Dodgers estimated at $4.5 million.[21] Twelve-year National League utility man Ray Knight was obtained for pitcher Mark Thurmond.

With the exception of Pettis and Knight, the 1988 Tigers' lineup changed little from the previous year. After starting on the road, Detroit opened the season at Tiger Stadium and hung on to third place, most days through June 11. After defeating Cleveland, 13–3, the team moved up to second. Within nine days' time, the Tigers took over the lead in the American League East and won 18 out of 27 games played in June, holding the premier spot all summer until September 5.

Rick appeared in Cooperstown for the Hall of Fame ceremonies that inducted Willie Stargell. Former Tigers pitcher Jim Bunning had missed Hall of Fame election by a mere four votes, but would be selected by the Veterans Committee in 1996.

The Chicago White Sox met Detroit at Tiger Stadium for a four-game series from August 18 to 21. When White Sox catcher Carlton Fisk, 40, came to town, he was just shy of breaking Rick's American League "most games caught" record of 1,806 games. On August 18, 1988, with Ferrell present in the seats, Fisk caught his 1,806th game to tie Rick's "most games caught." The game was halted, and Rick went to home plate to congratulate Fisk and have photos taken, just as Ray Schalk had congratulated Rick in 1945 on his record-breaking achievement in Washington, D.C., forty-three years earlier. The next day,

On August 18, 1988, in a game played at Tiger Stadium, White Sox catcher Carlton Fisk (left) broke Rick Ferrell's American League "most games caught" record by catching his 1,806th game against the Detroit Tigers while Rick watched from the stands. The pair posed for photographs much as Ferrell had posed with Ray Schalk upon breaking his record back in 1945. (Ilitch Enterprises; Detroit Tigers Baseball Archives)

Fisk caught his 1,807th game to surpass Rick's record and went 5-for-5 at the plate for the first time in his eighteen-year career, garnering four singles, a triple, and two RBIs. Despite the hoopla for Mr. Fisk, Detroit won the game, 5–4, sweeping Chicago.

After breaking Rick's record, Fisk remarked, "It's difficult to get terribly excited about something that took seventeen years to build. It's not something that boiled down to just one game or a single moment in a game, like a home run. I knew if I kept playing, it was going to happen." And later, he conceded, "What it means is that you have persevered over the odds."[22]

Executive consultant Ferrell told the *Detroit Free Press*, "I knew that it was going to be broken eventually. I'm not surprised that it's Fisk. He's been a fine catcher through the years. He's had his share of injuries, but he always came back to catch. Others may have decided to move to first base or the outfield." In the same article, Rick lamented the lack of new catching prospects. "We're not getting the good young catchers coming up like we used to. It's not a glamorous position, and the kids don't think there's a lot of popularity in it. I'm a little disturbed. The only good young catcher is the kid in San Diego (Benito Santiago)."[23]

From August 7 to September 6, the Tigers slumped with a record of 9–20, which cost them the lead for the first time since June. With a 9–3 record for the final twelve games, they ended the season in second, one game behind the Boston Red Sox, with an 88–74 record. By a single game, Sparky and the Tigers just missed clinching the division again. The Dodgers won the Series against the A's, with injured, pinch-hitting Dodger Kirk Gibson blasting his game-winning homer, considered by many as one of the most exciting moments in baseball history.

Meanwhile at the September 8 owners' meeting in Montreal, National League President Bart Giamatti was voted to replace Commissioner Peter Ueberroth when his term expired in April 1989. Later in the fall, arbitrator Nicolau found baseball owners guilty of collusion for a second time in not signing almost two hundred free agents for 1986, a verdict known later as "Collusion II."[24]

In December, Glenn Waggoner wrote in a *New York Times* article, "The death of collusion has already spawned a rebirth of stupidity.... The owners are unable to control their spending, offering huge, long-term contracts."[25] Additionally, Major League Baseball signed a four-year television deal with CBS for $1.05 billion, one of the largest sports broadcasting deals ever made. Starting in 1990, twelve regular season games and all post-season games would be televised. The previous contract for NBC's "Game of the Week" had been for thirty-two games per season. With more pay–TV games expected, Commissioner Ueberroth accurately predicted, "Cable is in 60 percent of the country now. It will go up to 70–80–90 percent. People will have cable TV the way they now have telephone."

Joe Falls wrote another Ferrell profile for the March 1, 1989, *Detroit News,* entitled, "Age-Old Quest Still Fun for Ferrell, 83." Interviewing Rick during early spring training at Lakeland, the old pro said, "I always get excited whenever I walk into a ballpark. You never know what's going to happen in a ballpark." He recalled his old playing days, when the team traveled by train and got six dollars a day for meals. "They didn't actually give us the money — we had to eat at the hotel where the team was staying and we could charge up to $6 a day for meals. If you went over $6, you had to pay for it. If you went under, the team kept the difference. Every day, we tried to make it come out as close to $6 as possible." Recalling the 100 degree temperatures in St. Louis and no such thing as air conditioning, he reminisced, "When we'd ride the trains, we'd open the windows to get some air. Pretty soon, there was soot over everything — our pillows, our sheets, and even our eyebrows. The dirt used to get in our ears. When you brushed your teeth, you'd clean your ears." But looking toward the future season, he surmised, "I'm afraid we're going to be out-homered this year ... and I see a few questions in our pitching staff." Falls wrote Rick reported to Bill LaJoie, who sought his wisdom as did Jim Campbell.

Bart Giamatti, 50, a former Yale University president, succeeded Peter Ueberroth as baseball commissioner in April, with good friend Fay Vincent becoming deputy commissioner. For years, Giamatti had endured continual legal probes into Pete Rose's gambling charges.

The Tigers' 1989 lineup lacked a few familiar faces. In March the front office had dealt Tom Brookens and Luis Salazar; Darrell Evans was gone too. Pitcher Eric King went to the White Sox for Ken Williams. Other newcomers on the Tigers' roster included infielder Torey Lovullo and outfielder Billy Bean.[26] Veterans Jack Morris, Dave Bergman, Lou Whitaker, and Alan Trammell from the 1984 World Series team remained on-board.

In 1989 at age 83, Rick was beginning his thirty-ninth season with the Detroit Tigers organization, and there was no slowing him down; he was present for every game time at Tiger Stadium from Opening Day through the final out of the season. During his off hours, he played tennis and golf, attended card shows, signed autographs, and answered fan mail.

But no one could have predicted the dreadful events of the coming months and the pathetic downward spiral his team would endure. After losing two games to start the season, the Bengals continued a slide backward, ending the month of April in fourth place with an 8–14 record. A May 7, 1989, *Washington Post* article summarized, "The Tigers are too old, have lost too much talent, and haven't done a good enough job in the farm system. A team that has averaged 89 victories over the last ten full seasons may, finally, be at the end of its run."[26]

One reality was that since Bill LaJoie had been promoted to GM from scouting director/assistant general manager in 1983, five men had held the position, each with their own scouts. Also, in the late '80s, Detroit's draft selections had been between fifteenth and twenty-sixth, yielding first-round picks like Rico Brogna (1988) and Greg Gohr (1989).

Having won only three more games by May 19, Detroit was entrenched in seventh — and last — place in the American League East, and their field boss began to show the strain. In his twentieth managerial season (and eleventh with the Tigers), Sparky Anderson, 50, suddenly collapsed from nervous exhaustion and was sent home to California under doctor's orders. Third base coach Dick Tracewski filled in for Anderson, but the entire organization — from players to front office — was shaken by the much-loved manager's sudden departure. When Sparky returned to the team seventeen days later on June 4, his team was still in seventh place, with a 22–32 season record. At the All-Star break a month later, they were 17 games out of first, winning only five games for the rest of July, while losing twelve. Rick and his children traveled to the Hall of Fame ceremonies in Cooperstown to welcome catcher Johnny Bench and infielder Carl Yastrzemski.

Unfortunately, events in baseball at-large became increasingly turbulent. On August 26, with support by a majority of the club owners, Commissioner Bart Giamatti banned Pete Rose from baseball for life for gambling, betting on his own baseball team, and other infractions. However, less than a week after his ruling, the 51-year-old Giamatti died suddenly on September 1, 1989, of a heart attack on Martha's Vineyard, shaking up the entire baseball world.

The owners quickly approved Deputy Commissioner Faye Vincent as the new baseball commissioner on September 12. Vincent promised to continue Bart Giamatti's vision for baseball: developing affirmative action and international baseball, implementing drug testing, developing talent, and improving stadium ambience by eliminating disrespectful fan behavior. Also in early September, an arbitrator fined club owners $10.5 million in damages for collusion after the 1985 season in restricting salary-bidding for free agents.[27]

Sparky Anderson's boys endured a 12-game losing streak during August, and October 1 finally brought a merciful end to 1989, the Tigers' most disastrous season in years. Detroit's $14 million player payroll had resulted in a dead-last finish, 30 games behind the division-leading Toronto Blue Jays. Twenty Tigers had been on the disabled list during the year. Only 1,544,000 fans attended the games, far below the two-million attendance standard in recent years. The only notable achievement belonged to outfielder Gary Pettis, who won a Gold Glove.[28]

Free agency had become increasingly prevalent and the Tigers' front office had been forced to pay out increasing sums of guaranteed money to acquire better players. They lost Pettis, Fred Lynn, and Hudson to free agency, with Tanana re-signing. Breaking with past tradition, the Tigers' LaJoie signed free agent infielder Tony Phillips to a three-year, $4 million contract, and free agent Lloyd Moseby to a two-year, $3 million deal, while releasing veteran pitcher Guillermo Hernandez.[29] To cap off the dismal year, on Christmas Day, former

Tigers manager Billy Martin was killed in a roll-over car crash in Johnson City, New York, at age 61.

To begin the New Year of a new decade in 1990, the Detroit Tigers' front office was once again restructured. Approaching 89 years of age, John Fetzer retired completely from baseball, assuming the title of Chairman Emeritus, while Jim Campbell replaced Fetzer as Chairman of the Board and Chief Executive Officer of the Tigers. A surprise choice was made when University of Michigan Athletic Director and legendary football coach Bo Schembechler, a close friend of Tigers owner Tom Monaghan, was tapped to run the Tigers as Chief Operating Officer and President. Rick remained on as executive consultant for the organization.

During that winter 161 major league ball players filed for arbitration. Jack Morris reached a deal with the Tigers for a salary estimated at $2.1 million for the season, with an option for 1991. Free agent Cecil Fielder, 26, signed with Detroit for two years at an estimated $3 million. Pitcher Dan Petry re-signed with the Tigers as a free agent. Bo Schembechler's player payroll totaled about $17,849,000.[30]

The collective bargaining agreement between the owners and the Players Association was due to expire and each side had stockpiled strike funds, with the players' strike fund totaling between $80 and $90 million. Without an agreement, owners threatened to lock-out spring training and forfeit the entire baseball season. Players blamed owners for the problems under debate: arbitration eligibility, owners' contributions to the pension fund and benefit plan, size of team rosters, and collusion protection. Owners seeking revenue sharing were perceived as union-busters by the Players Association. The owners wanted salary caps, no multi-year contracts, but rather salaries structured on a "pay-for-performance" scale to include a player's length of major league service.

During the off-season, Rick was back in the news. In a February 15, 1990, article "Owners: Golden Egg on their Faces," the *Washington Post*'s Shirley Povich questioned the validity of anyone putting too much value on a player's fielding statistics: "Another example of the perfidy of fielding averages is Rick Ferrell, a Hall of Famer and artist with the mitt. It was his ill luck to be catching the Senators' four knuckleballers: Dutch Leonard, Roger Wolff, John Niggeling, and Mickey Haefner. They put Ferrell in the record book more than once for committing the most passed balls." (The *Baseball Encyclopedia* lists that while catching 96 games pitched by knuckleball starters in 1944, Rick collected 20 passed balls, with nine errors for a .981 fielding average. During 83 games caught in 1945, his passed balls totaled 21, with four errors for a .990 fielding average.)

But in 1990, no meeting of the minds transpired between the owners and players union, and a 32-day baseball lockout occurred from February 15 to March 18 that prevented the scheduled start of spring training. The agreement reached between the union and team owners increased the owners' contributions to the players' pension fund to $55 million. Salary arbitration would be available to seventeen percent of the players with two-to-three years' experience. Minimum salary for a rookie was increased to $100,000.[31] Again the owners gained nothing.

The strike delayed the start of the 1990 season by a week so the players could get in shape. Working-class and wealthy fans, disillusioned and embittered with baseball, vowed to stay away from the big-league games. After 103 losses in 1989, only twelve Tigers had been retained for the 1990 season. Detroit's 40-man roster included 15 minor league and new players, like Cecil Fielder (1B), Tony Phillips (3B), Lloyd Moseby (CF), and Larry Sheets (RF). Gone were Doyle Alexander, Willie Hernandez, Keith Moreland, Fred Lynn, and Pat Sheridan. The starting rotation would be headed by Jack Morris, along with Dan Petry, Jeff Robinson, and Frank Tanana.

Still going to the ballpark every day for the games, Rick now drove to his office by late morning, ate lunch with the guys, and worked until game time at 7:05 P.M. Due to failing eyesight, he would watch the initial innings, but leave the ballpark at about 9:00 P.M. before nightfall to make the drive home on I-75 safely before dark.

Rick, family, and friends were at Tiger Stadium for the excitement of Opening Day on April 9. But the Tigers immediately got off to a poor start, losing the opener, and fell to seventh (last) place by April 30, at 8–12. From April 29 to May 8, Detroit lost nine of ten games played. During a May 6 game that Toronto won, 11–7, ten total homers cleared the fences, three by Fielder, two by Lemon, and five by the Blue Jays. Despite bouncing back during May 15–21 to win seven straights, Detroit finished the month in sixth. At the Seattle Kingdome on June 2, left-hander Randy Johnson pitched a 2–0 no-hitter against the Tigers, leaving them 6½ games out of first.

Seeking stronger pitching, the Tigers front office traded catcher Matt Nokes, 26, to the Yankees for hurlers Lance McCullers and Clay Parker. Their first-round draft pick was tall, switch-hitting first baseman, Tony Clark, 17, from El Cajon, California. By the All-Star break, Detroit had pulled themselves up to fourth in the A.L. East.

Ferrell did not attend the mid-summer classic due to the onset of glaucoma at age 84. In the late 1980s, he'd noticed his vision had become blurry during a golf game when he was unable to track his golf ball after hitting it. He missed an ophthalmologist appointment due to a baseball trip. When he finally did visit the eye doctor, the optic nerve in his left eye had been silently and severely damaged by glaucoma, as had his mother's, which would leave Rick essentially blind in that eye. Able to see mainly with his right eye, he continued to drive himself to the ballpark to watch games on a daily basis, going slowly in the right lane of the fast-moving traffic on the freeway, much to the dismay of his loved ones. "I made it!" he'd announce, after driving home from a night baseball game, instilling dread that one day, he might not. Even partial blindness did not keep him from the Tigers and baseball.

In Cooperstown with his daughters at the end of July, Rick appeared on the dais with the other Hall of Famers as Jim Palmer and Joe Morgan were inducted. The talk of the town was Commissioner Faye Vincent's banning of George Steinbrenner from baseball for one year for having paid $40,000 to a known gambler for negative information against Dave Winfield in an effort to discredit Winfield. George's son, Hank, 33, took control of the Yankees.

In Detroit, disinterested baseball fans were staying away in 1990 as the Tigers bounced around the standings in August to finish the month in third place, eleven games out of first. Creating some fan interest was 26-year-old Cecil Fielder's quest for fifty homers. In a 10–3 win October 3, the final game of the season, Fielder blasted two homers at Yankee Stadium, numbers 50 and 51, a feat last achieved by Yankee Roger Maris in 1961. After 1989's last place finish in the A.L. East with 103 losses, the Tigers' third place, 79–83 record showed an improvement of 20 wins in 1990. The Associated Press voted Cecil "Tiger Player of the Year." Even so, the attendance at Tiger Stadium — 1,495,785 — dropped to its lowest total in thirteen years.

Financial concerns and player transactions occupied Ferrell and the Tigers' brass that autumn. Collusion cases against the owners had resulted in $280 million in damages that owners owed the affected players, equal to $10.77 million per club.[32] With ticket revenue down, clubs were losing money and attempting a return to cost efficiency and developing talent slowly through the minor leagues, a philosophy long held by Ferrell. In addition to Pay TV subscriptions, new revenue sources were required, and oddly, baseball expansion was again on the table. Tiger free agents Dan Petry, Jack Morris, and Mike Heath re-signed contracts.

But Bo Schembechler made one regrettable PR move that fall by announcing that 1991 would be the final season for the revered Ernie Harwell, the much-loved Tigers' radio announcer for the past thirty years since 1960. Detroit baseball fans rioted in protest, newspapers criticized, and both Bo and WJR's Jim Long were on the hot seat for the unpopular decision. Upset with the Harwell firing himself, Rick commented, "I tried to tell 'em, 'This guy's pretty popular in Detroit,' but they wouldn't listen."

Hall of Fame sportswriter Joe Falls wrote a profile of Schembechler and the Tigers for the September 20, 1990, *Detroit News*, saying the new president needed to emulate Jim Campbell's rise to success. "Instead of trying to fool people or act like an expert, (Jim) took Rick Ferrell to his side and learned from him. Everywhere Campbell went, Ferrell went with him. They were inseparable. They were breakfast, lunch, and dinner companions. Campbell had the leadership qualities— the ability to get things done — and Ferrell provided him with the information needed to make his moves. No ego problems were involved with either side. It was a great relationship — one that produced two world championships in Detroit. You can talk about Denny McLain and Al Kaline and Willie Horton and Kirk Gibson and Lance Parrish and Jack Morris getting it done, but the direction that came from the front office — Campbell and Ferrell, Inc.— made it all possible. Now, Campbell is almost out of the picture. He'll probably hang around a while, but has allowed Schembechler to be his own man...."

January 1991 transactions by smart general manager Bill LaJoie sent pitcher Jeff Robinson, 29, to Baltimore for slugging catcher Mickey Tettleton, 30. Then the 56-year-old LaJoie, himself, resigned from the Tigers after six years in that position, saying cryptically in the January 13, 1991, *New York Times* that he wished to pursue "a more relaxed lifestyle." Perhaps the former GM had felt constrained in his authority to make deals. Tigers vice president of player development Joe MacDonald stepped in as interim general manager.

On February 20, the Tigers' organization was deeply saddened by the unexpected death of the highly regarded ex–Tigers owner John Fetzer, 89, in Honolulu. Fetzer's title had been Chairman Emeritus of the Detroit Tigers, but his real legacy was the creation of the Fetzer Institute in Kalamazoo, Michigan, dedicated to the promotion of world peace and holistic health, which continues its mission to the present day.

Good pitching eluded Detroit. Over the winter, they signed two 31-year-old veterans: right-hander Bill Gullickson and southpaw John Cerutti. Hopefully offense had been strengthened by the signing of power-hitters Rob Deer and Pete Incaviglia. Outfielder Chet Lemon, 35, was given his unconditional release. Youth prevailed, as Petry, Bergman, Whitaker, and Trammell remained as the only holdovers from the 1984 World Series team.

The Ferrells and friends attended the annual Tigers opener in early April 1991 to see Detroit beat New York. Holding their own, the team resided in third place by the end of April, only 1½ games out of first.

Rick continued his trips to his Tiger Stadium office every day, arriving sometimes later in the morning and staying until half way through the Tigers' night games. Like Rick, Tiger Stadium, the old gem standing at the corner of Michigan and Trumbull near downtown Detroit since 1912, was aging, and the ballpark badly needed refurbishing. The rust-covered steel infra-structure and the players' facilities needed updating, as did other amenities (upscale boxes, restrooms, suites, narrow corridors). Personnel exceeded space. Debate over where a new stadium might be built stalled due to resistance from traditional "Tiger Stadium lovers" and the city of Detroit's lack of cash. William Haase, the Tigers' Senior Vice President for Operations, told the April 8 *New York Times* that the Tigers hadn't ruled out Detroit as a site for a new stadium, but that some feared the Tigers might relocate to the suburbs as the Lions and Pistons had. Plans were still indefinite. Haase, who rose to become a National Baseball Hall of Fame vice president, publicly credited Rick with teaching him almost all he ever knew about the game of baseball.

The patriarch Rick assembles in Sarasota, Florida, during spring training in 1990 for lunch with several of his children, nieces, and nephews. Seated in front, left to right: Maureen Ferrell (Rick's daughter), George Ferrell, Jr., Rick (center), and Wes Ferrell, Jr. Standing, left to right: Jason Ferrell (George Ferrell Jr.'s son), Kerrie Ferrell (center), and Gwenlo Ferrell Gore (Wes' daughter).

May and June found the team humming primarily in third place, playing .500 ball despite two lengthy losing streaks. In late June, pitcher Dan Petry (125–104) — one of the last of the '84 World Series Champions — was traded to the Atlanta Braves, where Bill LaJoie now worked. By the All-Star break, Detroit was still in third, 41–40, seven games behind Toronto. At July's end, Rick attended the Hall of Fame ceremonies with new inductees Rod Carew, Gaylord Perry, and Fergie Jenkins.

As a team, the Tigers were near the top in runs because of their combined power hitters Fielder, Tettleton, and Deer. On September 8, the squad dropped to third place, six games out of first, 72–65, where it would finish the month. The Tigers battled Boston for second place in the American League East during the stretch, playing them at Fenway, October 1–3, splitting two games. On the last day of the season, October 6, Frank Tanana defeated the Orioles, 7–1. Detroit tied with Joe Morgan's Red Sox for second place in the American League

East, 84–78 (.519), seven games behind Toronto, the division winner. Detroit's super home-run production had compensated for its poor ERA and weak offense. Fielder hit 44 round-trippers to tie with Jose Canseco for major league lead and led the majors with 133 RBIs.

October 6, 1991, was sadly, also announcer Ernie Harwell's final radio broadcast. After joining the Tigers in 1960, he became one of the greatest announcers in baseball history and a Hall of Famer. An entire generation of radio listeners had grown up hearing Harwell's familiar voice calling the Tigers' games. Along with Ernie, his fellow announcer Paul Carey also retired after nineteen years with the Tigers. The National Trust for Historic Preservation launched a campaign to save the 79-year-old Tiger Stadium from demolition and preserve it for posterity.

In Detroit's front office, semi-retired Jim Campbell still held the title of Chairman and CEO of the Tigers, while Bo Schembechler was president and Joe MacDonald, general manager. Rick Ferrell, still executive consultant, turned 86 on October 12 and except for his dim eyesight, was going strong. The "big brass" had selected pitcher Justin Thompson (first) in the June draft. Back in June, Sparky Anderson had gotten a two-year extension to his managerial contract.

Before Christmas, Cecil Fielder rejected a four-year, $17 million contract offer from the Tigers, after being paid $1,750,000 in 1991. Eligible for free agency after 1993, he now sought a salary more like Bobby Bonilla's $29 million over five years. The Tigers offered Cecil $3.2 million for 1992, but he filed for arbitration, seeking $5,400,000, the highest demand in the sixteen-year history of arbitration. (Of the 136 players filing for arbitration, twenty wanted more than $3 million a year.) On January 28, both parties avoided arbitration by agreeing on $4.5 million for the year. As the largest one-year salary in baseball history, Fielder's contract represented 16 percent of the Tigers' $25 million payroll for 1992. Four days later, Pittsburgh's Barry Bonds signed for $4.7 million, breaking Fielder's record, an amount that Ferrell had difficulty relating to.

In late 1991, Detroit Tigers owner Tom Monaghan re-assumed presidency and control of Domino's Pizza, the national corporation he had started and owned. His strong Catholic faith had inspired him to put God and his religion first and gradually divest himself of his material possessions. In a December 10 *New York Times* article, he spoke of even selling the Detroit Tigers, with the surprising admission that "none of the things I've bought — and I mean none of them — have ever really made me happy." In spring training, word traveled through the grapevine that Monaghan was now selling off his Domino's stock and soon, his non-pizza investments would go too— meaning the Detroit Tigers Baseball Club.

On April 6, 1992, Rick attended his 63rd major league Opening Day with his children and friends. Deep down, everyone knew that this— his forty-third Detroit Tigers Opener since 1950 — would be their last at Tiger Stadium and a wistfulness pervaded the normal excitement. Disappointingly, the Tigers lost their first six games in sweeps by Toronto and New York and fell to sixth place where they stayed until the All-Star break in July. In the June draft, the Tigers signed infielders Chris Gomez and Frank Catalanotto and an outfielder named Bobby Higginson, among others.

At the July break, the Tigers were 41–48, 13 games behind the leader. Failing eyesight prohibited Rick from attending the classic, but he planned to attend in 1993 for the celebration of the 60th Anniversary of the first All-Star Game.

Baseball, itself, was on a precarious financial roller-coaster ride. Problems simmered among the Players Association, the owners, and Commissioner Fay Vincent over proceeds. Huge player salaries strained operating budgets. On June 16, a *New York Times* article by Claire Smith revealed that the Tigers had been "forced to borrow almost $5 million from the central baseball administration" to meet its June payroll. Two other clubs were rumored to have borrowed almost $35 million from the central bank.

On July 29, 1992, the announcement came that everyone had anxiously expected: The Detroit Tigers organization had been sold. Tom Monaghan had struck a deal with Little Caesar's Pizza owner Mike Ilitch to pay an estimated $85 million for the club he'd bought for $53 million back in 1983. The Detroit Tigers' "family" shake-up began August 3 when CEO Jim Campbell and President Bo Schembechler were suddenly fired by Monaghan. Campbell was impersonally notified of his termination by a fax received after he and Rick had attended the Hall of Fame induction of Tom Seaver and Rollie Fingers in Cooperstown. The *Detroit Free Press* headline screamed: "AXED BY FAX!" to describe his dismissal. After forty-three years with the Detroit Tigers as his only priority, Campbell remained shaken and shattered by the calloused treatment he'd received. Monaghan assumed presidency of the Tigers, citing differences between himself and Bo, but belatedly praising Jim Campbell's outstanding service to the club and to baseball. On August 24, major league owners unanimously approved the team's final sale and the deal was done. That was it. Rick's great run in baseball was nearing an end, as he submitted his resignation to the Detroit Tigers, effective December 31, 1992.

Yet in an August 28 *Detroit Free Press* article, 86-year-old Rick, the oldest member of the Tigers' staff, told sportswriter George Puscas that he was "looking forward" to the new owner's changes. "I was told to continue doing the things I've been doing." Rick noted that he had been with the Tigers forty-three years, "since the time Walter O. Briggs owned the team in the 1950s. Mike Ilitch was in our minor-league system at the time. I think I was a coach here then. I've been a farm director, a vice president, and a lot of things under four or five owners and a lot more general managers. This change in ownership with the Tigers is something we've long been expecting. I expect a lot of other changes, too. We've got to take the game away from the agents and give it back to the owners. It's gone too far the wrong way." Only this never happened.

The rest of the season passed, and his children enjoyed the autumn baseball games with special attention. The Tigers bounced between fourth and sixth place in September before finally settling into fifth during the last five games. On October 4, they finished one game out of fourth place with a 75–87 record, 21 games behind first-place Toronto.

The final Tigers home game on September 30 — a 4–2 victory over the Orioles — was also the last Tigers game for Rick and his kids. They bid farewell to the friends they'd made over the decades at Tiger Stadium — other Tiger "family" members, the stadium staff, the ushers and police officers, the ticket takers and concessioners, the sports reporters and photographers. The next day Joe Falls wrote in the *Detroit News* "It was so quiet in the ball park Wednesday night ... all those empty seats. A little sadness: Rick Ferrell is quitting at the end of the season. The old catcher-scout-friend is 86 and figures it's time to slow down."

Rick's prediction proved correct that there would be "a lot of other changes." Ilitch executed a top-to-bottom sweep of the Tigers' organization before bringing in staff from his hockey team, the Detroit Red Wings, to operate the club. Rick turned 87 on October 12, 1992, and with a few retained holdovers, continued reporting daily to his Annex office until the end of the year. Several Tigers filed for free agency, while the addition of the Florida Marlins and Colorado Rockies expanded the National League.

Just before the Christmas holiday, 1992, Rick Ferrell quietly cleared out his office of photos, files, memorabilia, and other belongings. No retirement party was held in his honor, no gold watch for sixty-six years of meritorious service to the game of baseball was given him, no back-slapping, hand-shaking farewell after all the decades of dedicated effort to the organization. He left his executive career as quietly as he'd departed his playing career. Rick simply said good-bye to the people that remained before quietly exiting Tiger Stadium for the last time, thus ending his long, successful tenure with the Detroit Tigers and professional baseball.

14

❖ ❖ ❖

1993–1995

Farewell and Epilogue

As 1993 began, Rick sailed into retirement as he had weathered other life changes—with grace and ease, and no visible regrets. Immediately he realized that by not going to the stadium each day, he would need to create a daily routine for himself. To that end, he set up an "office" in his dining room where he answered fan mail and signed autographs.

Jim Campbell, still smarting from his painful, public firing, phoned frequently to express his agitation. Rick patiently listened before advising Jim that their time with the Tigers was over and that so much had changed at Tiger Stadium, they no longer would fit in with the current organization. Jim's physical health began to decline.

Fan mail continued to pour in on a daily basis and, as part of Rick's new daily routine for retirement, answering all his autograph requests became a "cottage industry." He created a new price list to send when a fan had forgotten to send return postage or autograph fees. The list read: "From the Desk of Rick Ferrell: I receive hundreds of requests for autographs each week. Orders must include return packaging and postage or SASE. My discount fees are as follows:

My autographed HOF plaque $8.00	Your jersey $20.00
My autographed 8 × 10 picture $15.00	
Your baseball or minibat $12.00	
Your bat, glove, cap $15.00	All proceeds go to charity.

For the first time in their lives, Rick had time to sit around the kitchen table with his children and chat leisurely over coffee without having to rush out to the ballpark or airport. His daughter and he would read the *Detroit Free Press* in the morning to "cuss and discuss" current events.

One summer day, Rick's old friend, *Detroit News* sportswriter Joe Falls, a future Hall of Famer, called Ferrell to go to Joe Muir's Seafood Restaurant for lunch and an interview, which appeared in Falls' September 19, 1993, column entitled, "Former Tiger Official Ferrell Is a Man to Be Treasured." Falls wrote that, along with Detroit's civic treasures like the GM Building and the Detroit Institute of Arts, he wanted to add another local treasure: Rick Ferrell, the oldest living member of the Baseball Hall of Fame, who would turn 88 on October 12. "He is a true treasure because he hasn't changed one bit in all these years. He is as gentle as ever, soft-spoken and polite. But I must warn you: If you take him to lunch, you'd better come dressed because he will show up with a shirt and tie and a neatly pressed suit." Falls also noted that "I've seen [Rick] eat everything in sight, including two desserts, and he never gained so much as an ounce." Jim Campbell often wryly observed the same thing, as he battled weight gain, saying, "I eat the same thing Rick does, but Rick never gains an ounce!"

Contrasting the filthy conditions under which Rick caught to his modern GQ appearance, Falls described, "He played at a time when the games would start at 3 P.M. and the temperature would often be more than 100 degrees. He was a dust-bowl catcher playing with a dirty uniform. He played on major-league fields where there was no grass in the infield, just dirt, and you might get your uniform cleaned once a week."

The article highlighted Ferrell's baseball career, recalling the first All-Star Game, and the 1944–1945 Washington knuckleballers that Rick caught "with poise and also with very few passed balls." Over lunch, Rick related some of his favorite baseball stories in his slow, Southern style: the Joe DiMaggio incident in the middle of his 56-game streak, the time both Rick and Wes homered in the same game ("Stick a stick up on *that* one!"), his rookie story following veteran Lu Blue around Grand Central Station on his first trip to New York City. Falls included these tales, writing, "The Ricker keeps going on and on, and you will never meet a more pleasant man even if you live to be 100."

Upon the death of Tiger Hall of Fame second baseman Charlie Gehringer the previous year on January 1, 1993, Rick had been anointed with the dubious title of "oldest living member of the Hall of Fame." On November 12 in Little Rock, Hall of Fame Yankees catcher Bill Dickey died at age 86. He had broken into the major leagues in 1928, the year before Rick, and retired in 1943 with a career average of .313 over 1,789 games.

Sporting News writer Steve Gietschier profiled Ferrell for article in the January 24, 1994, issue entitled, "Classy Catcher." In it, Wes was quoted, talking about Rick, "Brother or no brother, he was a real classy catcher. You never saw him lunge for the ball; he never took a strike away from you. He'd get more strikes for a pitcher than anybody I ever saw because he made catching look easy."

Readers' mail to *The Sporting News* followed publication of the article. Richard J. Kosinski wrote in February 7, 1994, "I enjoyed your article, 'Classy Catcher,' about Rick Ferrell. Not only do these historical articles give fans a perspective of yesteryear, but also we are able to compare former sports greats with those of today. And the more I read about sports heroes from the past, the less I am impressed with the class exhibited by most modern sports figures."

Soon after, in late 1993, Rick began experiencing for the first time, extremely severe pain in his old catching hands. A catcher's joints are the first parts to go, and at this time, Ferrell was diagnosed with severe arthritis, causing him chronic burning pain and stiffness to the unusual point of complaint. Various medications prescribed by doctors suppressed his appetite, causing noticeable weight loss from Rick's already slender physique.

In early 1994, Rick decided to try physical therapy in an attempt to treat his sore stiffness. Over the 1994 winter the arthritis inflammation spread from his hands to his ankles, knees, neck, and shoulders, wracking his entire body with severe pain. In a most unusual turn of events, Ferrell found he lacked the energy to even get dressed to go outside. Without an appetite, he lost too much weight, felt tired and weak, and began to spend entire winter days indoors.

In a small, blue spiral-bound notebook, Rick began documenting his day-to-day health that spring. "April 27, 1994: No pills, no appetite, losing weight. Ate steak for dinner. Felt good all evening. Need something in stomach apparently, at all times to prevent nausea feeling." But his chronic pain persisted. During this period of ill health, his two concerned adult daughters, who lived and worked in Ann Arbor, fifty miles west, monitored Rick's health, calling him constantly, alternating personal visits to maintain the groceries and housekeeping, and regularly staying overnight with him at his apartment. Friends checked on him daily and dropped in with prepared dishes and conversation.

Ferrell began a program of Prednisone, physical therapy and whirlpool treatments to exercise and sooth his arthritis. He wrote, "May 9, 1994: Pain continued pretty bad. 2 weeks from mega-dose. Went to physical therapy at 3:00, then to store — took walk to golf course. Feel good at 6:00 before dinner." Twenty milligrams of Prednisone per day plus additional iron relieved Rick so that he gradually began gaining weight again, reaching 154 pounds, and felt well enough to get outside again.

A letter written by Kerry Keene of Raynham, Massachusetts, appeared in the July 4, 1994, issue of *The Sporting News*, referencing Ferrell: "In his book, *The Politics of Glory: How Baseball's Hall of Fame Really Works*, Bill James is unnecessarily harsh on Hall of Famer Rick Ferrell, among others, suggesting that he does not belong in Cooperstown. [*TSN*, June 20] Ferrell, the oldest living Hall of Famer and as classy a man who had ever played the game, does not deserve this type of criticism. Did it ever occur to James that Ferrell may have been rewarded for six decades of service to baseball as not only a player, but also a coach, scout, general manager, and vice president?" The criticism levied at Ferrell's career was certainly off-base and unjustified.

A July 27, 1994, *Detroit News* article stated that only a dozen Hall of Fame members from the 1930s were still alive, including Rick Ferrell, Joe DiMaggio, Bobby Doerr and Bob Feller, while several, like Ted Williams, Early Wynn, and

Buck Leonard, were in dire health straits. This Associated Press writer compared the old timers to the modern day players. "There was a different sense of manliness back then, an unwritten code of behavior, on and off the field, that seems quaint today." Players wore heavy flannel uniforms and would never been seen in a gold chain or earrings. "They'd be joked out of the league," Ferrell told the reporter. Back then, players didn't munch snacks in the dugout, never showboated after a home run, and never charged the mound if hit by a pitch. In fact, a player couldn't even acknowledge the sore spot by rubbing it, but rather, just dug in and tried harder to get a hit. Bobby Doer said, "Back then, if you got on somebody about knocking you down, why they'd come back and throw at you again. It's just inviting a shot at you." "Players are not stronger," Ferrell continued. "The baseball is a golf ball now. They've tightened it up now to where it just jumps out of the ballpark. The pitching isn't that bad. They've narrowed the strike zone to nothing." The writer concluded that "there is a consensus that the game was more fun when they played and a concern for the future of baseball amid serious talk of another strike." And a players' strike was, in fact, called on August 12, 1994, the fourth in-season strike in 23 years.

A September letter from Rick to his nephew "Little Rick" in North Carolina was printed in Dick Thompson's book, *The Ferrell Brothers of Baseball* (p. 257). Rick expressed, "I think the strike will be settled for the play-offs and World Series. Both sides are quite firm. However, the owners have never won a point. They usually cave in. The salary cap is a joke. Basketball and football both have it and they don't like it. Something has to be done about the salaries, though. They are out of line. I don't blame the players." But Rick's prediction proved inaccurate; the World Series was cancelled. Baseball did not resume play again for 232 days, until April 2, 1995.

However around September 10, 1994, another unfortunate reversal of aging occurred for Rick, this one with permanent consequences. While walking outside, he felt a snap in his hip, causing him to limp home in pain. X-rays revealed a severely damaged right hip joint on the old catcher. On October 15, just after his 89th birthday, he wrote, "Bad report on hip. Bone on bone thing, they say — 2 first-floor apts. available in complex on golf course — will check it to move to first floor." His doctor's report also discovered a fast heartbeat and fluid on his lungs, further negative developments in his overall health.

By mid–October 1994, although Rick was still getting out to run errands, he wrote, "Can't take stairways much now." His second-floor apartment had been arranged so that everything was in easy reach near the kitchen table and chair where Ferrell stationed himself: eyeglasses, medications and water, clock, portable telephone with speed dial to the children, battery-operated radio for listening to the news and Tiger games on WJR, old/new mail. His autographing supplies were collected together — baseball photos, Hall of Fame and other baseball cards, Sharpie pens, ballpoints — next to the bills, checkbook, and newspapers. By October 25, Rick had become essentially housebound within his Troy apartment and wrote, "10th day in apartment. I enjoy it, no problem. Not interested in going any place." He went out for a medical appointment, aided by one of his daughters, the next day, and entered, "Hip replacement discussed; don't like that — I'll go along for a while."

Using crutches had become the new norm. With his faulty eyesight, Rick had given up driving. On November 3, "Same schedule. Feel OK but not good — haven't tried to go out — Do the necessary things here slowly. Lie down several times a day to relax and rest. Paper and mail delivered to door. Hope to feel better to help myself more." A hernia and a persistent cough now accompanied his glaucoma, arthritis, swollen feet, and hip difficulty.

On January 1, 1995, Rick wrote in his notebook, "Good day again. Scared to drive yet. Hope to have a better year this time. 94 — not too good." In Rick's last entry in his notebook, May 5, 1995, doctors had removed cataracts from his eye, but failed to improve his blurry vision.

However, long story short, Rick's health worsened, his appetite ceased altogether, and his weight declined to 125 pounds. In July after a stay at nearby Beaumont Hospital, doctors directed Rick to a nearby Bloomfield Hills nursing home to recuperate. After two weeks with little progress, one evening, his daughter saw that he could not sign an autograph request and did not turn on the radio to listen to the Tigers game. Rick passed away the next morning, July 27, 1995, just shy of his 90th birthday, with Kerrie by his side. After outliving Wes by almost twenty years, and George by nine, the last of the seven Ferrell brothers, the oldest living member of the Hall of Fame, was gone.

After receiving friends at a local funeral home in Troy, Michigan, his children flew with Rick's body back to Greensboro, North Carolina, where he was laid to rest on a Wednesday morning in the Ferrell family plot in New Garden Cemetery beside Ruth and Janet. The graves of Wes, the other Ferrell brothers, and his parents were as close as the pitcher's mound is to home plate.

About fifty people turned out for the funeral service. Local resident Ralph Hodgin, an ex–White Sox player, was the only former major leaguer in attendance. For the simple ceremony, longtime broadcaster Charlie Harville delivered a brief eulogy, saying of Rick, "I like to think of coming home. I like to think his place is at Guilford and is also secured in the hearts of his family and friends. In baseball, when you come home again, you're safe. Rick Ferrell is home again." His children returned to Michigan with broken hearts, facing the agonizing adjustment of living without their precious father nearby.

Death respects no one, and life is unpredictable. In Lakeland, Florida, just three months after Rick's death, his staunch friend and business partner, 71-year-old Jim Campbell died of a sudden heart attack in Lakeland Regional Medical Center. Detroiters were dismayed despite the fact that Jim's health had been poor in recent years. His body was flown to Detroit for a heavily-attended memorial service at the Mariners' Church of Detroit on November 5, 1995, and then driven to his home state of Ohio for burial. Jim's birthday on February 5 had fallen just three days after Wes Ferrell's; Rick had been like an older brother and advisor to Jim for decades, as well, and had understood and assisted him in all his endeavors. Thus ended the Ferrell-Campbell team.

Epilogue

Following Rick's death, the Detroit Tigers moved from Tiger Stadium to brand new Comerica Park, built in downtown Detroit, to play the 2000 season. The "Save Tiger Stadium" group battled for preservation of the old ballpark for years until it was totally demolished in 2009.

Rick's name continued to appear in the news occasionally. The August 12, 2006, *Sports Illustrated* published a letter from Randall L. Chuck of Miami: "Recounting his days catching Phil Niekro's knuckler (Players, July 31), Bruce Benedict said, 'Phil could have pitched every day. I was the one who needed four days off.' I wonder how he would have felt had he caught the 1944–45 Washington Senators' staff, which boasted four knuckleballers: Mickey Haefner, Dutch Leonard, Johnny Niggeling, and Roger Wolff. That was Hall of Famer Rick Ferrell's job. Rick caught 179 games in those two season and was named to the American League All-Star squad each year — two of his eight appearances. Oh, yes, Ferrell was 38 at the start of the '44 season and didn't benefit from the hinged pillows that knuckleball catchers now wear."

Even back in early 1945, Rick Ferrell was being touted for Hall of Fame candidacy. A February 1945 *Baseball Magazine* article by Ed Rumill entitled "That Unsung Catching Star, Rick Ferrell," summarized the catcher's outstanding career, stating that during the upcoming season, Ferrell should break the A.L. record for most games caught. "The record, itself, is enough to put the fellow in the Hall of Fame at historic and beautiful Cooperstown."

When rating the best all-time catchers, he wrote that Bill Dickey and Mickey Cochrane's names were always mentioned, but rarely Rick's. Rumill asked, "Who could match [Rick's] all-around abilities as a receiver and hitter? And, of course, how many were there who could even approach his endurance mark?" He compared the 16 years it took Ferrell to reach his 1,800th game to the number of years for Dickey (16) and Gabby Hartnett (20). "Thus, even a northerner will agree that this slender veteran from North Carolina should soon have a niche in the attractive little shrine on the main street of Cooperstown. To date, of the 14 plaques in the Hall of Fame, not one belongs to a backstop. Ferrell, like a great many other top-notch ballplayers down through the musty years of baseball, has suffered because of his almost colorless makeup." He pointed out that "the dandy little catcher," as Moe Berg had called Ferrell, was single-handedly responsible for the success of knuckleballers Niggeling and Leonard when they found a catcher who could corral their pitches. Also, other catchers wouldn't call for the knuckler in a clutch because should they missed it, the statistic would show a passed ball on the catcher rather than a wild pitch by the hurler. Rumill asked again, "Unless there is somebody on the club who can don a mask and protector, squat behind the plate and catch it, what on earth good is [pitching the knuckleball] going to do a hurler on the team?" Also noted was the fact that Ferrell had "learned to catch the fluttering delivery, even though he has sometimes had to do it by the simple and crude process of stepping in front of it, letting it strike his chest protector, and fall dead at his feet. No, Rick is not afraid to call for the knuckler in the clutch...."

The modern catcher enjoys security on and off the field never imagined by catchers from the 1930s and '40s. Current catching equipment renders receivers like astronauts, they are so padded and protected by solid helmets, heavy face guards, thick chest and throat protectors, shin guards, and huge mitts. The meager, rudimentary older "tools of ignorance," had afforded little protection. Rather than enduring long, noisy, dirty, sleepless train rides before having to catch a doubleheader, the modern player jets to a game in first-class, quiet comfort. Instead of being at the mercy of an owner who determined a player's career, the modern catcher, with protection from the Players Association, can refuse to go to a team once he's traded. Like other old-time ballplayers, Ferrell fought for his contracts on an annual basis after his initial three-year deal and was not afforded the security of a long-term, multi–million dollar guaranteed salary.

From the perspective of 2010, long-term, guaranteed contracts have become the norm and baseball salaries have skyrocketed into the multi-millions. The highest paid player for the Detroit Tigers is currently Miguel Cabrera, with six years and $126 million left on his contract. Management is striving to lower its player payroll.

Through most of the twentieth century, Rick Ferrell was a devoted classic baseball man who played the game of baseball during the Great Depression and World War II and afterward, worked as a coach, scout and front office executive as an ambassador on its behalf. Relying on his own brains, brawn, sweat, and initiative, he maintained the highest professional standards throughout his career, always proud to play a small part in the preservation of America's great pastime.

Appendix A.
Hall of Fame Memberships

National Baseball Hall of Fame, Cooperstown, New York (1984)
North Carolina Sports Hall of Fame, Raleigh, North Carolina (1964)
Guilford College Athletics Hall of Fame, Greensboro, North Carolina (1970)
Boston Red Sox Hall of Fame, Boston, Massachusetts (1995)
Guilford County Sports Hall of Fame, Greensboro, North Carolina (2005)

Appendix B. Career Statistics

Ferrell, Richard Benjamin (Rick)

Born, October 12, 1905, at Durham, North Carolina. Died, July 27, 1995, at Bloomfield Hills, Michigan. Batted right. Threw right. Height, 5' 10". Weight, 170. Brother of pro baseball players George and Wes Ferrell. Elected to Baseball Hall of Fame, 1984.

Year	Club	League	Pos	G	AB	R	H	TB	2B	3B	HR	RBI	SB	PCT
1926	Kinston	Virginia	C	64	192	24	51	63	6	0	2	20	1	.266
	Columbus	Amer. Assoc.	C	5	14	4	4	5	1	0	0		0	.286
1927	Columbus	Amer. Assoc.	C	104	345	42	86	114	14	4	2	44	2	.249
1928	Columbus	Amer. Assoc.	C	126	339	51	113	160	31	5	2	65	4	.333
1929	St. Louis	American	C	64	144	21	33	41	6	1	0	20	1	.229
1930	St. Louis	American	C	101	314	43	84	113	18	4	1	41	1	.268
1931	St. Louis	American	C	117	386	47	118	165	30	4	3	57	2	.306
1932	St. Louis	American	C	126	438	67	138	184	30	5	2	65	5	.315
1933	St. Louis/Boston	American	C	140	493	58	143	184	21	4	4	77	4	.290
1934	Boston	American	C	132	437	50	130	170	29	4	1	48	0	.297
1935	Boston	American	C	133	458	54	138	189	34	4	3	61	5	.301
1936	Boston	American	C	121	410	59	128	189	27	5	8	55	0	.312
1937	Boston/W'ton	American	C	104	344	39	84	98	8	0	2	36	1	.244
1938	Washington	American	C	135	411	55	120	157	24	5	1	58	1	.292
1939	Washington	American	C	87	274	32	77	92	13	1	0	31	1	.281
1940	Washington	American	C	103	326	35	89	111	18	2	0	28	1	.273
1941	W'ton/St. Louis	American	C	121	387	38	99	130	19	3	2	36	3	.256
1942	St. Louis	American	C	99	273	20	61	69	6	0	1	26	0	.223
1943	St. Louis	American	C	74	209	12	50	57	7	0	0	20	0	.239
1944	Washington	American	C	99	339	14	94	107	11	1	0	25	2	.277
1945	Washington	American	C	91	286	33	76	93	12	1	1	38	2	.266
1946	Washington [Coach, did not play]	American												
1947	Washington	American	C	37	99	10	30	41	11	0	0	12	0	.303

Rick Ferrell, cont'd

FIELDING STATS

Team	POS	G	GS	OUTS	TC	TC/G	CH	PO	A	E	DP	PB	CASB	CACS	FLD%	RF	ZR
1929 Browns	C	45	-	-	182	4.0	175	140	35	7	3	2	-	-	.962	0.00	-
1930 Browns	C	101	-	-	409	4.0	402	336	66	7	5	2	-	-	.983	0.00	-
1931 Browns	C	108	-	-	512	4.7	498	412	86	14	11	6	-	-	.973	0.00	-
1932 Browns	C	120	-	-	572	4.8	564	486	78	8	9	3	-	-	.986	0.00	-
1933 Browns	C	21	-	-	108	5.1	107	91	16	1	1	0	-	-	.991	0.00	-
1933 Red Sox	C	116	-	-	582	5.0	576	500	76	6	9	1	-	-	.990	0.00	-
1934 Red Sox	C	128	-	-	609	4.8	603	531	72	6	7	6	-	-	.990	0.00	-
1935 Red Sox	C	131	-	-	612	4.7	599	520	79	13	12	8	-	-	.979	0.00	-
1936 Red Sox	C	121	-	-	619	5.1	611	556	55	8	5	1	-	-	.987	0.00	-
1937 Red Sox	C	18	-	-	104	5.8	103	93	10	1	1	0	-	-	.990	0.00	-
1937 Senators	C	84	-	-	388	4.6	383	341	42	5	5	6	-	-	.987	0.00	-
1938 Senators	C	131	-	-	592	4.5	581	512	69	11	15	8	-	-	.981	0.00	-
1939 Senators	C	83	-	-	382	4.6	373	327	46	9	9	19	-	-	.976	0.00	-
1940 Senators	C	99	-	-	504	5.1	494	427	67	10	5	17	-	-	.980	0.00	-
1941 Senators	C	21	-	-	100	4.8	98	85	13	2	1	3	-	-	.980	0.00	-
1941 Browns	C	98	-	-	393	4.0	391	340	51	2	11	6	-	-	.995	0.00	-
1942 Browns	C	95	-	-	419	4.4	413	356	57	6	7	10	-	-	.986	0.00	-
1943 Browns	C	70	-	-	384	5.5	379	327	52	5	7	2	-	-	.987	0.00	-
1944 Senators	C	96	-	-	483	5.0	474	403	71	9	8	20	-	-	.981	0.00	-
1945 Senators	C	83	-	-	399	4.8	395	331	64	4	3	21	-	-	.990	0.00	-
1947 Senators	C	37	-	-	157	4.2	156	134	22	1	5	1	-	-	.994	0.00	-

Career	POS	G	GS	OUTS	TC	TC/G	CH	PO	A	E	DP	PB	CASB	CACS	FLD%	RF	ZR
C Totals	C	1,806	0	0	8,510	4.7	8,375	7,248	1,127	135	139	142	n/a	n/a	.984	0.00	—
18 Years	C	1,806	-	-	8,510	4.7	8,375	7,248	1,127	135	139	142	n/a	n/a	.984	0.00	—

Chart courtesy Baseball Almanac (www.baseball-almanac.com)

Appendix C.
1929–1947: Catching Highlights

November 8, 1928	Judge Landis decision: Rick Ferrell granted free agency from the Detroit Tigers by baseball Commissioner Landis.
November 11, 1928	Signed with St. Louis Browns for $25,000 bonus
April 19, 1929	Major league debut: St. Louis Browns
April 29, 1931	In 8th inning, Rick almost broke up his brother Wes' no-hitter.
May 9, 1933	Rick, with pitcher Lloyd Brown, traded to the Boston Red Sox for catcher Merv Shea and cash.
July 6, 1933	First All-Star Game (Chicago): Rick caught entire nine innings for A.L. team, beating N.L., 4–2.
July 19, 1933	For the first time, brothers on opposite teams (Rick and Wes Ferrell) each hit a home run in the same game.
May 6, 1934	In the 4th inning, Boston Red Sox score 12 runs off Detroit Tigers with four consecutive triples by Carl Reynolds, Moose Solters, Rick Ferrell, and Bucky Walters to win 14–4; tied record.
July 10, 1934	All-Star Game (New York): American League roster (2nd time)
July 8, 1935	All-Star Game (Cleveland): American League roster (3rd time)
July 7, 1936	All-Star Game (Boston): American League (4th time)
June 10, 1937	Boston Red Sox trade Ferrell brothers to Washington Nationals for Bobo Newsom and Ben Chapman.
July 7, 1937	All-Star Game (Washington); American League (5th time)
July 6, 1938	All-Star Game (Cincinnati); American League team (6th time)
August 12, 1938	Wes released by Washington Nationals
May 15, 1941	Rick traded back to St. Louis Browns for pitcher Vern Kennedy.
September 26, 1941	St. Louis Browns catcher Rick gets a 5th inning bunt-sin-

gle to spoil Cleveland Bob Feller's no-hitter, but Feller wins, 3–2.

March 1, 1944	Browns trade Rick back to Washington Senators for outfielder Gene Moore and cash
July 11, 1944	All-Star Game (Pittsburgh); American League roster (7th time)
Season, 1945	At age 39, Rick catches the Nats pitching staff of four knuckleball starters: Leonard, Niggeling, Haefner, Wolfe.
July 6, 1945	Rick breaks Ray Schalk's A.L. record (1,721) for "most games caught" with his 1,722nd game behind the plate.
July 1945	Named to American League All Star roster for 8th time; no game played.
September 14, 1947	Rick plays his final major league baseball game after playing in 1,884 games.

Appendix D.
1950–1992: Executive Highlights

January 1950 — Rick joins Detroit Tigers organization as a coach at age 44; rises through front office ranks for 42 years.

January 1954 — Becomes scout for Carolinas and Southeast territory

August 2, 1958 — Promoted to Farm Director for Detroit Tigers

January 26, 1959 — Promoted to Acting General Manager of Tigers

April 10, 1959 — Named General Manager of Detroit Tigers

November 29, 1961 — Chosen by A.L. President Joe Cronin to join Major League Baseball Official Rules Committee; will serve 20 years

September 1962 — Named Vice President of Detroit Tigers

May 1964 — Inducted into the North Carolina Sports Hall of Fame, Raleigh, North Carolina, with Enos "Country" Slaughter

October 10, 1968 — Detroit Tigers win the World Series vs. St. Louis Cardinals two days before Rick's 63rd birthday

October 1975 — Named Executive Consultant for Detroit Tigers

March 4, 1984 — Rick Ferrell and "Pee Wee" Reese elected to Baseball Hall of Fame by its Veterans Committee

August 12, 1984 — Rick inducted into the National Baseball Hall of Fame, Cooperstown, New York

October 14, 1984 — Detroit Tigers win the World Series vs. San Diego Padres

August 20, 1988 — Chicago White Sox catcher, Carlton Fisk breaks Ferrell's A.L. record for "Most Games Caught"—1,807—at Tiger Stadium with Rick in attendance.

December 31, 1992 — Rick, 86, resigns from Detroit Tigers after 42 years with the organization.

Chapter Notes

Chapter 1

1. *Greensboro Daily News*, April 29, 1911.
2. Interview with Bonnie Ferrell Waynick, February 2009.
3. Harvey T. Brundidge, "Ferrell Brothers Make Game Profitable Business," *The Sporting News*, 1932.
4. Guilford College transcripts, Fall 1923.
5. Ibid.
6. Wilt Browning, "Guilford Athletics: Rich Tradition Despite Low Profile," *Greensboro News and Record*, May 20 1984, p. B-1.
7. *The Columbus Citizen*, September 26, 1927, p. 17.
8. *The Columbus Citizen*, May 14, 1928, p. 14.

Chapter 2

1. Josh Levanthal, *Take Me Out to the Ballgame* (New York: Black Dog and Levanthal, 2000), p. 84.
2. Ibid.
3. *St. Louis Post-Dispatch*, April 22, 1929, p. 15.
4. "Dan Howley to Quit as St. Louis Manager," *Washington Post*, October 6, 1929, p. M-21.
5. John McGraw, *Detroit Free Press*, May 1984.
6. Frank Young, "Manager Sees Pennant with New Punch," *St. Louis Post-Dispatch*, June 15, 1930.
7. Ibid.
8. "Rick Glad to Lose a Hit," *Chicago Tribune*, May 2, 1931.
9. *New York Times*, March 15, 1932, p. 27.
10. Damon Kerby, *St. Louis Post-Dispatch*, August 31, 1932, p. 2-B.

Chapter 3

1. On This Date: January 7, 1933, www.baseballlibrary.com.

2. *St. Louis Post-Dispatch*, March 19, 1933, p. 1-D.
3. "Rick Ferrell Loses His Business Touch," *The Sporting News*, March 23, 1933, p. 3.
4. *St. Louis Post-Dispatch*, May 10, 1933.
5. Melvin Webb, "Pitchers May Figure in Deal," *Boston Globe*, June 13, 1933, p. 21.
6. Ernie Harwell, "Ferrell Catches First All Star Game, *Detroit Free Press*, August 12, 1984.
7. "Babe Ruth Steals the Show," *Washington Post*, July 8, 1956, p. 1-B.
8. Shirley Povich, "Wes' Soft Stuff in Red Sox Debut Puts Brother on Rough Spot," *Washington Post*, April 6, 1949, p. 6.
9. Ibid.
10. Ibid.
11. Ibid.
12. Glenn Stout and Richard Johnson, *Red Sox Century* (New York: Houghton Mifflin, 2000), p. 191.

Chapter 4

1. Dillon Graham, "Wes Ferrell Sees Himself as a Leader," *Washington Post*, April 21, 1935, p. B-13.
2. Ibid.
3. National Chicle Co., Cambridge, Mass., 1935.
4. "Ferrell Keeps Skill in Family," *Los Angeles Times*, July 16, 1935, p. 7.
5. Lawrence Leonard. "Great Little Catcher Believes Red Sox Will Beat Out Others," *Greensboro Daily News*, December 31, 1935.
6. *Los Angeles Times*, March 10, 1936, p. 29.
7. Ibid.
8. *Boston Globe*, May 8, 1936, p. 29.
9. *Boston Globe*, May 27, 1937, p. 26.
10. UPI. "'Moneybags' Yawkey Optimistic," *The Washington Post*, June 2, 1936, p. 19.
11. *Washington Post*, August 22, 1936, p. X-14.
12. Ibid.

13. *Chicago Daily Tribune*, August 23, 1936, p. A-4.
14. Hy Hurwitz, "What About it?" *Boston Globe*, August 25, 1936.
15. Shirley Povich, "This Morning," *Washington Post*, August 31, 1936, p. X-16.
16. H.G. Salsinger, *Detroit News*, September 16, 1937, p. 25.
17. *Washington Post*, December 22, 1936, p. X-23.
18. *Los Angeles Times*, January 31, 1937, p. A-13.
19. *Washington Post*, June 11, 1937.

Chapter 5

1. Levanthal, *Take Me Out to the Ballpark*, p. 76.
2. *Washington Post*, June 29, 1937, p. 19.
3. *Washington Post*, July 1, 1937, p. 23.
4. *The Sporting News*, July 8, 1937, p. 23.
5. *The Sporting News*, January 27, 1938, p. 5.
6. *Los Angeles Times*, April 19, 1938, p. A-9.
7. Shirley Povich. "This Morning," *Washington Post*, May 11, 1938, p. 18.
8. Ibid.
9. *Washington Post*, July 2, 1938, p. 2.
10. Dave Camerer, "Wes Finds Brother No Aid Now," *World Telegram*, August 18, 1938.
11. Ibid.
12. Shirley Povich. "Rick Ferrell Hits Triple to Win Game," *Washington Post*, August 25, 1938, p. 18.
13. Shirley Povich, "This Morning," *Washington Post*, July 18, 1939, p. 10.
14. *Chicago Daily Tribune*, August 7, 1940, p. 23.
15. Shirley Povich, "This Morning," *Washington Post*, April 8, 1941.

Chapter 6

1. Peter Golenbock, *The Spirit of St. Louis: A History of the St. Louis Cardinals and Browns* (New York: HarperCollins-Avon, 2001) p. 279.
2. Joe Falls, *Detroit Free Press*, July 28, 1995.
3. *St. Louis Post-Dispatch*, July 22, 1941, p. 2-B.
4. *St. Louis Post-Dispatch*, July 30, 1941, p. 2-B.
5. Shirley Povich, "This Morning," *Washington Post*, March 24, 1942, p. 19.
6. Ibid.
7. Herman Wecke, "Club Ahead of 1941 Record," *St. Louis Post-Dispatch*, July 21, 1942, p. 8-A.
8. *The Sporting News*, October 22, 1942, p. 2.
9. Frederick Lieb, "Catchers in Game's Most Hazardous Job," *The Sporting News*, December 31, 1942, p. 2.
10. Baseball Today: April 22, 1943, www.baseballlibrary.com.
11. AP, "Browns Prepared for Anything," *New York Times*, April 17, 1943, p. 31.
12. Arch Ward, "In the Wake of the News," *Chicago Daily Tribune*, July 10, 1943, p. 15.
13. Golenbock, *The Spirit of St. Louis*, p. 293.
14. *Los Angeles Times*, November 17, 1943, p. 15.

Chapter 7

1. Shirley Povich, "This Morning," *Washington Post*, March 4, 1944, p. M-7.
2. Ibid.
3. Ibid.
4. *The Sporting News*, April 17, 1989, p. 17.
5. Shirley Povich, "This Morning," *Washington Post*, April 23, 1944, p. M-6.
6. Arthur Daley, "Sports of the Times: The Man in the Iron Mask," *New York Times*, June 22, 1944, p. 15.
7. Shirley Povich, *Washington Post*, July 27, 1944, p. 14.
8. Walter Haight, *Washington Post*, March 8, 1945, p. 10.
9. Buck O'Neil, "Weaker Hitters Best Against Knuckleballers," *The Sporting News*, June 14, 1945, p. 7.
10. *The Sporting News*, July 12, 1945, p. 17.
11. Bill Gilbert, *They Also Served: Baseball and the Home Front, 1941–1945*. (New York: Crown, 1992), p. 241.
12. Ibid., pp. 270–71.

Chapter 8

1. Shirley Povich, *Washington Post*, February 18, 1946, p. 10.
2. Shirley Povich, *The Sporting News*, March 7, 1946, p. 18.
3. Shirley Povich, *Washington Post*, January 5, 1947, p. M-6.
4. *Washington Post*, June 27, 1947, p. B-6.
5. *The Sporting News*, July 16, 1947, p. 18.
6. *The Sporting News*, "Letters," July 23, 1947, p. 38.
7. *Washington Post*, September 2, 1947, p. 17.
8. "Umpires Riding Us Since McGowan Case, Nats Say," *Washington Post*, August 5, 1948, p. 15.

Chapter 9

1. Anderson, William. *View from the Dugout* (Ann Arbor: University of Michigan Press, 2006), p. 116.

2. *Washington Post*, May 7, 1950, p. C-3.
3. Anderson, *View from the Dugout*, p. 113
4. Ibid., p. 198.
5. *The Sporting News*, March 28, 1951, p. 7.
6. Anderson, *View from the Dugout*, p. 201.
7. Virgil Trucks, *Throwing Heat: The Life and Times of Virgil Fire Trucks* (Dunkirk, Md.: Pepperpot, 2004), p. 159.
8. *Washington Post*, May 15, 1952, p 19.
9. *The Sporting News*, May 28, 1952, p 13.
10. Trucks, *Throwing Heat*, p. 159.
11. Walt Spoelstra, *The Sporting News*, October 14, 1953, p. 17.
12. Walt Spoelstra, *The Sporting News*, January 17, 1954, p. 23.
13. *The Sporting News*, January 16, 1957, p. 25.
14. *The Sporting News*, March 13, 1957, p. 17.
15. *The Sporting News*, April 10, 1957, p. 4.
16. Ibid.
17. *The Sporting News*, November 6, 1957, p. 21.

Chapter 10

1. Irving Smallwood, *Greensboro Daily News*, January 24, 1959.
2. *The Sporting News*, February 4, 1959, p. 8.
3. Irving Smallwood, *Greensboro Daily News*, January 24, 1959.
4. Ibid.
5. *The Sporting News*, April 29, 1959, p. 8.
6. Bob Addie, *Washington Post*, May 3, 1959, p. C-3.
7. Arthur Daley, *New York Times*, May 20, 1959, p. 41.
8. *The Sporting News*, May 27, 1959, p. 7.
9. *The Sporting News*, June 3, 1959, p. 19.
10. John Drebinger, *New York Times*, June 14, 1959, p. S-1.
11. Walt Spoelstra, *The Sporting News*, July 29, 1959, p. 11.
12. *The Sporting News*, August 26, 1959, p. 10.
13. David Condon, *Chicago Tribune*, November 20, 1959, p. C-1.
14. Walt Spoelstra, *The Sporting News*, December 16, 1959, p. 20.
15. *The Sporting News*, March 9, 1960, p. 13.
16. Schneider, *Bengal Tales*, p. 18.
17. *Detroit Free Press*, April 4, 2000.
18. Schneider, *Bengal Tales*, p. 19.
19. *The Sporting News*, April 19, 1961, p. 17.
20. Fred Katz, "Rick Ferrell: Free Thinking Front Office Man," *Sport Magazine*, May 1962.
21. Walt Spoelstra, *The Sporting News*, September 8, 1962, p. 17.
22. Walt Spoelstra, *The Sporting News*, October 6, 1962, p. 28.
23. *The Sporting News*, November 23, 1963, p. 26.
24. *The Sporting News*, March 21, 1964, p. 20.
25. Joe King, *The Sporting News*, May 9, 1964, p. 7.
26. *The Sporting News*, November 14, 1964, p. 5.
27. Ibid.
28. *Baseball Digest*, March 1965, p. 82.
29. Bill Veeck, *Los Angeles Times*, October 8, 1965, p. C-5.

Chapter 11

1. *Chicago Daily Defender*, August 24, 1966, p. 26.
2. Dan Ewald, *John Fetzer: On a Handshake* (Illinois: Sagamore Press, 1997), p. 140.
3. Telephone Interview between Kerrie Ferrell and Gene LaMont, 2008.
4. *The Sporting News*, January 20, 1968, p. 31.
5. *The Sporting News*, January 13, 1968, p. 38.
6. Ewald, *John Fetzer*, p. 136.
7. www.wikipedia.com, Detroit Tigers, 1968.
8. Ewald, *John Fetzer*, p. 75.
9. Fred T. Smith, *Fifty Years with the Detroit Tigers* (Detroit: Fred T. Smith, Russ Entwistle, John Duffy, 1983), p. 192.
10. *New York Times*, September 16, 1970, p. 64.
11. www.wikipedia.com, Detroit Tigers, 1972.
12. Ibid.
13. *Chicago Tribune*, January 12, 1973, p. C-1.
14. *The Sporting News*, January 20, 1973, p. 41.
15. *Los Angeles Times*, March 29, 1973, p. E-1.
16. www.retrosheet.org, Detroit Tigers, 1973, Ron LeFlore.
17. *The Sporting News*, July 28, 1973, p. 10.
18. www.baseballlibrary.com, Detroit Tigers, 1973.

Chapter 12

1. Telephone interview between Kerrie Ferrell and Ralph Houk, 2008.
2. Ibid.
3. The Fetzer Institute, Kalamazoo, Michigan. Detroit Tigers file.
4. www.wikipedia.org, Detroit Tigers, 1975.
5. James Edward Miller, *The Baseball Business* (Chapel Hill: University of North Carolina Press, 1990), p. 215.
6. Ibid, p. 200.
7. *The Sporting News*, September 16, 1976.

8. www.baseballreference.com, Detroit Tigers data/draft.

9. Ewald, *John Fetzer*, p. 114.

10. *New York Times*, July 19, 1977, p. L-19.

11. Bob Broeg, "Just How Good Was Brooksie?" *The Sporting News*, October 8, 1977, p. 8.

12. *The Sporting News*, December 3, 1977, p. 69.

13. www.retrosheet.org, Detroit Tigers, June draft, 1978.

14. *Los Angeles Times*, September 21, 1978, p. E-4.

15. *Atlanta Daily World*, November 28, 1978, p. 5.

16. *The Sporting News*, January 13, 1979, p. 2.

17. *Los Angeles Times*, February 25, 1979, p. C-2.

18. *Washington Post*, April 28, 1979, p. F-3.

19. Ewald, *John Fetzer*, p. 132.

20. Miller, *The Baseball Business*, p. 253.

21. *Los Angeles Times*, February 18, 1980, p. C-15.

22. *The Sporting News*, January 3, 1981.

23. Ewald, *John Fetzer*, p. 115.

24. Joe Durso, "Kemp Seeks Stability," *New York Times*, February 6, 1983, p. S-1.

25. *Los Angeles Times*, June 21, 1982, p. D-4.

26. *New York Times*, November 7, 1982, p. 217.

Chapter 13

1. Jerry Green, "1933: Straw Hats, Spats, and Rick Ferrell," *Detroit News*, July 1, 1983.

2. Ibid.

3. Ibid.

4. Joe Falls, "Rick Ferrell: The Quiet Roar Behind the Tigers," *MICHIGAN: Detroit News Magazine*, August 12, 1984, pp. 12–18, 24.

5. Mike Downey, "Tigers Look Terrific," *Detroit Free Press*, March 6, 1984.

6. Jerome Holtzman, "If the Tigers Don't Win, Neither Will Sparky's Books," *Chicago Tribune*, April 8, 1984, p. B-4.

7. George "Sparky" Anderson, *Bless You Boys* (Chicago: Contemporary Books, 1984), p. 123.

8. Gene Guidi, *Detroit Free Press*.

9. www.wikipedia.org, Detroit Tigers, 1984.

10. Ewald, *John Fetzer*, p. 78.

11. *Ann Arbor News*, September 3, 2007, p. 6.

12. *Detroit Free Press*, Sports Section, early December 1984.

13. Ibid.

14. *Detroit Free Press*, April 10, 1985.

15. Joe Durso, "4 Specialists Set to Step into Hall," *New York Times*, July 29, 1985.

16. *New York Times*, August 22, 1985, p. D-22.

17. Michael O'Donnell, "Age Can't Catch Up to Fisk's Rare Feat," *Chicago Tribune*, August 25, 1985, p. B-4.

18. "Morning Briefing," *Los Angeles Times*, August 16, 1986, p. B-2.

19. Mike Penner, *Los Angeles Times*, September 24, 1986, p. B-1.

20. Jerome Holtzman, "New Comiskey Park Stadium Approved by Owners," *Chicago Tribune*, December 8, 1986, p. B-3.

21. www.retrosheet.org, Trades/Detroit Tigers/1988.

22. Drew Sharp, "Fisk Says Record is No Big Deal," *Detroit Free Press*, August 19, 1988, p. 1-D.

23. Ibid.

24. *New York Times*, August 31, 1988, p. D-25.

25. Glenn Waggoner, "Death of Collusion Has Already Spawned the Birth of Stupidity," *New York Times*, December 18, 1988, p. S-7.

26. www.retrosheet.org, Transactions/Detroit Tigers/1989.

27. *Wall Street Journal*, September 1, 1989, p. B-3.

28. www.baseballchronology.com, Detroit Tigers/1989.

29. *www.retrosheet.org*, Transactions/Detroit Tigers/1989.

30. Murray Chass, *New York Times*, January 17, 1990, p. A-19.

31. www.si.com, Baseball/lockouts/1990.

32. *New York Times*, November 4, 1990, p. S-1.

Bibliography

Books

Anderson, Sparky, and Dan Ewald. *Bless You Boys*. Chicago: Contemporary, 1984.

Anderson, William M., ed. *The Detroit Tigers: A Pictorial Celebration of the Greatest Players and Moments in Tigers History*. 4th ed. Detroit: Wayne State University Press, 2008.

_____. *The View from the Dugout: The Journals of Red Rolfe*. Ann Arbor: University of Michigan Press, 2006.

Auker, Elden, and Tom Keegan. *Sleeper Cars and Flannel Uniforms*. Chicago: Triumph, 2001.

The Baseball Encyclopedia. New York: Macmillan, 2003.

Bevis, Charlie. *Mickey Cochrane: The Life of a Baseball Hall of Fame Catcher*. Jefferson, N.C.: McFarland, 1998.

Borst, Bill. *Still Last in the American League: The St. Louis Browns Revisited*. West Bloomfield, MI: Altwerger & Mandel, 1992.

Dickey, Glenn. *Great No-Hitters*. Radnor, PA: Chilton, 1976.

Dolson, Frank. *Jim Bunning, Baseball and Beyond*. Philadelphia: Temple University Press, 1998.

Ewald, Dan. *John Fetzer: On a Handshake*. Kalamazoo, MI: Fetzer Institute, 1997.

Falls, Joe. *Baseball's Great Teams: The Detroit Tigers*. New York: Macmillan, 1975.

Gilbert, Bill. *They Also Served: Baseball and the Home Front, 1941–1945*. New York: Crown, 1992.

Golenbock, Peter. *The Spirit of St. Louis: A History of the St. Louis Cardinals and Browns*. New York: Spike/Avon, 2000.

Green, Paul. *Forgotten Fields*. Waupaca, WI: Parker Press, 1984.

Harwell, Ernie. *Diamond Gems*. Royal Oak, MI: Momentum, 1991.

_____. *Stories from My Life in Baseball*. Detroit: Detroit Free Press, 1992.

Honig, Donald. *Baseball When the Grass Was Real*. New York: Coward, McGann, and Geoghegan, 1975.

_____. *The Greatest Catchers of All Time*. Dubuque, IA: William. C. Brown, 1991.

Kaplan, Jim. *Lefty Grove: An American Original*. Cleveland: Society for American Baseball Research, 2000.

Miller, James Edward. *The Baseball Business*. Chapel Hill: University of North Carolina Press, 1990.

Neft, David D., et al. *The Sports Encyclopedia: Baseball*. New York: St. Martin's, 2003.

Reidenbach, Lowell, and Joe Happel, eds. *Baseball's Hall of Fame: Cooperstown*. New York: Gramercy, 1999.

Smith, Fred T. *Fifty Years with the Tigers: A Fifty Year History of the Detroit Tigers*. Detroit: Fred T. Smith, 1983.

Spink, J.G. Taylor. *Judge Landis and 25 Years of Baseball*. St. Louis: *The Sporting News*, 1974.

Stout, Glenn, and Richard A. Johnson. *Red Sox Century*. Boston: Houghton Mifflin, 2000.

Thompson, Dick. *The Ferrell Brothers of Baseball*. Jefferson, N.C.: McFarland, 2005.

Trucks, Virgil O. *Throwing Heat: The Life and Times of Virgil Fire Trucks*. Dunkirk, MD: Pepperpot, 2004.

Werber, Bill, and C. Paul Rogers, III. *Memories of a Ballplayer*. Cleveland: Society for American Baseball Research, 2001.

Articles

Abatt, Co. "Hall of Famer Ferrell Adjusts to Retirement." *Detroit News*, August 24, 1993.

AP. "Browns Need Relief for Catcher Ferrell." *St. Louis Post-Dispatch*, August 5, 1942.

_____. "Browns Prepared for Anything." *New York Times*, April 17, 1943.

_____. "Browns Trade Vernon Kennedy for Rick Ferrell." *St. Louis Globe-Democrat*, May 16, 1941.

_____. "Browns' $25,000 Beauty." *St. Louis Post-Dispatch*, April 8, 1929.

_____. "Code of Behavior Changes." *Detroit News*, July 27, 1994.

_____. "Ferrell Brothers Each Homer; Indians Win in 13 Innings." *Boston Globe*, July 19, 1933.

_____. "Ferrells Pull the Big Brother Act with 'Cats.'" *Boston Globe*, May 4, 1936.

_____. "Gehrig, Baseball's 'Iron Man' Dies After Two-Year Illness." *St. Louis Post-Dispatch*, June 3, 1941.

_____. "Howley Will Quit Berth as Browns' Boss." *Los Angeles Times*, October 6, 1929.

_____. "I'm to Blame, but Also the Goat, Says Wes." *Chicago Tribune*, August 23, 1936.

_____. "No Hits—No Brotherly Love." *St. Louis Post-Dispatch*, May 2, 1931.

_____. "Wes Ferrell Is Suspended for Ten-Day Period." *St. Louis Post-Dispatch*, August 31, 1932.

_____. "Wesley Ferrell Released by Washington; Through for the Season." *Washington Post*, August 13, 1938.

Broeg, Bob. "Catchers Get Special Drill from Ferrell." *The Sporting News*, March 27, 1957.

_____. "Cronin Sheds Light on Ferrell." *St. Louis Post-Dispatch*, August 12, 1984.

Browning, Wilt. "A Catcher Laid to Rest—At Home." *Greensboro News and Record*, August 3, 1995.

_____. "A Special Day in History for Greensboro Brothers." *Greensboro News and Record*, July 19, 1988.

_____. "Baseball Has Lost a Great Treasure." *Greensboro News and Record*, July 28, 1995.

_____. "Ferrell Recalls Gehrig: Can It Be 50 Years Ago?" *Greensboro News and Record*, July 4, 1989.

_____. "Hall of Famer: Greensboro's Rick Ferrell, Former Catcher, to Be Inducted Today." *Greensboro News and Record*, August 29, 1984.

_____. "HOF Career Supplants Fling in Boxing Ring." *Greensboro News and Record*, late September 1984.

Camerer, Dave. "Wes Finds Brother No Aid Now." *World Telegram*, August 18, 1938.

Chass, Murray. "161 Players File for Arbitration." *New York Times*, January 17, 1990.

Corio, Ray. "Rick Ferrell, Hall of Famer, 89, Catching Half of Brothers' Pair." *New York Times*, July 28, 1995.

Crutchfield, Moses. *Greensboro News & Record*, March 8, 1984.

Daley, Arthur. "Sports of the Times: Man in the Iron Mask." *New York Times*, June 22, 1944.

Drebinger, John. *New York Times*, June 14, 1959.

Drohan, John. "Dick Ferrell One of Four Brothers in Organized Baseball." *Boston Traveler*, June 21, 1930.

Durso, Joe. "4 Specialists Set to Step into the Hall." *New York Times*, July 29, 1985.

Edwards, Henry P. "Rick Ferrell Forsook Ring Career to Star in Majors." *Washington Post*, January 18, 1931.

Falls, Joe. "Age-old Quest Still Fun for Ferrell, 83." *Detroit News*, March 1, 1989.

_____. "Bo Implements His Plan Quietly." *Detroit News*, September 30, 1990.

_____. "Ferrell Dies, but Not the Memory of His Response When He Thought DiMaggio Was Out of Bounds." *Detroit News*, July 28, 1995.

_____. "Former Tiger Official Ferrell Is a Man to Be Treasured." *Detroit News*, September 19, 1993

_____. "Rick Ferrell: The Quiet Roar Behind the Tigers." *Detroit News (MICHIGAN: Magazine)*, August 12, 1984.

_____. "So Many Empty Seats in Home Finale." *Detroit News*, October 1, 1992.

Gage, Tom. "Ferrell Will Catch Up With All-Star Festivities Next Year." *Detroit News*, July 12, 1992.

Garber, Mary. "Scouts and Gentlemen Help Rookie Learn Her Trade." *Greensboro News and Record*, undated 1950s.

Gietschier, Steve. "Classy Catcher: Rick Ferrell, the Oldest Living Member of the Hall, Didn't Knuckle Under." *The Sporting News*, January 24, 1994.

Graham, Dillon. "Wes Ferrell Sees Himself as a Leader." *Washington Post*, April 21, 1935.

Green, Jerry. "1933: Straw Hats, Spats, and Rick Ferrell." *Detroit News*, July 1, 1983.

Gould, James M. "Rick Ferrell Hits Homer, Also Drives in Four Runs." *St. Louis Post-Dispatch*, June 15, 1930.

Harwell, Ernie. "All Star Game Still Alluring 71 Years Later." *Detroit Free Press*, July 12, 2004.

_____. "Animal Crackers Are Banned; First Free Agent Is Born." *Detroit News*, March 8, 1991.

Hershberger, Chuck. "Rick Ferrell: Baseball's First Free Agent." *Old-Tyme Baseball News*, Vol. 5, Issue 1, 1993.

Holtzman, Jerome. "New Comiskey Park Stadium for Chicago White Sox Approved." *Chicago Tribune*, December 8, 1986.

Hurwitz, Hy. "Lefty Grove All Smiles." *Boston Globe*, April 18, 1936.

_____. "Rick Ferrell's Home Run Saves a Shutout." *Boston Globe*, August 22, 1936.

_____. "What About It?" *Boston Globe*, August 25, 1936.

Justice, Richard. "Baseball: Weaknesses." *Washington Post*, May 7, 1989.

Katz, Fred. "Rick Ferrell: Free Thinking Front Office Man." *Sport Magazine*, May 1962.

Keidan, Bruce. "Mitts Were the Pitts When Rick Ferrell Caught." *Pittsburgh Post-Gazette*, July 31, 1995.

Leonard, Lawrence. "Great Little Catcher Believes Red Sox Will Beat Out Others." *Greensboro Daily News*, December 31, 1935.

Lieb, Frederick. "Catchers in Game's Most Hazardous Job." *The Sporting News*, December, 31, 1942.

Mack, Gene. "Old-Timers Say Ferrell's Throwing Nearest Thing to Criger's They've Seen." *Boston Globe*, May 24, 1933.

Moore, Gerry. "Homers by Werber and Rick Win Game." *Boston Globe*, May 18, 1936.

O'Donnell, Michael. "Age Can't Catch Up to Fisk's Rare Feat." *Chicago Tribune*, August 25, 1985.

O'Neil, Buck. "Rick Knocks Wood on Nats Knuckleballers." *The Sporting News*, April 6, 1944.

_____. "Weaker Hitters Best Against Knuckleballers." *The Sporting News*, June 14, 1945.

Puscas, George. "Ferrell, 86, Welcomes Tigers' Plans." *Detroit Free Press*, August 28, 1992.

Povich, Shirley. "A True Love for Baseball." Washington Post, March 24, 1942.

_____. "Ferrell Ties Record with 1721 Game." *Washington Post*, July 5, 1945.

_____. "Iron Horse Breaks as Greats Meet in His Honor." *Washington Post*, July 5, 1939.

_____. "Neither Nats, Red Sox Gained by Trade." *Washington Post*, June 11, 1937.

_____. "Owners: Golden Egg on Their Faces." *Washington Post*, February 15, 1990.

_____. "Rick Ferrell Hits Triple to Win Game." *Washington Post*, August 25, 1938.

_____. "Rick Ferrell's Foul in Tribe's Park Will Cost Him $300." *Washington Post*, June 3, 1938.

_____. "This Morning." *Washington Post*, March 4, 1944.

_____. "Wes Ferrell Trims Lefty Grove in Duel." *Washington Post*, August 16, 1937.

Ray, Bob. "Bobby Doerr Only 18, but He's Ready for the Red Sox." *Los Angeles Times*, January 31, 1937.

Reston, Scott. "Dearth of Good Catchers Stump AL Managers." *Los Angeles Times*, January 13, 1937.

Rumill, Ed. "That Unsung Catching Star, Rick Ferrell." *Baseball Magazine*, February 1945.

Sharp, Drew. "Fisk Says Record No Big Deal." *Detroit Free Press*, August 19, 1988.

Siegel, Morris. "Suspension Faces Grumbling Players." *Washington Post*, August 21, 1947.

_____. "Umpires Riding Us Since McGowan Case, Nats Say." *Washington Post*, August 5, 1948.

Smith, Claire. "Some Major Feuds Stand in the Way of Problem Solving." *New York Times*, June 16, 1992.

UPI. "Moneybags Yawkey Optimistic." *Washington Post*, June 2, 1936.

Waggoner, Glenn. "Death of Collusion Has Already Spawned the Birth of Stupidity." *New York Times*, December 18, 1988.

Ward, Charles P. "Billy and Red Sox Catcher Stage Fight in Second." *Detroit Free Press*, September 14, 1936.

Webb, Melvin. "Ferrell Brothers Form a Red Sox Battery." *Boston Globe*, May 26, 1934.

_____. "Rick Ferrell Puts Fight in Red Sox: Backstop Has Improved His Batting 103 Points." *Boston Globe*, July 6, 1933.

Wecke, Herman. "Club Ahead of 1941 Record." *St. Louis Post-Dispatch*, July 21, 1942.

Newspapers

Boston Globe
Chicago Tribune
Columbus Dispatch
Detroit Free Press
Detroit News
Greensboro News and Record
Los Angeles Times
New York Times
Old-Tyme Baseball News
Pittsburgh Post-Gazette
St. Louis Globe-Democrat
St. Louis Post-Dispatch
The Sporting News
Wall Street Journal
Washington Post

Websites

www.baseball-almanac.com
www.baseball-reference.com
www.baseballchronology.com
www.baseballhalloffame.org
www.baseballlibrary.com
www.cbssports.com/teams
www.fenwayfanatics.com
www.homepages.rootsweb.com
www.paperofrecord.com
www.proquest.com
www.retrosheet.org
www.sabr.org
www.si.com
www.wikipedia.org

Index

Numbers in *bold italics* indicate pages with photographs.

283

Index

293

Index